RÁNQUIL

RÁNQUIL

Rural Rebellion, Political Violence, and
Historical Memory in Chile

THOMAS MILLER KLUBOCK

Yale
UNIVERSITY PRESS
New Haven and London

Published with assistance from the Kingsley Trust Association
Publication Fund established by the Scroll and Key Society
of Yale College.
Published with assistance from the Mary Cady Tew Memorial Fund.

Copyright © 2022 by Thomas Miller Klubock.
Maps by Nick Springer, Springer Cartographics, LLC.
All rights reserved.
This book may not be reproduced, in whole or in part, including illustrations, in any form (beyond that copying permitted by Sections 107 and 108 of the U.S. Copyright Law and except by reviewers for the public press), without written permission from the publishers.

Yale University Press books may be purchased in quantity
for educational, business, or promotional use. For information,
please e-mail sales.press@yale.edu (U.S. office) or sales@yaleup.co.uk
(U.K. office).

Set in Janson type by IDS Infotech, Ltd., Chandigarh, India.
Printed in the United States of America.

Library of Congress Control Number: 2021937099
ISBN 978-0-300-25313-9 (hardcover : alk. paper)

A catalogue record for this book is available from the British Library.

This paper meets the requirements of ANSI/NISO Z39.48-1992
(Permanence of Paper).

10 9 8 7 6 5 4 3 2 1

Contents

Acknowledgments vii
Glossary ix
Maps xi

INTRODUCTION 1
1. San Ignacio de Pemehue: Building an Hacienda on the Southern Frontier 26
2. Campesinos, *Indígenas,* and Early Challenges to the Hacienda 44
3. The *Inquilinos* Organize: Rural Labor and Social Unrest in Southern Chile 69
4. Populism in the Countryside: The Sindicato Agrícola Lonquimay and Carlos Ibáñez 98
5. Agrarian Reform Arrives in Alto Bío Bío 117
6. The Fall of Ibáñez and Political Radicalization in Southern Chile 142
7. Expulsion from the Nitrito Valley 168
8. "All You See Is Yours": The Sindicato Agrícola Lonquimay's Road to Revolution 188

9. Rebellion and Repression   214
10. History, Memory, and the Question of Campesino Insurgency   243

Notes   271
Index   309

Acknowledgments

I AM HAPPY TO recognize all those who have contributed to this book over the years. First and foremost, I would like to thank the staffs of numerous archives and libraries in Chile, including the Biblioteca del Congreso Nacional, the Biblioteca Nacional, the Archivo Nacional and Archivo Nacional de la Administración in Santiago, the Archivo Regional de la Araucanía and Archivo de Asuntos Indígenas in Temuco, and the office of the Registro Civil in Lonquimay. I am also pleased to recognize the assistance of those who facilitated access to judicial records held by the Corte de Apelaciones and the Conservador de Bienes Raíces in Temuco and the Juzgado Criminal in Victoria. Without the patience and, at times, heroic diligence of these archivists and librarians, especially staff members who searched dusty shelves for uncatalogued and long-ignored volumes, I would have never been able to locate many of the documents that provide the book's foundation. I would also like to thank Alberto Harambour Ross, Karen Donoso Fritz, and Pamela Nahuelcheo for their research assistance over the years.

I am grateful for the support of Jaya Chatterjee of Yale University Press. The book benefited from Lawrence Kenney's superb copyediting. Anonymous reviewers for Yale provided helpful comments and suggestions at different stages while I completed the manuscript. I owe an enormous debt of gratitude to Brian Loveman for his thoughtful comments on the manuscript as it reached its final stages. The book is much improved because of his meticulous reading, informed by his encyclopedic knowledge of Chilean history. I thank Heidi Tinsman and Peter Winn for years of friendship and intellectual exchange as well as for the very helpful comments both provided on the manuscript.

I presented some of the preliminary ideas for this book at a seminar at the Universidad de la Frontera in Temuco. I thank the historians Jaime Flores Chávez and Jorge Pinto for their comments. I am especially grateful to Jaime Flores Chávez for the helpful conversations we had about the Ránquil rebellion. His 1993 Universidad de Santiago de Chile master's thesis on Ránquil stands as a pioneering piece of research on Chile's social history. I had the opportunity to present some of the research in this book at the Norbert Lechner Seminar and Jornadas de Historia de Chile conference hosted by the Universidad Diego Portales in Santiago, where I received insightful comments from the attendees. I have also benefited from influential conversations I had with a number of historians in Chile. For their many years of friendship and intellectual inspiration I thank Julio Pinto Vallejos, Verónica Valdiva de Ortíz, Alberto Harambour Ross, and Consuelo Figueroa Garavagno. I would also like to thank forester Frida Schweitzer for her assistance and support in Lonquimay and Ránquil.

A semester sabbatical research leave from teaching and research funding from the University of Virginia provided the essential time and resources I needed to complete the book. I am grateful to Chris Gist of the University of Virginia Scholar's Lab, who produced drafts of three of the book's maps, and Nick Springer of Springer Cartographics, who designed and produced final versions of all four of the maps included here. This book grew out of research I did for a chapter of my book *La Frontera: Forests and Ecological Conflict in Southern Chile* and for a chapter in *A Century of Revolution: Insurgent and Counter-Insurgent Violence during Latin America's Long Cold War*, edited by Greg Grandin and Gilbert Joseph, and includes material from parts of those chapters.

Finally, my parents, Daniel Klubock and Dorothy Miller, and my sister Katharine Klubock contributed to this book with their unfailing support and years of lively conversation and debate. I thank Sandhya Shukla for her love, wisdom, and humor and our sons, Ishan and Kiran, for the great happiness they have brought us.

Glossary

arrendatario	renter
cabecilla	leader; ringleader
cacique	chief; head of an indigenous community
campesino	peasant
carabineros	police; branch of the armed forces
colono	settler; colonist
empleado	employee; servant
enganche	hook; labor recruitment
estancia	ranch
fiscal	public prosecutor
fundo	estate
gañan	estate laborer
hacienda/hacendado	estate/estate owner
hijuela/hijuelero	small plot of land/owner of a small plot of land
indígena	indigenous person
inquilino	resident estate laborer; service-labor tenant on an estate
inquilinaje	tenant estate labor system
invernada	winter pasture
jornalero	day laborer
lanzamiento	eviction
latifundista	owner of a large estate or latifundium
levantamiento	uprising
lonko	leader or head of a Mapuche community
mayordomo	administrator; manager

mediero	sharecropper
mediería	sharecropping
mejoras	improvements
nguillatún	indigenous Mapuche religious ceremony
obligado	inquilino who provides labor to an estate
obrero	worker
obrero agrícola	agricultural worker
ocupante	land occupier; squatter
olvido	forgetting; oblivion
parcela	parcel; plot of land
patrón	landowner; landlord; boss; master
piñón	nut of the *Araucaria araucana* pine (*pehuén*)
poblador	resident
proclama	manifesto
pulpería	company store
reducción	indigenous community
revoltoso	rebellious one; troublemaker
revuelta	revolt
sindicato	union
sindicalista	union member
sublevación	uprising; revolt
suceso	event; incident
trabajador	worker
vecino	resident; neighbor
veranada	summer pasture

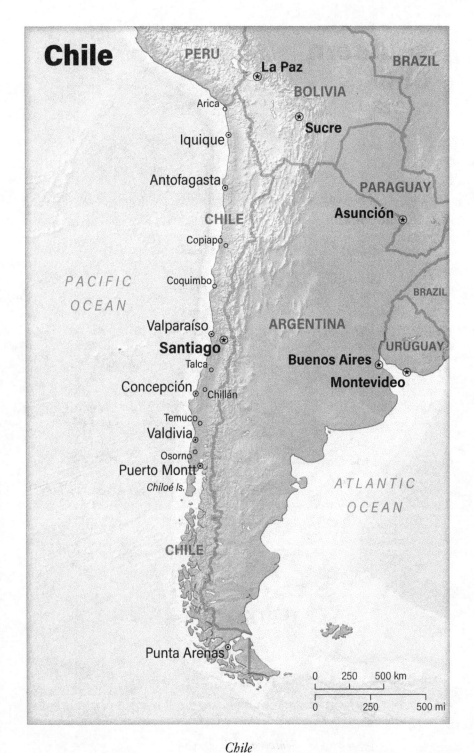

Chile

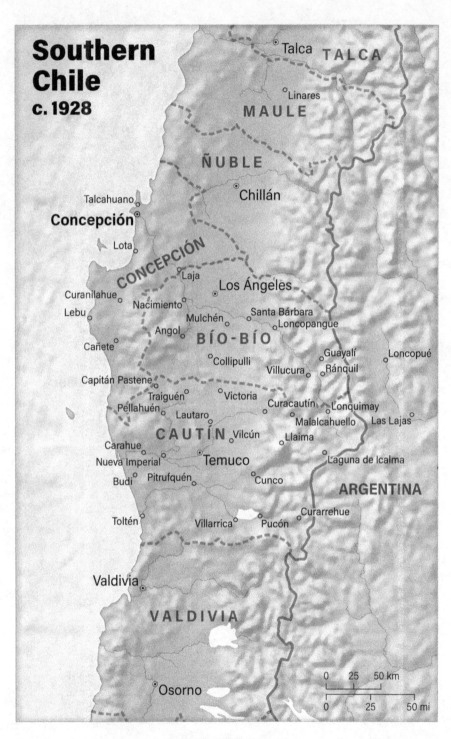

Southern Chile, c. 1928

Alto Bío Bío and the Araucanía, c. 1928

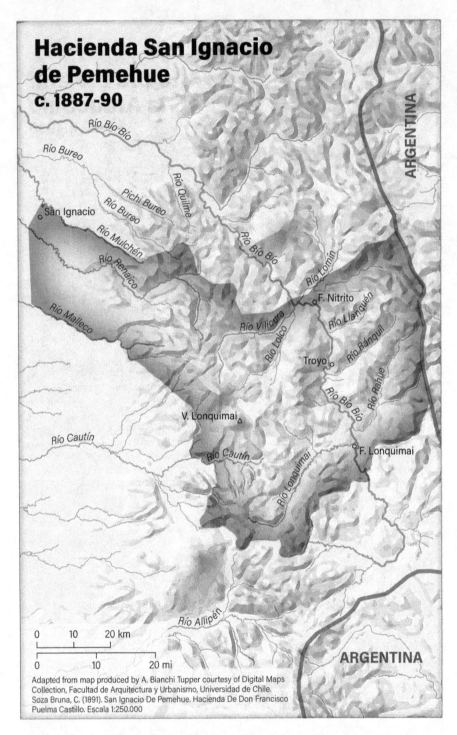

Hacienda San Ignacio de Pemehue, c. 1887–90
Adapted from map produced by A. Bianchi Tupper, courtesy of Digital Maps Collection, Facultad de Arquitectura y Urbanismo, Universidad de Chile. Soza Bruna, C. (1891). San Ignacio de Pemehue. Hacienda de Don Francisco Puelma Castillo. Escala 1:250,000.

RÁNQUIL

Introduction

IN LATE JUNE 1934 rural laborers rose in rebellion in the southern Chilean region known as Alto Bío Bío, led by the country's largest union of agricultural workers, the Sindicato Agrícola Lonquimay. As winter snowstorms blanketed the Andean valleys, a group numbering between three hundred and five hundred men and a handful of women, including some who hailed from local indigenous Pehuenche communities, assaulted the region's haciendas, killing estate owners and managers, the owners of stores located on the estates (*pulperías*), and three *carabineros* (police). The rebellion's leaders intended their movement to inaugurate a nationwide socialist revolution in which estate land would be distributed to "those who work it," in the words of the union's leader, Juan Segundo Leiva Tapia.

Over the course of the next week the campesino rebels confronted troops sent from around the country in pitched battles across a large region that straddled Malleco (formerly Bío-Bío) and Cautín provinces. Ultimately many surrendered, while others fled into the mountains or across the border to Argentina. The number of detainees remains unclear but certainly reached into the hundreds. However, only fifty-six arrived in jail in the city of Temuco. The rest were disappeared, a phrase used during the 1930s long before forced disappearance became internationally known as a tool of state terror employed by the military dictatorship of Augusto Pinochet (1973–90). Most were in all likelihood executed by carabineros in one of the most infamous massacres in Chilean history. The number of dead and disappeared is still unknown, but reasonable estimates range from eighty to more than two hundred. The Ránquil rebellion, named for one of the estates where laborers had first organized a union in 1928, was the largest rural uprising in Chilean history. The deaths of the detainees joined a long list of massacres of workers in northern Chile's nitrate mines as one of the most brutal acts of state violence in Chile until the horrors unleashed by the Pinochet dictatorship.

Since 1934 Ránquil has been enshrined in popular memory as both an iconic moment in the long history of campesinos' struggle for land and another episode in the Chilean state's history of violent repression of popular movements.[1] Over the years, the rebellion has received literary treatment in novels and plays, including most notably *Ránquil: novela de la tierra* by Reinaldo Lomboy (1942); *Los que van quedando en el camino* by Isidora Aguirre (1969); and *Actas del Alto Bío-Bío* by Patricio Manns (1985). During the 1960s the rural labor federation Confederación Nacional Campesina e Indígena Ránquil, led by the Communist Party, adopted the name both to honor the victims of the massacre and to celebrate what had been until that decade the most successful instance of rural labor organizing in Chilean history. Yet despite Ránquil's enduring presence in Chile's cultural memory there is a paucity of historical studies of this landmark event, Chile's most important campesino rebellion. When historians have examined Ránquil, they have interpreted it as unique, an aberration in Chile's otherwise long history of rural peace lasting until the wave of land invasions during the 1967–73 agrarian reform. The rebellion has been viewed as the exception that proves the rule of agrarian social stability in Chile.[2]

This book, the first major historical study of the Ránquil rebellion, tells the story of how and why campesinos in Alto Bío Bío turned to revolution. Rather than view the rebellion they made as quixotic or idiosyncratic, it locates their revolutionary movement in the context of rural social relations throughout the frontier territory that lies south of the Biobío River. Viewed from the perspective of the broader social history of southern Chile, the Ránquil rebels' radical challenge to the authority of the hacienda stands out not as an exception, but as the most visible and pronounced clash in a long history of conflicts between campesinos and estate owners. Rather than an unusual moment of violent rural protest, the Ránquil rebellion was one of many similar movements of rural laborers to claim estate land throughout southern Chile during the first three decades of the twentieth century. Similarly, the massacre that brought a bloody end to the rebellion was only an extreme instance of state violence directed at both indigenous and nonindigenous campesinos that had its origins in the military conquest of the southern frontier territory known as the Araucanía during the second half of the nineteenth century.³

While most writing on Ránquil focuses on the immediate causes of the rebellion, my book traces campesinos' decision to take up arms in 1934 to a long history of conflict over property rights that dated back to the late nineteenth century. Campesinos embraced revolution only after years of struggle for land on seven enormous estates, including Ránquil, with well over 200,000 hectares belonging to the aristocratic Puelma and Bunster families (a hectare is 2.47 acres). Their efforts had taken them on a long journey to local and regional courts, the offices of lands ministers and presidents in Santiago, and even Chile's supreme court. As they traveled through state institutions, Alto Bío Bío's campesinos allied themselves first with Chile's social reformist Democratic Party, then the dictatorial regime of Carlos Ibáñez (1927–31), and finally the Chilean Communist Party, moving from a pragmatic strategy of working through the legal system and petitioning authorities in Santiago to revolutionary insurrection. This was a journey marked periodically by brief and unresolved episodes of violence. Beginning in the early twentieth century, Chilean governments, at the behest of landowners, sent troops repeatedly to expel campesinos from the region's estates.

Chile has often been viewed as an exception in Latin America for its apparent political stability and flourishing multiparty democracy during the twentieth century. From 1932 until the 1973 military coup, while many of its neighbors experienced military interventions in politics and years of authoritarian rule, Chile maintained its democratic institutions largely intact while the military remained in its barracks. Salvador Allende's democratic road to socialism, or "via chileno al socialismo," in 1970–73 appeared to confirm Chile's unusually stable democratic institutions and political culture. Even when the 1973 military coup dealt a death blow to this experiment in building socialism at the ballot box and Chile became infamous around the world for the Pinochet dictatorship's systematic violation of human rights, few scholars sought the roots of state terror in the country's long history of political violence and bitter social conflict. Chile's supposed model transition to democracy after 1990, characterized by political stability and steady rates of macroeconomic growth, appeared to reaffirm the resilience of its democratic political culture. Like the Ránquil rebellion, the seventeen years of dictatorship under Pinochet appear to be an outlier in an otherwise peaceful history of multiparty democracy that has made Chile an exception in Latin America.⁴

I argue here that Chile's democratic politics during the twentieth century were built, at least in part, on a foundation of political violence and authoritarian rule.[5] The history of the Ránquil rebellion, and the politics of the 1930s more generally, allow one to see Chile as similar to, rather than different from, many of its Latin American neighbors. In 1933 sugar workers in Cuba engaged in revolutionary strikes, occupied sugar mills, and organized soviets, driving a radical rural laborers' movement in alliance with the urban working and middle classes and sectors of the military that opposed the dictatorship of Gerardo Machado. In El Salvador in 1932 campesinos organized by the Communist Party led a rural revolution that ended in the infamous *matanza* (massacre) of thirty thousand people. And in Colombia during the early 1930s campesinos organized *ligas agrarias* (agrarian leagues) and unions, invaded estates, and pushed to appropriate land in frontier areas that had seen the expansion of commercial coffee cultivation. Chile is not often considered in the company of Cuba, El Salvador, and Colombia, but the Ránquil rebellion and the broader pattern of rural social upheaval and political violence throughout southern Chile in the late 1920s and 1930s of which it is representative reflect the ways in which Chile resembled its Latin American neighbors more than is customarily thought.[6]

In part, the spread of revolutionary rural insurrections from Cuba and El Salvador to Colombia and Chile during the early 1930s had a global dimension, following as they often did the strategy of the Soviet Comintern and Third International. If anarchism and anarcho-syndicalism provided an international language for revolution during the 1910s and 1920s, by the early 1930s, as anarchist movements were brutally repressed throughout the hemisphere, Communist parties came to play an increasingly important role in rural social movements, the urban labor movement, and popular revolutionary politics in Latin America.[7] Unlike anarchists, who found their base of support among workers in ports, cities, and mines, Communist parties, along with more social reformist political movements—including, in Chile, the Democratic Party—began during the 1920s to make concerted efforts to organize in the countryside as well as in urban areas. While the Ránquil rebellion was deeply rooted in regional history, its leaders, who had ties to the Chilean Communist Party, were profoundly aware of both national and global events. They saw their rebellion as both meeting local demands for land and as part of a larger movement to usher in the end of liberal capitalism and the authoritarian rule that upheld its deeply unequal social order across the

Americas. When viewed comparatively alongside Cuba, Colombia, and El Salvador, where campesinos also pursued insurrection as a tool of socialist revolution, one can see the Ránquil rebellion as belonging to a broader hemispheric moment shaped by the post-1929 crisis in export-led capitalist development and Communist parties' commitment to overturning despotic oligarchic regimes through revolutionary strikes, land invasions, and popular insurrections.

In Chile the leaders of the Ránquil rebellion hoped their uprising would inaugurate a nationwide socialist revolution and bring down the democratically elected government of Arturo Alessandri (1932–38), which they viewed as authoritarian and illegitimate. They failed, but the threat of imminent revolution in the countryside that accompanied the collapse of the economy after 1929 pushed Chile's traditional political parties to implement both social and democratic reforms. The democratic politics of the "populist era," which incorporated urban working- and middle-class sectors and in which the Communist Party was a dynamic participant following its antifascist Popular Front policy after 1935, rested on the repression of the 1930s revolutionary challenge to electoral democracy. As Brian Loveman has pointed out, the social reforms that benefited urban labor and middle-class sectors and underwrote a thriving multiparty democracy in Chile from the 1930s to the early 1970s were predicated on the exclusion of rural labor and the maintenance of landed inequality in the countryside.[8] They were also founded on the violent repression of rural workers' movements to unionize and appropriate estate land throughout southern Chile. When rural workers organized unions under a new campesino unionization law and invaded large estates during the 1967–73 agrarian reform, the result was much the same as in the 1930s: violent repression and state terror. From this perspective, the Ránquil rebellion and the massacre that brought it to an end were not exceptions in Chilean history but rehearsals for the revolutionary agrarian movements of the 1960s and early 1970s and the Pinochet dictatorship's counterrevolution, which would direct some of its worst violence against campesinos in the southern countryside.

Ránquil and the Rural Labor Movement

The Ránquil rebels' revolutionary threat to the status quo lay not only in their attacks on carabineros and invasion of haciendas but also in the fact that most had been estate laborers who had organized a union to challenge the authority of their patrones. Historians have described the events in

Ránquil as a campesino uprising. But the term *campesino* elides more than it explains. Campesino is most easily translated as peasant or, more literally, person from the countryside, but the word does not suffice to describe the complex land and labor relations that shaped rural society in southern Chile. In the south, as in central Chile, rural people did not reside in villages or long-standing communities. Chile, unlike Mexico, Central America, or many of its Andean neighbors to the north, had no deeply rooted villages with generations-old ties or titles to commonly held land. Land in southern frontier territory was monopolized by large estates, which had been formed by force and fraud following military campaigns to defeat independent indigenous Mapuche groups between 1861 and 1883.

Because the Araucanía was frontier land, recently wrested from Mapuche control by military conquest, land not acquired by large estates or occupied by legally titled indigenous Mapuche communities in small *reducciones* (land-grant communities) remained public property. Numerous landless laborers migrated across the Biobío River and often settled on small plots of what they considered to be public land, hoping to be granted titles as *colonos* (settlers). Most remained in uneasy possession of their parcels without legal titles as *ocupantes*, confronting the constant threat of losing their land to large estates and expulsion by the police. While *colono* signified a settler smallholder with legal title to a small plot of land or membership in an actual colony organized by the state colonization services on public land, *ocupante* held a more ambiguous meaning. In its literal meaning it could signify the rights held by an occupier of public land based on a number of years of material possession and the introduction of improvements, mainly clearing forest, erecting fences, and planting crops. But, ocupantes were not colonos, and the term held another meaning: squatter. While many ocupantes hoped to transform their labor on public land into legal titles as colonos, they frequently found their property claims contested by large estates with whom they did battle for southern land. Conversely, estate owners throughout southern Chile, unlike their counterparts in central Chile, encountered challenges to their property rights from ocupantes who squatted within the borders of their estates and claimed the land based on rights derived from material occupation and frontier land's status as public.

As in central Chile, southern landowners employed tenant farmers known as *inquilinos* on their large estates. Typically, inquilinos received a plot of land where they could grow crops and pasture livestock in exchange for their labor. Estates supplemented their resident inquilino labor force with seasonal workers known as *gañanes*. These tended to be transient workers who migrated from estate to estate, across the border to Argentina, and, until 1930, to Chile's northern nitrate mines in search of work. Not infrequently, Alto Bío Bío's gañanes were the children of more permanent inquilino laborers or came from indigenous Pehuenche communities neighboring large estates. These categories of the rural laboring population in Alto Bío Bío were not absolute. Rural laborers frequently migrated between these different social positions and legal identities as often as they migrated across the border to Argentina, to the nitrate mines, or between estates. Inquilinos might become ocupantes and aspiring colonos by claiming the plots of estate land granted them in exchange for providing labor to or working on shares with their patrones. Further muddying social categories in frontier territory, ocupantes and even colonos often entered into *mediería* (sharecropping) and *inquilinaje* labor arrangements with large estates as a means of acquiring land for crops or pasture. Once established on an estate and contracted as a laborer, whether as an inquilino or *mediero* (sharecropper), they could claim the land they worked, transforming themselves into squatter ocupantes, but also, in the official language of the time, aspiring colonos who sought titles to their plots from the state.

This tangle of social arrangements surrounding land and labor confounded contemporary observers of the Ránquil rebellion from across the political spectrum, who described the rebellion's protagonists as either campesinos or colonos or both. To a one, historians have followed suit and identified the campesino rebels as colonos and campesinos, but never as inquilinos, gañanes, or agricultural laborers (*obreros agrícolas*).[9] This book demonstrates that most of the Sindicato Agrícola Lonquimay's members and participants in the rebellion the union led, including members of Pehuenche communities, had labored on the region's estates as inquilinos and in a number of cases worked as gañanes. Organized in union councils on large properties in Alto Bío Bío beginning in 1928, inquilinos began to disobey their patrones and work the small plots of estate land granted them in exchange for their labor as if they were their own. When landowners attempted to evict them, they simply refused to leave, claiming that estates lay on public land and that they enjoyed rights to be settled as colonos because of their material occupation and improvements they had introduced by clearing and cultivating their plots. This process was not unique to Alto Bío Bío. Throughout the south, from Llanquihue and Valdivia to Cautín, and Bío-Bío provinces inquilinos claimed estate land and petitioned the state for titles as colonos, while landless laborers invaded estates, which they similarly claimed lay on public frontier land. Rural workers also went on strike to demand improved work conditions and better salaries and petitioned the labor authorities for support in their conflicts with their patrones.

This history of rural workers' labor organization and collective movements to appropriate hacienda land in southern Chile has gone largely unwritten. More generally, the historiography of rural Chile has not yet recognized the degree to which inquilinos challenged landowners' authority over both land and labor during the first decades of the twentieth century. As a movement of inquilinos, the Ránquil rebellion belongs to a broader history of rural labor organizing during the 1920s. Brian Loveman's pioneering work, *Struggle in the Countryside*, uncovers rural workers' efforts to organize unions on haciendas and describes numerous collective conflicts over wages, payments in kind, and labor conditions on estates in central Chile during the 1920s and 1930s.[10] More recently, Claudio Robles has shown that between 1870 and 1930 some haciendas in central Chile invested in the modernization of production, introducing new machinery and expanding irrigation, which led to greater degrees of proletarianization in the inquilino–patrón relationship, including the replacement of in-kind payments with wages. Robles sees these changes in relations of production on central Chilean estates as driving new movements by laborers to organize unions in the 1920s and sparking a number of rural workers' strikes early in the decade.[11]

The history of the Sindicato Agrícola Lonquimay stands in sharp contrast to this history of agricultural modernization, proletarianization, and labor organization in the central Chilean countryside. Estates in Alto Bío Bío were notable for their lack of modernization. Most landowners invested little in making their properties productive, employing their vast landholdings, which could range from twenty thousand to forty thousand hectares, to pasturing relatively small herds of cattle and sheep. Most left their estates in charge of administrators and resided elsewhere. As was the case of the Puelma properties, whose owners lived in Santiago, estate owners in Alto Bío Bío employed their haciendas mainly as instruments for acquiring credit or as opportunities for speculation in a region where land values rose rapidly following the final military conquest of the territory's independent Mapuche groups during the early 1880s.

Unlike rural movements in which workers organized unions, strikes, and insurrections as a result of the capitalist modernization of agricultural production in zones producing export crops like sugar (Cuba), bananas (Colombia), and coffee (Colombia and El Salvador), the Ránquil rebellion erupted in the least developed sector of the economy and Chile's most marginal region, economically and geographically isolated on the eastern side of the Andes cordillera. The Ránquil rebellion's participants did not organize their union or pursue armed insurrection as a response to the expansion of the market and the pressures of proletarianization on increasingly modernized rural estates. Nor did they come from recently formed communities on the edges of modern capitalist agricultural enterprises.[12] Agricultural workers were able to organize a union in distant Alto Bío Bío because the region remained, even during the late 1920s, frontier territory where landowners exercised far less hegemony at both the national and local levels. Unlike in central Chile, in southern Chile estate owners' powers of paternalist persuasion and coercive control over their workers were relatively weak.

Both the fact that many rural properties lay on public land appropriated from the state, often via healthy doses of fraud, and landowners' minimal investments in introducing improvements on their land made them easy targets for rural laborers seeking to expropriate them. The frontier region was also an ideal place for Chilean governments to experiment with early agrarian reform policies and extend labor legislation into the rural sector, policies furiously rejected by central Chile's landed aristocracy, well-represented in congress by the Liberal and Conservative parties. Colonization laws designed to settle southern frontier territory with productive smallholders would animate workers' struggles to appropriate southern estates based on the principle that land belonged to those (men) who improved it through their labor. That estates were viewed as occupying public land and landowners as having done little to make their properties productive shaped inquilinos' and ocupantes' understanding that they had earned legal rights to the land based on their work in clearing forest and making the soil fallow.

Decades before Chile's agrarian reform of 1967–73 rural laborers contended that the state should expropriate unproductive estates and distribute their land to those who worked it. They were backed by the Ibáñez regime, which viewed the southern frontier region as a place where it could begin the necessary process of producing agricultural modernization by breaking up large estates. Two other concepts that would shape agrarian reform later in the century also emerged from conflicts over southern land during this period. By the early 1930s colonization laws, pushed from below by campesinos' land occupations, recognized that the state had the authority to expropriate large estates in the public interest and to resolve social conflicts. These principles guided the Ibáñez regime's efforts to expropriate land belonging to the Bunster and Puelma estates and distribute it to members of the Sindicato Agrícola Lonquimay. The 1930 expropriation of the Puelma family's Ránquil estate and distribution of its land to its former inquilinos marked the first step on what would be a long road to agrarian reform in Chile.

Moral Economy and the Path to Insurrection

Alto Bío Bío's rural laborers did not come from long-standing agrarian communities. Nor did they inhabit a world shaped by paternalist relations with their aristocratic patrones on large estates. Most estates had been recently organized during the late nineteenth century, and while a number of the region's inquilinos had been born on estates, just as many were more recent arrivals. Furthermore, a sizable number of inquilinos were members of recently formed neighboring Pehuenche communities. As I demonstrate in this book, a small core of lifelong inquilinos was supplemented by a significant number of workers who had settled on the estates during the late 1920s and early 1930s. These recent arrivals participated in the flows of labor migration that characterized rural Chile during this period. Rather than remaining isolated in the southern cordillera in millennial villages or as a permanent resident labor force on well-established estates, many of Alto Bío Bío's rural laborers had moved around the country in search of work, often to the other end of the country. During the 1920s, for example, not a few laborers in Alto Bío Bío were "hooked" with advances from labor recruiters sent by northern nitrate mining enterprises, provoking consternation about labor shortages among the region's landowners. Other agricultural laborers traveled from estate to estate or to cities like Santiago and Valparaíso or across the border to Argentina in search of work. Although most of the Ránquil rebels had been born in the region, they came from a laboring population that was used to movement, not permanence, and that was therefore less reliant on and less subordinated to large landowners than its counterparts in central Chile. They did not, therefore, inhabit a world shaped by precapitalist communal norms and traditions.[13] Nor would the Ránquil revolutionaries look backward to a moral economy shaped by past customs and values to judge social relations in the southern countryside as unjust and collective action to right the social order as legitimate.

With the collapse of Chile's nitrate economy after 1930, a number of former miners also migrated from the north to Alto Bío Bío, changing the complexion of the region's rural working class. They were drawn to the southern cordillera by government programs designed to reignite mining in gold placers as a response to the dislocations caused by the Great Depression. A number of gold placer concessions were located within the boundaries of the Puelma and Bunster families' estates, and many inquilinos, ocupantes, and colonos joined miners panning for gold, which they exchanged for goods at pulperías on the estates. Thus during the early 1930s rural workers in Alto Bío Bío lived and labored alongside unemployed workers from the northern nitrate mines. The Ránquil rebels came from a mobile rural working class that had lived and labored in a number of economic sectors and that included members of local Pehuenche communities as well as miners.

If the disruptions caused by the expansion of the market do not explain the rebellion, and there were no traditions of community access to land or precapitalist traditions of paternalist relations with patrones that were abrogated, why did Alto Bío Bío's rural laborers pursue the path of rebellion? Commentators sympathetic to the rebels hit on two explanations. The first was the extreme deprivation and misery a number of campesino families confronted after their violent expulsion from land in the Nitrito Valley claimed by the Bunster family's Guayalí estate. This rendition of the rebellion's origins depicts the revolutionary movement as a spontaneous eruption of protest provoked by the profound deprivation campesinos confronted during the harsh Andean winter, when heavy snowfall made work in gold placers impossible.

However, as E. P. Thompson and James Scott argue, deprivation and exploitation alone cannot explain why people choose to rebel, riot, or engage in collective action.[14] They have to judge their deprivation and the social relations in which it is embedded as unjust. In this book I ask what historical process moved the members of the revolutionary movement to see the extreme hardship they faced and, more generally, land and labor relations in Alto Bío Bío as unjust in the absence of a moral economy rooted in customary community norms or paternalist relations with patrones. How did campesinos move in 1934 from legal strategies of challenging hacienda owners' authority over land and labor to organized violent insurrection?

A second explanation seized on by politicians across the political spectrum as well as by the regional and national press was that innocent, hardworking colonos had been instigated by Communist agitators who seized on their eviction and imminent starvation to instigate the movement. Much of the scant historical writing on the Ránquil rebellion has focused on this question. Germán Palacios, for example, argues that the Communist Party played no role in fomenting the rebellion because it had been decimated by repression during the Ibáñez dictatorship, had suffered internal factionalization, and had only a weak presence in the countryside. The party lacked the infrastructure and cohesion to organize and lead a rebellion.[15] Sebastián Leiva and Olga Ulianova have employed declassified Comintern documents to revise Palacios's interpretation of the Communist Party's role in organizing the rebellion. Both demonstrate the party's active efforts to organize rural workers, indigenous communities, and miners in Alto Bío Bío but conclude that the party's leadership in Santiago played no role in planning the insurrection.[16]

I show that there is considerable evidence that a number of the Sindicato Agrícola Lonquimay's leaders were aligned with the Communist Party and articulated its ideological discourse, though with some variance from the party's formal positions. These local union leaders were active in the Federation of Chilean Workers (Federación Obrera de Chile, or FOCH), which was led by the Communist Party, and probably to some degree in the Communist Party but acted independently of the party leadership and Comintern in planning the insurrection. However, while neither the Comintern nor the party's leaders in Santiago played a role in organizing the campesino movement in Alto Bío Bío, their revolutionary rhetoric influenced the decision made by local union leaders to organize an armed movement to overthrow the government. National party and FOCH leaders adopted a fiery language of insurrection that followed the Comintern's policy of promoting anti-imperialist and agrarian revolution in Latin America, exhorting campesinos and Mapuche communities to organize unions and soviets, go on strike, and occupy estates.

Yet the question remains: What led campesinos to find the Communist Party's call for revolutionary strikes and insurrections meaningful? To understand how Alto Bío Bío's campesinos arrived at revolution requires accompanying them on their decades-long struggle to wrest estate land they deemed public from its aristocratic owners. As early as the 1890s, rural laborers claimed land on the region's estates, which they occupied as squatters. The Puelmas' and Bunsters' properties, they claimed, had been usurped from the state and from indigenous communities, which held true dominion over public frontier land. They based their case for the estates' status as public rather than private property on Chilean governments' efforts to reclaim the properties from their putative owners. The Puelma family was repeatedly forced to defend its property rights in legal battles with both Chilean governments and squatter ocupantes. Well over a decade before Juan Segundo Leiva Tapia organized the Sindicato Agrícola Lonquimay, the Puelmas had faced numerous challenges to their property rights in court and in congress and, on the ground, by squatter ocupantes, many of them inquilinos, who claimed plots of estate land as their own.

The Ránquil rebellion reflects the violence endemic to rural social relations in southern Chile, yet it also reveals another side of Chilean politics: a long tradition of appealing to the law and petitioning the state that extended even into the distant mountain frontier territory of Alto Bío Bío. To southern campesinos, the apparatus and agents of the state in southern Chile—courts, land agencies, labor inspectors and tribunals, and surveyors—operated as more than instruments of landowner power and state domination. At times both the legal system and government agencies provided southern campesinos a toolkit of resources and rights and even an understanding that the state could mete out justice in their conflicts with large estates. The history of the Ránquil rebellion demonstrates a fundamental tension in Chilean history between the power of law, the state, and the institutions of democratic rule on the one hand, and, on the other, Chilean governments' periodic resort to repression to quell challenges to the social order and limit the possibilities of democratic participation.

Yet the stark contrast between law and violence does not do justice to the authoritarian legal traditions that imposed limits on Chilean democracy. On the frontier Chilean governments established new executive powers to make law by simple decree, a tradition of authoritarian governance that would be expanded nationally during the twentieth century. Governments from across the political spectrum periodically resorted to so-called decree-laws of dubious constitutional standing to impose policy.[17] In addition, democratic governments were often accorded extraordinary faculties by congress that allowed the executive to abrogate basic constitutional rights, including rights to free speech and assembly, as was the case during the second government of Arturo Alessandri (1932–38). Chilean governments also employed draconian internal security of the state laws throughout the twentieth century, including during the second Alessandri government, to repress labor organizing, radical speech, and leftist publications as well as to jail political dissidents. In this sense the

Alessandri government, often heralded as restoring democratic rule following the demise of the Ibáñez dictatorship, represented continuities in Chile's authoritarian political traditions as well as in the persistent use of violent repression to quell popular protest and leftist movements.[18]

Even in its most authoritarian incarnation, however, law could also work as a tool of reform. Although he established a dictatorship backed by a pliant congress and employed the police to persecute his political opponents and crack down on unions, anarchists, and the Communist Party, Ibáñez introduced key social reforms. Among these were new labor legislation and a series of measures designed to break up unproductive rural estates in southern Chile and distribute their land to colono smallholders. Unlike his predecessors, Ibáñez on a number of occasions threw his support to inquilinos, ocupantes, and colonos in their conflicts with large estates and expressed hostility to southern Chile's *hacendados*. He also endorsed the extension of labor laws and unionization into the countryside. His support for inquilinos' right to organize unions has gone unnoticed by historians, but it marked a major blow to landowners' authority in the southern countryside and a potential seismic shift in rural labor relations. In Alto Bío Bío, Ibáñez intervened directly to back rural workers' rights to organize. He also implemented the 1928 Southern Property Law, which appeared to hold the promise that inquilinos and ocupantes might win rights to land on estates that could not prove their titles were legitimate and could therefore be expropriated by the state.

Campesinos throughout southern Chile found in these Ibáñez-era laws a set of labor rights and rights to both estate and public land that would shape a robust rural social movement during the late 1920s. In the absence of the bonds and traditions of settled communities with access to communally held land, the Ibáñez regime's reforms afforded campesinos a moral and legal language to judge estates' monopoly of southern land and exploitation of rural labor as unjust. The fundamental principle, enshrined in colonization laws, that frontier land was public and that those who had material occupation of the land, demonstrated by the improvements they had made, enjoyed property rights shaped campesinos' struggles to wrest land from large estates throughout southern Chile.

When campesinos took up arms to defend their rights to both estate and public land in Alto Bío Bío, they did so as men who were heads of families, claiming patriarchal rights encoded in agrarian laws for almost a century. While many campesina women accompanied their male relatives as they occupied estate land in Alto Bío Bío during the 1920s and 1930s, few women would participate directly in the Ránquil rebellion, a reflection of both the patriarchal organization of campesino households and the rural labor movement as well as the legal codes that shaped campesinos' understanding of their land and labor rights. The earliest nineteenth-century land laws, dating back to 1845, and the colonization laws that followed well into the twentieth century prescribed a patriarchal social order in which only male heads of household were granted rights to public land. Colonization laws dictated that men who were heads of households and settled on public land were eligible for additional allotments for each of their male children above a certain age. Women and single adult men received no land rights under agrarian and colonization law. As Heidi Tinsman has shown, an array of additional laws granted male campesinos authority over their wives' labor, including the 1931 Labor Code's requirement that women have their husbands' permission to engage in wage labor and laws making husbands their wives' legal representatives in commercial and land transactions; these statutes shaped the process of agrarian reform and campesinos' struggle for land in the 1960s and early 1970s in profound ways. Just as the agrarian laws setting out the terms for the colonization of southern frontier territory were a template for later agrarian reform laws, colonization law similarly shaped the gendered terms in which land rights were defined by both the state and campesinos themselves during the years of Chile's agrarian reform between 1966 and 1973.[19]

There is some debate about the participation of Pehuenche communities in the Ránquil rebellion. The historian Jaime Flores, on the basis of an analysis of the last names of prisoners detained following the rebellion's repression, argues that only a small minority (close to 15 percent) of the rebels belonged to the region's Pehuenche communities. This statistic may not do justice to the role played by members of Pehuenche communities in the rebellion. Well before 1934 members of Pehuenche communities had joined the Sindicato Agrícola Lonquimay, and the union had established councils on estates neighboring Pehuenche communities where community members labored as inquilinos and gañanes. At least one of the union leaders during the early 1930s was Pehuenche, reflecting the presence of the region's indigenous communities in the union. There is evidence in detained rebels' testimony that male members of Pehuenche communities joined in assaults on a number of estates, where substantial numbers of Pehuenche inquilinos labored. Members of the Ralco community, led by their *lonko* (head or leader), Ignacio Maripi, joined the union, attended the union assembly at which the rebellion began, and took part in the rebellion. A number were killed, while others, including Maripi's son, were detained and jailed. The Ránquil rebellion was not the Indian uprising, or *indiada*, described in some fairly hysterical contemporary press accounts. But members of Pehuenche communities, especially the Ralco community, did play a role in both the union and the insurrection, a notable early experience of alliance between non-Mapuche (*huinca*) campesinos and Mapuche communities in the rural labor movement. This points to the ties between members of the community and their poor huinca neighbors; many worked together as inquilinos and gañanes on the region's estates.[20]

The Chilean Communist Party viewed Pehuenches' participation in the rebellion as a sign of its successful organizing of a revolutionary alliance of obreros, campesinos, and *indígenas*, as well as Mapuche communities' revolutionary potential and support for the establishment of an independent indigenous republic, a *república araucana*. However, the available evidence does not support the contention that Ralco or other Pehuenche communities supported the ideological project of organizing soviets or building an autonomous Araucanian Republic. Rather, Ralco's leaders adopted the same strategies as the nonindigenous members of the Sindicato Agrícola Lonquimay. They forged alliances with political parties, went to court to defend the community's land rights, traveled to Santiago to meet with ministers and the president, and worked with the union to win rights to land usurped by the Bunster family's estates. Like many of the Sindicato Agrícola Lonquimay's members, Ignacio Maripi wagered that with the backing of the union Ralco would finally win legal title to land held by the Bunster family because of the reforms introduced during the Ibáñez regime. When these hopes were dashed following Ibáñez's fall from power, new, revolutionary alternatives emerged. The socialist revolution advocated by Leiva Tapia and other union leaders appeared to hold the promise that Ralco and its members would finally recover land appropriated by the Bunsters' Guayalí and Ralco estates.[21]

Violence and Oblivion

The violence embraced by Ránquil's campesino rebels and the massacres committed by carabineros in the subsequent repression did not constitute an unusual case. Rather, Alto Bío Bío's *sucesos* (events), as they are often euphemistically called, belonged to a long, widespread history of rural violence throughout southern Chile. From the military conquest of the frontier and forcible appropriation of Mapuche territory to the formation of large estates and dispossession of campesino smallholders, property relations were shaped by acts of violence committed by the state and landowners and often opposed by campesinos, who not infrequently took up arms themselves to protect their land. In numerous cases Mapuche communities and Chilean campesinos battled for land with large estates that were supported by carabineros. As I demonstrate in this book, the historical processes that exploded in the Ránquil rebellion were repeated throughout the south. In Pellahuén, Nueva Italia–Capitán Pastene, Llaima, Budi, Toltén, and Pucón, among many other regions, estate owners confronted land invasions, recalcitrant squatter ocupantes, and small-scale rebellions of their inquilino laborers.

Historians to a one have identified campesino violence in Ránquil as an uprising, a spontaneous reaction to immediate conditions of exploitation and misery rather than an organized collective movement and armed insurgency. As in the case of colonial South Asia described by Ranajit Guha, where leftist historians described peasant rebellions as local uprisings or mob actions, the precursor to more modern political movements led by nationalist and Marxist parties, in Chile historians have tended to follow contemporary narratives of the Ránquil rebellion in language that emphasizes the campesino movement's nonpolitical nature, in distinction to the radical leftist politics of central and northern Chile's working-class movements: the sucesos or episode in Ránquil; the Lonquimay *levantamiento* (uprising).[22] "Uprising" and "events," rather than "insurgency" or even "rebellion," preserve the movement's local and immediate nature, even its exceptional quality, reducing it to Alto Bío Bío's unique concatenation of circumstances. As William Taylor notes with regard to colonial Mexico, peasant insurrections "are regional in scope," "offer new ideas or a vision of a new society," and aim for a "reorganization" of the social order, whereas revolts and uprisings are local and seek to reestablish a past social equilibrium. Historians, following contemporary observers, have tended to place the Ránquil rebellion in the camp of uprisings rather than insurrections, implicitly underlining its prepolitical, unplanned, and local nature. As Guha demonstrates in the case of colonial India, this characterization of peasants' collective movements impedes a serious historical engagement with their political consciousness.[23]

Much historical ink has been spilled on workers' movements in the nitrate zone in northern Chile, from the general strike and then infamous

1907 Escuela Santa María massacre in Iquique to the strikes, protests, and massacres in San Gregorio and La Coruña in the 1920s. Because nitrate production drove the Chilean economy from the 1870s until 1930 and because the nitrate mines were the birthplace of Chile's labor movement and Left, Chile's northern mining frontier has received a great deal of attention from historians.[24] Unlike nitrate workers' organizations and strikes, Ránquil and other southern rural rebellions have been largely relegated to historiographical oblivion. Northern Chile's working-class movements, led by Democrats, anarchists, and, later, Socialists and Communists, left a deep cultural and political footprint and an abundance of historical sources. In contrast, rural laborers in the south were dispersed and toiled on difficult-to-access estates that often lay on mountainous terrain or land covered with dense native forest. Whereas northern Chile's nitrate ports, Antofagasta and Iquique, linked the nitrate mines to the nation and the international economy, rural workers in southern Chile, especially in geographically isolated regions like Alto Bío Bío, were only tenuously connected to the rest of the country. They lacked the social and cultural institutions of the northern nitrate zone's mining and urban working class. As a result, they left a paucity of historical sources. Having access to few newspapers, unions, political parties, or cultural institutions they could call their own, they made their biggest historical impression in the uncatalogued and often lost archives of regional governments (intendencies), courts, and the police.

In part, the lack of readily available sources has meant that historians have too often ignored southern Chile's history of militant campesino movements. They have as well implicitly accepted the social-scientific argument that mine workers composed the vanguard of the Chilean labor movement and the pillar of Chile's revolutionary Left; if radicalization occurred in the countryside, it came from the outside, from the leftist parties and unions organized in cities or mining zones.[25] In the case of the Ránquil rebellion historians have confronted the challenge of locating sources beyond published memoirs or accounts in the regional and national press. Jaime Flores's 1993 master's thesis employed three important sources: the Curacautín newspaper *El Comercio*, the sentence delivered by the judge charged with investigating the crimes committed during the rebellion in the archive of the Temuco appeals court, and oral histories. In this book I build on Flores's work by adding new research in hitherto unexamined archival collections containing the documents of the interior ministry, the intendencies of Bío-Bío, Malleco, and Cautín provinces, labor courts, the Ministerio de Bienes Nacionales, whose report of a government commission charged with investigating the history of the Puelma estates is invaluable, military courts, and local and regional courts, including that of Temuco's appellate court, as well as in newspapers from local towns.

Most important, I was able to review four volumes of documents containing a wealth of information produced during the judicial investigation of the rebellion by the appellate court justice Franklin Quezada Rogers. Documents in these volumes describe in detail the campesino rebels and the rebellion itself. They were originally held in the archive of Temuco's appellate court, but for reasons unknown were transferred for storage to the city's Conservador de Bienes Raíces, a privately operated property registry office. A great deal of persistent negotiation finally allowed me to gain access to these volumes, which appear in no catalogue and whose existence the conservador repeatedly denied. There are at least seven volumes in the collection; the conservador provided access to only four of these, claiming ignorance of the remaining volumes' location. My hope is that the three volumes are recovered and that all seven volumes are transferred to Chile's national archives, where they can be made available to future researchers.

The difficulties I encountered in tracking down and then reviewing the records of the judicial inquiry into the Ránquil rebellion reflect the lamentable state of Chile's judicial archives, but also perhaps the Chilean state's efforts to erase the insurrection and its bloody repression from the historical record, to consign it to *olvido* (oblivion), as part of the political process of national reconciliation based on a blanket amnesty passed in September 1934. The amnesty covered both the campesino rebels who sought to produce a violent overthrow of the government and the carabineros who responded with the kinds of counterinsurgent violence that one might associate with the Cold War in Latin America. Eventually, the campesinos' crimes were all deemed by the courts to be part of a political conflict and thus, rather than matters of criminal investigation and penalty, acts that should be amnestied. Less of a surprise is that legal accusations against carabineros received only summary investigations by military courts and that serious investigation of the Ránquil massacre was foreclosed by the same amnesty law.[26]

The challenges of accessing the judicial records, which include transcripts of interrogations of detained campesinos, might be viewed as representative of the larger methodological problem of how to enter the realm of campesinos' lived experience and build some understanding of their motivations and goals, their political consciousness. The judicial inquiry into the rebellion contains a great deal of information about its origins and the events that took place during late June and early July 1934 in Alto Bío Bío. But as in the case of all police and judicial records, this information is marked by elisions and distortions. While one can hear campesinos' voices in their testimony under questioning, their words offer only a partial and fragmented view of the rebellion and its root causes.

Carabineros' torture and execution of detained prisoners during the rebellion's repression constitutes one obvious obstacle to establishing a clear historical record. Extreme violence caused trauma and certainly made campesinos reluctant to testify openly and explicitly either following their arrest or later while held prisoner under miserable conditions in Temuco. A number of detained campesinos confessed after being tortured. Some attempted to recant their coerced testimony but without success. In general, campesinos understandably tried to deflect responsibility by claiming they had been coerced by a small group of *cabecillas* (ringleaders) and by denying they had supported the movement's revolutionary goals.

Two contradictory but complementary approaches to representing the rebellion shaped campesinos' testimony and mediated the directness with which they speak in the judicial records. First, both police reports and the judicial inquiry reduced the rebellion to a collection of common crimes, eliding its revolutionary insurgent character. This was coupled with a narrative repeated in both the press and congress describing campesinos as credulous or backward or both and as being either coerced or instigated by a handful of communist agitators. The rebellion was nothing more than an assortment of criminal acts committed by an unruly mob of otherwise peaceful campesinos led astray by communist agents. Second, the amnesty law precluded any investigation of political crimes and any consideration of the commitment to a collective revolutionary process that might have inspired campesinos who joined the rebellion. In both cases, either by defining the rebellion as a matter for the criminal courts or applying an amnesty to all imprisoned campesinos, the effect was to prevent any coming to terms with the Ránquil rebels' revolutionary challenge to the status quo in the southern countryside. The judicial inquiry raises the question of how to read, in Guha's words, the "prose of counterinsurgency," which shaped judicial, police, and press reports' characterization of the rebellion as criminal banditry and campesinos as common criminals, "against the grain" to come to some understanding of campesinos' political consciousness, their engagement with the movement's insurrectionary strategy and revolutionary goals.[27] The amnesty presupposed that all crimes committed during the rebellion were political, contradicting the tenor of police reports and the judicial investigation, yet it similarly preempted any investigation of the movement's revolutionary dynamics.

The Pinochet regime's infamous 1978 "auto amnesty"—imposed as a decree-law following five years of the worst state terror the country had ever seen—had a long genealogy in amnesties going back to the wars of independence and nineteenth-century civil wars. As Elizabeth Lira and Brian Loveman have demonstrated, amnesties and pardons of crimes associated with political violence have produced the historical amnesia, the olvido, necessary to national reconciliation, functioning as a precondition for Chilean democracy and the legitimacy of the state.[28] In the case of the 1934 amnesty law, foreclosing a full accounting of campesinos' insurrectionary violence was necessary to extending the amnesty to carabineros for the massacres committed during the suppression of the insurrection. At a more general level, the amnesty served to establish the olvido necessary to restoring social and political stability. The amnesty closed the books on the violent social conflicts that had shaken southern Chile and swept under the rug the state's use of extraordinary violence to quell the rebellion. Similarly, it operated to wipe from the legal record a series of military coups and interventions that had defined Chilean politics since 1931, including a 1932 coup that ushered in a brief Socialist Republic. The amnesty and subsequent olvido, like the bloody repression in Alto Bío Bío, laid the foundation of the stable multiparty democracy established in 1932 with the election of Arturo Alessandri, which lasted until the 1973 military coup.

In the end, detained rebels' testimony raises the question of how to understand the causes and dynamics of the Ránquil rebellion. How to interpret campesinos' turn to armed insurrection? The fact of the massacre has dominated both popular memory and the historiography of Ránquil, eclipsing any analysis of the violence committed by the campesino movement. In part, both the disproportionate size of the massacre of possibly hundreds of prisoners and the hysterical accounts of the rebels' acts of criminal barbarity, all part of a general campaign in the press and congress to depict the campesinos as barbarous, depraved, communist *indios*, produced a backlash in popular cultural representation and in the work of historians, which largely portrays the rebels as innocent victims of state violence. Historians' response to the hyperbolic, and mostly invented, descriptions of the rebel bands' atrocities has been to ignore the acts of violence committed by the revolutionary movement as well as campesinos' commitment to an armed insurrectionary path to socialist revolution. Most descriptions portray the rebels as the victims rather than the perpetrators of violence. The slim historiography of the rebellion has mostly failed to come to terms with the question of both campesinos' agency and the character of their revolutionary politics.

A close reading of the rebellious campesinos' actions, including their use of violence and their testimony to the court during the judicial investigation, opens a way of understanding their values, ideas, and motivations, even a rough sense of their political consciousness. The rebels' crimes could easily appear to constitute the criminal acts of a mob driven by deprivation and hunger, a common portrayal in the press and congress at the time. Yet hunger does not suffice to explain the violence. Campesinos acted because they were animated by a sense of justice rooted in decades of engagement with state agencies and the legal system. In assaulting estates and pulperías, they did not simply engage in banditry or looting. They viewed their actions as recovering provisions that were rightfully theirs and acquiring land to which they held legal rights. The rebels' acts of violence also reveal a dimension of symbolic social subversion, of turning the world upside down, an inversion of established social hierarchies that would have given concrete meaning to the Communist Party's more formal ideological promise of revolutionary transformation. What appeared to outside observers to be criminal acts of banditry had a practical purpose as well. The revolutionary movement's leaders targeted pulperías and estates for assault because they sought provisions and arms. The goods stored in estates' storehouses and pulperías would allow them to survive the months of harsh winter weather until, they believed, a nationwide revolution deposed the Alessandri government.

One is left to piece together from the shards of evidence the insurrection's revolutionary character and the ways in which the region's campesinos, described as sober and hardworking in numerous accounts, came to see armed insurrection as a legitimate response to the abuses inflicted by carabineros and the violence inherent in a rural social order in which large estates accumulated tens of thousands of hectares of land while campesinos were either left landless or relegated to small plots on the most rocky and inhospitable high-altitude terrain, where winter winds blew hard and snowfall accumulated by the meter. During 1934, having tried every legal means at their disposal and having exhausted every political appeal on their many trips to Santiago and now facing eviction from their land, the rebels began to see that the Communist Party's depiction of the Alessandri regime as illegitimate and guilty of bloody acts of repression made more and more sense. What is more, given the Sindicato Agrícola Lonquimay's success in building a powerful campesino movement and the political turmoil of the last years with its military coups and uprisings, the party's advocacy of armed self-defense and the occupation of large estates as the first steps to overthrowing a government identified with both landowners and a long history of massacres would have appeared as a practical possibility. In Alto Bío Bío, after years of collective organizing to build unions and appropriate the region's estates it would not have been difficult for campesinos to see revolution on the horizon.

One is left, too, with the difficult question of the executions of the more than one hundred campesinos who surrendered. Numerous accounts allow one to both piece together the acts of violence and establish a rough estimate of the numbers of dead. At their most impressionistic, descriptions of Alto Bío Bío after the rebellion and carabineros' successful counterinsurgency paint a picture of desolation, burned houses, women and children abandoned without food and shelter, perhaps hundreds widowed and orphaned, many hiding from carabineros in the mountains. Following the rebels' final surrender, carabineros reported triumphantly that they had detained four hundred prisoners and were prepared to march them to Temuco, where they would be tried for their crimes. But only fifty-six arrived, and eventually sixty-two people were imprisoned in Temuco. Carabineros' explanations for this discrepancy foreshadow the explanations given by the Pinochet regime for its forcible disappearance of leftist militants in the 1970s. Many, they reported, had been killed in crossfire with bands of roaming insurgents. Others, who had attempted to flee, flung themselves into the Biobío River, and had presumably either died or escaped to freedom. No cadavers were ever located. They all simply disappeared, confirmation perhaps of some accounts that described carabineros' lining up prisoners on the banks of the Biobío River, where they faced the firing squad.

Police reports stated that numerous rebels had fled into the mountains and across the border to Argentina, another explanation for the whereabouts of *desaparecidos* that would reemerge during the darkest years of the Pinochet dictatorship. Sober estimates since the 1940s range from eighty executed and disappeared to two hundred. The government convened no truth commission, however, to investigate carabineros' crimes, and the 1934 amnesty law precluded any further judicial inquiry. Revolutionary challenges to the Alessandri regime remained quelled, Chilean security forces' first successful counterinsurgency in the countryside. Four decades of populist social reforms would follow, winning Chile the reputation as Latin America's most reliable multiparty democracy. This democracy would not accommodate any challenges to the rule of large estates in the countryside. For campesinos, the labor and agrarian reform legislation crafted during the 1920s to establish social peace—and tentatively introduced onto a handful of southern estates during the late 1920s—remained unimplemented. Democracy and social reform did not make it out of the city to the countryside.

But southern campesinos' movements to appropriate privately held property, their long history of clearing forests, planting crops on inhospitable soil, erecting fences, and pasturing their livestock in the mountains, staking a claim to frontier land based on their labor, would reemerge, this time at the national level during the agrarian reform implemented by the Christian Democratic government of Eduardo Frei Montalva (1964–70) and the socialist government of Salvador Allende (1970–73). The basic concepts of this period, namely, that the land belonged to those who worked it and that large, unproductive estates that did not fully cultivate their land or were embroiled in social conflicts might be expropriated by the state in the public interest, had been tried before, however tentatively, during the late 1920s and early 1930s in southern Chile. Now, however, the wave of land occupations and union organizing among campesinos swept rural Chile from south to north, inspired by the revolutionary politics of the 1960s. As in 1934, the response was draconian. Among the worst, most hidden, and hard to reveal atrocities committed following the 1973 military coup were directed at southern campesinos.

The Ránquil massacre left possibly hundreds dead and disappeared, but the violence visited on the countryside by the military regime led by Pinochet, now armed with Cold War national security ideology and more modern technologies and techniques of counterinsurgency propagated by the United States, marked a new chapter in the Chilean state's repression of popular movements. If repression in the countryside in 1934 was the prerequisite for populist social and labor reforms during the 1940s, state terror after 1973 was directed toward an entirely different purpose: to unravel those same reforms and establish the social order and political stability required by the military regime's radical experiment with free-market economic reform. In the end, Ránquil is a reminder that political violence and state terror have a long history in Chile and that the profound socioeconomic inequalities in the Chilean countryside today, one of the grim effects of Chile's supposed free-market economic miracle, are rooted in the repression of campesinos' recurrent struggles to build a more free and just society.

CHAPTER ONE

San Ignacio de Pemehue
Building an Hacienda on the Southern Frontier

IN THE FRONTIER TOWN of Los Ángeles in March of 1863 an indigenous Pehuenche, referred to in legal documents as the "indígena named Nahuel," transferred rights to an ill-defined tract of land just south of the Biobío River to José María Rodríguez. This was not a simple land sale however. Nahuel used the land to pay off a supposed debt of an equally imprecise "quantity of pesos" he owed Rodríguez. The deed produced during the sale of Nahuel's land, which he had allegedly used as collateral for a loan, did not describe the size of the property, but the judicial proceedings to seize it to pay off the debt did delineate vague boundaries. They described the land's northern border as the Llolenco and Curaco estuaries, the southern border as the Lirque estuary, "following this estuary to the east until it arrives at a road," the southeastern border as Agua de los Padres, "bordering on the south this same path until it hits the Renaico River and following the Puelche River until it hits the cordillera." The eastern border was given as the Andes cordillera, as if the intertwined mountain chains that compose the cordillera were a simple line, and the western border the confluence of the Mulchén River and the Lirque and Llollenco estuaries, a point rather than a line.[1] This property transfer laid the groundwork for the formation of what would become one of Chile's largest haciendas, the 180,000-hectare San Ignacio de

Pemehue estate. It planted the seed of decades of bitter conflict over land and property rights in Chile's Alto Bío Bío region that would explode in a bloody campesino insurrection in 1934.

When Nahuel ceded this land to pay off the debt to Rodríguez, the transaction reflected the new push by Chilean settlers and land speculators to occupy independent Mapuche territory, the frontier region known as the Araucanía. Only a decade earlier the government of Manuel Montt (1851–61) had begun to make the state's presence felt in the territory controlled by independent indigenous Mapuche groups between the Biobío River on the north and the Toltén River on the south. In 1852 it established Arauco province and made the town of Los Ángeles its capital, installing the embryonic institutions of governance: a provincial intendancy, department governerships, and local courts. The law also delegated to the president the authority to govern the new province by decree, an assumption of presidential power and mode of governance that would become increasingly frequent over the course of the nineteenth and twentieth centuries when regimes across the political spectrum would resort to rule by decrees, decree-laws, and decrees with power of law (*decretos con fuerza de ley*).[2]

During the first half of the nineteenth century Arauco had been governed by a number of indigenous groups loosely grouped together under the term "Mapuche" or "*araucano*." Pehuenches had historically constituted their own ethnic group, but through increasing trade and contact with Mapuche groups to the west in the central valleys and littoral they had become "araucanized" during the eighteenth century, integrated culturally and linguistically into Mapuche society. At the beginning of the nineteenth century Pehuenche territory stretched from Laja to Lonquimay, straddling the Andes cordillera. Mapuche groups to the south and west engaged in sedentary agriculture and established permanent settlements, while Pehuenches were largely nomadic, moving back and forth from the mountain valleys on the Chilean side of the cordillera to the Argentine pampas. Following the Spanish conquest, Pehuenches adopted European horses, cows, and sheep, building a robust livestock economy. They also collected salt from the eastern slopes of the Andes and the seeds of cones from high-altitude *Araucaria araucana* pine (known as *piñones*, or pine nuts), a major staple of their diet and trade that served as an alternative to the grains and garden crops cultivated by more sedentary Mapuche groups.[3]

Pehuenches' transhumance meant that they had no fixed relationship to land but relied on movement between diverse ecological niches. They also depended on trade with other Mapuche groups and Spanish or Chilean merchants. They built extensive commercial networks linking the eastern side of the Andes in Argentina to the western side of the cordillera in southern Chile, descending into the fertile plains of the central valley.[4] During the eighteenth century Pehuenches traded horses, salt, skins, ponchos, and ostrich feathers with Spanish merchants.[5] Until the mid-nineteenth century, with the brief interruption of the independence wars, *parlamentos*, parleys and peace treaties hammered out between Mapuche leaders and Spanish and then Chilean authorities, religious missions, and dynamic trade defined Pehuenches' relation to the colonial and then to republican governments.[6] As late as the 1850s caravans of Chilean merchants traded tools, wheat and corn, and beads with Pehuenche groups in the Andes in exchange for salt and livestock.[7]

Pehuenches' transcordillera trade was possible because the Andes cordillera becomes lower in southern Chile, reaching altitudes of only two thousand to three thousand meters at its highest points. In Alto Bío Bío a number of mountain passes lying between seventeen hundred and twenty-four hundred meters above sea level allowed Pehuenches movement across the cordillera from Chile into the Argentine pampas.[8] Andean glacial lakes give rise to numerous rivers and estuaries descending to the west into lowland valleys and are fed by winter rains and spring snowmelt, running through steep ravines and gorges.[9] On the western side of the cordillera at lower altitudes lie sheltered valleys and river basins where winter snows are scarce. These valleys are protected by forests of the Chilean beech known as *coigüe* (*Nothofagus dombeyi*) and *roble* (*Nothofagus obliqua*) as well as *rauilí* (*Lophozonia alpine*), cypress, and the evergreen conifer *lleuque* (*Prumnopitys andina*). In the winter Pehuenches took their cattle to graze in these valleys, known as *invernadas* (winter pastures). During the summer they pastured their livestock further up the cordillera in high-altitude valleys known as *veranadas* (summer pastures), which were covered with snow during the winter. There, their animals found sustenance in *quila*, a wild bamboo, *coirón*, a hardy thatch grass that evolved to survive low temperatures and the strong winter winds, and the bark and branches of shrubs, including *yaqui* (*Colletia spinosa*), *chacay* (*Discaria trenervis*), and *michay* (*Berberis darwinii*). At higher altitudes, where the vegetation was sparser, both people and livestock fed on *piñones*.

In 1853 the Montt government took up the question of what to do with frontier territory south of the Biobío River. An 1845 colonization law had established the legal framework for settling foreign and Chilean settlers (colonos) on *terrenos baldíos* (empty lands), effectively ignoring the frontier's large Mapuche population and its territorial sovereignty. It enabled the state to grant men who were heads of households up to twenty-five *cuadras* of land (a cuadra is about 1.7 hectares) and to each of their sons up to twelve cuadras on frontier land. Settling male-headed households of colonos in the frontier would establish the basis for social order and a productive agricultural economy. As President Manuel Bulnes noted in 1850, the goal of the law was to populate the putatively empty lands of the southern provinces, especially with European immigrants.[10] By decree the Montt government then established the legal protocols for building a regime of private property and transferring land from indigenous persons. Sales and rentals of untitled indigenous land were made legal, but a set of restrictions applied. The province's intendant or governor of the department where the land was located had to approve the transaction. Article three of the decree required that sales of properties larger than one thousand cuadras (which would have been the case in the transfer of Nahuel's supposed property in Alto Bío Bío) be approved by the government in Santiago. The decree was intended to introduce government regulation of a process defined by widespread appropriation by force and fraud in which frontier territory was sacked by opportunistic Chilean speculators who accumulated enormous properties, thereby depriving the state of a crucial source of potential revenue and imposing an obstacle in the way of European immigration.[11] There is no indication that, in 1863, either the intendant or governor authorized Nahuel's transfer of what he said was his land to Rodríguez to pay off a putative debt.[12] Even in the Chilean state's own terms, the sale was clearly illegitimate.

In addition, Nahuel held no rights to sell property and probably understood the transfer of land to Rodríguez, if he understood the contract, which was written in Spanish, or had been assigned a translator (for which there is no evidence), as a grant of usufruct rights. Pehuenches did not own property as individuals or even as groups defined by kinship networks. Their transhumance and mobility meant that they viewed land not in terms of ownership but as a variety of ecological niches to which they enjoyed customary rights. In no circumstance would one indigenous person, even a lonko representing a larger kinship group or community, be able to claim property rights to thousands of hectares of land that could be sold, transferred, or rented to non-Mapuche Chileans (huincas). Land sales at best would have been understood as rentals or as grants of nonexclusive usufructory rights to land historically used by Pehuenche groups to graze livestock and collect forest products.

Nahuel's 1863 sale of his land to Rodríguez came at an opportune time, just as frontier military campaigns opened up new territory south of the Biobío River for settlement. In 1861 the Chilean state began to make its governance of Arauco province reality through the process of military conquest and occupation. That year the Chilean military, advancing from the north, reestablished the frontier city of Angol, which had been destroyed during indigenous rebellions in 1723 and 1766. From there it began to build a line of forts, known as the Malleco line, stretching along the Malleco River that began, step by step, to squeeze indigenous territory from the north. Rodríguez probably seized on the Chilean military push south of the Biobío River to acquire Pehuenche land, establishing a fraudulent claim to pasture whose value would increase as Alto Bío Bío was integrated into Chilean territory.

Despite the apparently illegitimate origins of Nahuel's transfer of land to Rodríguez, the title to this property was registered in the Conservador de Bienes Raíces in Nacimiento. Rodríguez's intentions were clearly speculative, as was the case in many equivalent transactions. In October 1864, just months after he had stepped down from his positions as intendant of Arauco and commander of Chile's military forces on the southern frontier, Cornelio Saaverda purchased the land from Rodríguez, eventually turning it into an hacienda, San Ignacio de Pemehue.[13] He paid for the land in Los Ángeles by transferring to Rodríguez an IOU of $7,184 pesos that he held from Joaquín Fuentealba. In exchange for this assignment of a debt owed to him by a third party, Rodríguez agreed to give Saavedra his choice of four thousand cuadras of land.[14]

Cornelio Saavedra's purchase of the land acquired from Nahuel reveals a great deal about both state governance and the formation of private property in southern Chile's frontier territory. During the late 1850s Saavedra had held the highest political and military positions in Arauco province as intendant and military commander. In 1861 he initiated a reorientation of the state's approach to indigenous territory. Until that year Chilean governments had more or less continued the existing policy handed down from the Spanish colonial state of colonizing indigenous territory with religious missions and building profitable commerce with independent Mapuche groups. At the same time, by the 1840s and with increasing volume during the 1850s, Chilean settlers began to cross the Biobío River and acquire indigenous land in an informal and unregulated process, purchasing and renting land from Mapuches or appropriating it by force.

As the historian Jorge Pinto argues, two crises, one economic and the other political, sparked a change in state policy toward indigenous territory. First, during the 1840s and 1850s Chile had ridden the wave of an economic boom, driven by silver mining and wheat exports to emerging Pacific markets in California and Australia. By the late 1850s silver production had declined, and the United States and Australia had begun to supply their own wheat, leading to a major economic crisis in Chile in 1857.[15] Leading Chilean Liberals, including José Bunster, a Valparaíso merchant who had invested in land across the Biobío River, and Benjamín Vicuña Mackenna, led the movement to pressure the government to conquer the Araucanía by force during the late 1850s and 1860s. They argued that once pacified and settled the southern frontier would yield a bonanza of wealth that would resuscitate Chile's agricultural economy.[16] Second, an 1859 Liberal revolution against the government of Manuel Montt provoked a rupture in Mapuche–Chilean relations. A number of Mapuche groups allied themselves with the forces of southern revolutionaries against the central government in Santiago, taking advantage of the political schism produced by the civil war to rebel against encroachments into their territory by Chilean settlers.[17]

In the context of the economic and political crisis of the late 1850s, Saavedra proposed a military strategy for incorporating independent indigenous territory into the nation. Following his design, the Liberal–Conservative alliance government of José Joaquín Pérez (1861–71) began to push the Chilean military line southward. Saavedra's goal was to populate the region with industrious smallholders, often former solders, protected by a chain of forts.[18] Saavedra was also concerned with the fraudulent dispossession of indigenous peoples, unlike the Liberal exterminationist position articulated forcefully by the voice of Valparaíso's merchant elite, *El Mercurio de Valparaíso*, and Santiago's Liberal *El Ferrocarril*. *El Mercurio* proposed in 1859 that the government "defeat and exterminate the indígenas" in order to "take control of the vast and wealthy territories of the Araucanía" via military conquest. *El Ferrocarril* argued that same year that "the araucanos are barbarians ... [and] they do not have the right to be treated as men, they should be dispossessed of their land and must be exterminated or enslaved."[19] While advocating military conquest of the Araucanía's indigenous population, Saavedra sought to settle Mapuches on small plots of land and place them under state protection with the goal of making them productive, civilized farmers, assimilated into Chilean society. To Saavedra, protecting indigenous land from fraudulent and forcible appropriation by land speculators was also essential to guaranteeing both state dominion over frontier territory and settling newly acquired supposedly public land with small and midsize farmers. Saavedra proposed the subdivision of frontier land into plots of five hundred to one thousand cuadras to be sold at public auction, which would produce a large number of smaller properties and produce a new source of agricultural wealth and stream of revenue for the state.[20]

Rampant land fraud undermined Saavedra's project of settling the frontier with small farmers. In 1861 he described one of the methods employed by speculators to rob both "indios" and the state of their land and form large estates. He noted that throughout frontier territory there were numerous contracts in which indios appeared as debtors for "large quantities of pesos." These debts were then taken to local courts, where Mapuches surrendered what they called their property, land they had purportedly employed as collateral. Saavedra reported that "in general these contracts are simulated. The lands that they seize through debt, either do not belong to the supposed debtors or they are empty and thus belong to the State." "In these contracts," he continued, "it is common to find an indio receiving interest-bearing loans of four, six, and ten thousand pesos, with a term of two, three, and even fifteen days, with loans taken out on vast expanses of land." According to Saavedra, "It wasn't bad speculation, they looked for anyone wearing a *chamal* [woolen blanket] who spoke indio, they gave him one or two pesos to go to a scribe and swear they were owners of large extensions of land and to say that they had received some quantity of thousands of pesos." This was how, he concluded, land speculators "defrauded scandalously the State."[21] The fraud committed in the alienation of indigenous land had produced "chaos in the legitimacy of property rights."[22]

A decade later Saavedra noted that "in a number of reports I have had occasion to speak of the damages done to the State and the indígenas by private parties who usurped land that came under the protection of our advancing frontiers." In part, this fraud was committed via translators. An 1856 account described how "speculators bring with them selected translators who transmit to the public scribes distinct concepts from those the indígenas communicate." In Alto Bío Bío, Pehuenches like Nahuel were brought before scribes and notaries; the party purchasing the land provided a translator, who participated in the fraudulent appropriation of indigenous land. According to Raúl Molina and Martín Correa, this method of stealing Pehuenche land was used in the purchase of a number of estates in Alto Bío Bío, including Ralco and Guayalí. Other reports noted that Mapuches, who had little understanding of the Spanish terms used to describe distance or even of the legal meaning of private property, sold vast spaces in return for a small number of pesos.[23]

Rampant land fraud became so acute that in 1863 and again in 1873 the government banned notaries and scribes in Nacimiento, Arauco, and Mulchén from registering land sales from Mapuches because since 1853 numerous land titles had been issued to pay off Mapuches' debts without the approval of intendants, governors, or, after 1866, indigenous protectors, who could guarantee that the indígenas "understand the contracts they attempt to grant." Despite these clear regulations, notaries and scribes throughout Arauco province continued to issue deeds in which "indígenas ... admit that they owe debts of large sums to third parties" without government oversight. As the 1873 decree noted, in most cases the Mapuches who signed these contracts handing over their land had little comprehension of what the transaction meant, which "calls into question the legitimacy of the loans."[24] Given this rampant fraud, Cornelio Saavedra argued for regulations to guarantee the state's right to the frontier land being opened up by the military and to prevent "abuses of indios."[25]

It is thus ironic that in October 1864 Saavedra purchased the land Nahuel had transferred to Rodríguez the previous year. His description of the use of fictitious debt to appropriate indigenous land is almost a literal description of Nahuel's transfer of his land to pay off a debt of "a quantity of pesos." Yet Saavedra saw no problem in purchasing this same land from Rodríguez, participating in the bonanza of land speculation that had been the business of military commanders in southern frontier territory for decades. In fact, Saavedra was joined by another southern military official in the land grab in Alto Bío Bío. On 15 October 1873 Rodríguez sold another piece of land he had acquired from Nahuel to Manuel Bulnes Pinto, the son of the Chilean president Manuel Bulnes Prieto (1841–51). In 1867 Bulnes Pinto had led a National Guard unit of 375 men, which he had organized and funded himself, from Mulchén into the mountains to combat independent Mapuche groups known as *arribanos*.[26] By 1870 he had become a sergeant major in the regular army, leading troops in frontier battles with recalcitrant Mapuche groups. Bulnes Pinto, like Saavedra and other military commanders, viewed land on the southern frontier as an excellent place for speculation and leveraged his military position and political contacts to acquire inexpensive property. In 1872, a year before he purchased a piece of Nahuel's land from Rodríguez, he had been sent to Antuco to guarantee Pehuenche groups' loyalty and convince them to celebrate a formal surrender to the Chilean government.[27]

Bulnes Pinto was simply following in his father's footsteps. In the 1840s Manuel Bulnes Prieto had commanded Chile's troops along the southern border with Mapuche territory and acquired a large hacienda near the frontier town of Nacimiento.[28] Eighteen seventy-three would have been a good year for his son to purchase land in Alto Bío Bío. That year, after decades of warfare and violence, fifty Pehuenche *caciques* (chiefs or leaders) signed a peace treaty and recognized the authority of the Chilean government under Bulnes Pinto's supervision as a commander in the southern army. Only five years earlier Cornelio Saavedra had completed his campaign to push the Chilean military line southward to the Malleco River.[29] The military "pacification" of the Araucanía had also opened the door to the extension of the railroad into frontier territory. In 1873 a line connecting Los Ángeles to the town of Angol was built, integrating Alto Bío Bío into national markets and pushing up property values.

Both Bulnes's and Saavedra's interests in acquiring Pehuenche land in Alto Bío Bío were clearly speculative, reflecting the ways in which the military leaders in charge of conquering frontier territory viewed indigenous land as a profitable investment. Neither appears to have built fences, pastured livestock, or hired inquilinos to work on their new properties. Both continued, however, with their military careers during the 1860s and 1870s. In August 1879, fifteen years after he had purchased the hacienda he called San Ignacio de Pemehue from Rodríguez, Saavedra sold the property to Francisco Puelma Castillo for $86,000 pesos.[30] For his part, Bulnes, who had divided his property, now known as the Santa Elena hacienda, into several lots, sold them in 1881. Puelma Castillo purchased the easternmost lot, which bordered the land he had purchased from Saavedra, for $11,000 pesos.[31]

On the eve of the 1879 land sale Saavedra wrote to Puelma Castillo to say that the price of the sale would be ten pesos per cuadra for the first four thousand cuadras and eight pesos for the remaining four thousand cuadras. He added that in terms of the rest, "from the Alto de Cule that forms the first *cordón de serranía* [mountain chain] with vegetation and grass ... to the high altitude part, which can only be considered as pasture and that continues then into the Cordillera with its valleys, *señor* Saavedra will fix the value with prudence."[32] A question immediately arises: How did the four thousand cuadras Saavedra purchased from Rodríguez in 1864 become, fourteen years later, well more than eight thousand cuadras, extending eastward into the Andes cordillera? The Altos de Cule toward the east were an important landmark. The peaks are north of the Renaico River in the cordillera and west of the Biobío River, confirming that, despite the hacienda's expansion to over eight thousand cuadras, in 1879 the southern border remained the Renaico River, as set down in the 1863 transfer of Nahuel's land, and the eastern border the highest peaks of the cordillera.

The sales from Rodríguez to Bulnes Pinto and Saavedra, and from the latter two to Francisco Puelma Castillo, each successively enlarged the size of the hacienda that Puelma Castillo would call San Ignacio de Pemehue. The property expanded northward to the Mulchén River, which had not been defined during the original property transfer from Nahuel; eastward to the highest peaks of the Andes cordillera, which were the Lonquimay, Chilpa, and Tolhuaca volcanoes and the border dividing Chile from Argentina; and southward to the Renaico River. According to the telling of his son Francisco Puelma Tupper, Francisco Puelma Castillo took immediate possession of the property he had purchased from Saavedra and Bulnes and, unlike the two military commanders, introduced improvements on the land, a key measure of legal dominion. He built houses, roads, bridges, and corrals, cultivated fields, pastured a considerable number of cattle, and installed families of inquilinos and *empleados* (employees).[33]

Francisco Puelma Castillo came from the upper echelons of Chilean society. Born in 1828, he attended the prestigious Instituto Nacional, where he studied engineering with the Polish scientist Ignacio Domeyko, focusing on mining. He continued on to the University of Chile, where he studied law. Probably influenced by his studies with Domeyko, he chose to pursue a career in mining and found a position administering the Descubridora copper mine in Chañarcillo in northern Chile at a time when Chile was becoming the world's largest copper producer. Puelma Castillo translated his experience in copper mining to the development of Chile's nitrate industry in the Bolivian province of Antofagasta. In partnership with José Santos Ossa, he located rich deposits of nitrates near the city of Antofagasta and secured a mining concession from the Bolivian government, founding the Compañía Explotadora del Desierto de Atacama. The company received investments from the Valparaíso merchant Agustín Edwards Ossandón as well as from the British merchant William Gibbs, who had already established nitrate enterprises in the Peruvian province of Tarapacá. The renamed company, the Compañía de Salitre y Ferrocarril, would become one of Chile's major nitrate producers in 1872 after acquiring a concession from the Bolivian government to exploit Antofagasta's nitrates.[34]

Puelma Castillo parlayed his financial successes in mining into a long career in politics. He served as intendant of Chiloé and Arauco in 1857 and as deputy in congress between 1858 and 1870. As the intendant of Arauco, just two years before Cornelio Saavedra occupied the position, he "dedicated himself to consolidating the defensive line of the frontier and countering the expansion of indigenous [territory]." Like Saavedra and Bulnes Pinto, he was an advocate of the military "pacification of the Araucanía" and the project of bringing independent Mapuche territory into the domain of the expanding Chilean state.[35] It seems that he invested some of his nitrate fortune as well as the power of his political positions as intendant of Arauco and Chiloé, deputy for Nacimiento and Arauco, and then senator for the province of Ñuble into the purchase of the properties that would come to compose his San Ignacio de Pemehue hacienda.[36]

In 1878 and 1879 the Argentine military initiated operations against indigenous groups on the western frontier in what was known as "the campaign of the desert." By 1883 the offensive had succeeded in defeating independent Pehuenche groups, many of whom fled into the Andes cordillera and across the porous border with Chile into the mountain valleys of Alto Bío Bío, settling in Trapa Trapa, Queco, Guayalí, and Lonquimay.[37] At the same time, the Chilean military continued its push southward and eastward, moving its line of forts from the Malleco River until arriving finally at the Cautín River in 1881. This incremental military conquest of independent Mapuche territory ended with the retaking of Villarrica in 1883. During 1882 and 1883 the Chilean military entered Alto Bío Bío's cordillera, building forts in the Nitrito, Lonquimay, Lincura, and Maitchi valleys.[38] Puelma Castillo's purchase of San Ignacio coincided conveniently but not coincidentally with the final defeat of the remaining independent Mapuche groups and the establishment of Chilean military control over Alto Bío Bío.

Military violence played an essential role in allowing Puelma Castillo to enjoy the fruits of his property. In 1882, as Pehuenche groups fled westward across the cordillera from Argentina into Alto Bío Bío, Chilean forces stationed at the fort in Lolco massacred a large group of Pehuenche men, women, and children. The victims included a number of Pehuenches who had been sent as messengers by "the cacique of Lonquimay" on the

Chilean side of the Andes to meet with Martín Drouilly, the commander of Chilean troops in Alto Bío Bío. The soldiers were instigated by two administrators of Puelma Castillo's San Ignacio de Pemehue hacienda. Drouilly said that when he arrived in Nitrito he found that "the friendly indios had all fled because of the cruel and hidden massacres that had been committed in November by the Lolco fort's forces, massacres directed by the empleados of San Ignacio." Among the dead, according to Drouilly, were "nineteen women and children assassinated and incinerated three leagues from Nitrito" as well as "seven unarmed indios sent to Nitrito" who were shot and then thrown into the Biobío River in order "to make the crime disappear." The bloody massacre cleared Puelma Castillo's newly acquired hacienda of Pehuenche groups who had settled in the fertile Nitrito Valley. The massacre might be viewed as a precondition for the so-called improvements Puelma Castillo then introduced on his property: roads, bridges, fences, cleared forest, and a labor force of inquilinos.[39]

Ironically, the final violent conquest of Alto Bío Bío's mountain valleys in 1882–83 did not help Francisco Puelma Castillo consolidate his dominion over his new property, despite his economic position and political influence. Instead, during the Liberal regime of José Manuel Balmaceda (1886–91) the state began to assert its rights to recently pacified frontier land, which it defined as public, in part by creating new administrative divisions, which included the establishment of Cautín and Malleco provinces. A month into his administration, Balmaceda, who had served as colonization minister between 1881 and 1883, promulgated new instructions to the lands inspectorate to survey and distribute frontier territory in fifty-hectare lots to colonos in Victoria, Purén, and Traiguén. Two years later the Balmaceda government attempted to create a lands and colonization directorate to establish state oversight over colonization in the territory south of the Biobío. When this measure was blocked in congress, Balmaceda decreed the reorganization of the office of Lands and Colonization "to guarantee the conservation of the State's lands, organize the measurement and division of these lands, and oversee the constitution of indigenous property and the installation of colonos." The frontier would generate revenue for the state through auctions of public land and by becoming a new source of agricultural wealth produced by colonos on small to medium-size plots of land. State ownership of public land was also a precondition of frontier colonization by European immigrants, a central element of Balmaceda's program for promoting southern Chile's economic development.[40]

In 1887, after only a decade of ownership, Puelma Castillo encountered the first challenge to his property rights. The Balmaceda government initiated auctions of leases of pasture lying on public land in Alto Bío Bío in order to raise revenues and promote the colonization of mountain regions bordering Argentina. The land to be auctioned covered a huge territory in Alto Bío Bío, including almost all of the land claimed eventually by Puelma's San Ignacio de Pemehue estate. One lot (Lot A) was defined by the estuaries and springs that flowed from the southeastern bank of the Biobío River, from Contraco to the Lonquimay valley. Lot B incorporated the Lonquimay valley and the tributaries of the Lonquimay River. Lot C contained the land bordered by the southeast bank of the Biobío River and its tributaries, from the Lonquimay valley to the Galletué Laguna to the north. Lot D contained the lands "bathed by the estuaries and springs" that flowed into the Biobío River from the northeast, from Nitrito to the Ránquil valley. Lot E was bordered by the estuaries and springs that emptied into the Biobío River from the Ránquil Valley to Lincura. Lot F included the lands "bathed by the estuaries and springs that flow from the Biobío River to the Lincura Valley," including the Galletué Laguna. Lot G was bordered on the north by the Renaico River, on the east by the first mountain chain in the Andes cordillera, dividing the springs which empty into the Biobío River, and on the south by the Malleco River.[41]

Before the auctions, Francisco Puelma Castillo went to the government to ask that three of the lots, A, D, and G, be left out of the auctions because, he contended, they belonged to his San Ignacio hacienda. This assertion of rights to the enormous lots contradicted his earlier acceptance of the estate's southern border as the Renaico River and his recognition of this border in the deeds produced during the sales from Saavedra and Bulnes Pinto. It is unclear why, but perhaps because of Puelma Castillo's opposition and political prominence, the auctions were postponed until 1889, when a new decree announced auctions of leases to the same lots of Alto Bío Bío's pasture. Puelma Castillo again went to the government to complain that land belonging to his hacienda had been included in the auction.[42] His efforts bore little fruit, however, probably because his claims to the three lots were ill-founded and the size of his property still badly defined and unsurveyed. Puelma Castillo appeared to be relying on the absence of cadastral maps of the region to make his claims to well over a hundred thousand hectares of land. In 1889 the Balmaceda government proceeded with the auctions.

Puelma Castillo then pursued a two-pronged approach. First, he purchased the leases to lots A, D, and G at public auction.[43] Then, in December 1890, he initiated a legal case against the state, requesting definitive demarcation of the borders separating San Ignacio from neighboring public land. The case arrived at the Supreme Court, but no sentence was ever issued since the government and Puelma Castillo agreed to an independent arbitrator, a surveyor who would study San Ignacio's deeds and draw its boundaries. The most important issue was the property's southern and southeastern borders.[44] A question remained: Why did Puelma Castillo lease lots A, D, and G if he considered that the land legally belonged to his hacienda? This action suggests that he recognized certain ambiguities in the definition of his property's borders, even, perhaps, the dubious legitimacy of his land claims.

Two years later the surveyor, Alberto Larenas, handed in his report on the Puelma estate. Puelma Castillo was now a senator for Ñuble and had held a seat in the senate since 1882. His career in congress stretched almost four decades. He had exercised key functions in government as intendant of Arauco province and as Chile's diplomatic representative in negotiations with its neighbors. He had also founded the country's most important nitrate mining company in Antofagasta. This is to say he figured among Chile's most wealthy and politically influential elites. Perhaps not surprisingly, Larenas's report supported Puelma Castillo's land claims. The surveyor's report became a key document in the tangled history of San Ignacio de Pemehue but disappeared from all archives by 1916 and is still missing today. But in 1919 Francisco Puelma Tupper, Puelma Castillo's son, described the report to bolster his family's land claims. According to Puelma Tupper, Larenas studied the available documentation but could not locate the deeds from the original sales and did not travel to Alto Bío Bío, a still largely unmapped territory, to study the region's topography on the ground. Larenas did not weigh in on the validity of the original land sales and deeds but offered a general description of San Ignacio de Pemehue's borders. According to the surveyor, the property was bordered on the north by the Mulchén River, on the east by the Andes cordillera, and on the south by the Pemehue cordillera to the Rucachurue spur, to the Biobío River, and from there the spur separating the Aillinco and Rahue Rivers.[45] The report was a key turning point in the decades-long expansion of Nahuel's property. By pushing the southern border from the Renaico River to the Rahue River and eastward into the cordillera, incorporating the lots Puelma Castillo had leased in 1889 into the estate, Larenas built on paper a new estate whose size reached more than 130,000 cuadras. It appears that at this time the San Ignacio hacienda was also divided into five smaller estates, or *fundos*, each with roughly 30,000 to 40,000 hectares: Ránquil, El Rahue, Chilpaco, Lolco, and Villucura.

In May 1893, the same year Larenas released his report on San Ignacio's contested borders, Puelma Castillo died, leaving his property in Alto Bío Bío to his widow and children, who formed a public company, Puelma Tupper and Company, to administer their inheritance. The company's shareholders included his sons Francisco, Alfredo, and Manuel Puelma Tupper and his daughter-in-law, Sara Navarro Puelma, who served as legal guardian for her son with Guillermo Puelma Tupper. Manuel Barros Borgoño, Enrique Rodríguez Cerda, Juan Antonio Orrego, and Jorge Federico Bussey, the legal representatives of their wives, Puelma Castillo's daughters, respectively, Elisa, Rosa, Teresa, and Adelaida Puelma Tupper, also held stock in the Puelma Tupper company.

Puelma Tupper and Co.'s owners reflected the tightly woven web of social ties binding Chile's Liberal oligarchy. Francisco Puelma Tupper was a doctor, educated, like his father, at the Instituto Nacional as well as at the University of Chile and in Germany. He taught at the University of Chile's medical school and served as a Liberal Party deputy during the 1880s, although by the late 1880s he had become a leading figure in the Radical Party. His brother Guillermo also studied at the Instituto Nacional and the University of Chile and continued his medical education in Germany. Like his brother Francisco he was a Radical, serving as a deputy until his death in 1895. Their brother-in-law Manuel Barros Borgoño was also a doctor, educated at the Instituto Nacional and the University of Chile as well as in France, and became the head of the University of Chile's medical school. He was the nephew of Diego Barros Arana, a prominent Liberal intellectual, the director of the Instituto Nacional, and arguably Chile's most eminent historian during the nineteenth century. Finally, Juan Antonio Orrego, a distinguished Liberal lawyer involved in banking and mining, served as a deputy from 1879 until 1888 and occupied a number of high government positions, including minister of war in 1893.[46]

Not surprisingly, Barros Borgoño, Orrego, and Guillermo Puelma Tupper all joined the congressional opposition to Balmaceda during Chile's 1891 civil war, as did Francisco Puelma Castillo while he still lived and held a seat in the senate. Puelma Castillo and his family had direct conflicts with the Balmaceda government over the leases of lots they claimed as their property. They also opposed the Balmaceda government's efforts to requisition livestock and other goods from wealthy landowners during the civil war. In fact, perhaps because Puelma Castillo was a powerful political enemy, the Balmaceda government requisitioned livestock from San Ignacio for the war effort. In response, Puelma Castillo resorted to fraud. He sold all of San Ignacio's livestock and machinery to his son-in-law Jorge Bussey and entered into a fictive rental contract, transferring San Ignacio to Bussey as a rental property. Like so many documents in this history, this rental contract disappeared almost immediately from government archives, as government lawyers would point out later when Bussey sought compensation from the state for the losses he had incurred as the estate's renter during the civil war. Tellingly, before the civil war Bussey had been designated as San Ignacio's *mayordomo* (manager or administrator) in public documents and lived on San Ignacio with his wife, Puelma Castillo's daughter Adelaida. As government lawyers contended, Puelma Castillo had devised the rental and sale contracts to avoid his estate being targeted by the government since he was a well-known political enemy of Balmaceda.[47] Apparently, the fraud was ineffective in that, as Bussey's claims indicated, the Balmaceda government had proceeded to requisition livestock from San Ignacio during the war.

When Elisa Tupper de Puelma died on 21 May 1886, the Puelma Tupper company was dissolved. Eliodoro Yáñez, a lawyer, Liberal Party leader, and member of congress, took charge of dividing the company's property among the Puelma heirs. He contracted Alberto Larenas, now in a private function, to survey San Ignacio de Pemehue. Larenas then organized San Ignacio into 21 plots covering 130,000 cuadras. The new survey and map consolidated the hacienda's expansion, establishing as its borders the Mulchén River to its origins to the Cerro Bonete in the Andes cordillera on the north, on the east the Andes cordillera, which divided Argentina and Chile, and on the south the border of the department of Mulchén to the Biobío River then to the Rahue and Mitraquén Rivers.[48] As a quick glance at a map would have shown, these borders expanded the estate both southward and eastward, increasing its size exponentially.

The leases of pasture in Alto Bío Bío auctioned by the Balmaceda government expired in 1896. A new colonization law had been passed that year designed to induce landless Chilean laborers who had crossed the cordillera in search of land and work in Argentina to return and populate the mountain valleys lying on the border, thereby "chileanizing" a contested frontier region. A government decree ordered the lands and colonization inspectorate to take possession of the land in Alto Bío Bío that had been leased in 1889 in order to settle Chilean laborers who had recently returned from the Argentine province of Neuquén.[49] All the lessees fulfilled their obligation to return the land rented from the state, save for Puelma Castillo's heirs, who refused to return lots A, D, and G, which, they maintained, lay within the original borders of San Ignacio de Pemehue. In addition, the Puelmas claimed part of Lot E, which had been leased by Olegario Cortés. Lot E contained land lying between the Ránquil River on the north, the Mitraquén spur on the south, the Andes cordillera on the east, and the Biobío River on the west.[50]

In 1896 the Puelma family petitioned the lands and colonization inspectorate to map the borders between San Ignacio and adjacent public land, employing their deeds and Larenas's 1893 report. A new study by a surveyor, Francisco Muñizaga, confirmed the borders of San Ignacio established by Larenas in 1893. Muñizaga drew the first map of the property, laying out in detail the sprawling hacienda.[51] Nonetheless, the Puelmas still confronted challenges to their dominion in Alto Bío Bío. On 10 January 1900 the Liberal president Federico Errázuriz Echauren issued a decree once again ordering auctions of leases to pasture in Alto Bío Bío. In response to this renewed threat to the family's property claims, Francisco Puelma Tupper petitioned the lands inspectorate to issue a deed to San Ignacio de Pemehue based on a favorable report issued by the inspector general of lands, dated 1 July 1901, and on a lands ministry order dated the same day. The government accepted his petition and issued the deed on 9 December 1901. The deed was signed by Inspector General of Lands Agustín Baeza, representing the state, and Eliodoro Yáñez, representing the Puelma family, as he had in 1896 when the Puelma Tupper company was liquidated.[52] Now, however, Yáñez was minister of lands and colonization and Baeza's boss. As critics in congress would later note, this represented an extraordinary conflict of interest, if not outright fraud, given Yáñez's dual role as the Puelmas' legal representative and the cabinet minister in charge of lands and colonization, the ministry responsible for determining the legitimacy of property titles in Chile's southern territory.

The legal agreement represented a critical victory for the Puelma family in its ongoing efforts to establish the legitimacy of San Ignacio's ever-expanding borders. But the new deed to the property was still only a piece of paper, and as clear as the borders appeared in Larenas's reports and Muñizaga's 1896 map, on the ground things were murkier. During the 1890s the major challenge to Francisco Puelma Castillo's land claims in Alto Bío Bío came from the state's leases of pasture in the valleys of the cordillera, but by the turn of the century his heirs confronted a new opponent. A large number of Chilean campesinos had settled within San Ignacio de Pemehue's borders, drawn by 1896 and 1898 laws on national colonization designed to populate Alto Bío Bío's mountain valleys. The fact that Chilean governments had challenged the legitimacy of the Puelma family's property rights and asserted that most of San Ignacio lay on public land allowed these laborers to view land on the gigantic hacienda as a place where they could settle and earn legal titles to small plots of land as colonos. By the first decade of the twentieth century the Puelma family faced an ongoing conflict with the local campesino population, which occupied both public land bordering San Ignacio and land within the estate itself. This struggle between the politically powerful Puelmas and rural laborers who had left Chile for Argentina and then returned or had migrated from within Chile into Alto Bío Bío—animated by the hope that they might acquire land to call their own—set the terms for decades of protracted and often violent social conflict that would explode in 1934.

CHAPTER TWO

Campesinos, *Indígenas*, and Early Challenges to the Hacienda

BY THE 1890S THE Chilean population across the border from Alto Bío Bío in the Argentine province of Neuquén had reached thirty thousand, the majority of the province's residents. Chilean laborers either worked on the region's cattle *estancias* or occupied small plots on the eastern slopes of the Andes cordillera engaging in the booming transandean livestock trade. In 1896 and 1898 the Chilean government passed two new colonization laws. The first dictated that Chilean laborers who were fathers of families, knew how to read and write, and returned from Argentina to settle on public land in southern frontier territory could receive titles to eighty hectares for male heads of families and forty hectares for their sons older than twelve. The second established similar provisions for Chileans who were not repatriated but who settled on public frontier land. In part, these laws were designed to extend to Chileans the legal rights to settle southern frontier land that had been granted to European immigrants in the foundational 1845 colonization law. In 1902 new regulations required these *colonos nacionales* to live and work on their land for five years and fence it in return for titles to their plots. Finally, in 1908 a new law granted similar rights to Chileans who had simply occupied public land (ocupantes nacionales) for more than three years. Generally, as long as aspiring colonos resided and worked on their land for a number of years, demonstrated by clearing forest, building fences, pasturing livestock, and cultivating crops, colonization officials were inclined to recognize their rights to legal titles.[1]

The new colonization laws built on the 1845 law's granting of property rights and colono legal status to men who were heads of households and their sons. The state's goal, following Cornelio Saavedra's blueprint, was to establish a population of small- to medium-size farmers who would settle with their families in frontier territory. Like the 1845 law, the new colonization laws excluded men without families and women from acquiring legal titles to frontier land as either ocupantes or colonos. Even if male campesinos' female family members helped in the hard work of introducing improvements in frontier territory, they acquired legal access to land only through their fathers and husbands. Implicit in the colonization legislation was the understanding that male-headed families would introduce order and progress into the anarchy of untamed frontier social relations. In practice, colonization laws shaped the ways Chilean campesinos in the south came to see their rights to frontier land. They would settle both putatively empty public land and privately held estate land not as individuals but as heads of families, men whose legal rights derived from their authority over their households as well as from the improvements they and their family members introduced into the unruly wilderness of the frontier.

In the late 1890s and early 1900s numerous Chilean campesinos returned to Chile from the Argentine province of Neuquén to claim land. Moreover, a number of campesinos who had moved into frontier territory across the Biobío River claimed public land under the new national colonization laws. In accordance with the colonization laws, these campesinos settled in frontier territory with their families. In Alto Bío Bío and Lonquimay 70 families, comprising 362 people, had received titles as either colonos repatriated from Argentina or colonos nacionales who had settled on public land by 1910. In 1898 a colony of 323 families was established in Lonquimay with colonos repatriated from Argentina, though many of them abandoned their land in 1898 after a winter of harsh blizzards.[2] A number of aspiring colonos, or ocupantes nacionales, also settled with their families on land in Alto Bío Bío they believed to be public, land the Puelma family claimed as part of its enormous holdings.

During the first two decades of the century the Puelmas engaged in a protracted battle with these ocupantes, one that would wind its way through the judicial system and reach the highest spheres of the government and congress in Santiago. Many ocupantes asserted that they were repatriated colonos who had returned from Argentina to settle on public land. The Puelmas countered by claiming that many of the ocupantes had invaded San Ignacio de Pemehue. They marshalled deeds from the original sales as well as the 1901 agreement with the state recognizing the legitimacy of their property rights. They also contended that a sizable number of the ocupantes had originally been contracted as inquilinos to provide labor to their estates in return for small pieces of land on which they could pasture their livestock and grow crops. Government agencies, from the general lands inspectorate to the lands measurement office, backed the Puelmas in their struggles to evict the ocupantes and inquilinos from San Ignacio, but the campesinos persisted for well over a decade, refusing to leave their land or desist from making claims to be settled as colonos within San Ignacio's borders.

This dispute over whether estate land was public or private and whether campesinos were ocupantes with rights to settle on public land as colonos or inquilinos who owed their obedience to estate owners endured. It shaped rural land and labor conflicts for decades in southern Chile as the frontier was opened to settlement and lay at the heart of the tensions that erupted in the Ránquil rebellion in 1934. The frontier's status as public land and the often fraudulent formation of southern estates like San Ignacio meant that landless laborers often viewed estate land as public. They invaded and squatted on estates, demanding titles to small plots as colonos. Or, if they had been contracted as inquilinos, they asserted ownership rights to the plots granted by landowners. They based their claims on their material occupation and the improvements they had made and invoked colonization laws and estates' status as public property. In Alto Bío Bío, as throughout southern Chile, the dubious legitimacy of estate owners' property rights undermined their authority over both land and labor.

As early as 1893 the Puelmas' conflict with the state over the legal status of San Ignacio had involved Chilean laborers who claimed they were colonos returned from Argentina. An 1893 report written by the surveyor Muñízaga described these putative colonos as ocupantes of land on the El Rahue estate, "property of don Francisco Puelma Tupper." Apparently these rural laborers remained on Puelma property while the legal battles over the hacienda's status persisted through the 1890s. In late 1906 the customs authorities in Lonquimay reported that on land belonging to the Staeding colonization concession, which neighbored San Ignacio, and on land in the Cajón de Rahue on Francisco Puelma Tupper's El Rahue estate a number of ocupantes had established themselves as colonos, contending they had returned from Argentina. But rather than engage in the agricultural labor required of colonos, they dedicated themselves exclusively to bringing livestock over the border clandestinely. Despite Puelma Tupper's appeals to the lands inspectorate to evict them, they remained on the land well into 1907, "exercising the lucrative profession of *contrabandista* [smuggler] with impunity."[3] In 1907 the government attempted to evict many of these same ocupantes from land on El Rahue. But the ocupantes persisted. In 1909 the lands measurement office weighed in on the subject by reaffirming that the land on El Rahue, still occupied by the group of aspiring colonos, was not public but belonged to Puelma Tupper. The lands inspectorate rejected the ocupantes' petition to be settled on public land as colonos repatriated from Argentina.[4]

Despite the intendancy's efforts to expel them, this group of ocupantes must have remained on El Rahue for a number of years because in 1916 once again a judicial order for their expulsion was issued to police in Lonquimay, this time by a court in Lautaro, at the behest of Francisco Puelma Tupper. In a conversation with the lands inspector, Puelma Tupper underlined that the ocupantes not only had no rights to be settled on his estate, since it was private rather than public property, but also had been his inquilinos and empleados. The ocupantes had taken over land assigned to them as inquilinos and were now claiming it as their own, using their material possession and improvements to demonstrate their rights to be settled as colonos within El Rahue's borders.[5]

The case of Puelma Tupper's inquilinos is illustrative of rural labor relations during the early years of frontier expansion in southern Chile. The inquilinos were free to occupy plots on the estate as if the land was their own and disobey their patrón for a number of reasons. First, neither landowners nor the state exercised much power over land and labor in the region since repeated efforts to expel both ocupantes and inquilinos who had become ocupantes by claiming colono status had failed over two decades. Second, as Puelma Tupper noted, his estate laborers did not rely on work and wages but mostly engaged in the contraband livestock trade. In fact, not only did Puelma Tupper exercise little authority over his labor force, but also the workers were not entirely dependent on their patrón for food, land, or salaries, unlike their counterparts on estates in central Chile. Smuggling livestock across the border with Argentina made them economically independent. And most inquilinos possessed their own livestock, which they pastured on both public land and within the supposed borders of the estates where they were employed.

Because the estates bordered public land inquilinos had access not only to the frontier with Argentina and the transandean livestock trade but also to land not claimed by private estate owners. The Puelmas' former inquilinos occupied both estate and neighboring public land in Alto Bío Bío. In Puelma Tupper's words, it was precisely in the borderlands between privately held and public land and in the legal space between colono and inquilino that the rural laborers "live their lives aimlessly" (*indistintamente pasan su vida*). The existence of public land in the region and the ill-defined borders between private and public property undermined landowners' control over their workers who could move off estates, settle on public land, and demand titles as colonos. In addition, because El Rahue's status as private property was still somewhat less than decided and because the Puelma family's property rights in the region were still in dispute, the inquilinos could maintain that the estate was public land rather than private property and petition to be granted titles to their plots as colonos.

Despite the 1916 verdict of the Lautaro court authorizing police to evict the ocupantes from San Ignacio de Pemehue, the conflict continued unabated. It appears that courts' power to enforce their decisions was limited in isolated Alto Bío Bío, where the state's administrative and police powers were weak. That same year Roque Fernández, Vicente Adrian, and Bernardo Quiroga brought a civil suit against both the Puelma family and the Bunster family, who owned two large estates bordering San Ignacio. Fernández had engaged for a number of years in a campaign to settle Lonquimay's valleys with both repatriated Chilean campesinos and members of local Pehuenche communities. Flores writes that the director of the Lonquimay colony accused Fernández around 1900 of "living among Lonquimay's *indios*" and settling them in the Rahue and Ránquil valleys, that is, within the borders of the Puelmas' El Rahue and Ránquil estates. Fernández was engaged in a lawsuit with the Puelmas over the valleys and, according to the director of the Lonquimay colony, had counseled "the indios" "to disobey the authorities and harass members of the colony."[6]

In 1916 Fernández and his fellow plaintiffs, representing the region's ocupantes, argued that both the Bunster and Puelma families had engaged in fraud to accumulate tens of thousands of hectares of public land south of the Biobío River and along the mountain border with Argentina in Alto Bío Bío. They dug deep in local and national archives to make their legal case. First, the plaintiffs argued that Luis Bunster controlled a large property known as Lot D that Francisco Puelma Castillo had rented from the state in 1889. Although Bunster had purchased the lot, the sale was illegal since Puelma Castillo had no ownership rights to the land he had leased from the state to pasture livestock. This lot included parts of two fertile valleys that would lie at the heart of the 1934 rebellion: Nitrito and Ránquil. The plaintiffs demanded that this vast stretch of land be restored to the state so that it might be settled by Chilean colonos. Second, Fernández, Adrian, and Quiroga argued that other lots and fundos owned by the heirs of Puelma Castillo had also been leased to Puelma Castillo in public auctions and, like Lot D, should be returned to the state. According to the plaintiffs, when the Sociedad Puelma Tupper was liquidated in 1896, a number of lots Puelma Castillo had rented from the state had been handed over to his heirs as family property. They asked that deeds to San Ignacio de Pemehue, which had been registered following the deal struck between Agustín Baeza, representing the state, and Eliodoro Yáñez, representing the Puelma family, be voided.[7]

For their part, the Puelmas marshaled the Nahuel land sales to Rodríguez and from Rodríguez to Saavedra and Bulnes in their defense. They argued that the only reference in the original titles to the size of what would become the San Ignacio hacienda was in the deed of the property Rodríguez sold to Saavedra, the estate's original 4,000 cuadras. But, they contended, in a second transaction Rodríguez sold to Saavedra "all the rest of the land acquired from Nahuel that remains." The Puelma family essentially maintained that "all the land ... that remains" amounted to roughly 126,000 cuadras, employing the 1890s surveys by Larenas to make their case. This patently absurd assertion incited much of the interminable litigation around San Ignacio de Pemehue. Given how difficult it was to define the estate's borders and the dubious legitimacy of its titles, the Puelmas resorted to two final legal arguments to substantiate the legitimacy of their ownership of the enormous estate.

First, regardless of the legitimacy of the borders in their estates' various deeds, the Puelma family had enjoyed uninterrupted possession of the land comprising San Ignacio for more than thirty years. Under the colonization laws such uninterrupted possession, along with the improvements they had made on the land, gave them ownership rights. And second, the estate's borders and deeds had been recognized given that San Ignacio had been employed as collateral when the family took out loans from the Caja de Crédito Hipotecario de Chile, the Banco de Chile, and the Banco Hipotecario de Chile, both when the estate was one integrated property and later, when it had been divided into a number of plots. This fact demonstrated the true reason Francisco Puelma Castillo had invested his nitrate profits in Alto Bío Bío. He astutely read the future of rising property values as the Chilean military pushed southward during the 1870s and early 1880s. But landownership also served as a means to acquiring credit. The property's value lay less in the herds of livestock grazing on Alto Bío Bío's mountain pasture than in the loans Puelma Castillo and his heirs had been able to obtain by employing San Ignacio as collateral.[8]

When the government Consejo de Defensa Fiscal (Council on Defense of the Public Interest) reviewed the competing claims in the 1916 lawsuit, including the maps, bills of sale, and land titles, it concluded that "the borders designated in the deeds are not, as we have seen, determined with precision. This is a fact that can be affirmed absolutely because it has been recognized by both the state and Puelma."[9] The consejo essentially called into question the legitimacy of the 1901 settlement engineered by Eliodoro Yáñez and Agustín Baeza. Nonetheless, in 1916 the consejo upheld Puelma's position and accepted as legitimate the borders drawn by Larenas and Muñizaga in the 1890s.[10] This fit a pattern of government agencies and officials recognizing the dubious nature of San Ignacio de Pemehue's borders but nevertheless supporting the Puelma family's claims to more than 130,000 cuadras of land in Alto Bío Bío.

Despite the Consejo de Defensa Fiscal's 1916 ruling, the conflict continued to simmer in Alto Bío Bío. In 1918 Roque Fernández, Eujenio Saez, José Ignacio Zurita, Paulo Parra, Juan Pablo Alegría, Otilia Pérez, and Manuel Antonio Hermosilla, who had now been engaged in a protracted legal battle with the Puelmas for well over a decade, sent a telegram to the lands ministry denouncing Francisco Puelma Tupper for seizing their land and "fence running," folding their small plots into his hacienda by erecting fences.[11] Despite local courts' orders that they be evicted and the instructions of the lands inspectorate authorizing police to expel them in 1907, 1908, and 1916, they apparently had remained on their land within San Ignacio's borders. The lands inspectorate took the Puelmas' side, as it had during earlier conflicts. Rather than running fences onto his former inquilinos' land, it reported, Puelma Tupper was building a fence on the border between land he acquired when he purchased the Staeding colonization concession from the state in 1910 and neighboring public land. It was imperative, the lands inspector argued, to expel the former inquilinos "by all means at our disposal, from the lands they are occupying, with the end of preventing their defrauding the interests of the state with the continuous contraband to which they are dedicated." Their smuggling of livestock across the border had damaged the interests of the region's estate owners because to move their herds they needed to "breach fences and destroy crops."[12] Worse, according to Puelma Tupper, four years earlier the inquilinos turned contrabandistas and bandits had killed four policemen in Lonquimay. Nonetheless, these alleged miscreants continued to defy the government and to appropriate large sections of the fundos that had comprised the San Ignacio Pemehue hacienda as well as the neighboring Guayalí fundo, which belonged to the Bunster family and included land in the Nitrito Valley.[13]

In fact, contraband trade drove much commercial activity in southern provinces along the frontier with Argentina. In Bío-Bío province, police and customs officials were powerless well through the 1920s to prevent the constant movement of people and goods across the border. A 1926 report in *El Siglo de Los Ángeles* described the carabineros' impotence in the face of audacious smugglers, who engaged in their trade with impunity. A reporter interviewed a carabinero lieutenant who had recently returned from an inspection of the Trapa Trapa cordillera in Alto Bío Bío. The carabinero reported that near the Trapa Trapa volcano he "began to see the abuses that are committed in this region, that, owing to the distance from the last detachment of carabineros and the small number of troops, it is almost impossible to avoid. Before we arrived at the volcano we surprised two individuals with contraband liquor, who, when they became alerted to our presence, fled in the direction of Argentina, leaving behind four barrels of liquor." The carabineros also reported on a thriving contraband commerce in timber extracted from the region's native forests and sold in Argentina.[14]

Contraband in livestock, lumber, and liquor was the clandestine side of a booming transandean regional commerce that linked the Argentine province of Neuquén to towns throughout southern Chile. As Susana Bandieri notes, by the early twentieth century Neuquén sold livestock to Chilean markets and received in return an array of consumer goods, including wine, beer, sugar, tea, coffee, flour, and soap.[15] Chilean and Argentine merchants built a dynamic transandean economy, one which established the context for the migrations of Chilean campesinos back and forth across the cordillera. Numerous Chilean campesinos, excluded from landownership in the south by the formation of large estates acquired fraudulently from indígenas, purchased at auction, or granted as concessions by the state, followed paths through the cordillera's mountain passes in search of work and land in Neuquén. Like Pehuenche groups, they practiced transhumance, moving their livestock from winter invernadas to summer veranadas, and although they established themselves in Argentina they returned to the Chilean side of the border frequently to sell livestock, buy goods, and visit family members.[16] The repatriated campesinos who occupied land on the Puelmas' estates, whether they were inquilinos or ocupantes, were active in this lively cross-border movement of goods, animals, and people, both licit and illicit.

In 1918 the lands and colonization inspector sent a note to the interior minister requesting that contrabandistas on the Puelma estates be expelled once again since they were impeding the construction of fences demarcating lots belonging to the state that were going to be put on auction. According to Puelma, some of the contrabandistas were inquilinos on his El Rahue estate; he had expelled them because he did not want to commit the crime of being complicit in their illegal activities. However, on 26 April 1919 Puelma went to the offices of the lands and colonization inspectorate to ask that the contrabandistas be settled as colonos on public land that had belonged to the Staeding colonization concession, land he had rights to since he had leased the concession in 1910. He would cede 240 hectares for this purpose, he said, "since I renounce taking land that is occupied by invaders, because I don't want to provoke problems."[17] Puelma Tupper's rights to the Staeding concession, however, had ended in 1917 when the colonization contract with the state was concluded. In effect, Puelma Tupper was telling government officials that he would be happy to settle the former inquilinos he had described as criminals, bandits, and murderers on a small piece of public land to which, despite his assertions to the contrary, he had no right.

The alleged contrabandistas found defenders in congress. The Democratic Party senator Zenón Torrealba stated that they were not smugglers but "honorable colonos nacionales and ocupantes of public land." Torrealba also contended that the Puelmas' titles to San Ignacio de Pemehue were illegitimate. He argued on the floor of congress what had now become a well-known position: Francisco Puelma Castillo had originally purchased only four thousand cuadras of land but had bequeathed to his children an estate of more than two hundred thousand hectares. In 1919 Torrealba requested that the foreign relations ministry, which was in charge of southern colonization, conduct a complete revision of the deeds to both the Puelma estates and the neighboring Staeding colonization concession. Torrealba offered a detailed narrative of how the Puelma family had acquired land by purchasing the leases to pasture in Alto Bío Bío and then converting them into private property. Furthermore, despite failing to fulfill the requirements of the Staeding colonization contract, the Puelmas had, he argued, redefined that land as private property also, expelling numerous ocupantes who had rights to be settled as colonos. Despite the ocupantes' repeated petitions to the interior and colonization ministry for land titles, the government had authorized the intendant to send carabineros to evict them.[18] Torrealba asked that the lands and colonization ministry "suspend a decree that is being implemented in Alto Bío Bío in which they are proceeding to fence off some extensions of land, affecting seriously a group of colonos who settled there more than twenty years ago." The aspiring colonos, Torrealba contended, "occupy with perfect right under the colonization laws the land they have settled on." He went on to denounce the "abuses of ocupantes who settled in this region a long time ago."[19]

Torrealba described sixty-five families who had occupied their plots for twenty, twenty-five, even thirty years. "Those families," he observed, "have built good houses, they have livestock, crops, and plantings and have overcome the difficulties of life [in the cordillera] through constant hard work." They had returned from Argentina with their tools and livestock to take advantage of the new laws on national colonization. The aspiring colonos had petitioned the lands ministry and inspectorate for titles ever since they had settled in the region but had met with little success. According to Torrealba, the land they occupied bordered the four thousand hectares of the San Pemehue estate, but as the property expanded to two hundred thousand hectares it swallowed up their small plots. Following the appropriation of the aspiring colonos' land, San Ignacio de Pemehue's owners had "persecuted and dislodged" both "indios" and ocupantes.

Francisco Puelma Tupper visited congress to present a lengthy, vigorous response to Torrealba. He rejected Torrealba's accusations that his family had "appropriated enormous expanses of public land," arguing that his father had bought the San Ignacio de Pemehue hacienda forty years earlier. As for the ocupantes: "I have never bothered even one of these ocupantes. Far from it, I have protected them decidedly, conceding plots on the Schmidt and Staeding concessions to nearly one hundred national families."[20] This was a revealing statement and subtle rhetorical device. Puelma Tupper contended that rather than evicting the ocupantes from San Ignacio he had settled them on two colonization concessions he had leased from the state. Not only did Puelma Tupper and his family claim the five fundos composing San Ignacio, but Puelma Tupper had also leased the Schmidt (in Valdivia) and Staeding (in Lonquimay) colonization concessions, considerably expanding his family's landholdings. Indeed, because the Staeding concession bordered San Ignacio on the southwest, it grew the Puelma family's landholdings in Alto Bío Bío to well over 200,000 hectares.

Puelma Tupper presented himself to his former colleagues in congress as no ordinary aristocrat. Like his father, he was well educated and had an abiding interest in science. His brother Guillermo Puelma Tupper had been one of Chile's leading exponents of positivism. Francisco Puelma Tupper had studied medicine in Europe and was an important figure in Chile's Radical Party. In addition, like his father, Puelma Tupper harbored an interest in geology and had an eye for investing his fortune in southern land. He acquired state colonization concessions with more than speculation in mind; he had entrepreneurial goals as well. In Valdivia he hoped to cultivate fields of beets for the sugar beet industry on the former Schmidt concession. Roberto Schmidt had received the concession to colonize seventy thousand hectares of land just south of the Toltén River with German settlers in 1904 and 1905. Schmidt's colonization contracts with the state required him to install a sugar beet factory; in exchange, the state agreed to advance the passages of the German colonos. However, Schmidt had never been able to take possession of the land because it was tied up in endless litigation with "private parties [*particulares*], who claimed rights to the land."[21]

According to Puelma Tupper, after acquiring the Schmidt concession he arrived at settlements with some of the litigants and was able to install twenty-seven foreign colonos and more than fifty Chilean, or national, colonos on the land in Valdivia, assigning each forty hectares for male heads of households and twenty hectares for their sons who were older than twelve, as established in the colonization laws. But Puelma Tupper insisted on one requirement of the colonos that was not mandated by the law: they had to cultivate three hectares of their land with sugar beets and sell him their harvests. However, the colonos had no interest in planting beets. They preferred to dedicate their labor in the fields to cultivating potatoes, which fetched a higher price on local markets. Nonetheless, Puelma Tupper signed contracts with the colonos that dictated that after ten years of cultivating sugar beets they would receive official titles to their land. This also was not prescribed by the colonization laws.

But it was not purely an exploitative relationship, Puelma Tupper argued, because he paid the colonos for their sugar beets, ten pesos per ton of material with 10 percent sugar content. Yet no colonization law gave concessionaires the right to obligate colonos, foreign or Chilean, to cultivate a particular crop or to sell this crop to the concessionaire. No law stipulated that if they fulfilled this arrangement, they would receive legal titles after ten years. These were extralegal methods of labor coercion devised by Puelma Tupper to force his colonos to produce sugar beets. The colonization contract provided Puelma Tupper two key instruments: one to acquire land, the huge property in Valdivia, and the other to acquire labor for his sugar beet business, the colonos themselves.[22]

While waiting for his recently acquired land to produce sugar beets, Puelma Tupper engaged in the region's booming timbering business. He owned his own train cars to transport wood from southern forests to Santiago and Valparaíso, selling sleepers from the "inexhaustible" southern forests to the state railroad. As the railroad expanded its network into southern Chile, it created a dynamic market for sleepers. And Puelma Tupper had three sawmills producing lumber, with stacks of boards piled high in railroad stations in Pitrufquén, Gorbea, and Lastarria. He earned healthy profits from logging the southern forests on the Schmidt concession and had accumulated "more than enough capital," which he planned to invest in sugar beets.[23] In fact, like most colonization concessionaires in southern Chile, it appeared that Puelma Tupper's major source of earnings was the region's abundant native forests. As in the cases of the notorious Silva Rivas (Llaima), Nueva Italia, and Budi colonization concessions, the state handed over literally tens of thousands of hectares of land covered with native forest on which European immigrants were to be settled. These had to be cleared to make way for crops and pasture, but until this labor could be done (usually by inquilinos or *arrendatarios*), colonization concessionaires made healthy profits by sending the lumber from their valuable forests north. Indeed, logging was the main business of both smallholder colonos and colonization concessions throughout the south.[24]

In his appeal to congress Puelma Tupper presented himself as distinct from the traditional estate-owning aristocrat. His investments in logging, rail transport, and sugar beets made him an entrepreneurial agent of frontier development, not a feudal obstacle to agricultural production. His contracts with his colonos distinguished him from landowners in central Chile who treated their inquilinos as serfs, dependents whose families owed labor to their patrones over the course of generations, in exchange for small plots of estate land. Yet Puelma Tupper had accumulated seventy thousand hectares in Valdivia, an enormous stretch of land that dwarfed haciendas in central Chile.

In the end Puelma Tupper's sugar beet dreams came to nothing. In his account, the Democratic Party was largely responsible. A Democratic Party congressman had encouraged Puelma Tupper's colonos to break their commitment to cultivate sugar beets with "subversive propaganda." Puelma Tupper alleged that during a senatorial campaign in Valdivia, the Democratic Party candidate, Darío Sánchez, had offered the colonos definitive titles to their land in exchange for their votes. The details are murky and there is no evidence of any quid pro quo between the senator and the colonos. However, in the end Sánchez won the elections and the colonos received their titles, but no sugar beets were cultivated, since the colonos understood that the quickest route to obtaining titles to their land was to plant potatoes and introduce livestock on their plots. Puelma Tupper's plans for the sugar beet operation failed, and the colonos got their land. Worse still, he claimed, they also continued to occupy land that was his personal property in Valdivia, land that had been part of the Schmidt concession and that he had received from the state in exchange for introducing colonos on the concession's land grant.[25]

Puelma Tupper's struggles with colonos on the Schmidt concession in Valdivia foreshadowed the conflict that would erupt further north in Alto Bío Bío two decades later. They also reflected a broader pattern of social conflict that swept southern Chile during the first decades of the twentieth century. Colonization concessions granted by the state to bring European settlers to populate southern Chile did constant battle with Chilean campesinos, often referred to as ocupantes, and Mapuche communities that occupied and claimed land granted to the concessions. Colonization concessions acquired landholdings of anywhere from twenty thousand to seventy thousand hectares to settle relatively small numbers of European immigrants but were often unable to exercise control over the property they leased from the state. They frequently devoted their energies to evicting campesinos and refused to respect stipulations in their contracts that they recognize the rights of Mapuches and ocupantes within the borders of their massive holdings. Expelling Chilean and Mapuche campesinos from their concessions was a central part of transforming land leased from the state to populate southern frontier territory with immigrants into large haciendas. Colonization concessions like Budi, Nueva Italia, and Luis Silva Rivas's Llaima concession engaged in constant campaigns to expel ocupantes and Mapuche communities from their land. Yet they ended up settling few European immigrants on the concessions. Instead, they converted their leases into enormous estates devoted to raising livestock and logging native forests.[26]

Having failed in Valdivia and in the sugar beet business, Puelma Tupper turned north to his family's estates in Alto Bío Bío. Again, he presented himself as an entrepreneur, inspired, as his father had been when he pioneered the development of northern Chile's nitrate mines, by science and industry. Whereas other landowners might have seen in Alto Bío Bío's estates pasture for their livestock and lumber to be cut from mountain forests, Puelma Tupper discovered in the cordillera oil-producing schists (metamorphic rocks sometimes referred to as shale) similar to those, he claimed, found in Scotland. Properly exploited, he believed, the Andes cordillera's shale could offer Chile a profitable supply of petrol. In 1903 he followed in his father's mining footsteps by staking a legal claim to the subsoil rights to the shale lying within and underneath San Ignacio de Pemehue.[27] It may be that Puelma Tupper's entrepreneurial plans for his inherited property were sincere, but it is as likely that the legal claims, or *denuncias*, served as another arrow in the family's legal quiver as they fought to establish dominion over their father's enormous property in Alto Bío Bío. Over the following decades the Puelmas made no discernable effort to develop San Ignacio's schists.

Puelma Tupper also purchased the lease to the neighboring Staeding colonization concession in Lonquimay and struck claims to subsoil rights within its borders with the alleged goal of exploiting its shale. The Staeding concession was typical of colonization concessions in southern Chile. In 1904 the Chilean state had granted Juan Staeding twenty-eight thousand hectares in Alto Bío Bío bordering the San Ignacio de Pemehue hacienda. Staeding's contract obligated him to settle five foreign colonos and five Chilean colonos on the concession's land. But, as on the estates composing San Ignacio de Pemehue, the land was not empty. Rather, it was already occupied by at least fifty-three campesino families who called themselves ocupantes of public land.[28] A congressional committee noted in 1912 that Staeding had settled only one family of European immigrants— who had traveled from Buenos Aires—but that the concession's land had been occupied by "many colonos or ocupantes nacionales[,] some since 1896 and many from before the year of the concession."[29] In 1910 Alfredo Irarrázaval Zañartu, a Liberal Democratic Party deputy for Angol and the editor of *La Tarde*, denounced the "enormous expanse of land" in Alto

Bío Bío controlled by the Staeding concession. He noted that the powers of the police, judiciary, and positions in the local government had been placed in power of one person, the concession's administrator. The Staeding concession had never fulfilled any of its obligations to settle colonos on the land. Instead, like most colonization concessions throughout the south, it had employed its control of local institutions to expel numerous ocupantes, repatriated from Argentina, who had settled on land they believed to be public and to which they had rights under the colonization laws.[30]

Puelma Tupper had not only acquired twenty-eight thousand hectares with which to expand his family's holdings in Alto Bío Bío, but also faced a bitter conflict with over fifty families of ocupantes. As in Valdivia, his entrepreneurial plans collided with a rocky social landscape. To exercise control of the twenty-eight-thousand-hectare concession he would have to evict the ocupantes. While Staeding's evictions were sporadic and unsuccessful, Puelma's were aggressive. Until he took over, Irarrázaval noted, "it was a question of isolated abuses that were committed once in a while and that always found a painful echo in the press." Now it was a question of "a true crusade against [the ocupantes]." In a precursor to the events that would precipitate the 1934 uprising two decades later, the government dispatched thirty carabineros to evict the aspiring colonos from land within the Staeding concession. Irarrázaval received a telegram from the ocupantes stating that "government surveyors, carabineros have gone, at the orders of don Francisco Puelma Tupper, to evict them from public land that they have occupied in Lonquimay Alto Bío Bío for more than ten years."[31]

Puelma's telling of this conflict differed. He had, he said, taken over the Staeding concession in order to exploit the oil-producing shale. However, more than sixty families had taken possession of the land without "my having ever harassed them." Eventually he had restored the concession to the state, and the Consejo de Defensa Fiscal had canceled the colonization contract in 1917. In a confusing rhetorical move, Puelma Tupper then conflated these sixty ocupante families with the contrabandistas he had been struggling with on his El Rahue estate. Now that the Staeding concession was canceled, Puelma Tupper argued, the contrabandistas would once again invade his land on El Rahue. They were holed up in the Cajón de Rahue on the estate, where customs officials could not find them. According to Puelma Tupper, "In one night one thousand head of livestock pass over the border" without paying tariffs. In this case, as in the case of the Schmidt concession and his enduring conflict over the titles to San Ignacio, the government authorities friendly to his enemies resided in the Democratic Party. A Democratic Party senator in Valdivia had organized the colonos on the Schmidt concession against him, destroying his plans to develop a sugar beet industry. Now another Democratic Party senator, Zenón Torrealba, wanted "to prevent his study of Lonquimay's shale by giving his support to individuals who have located themselves on the mineral claims on my property."[32]

Presumably none of the challenges to the Puelma Tupper family's property rights in Alto Bío Bío prospered, despite the support of local and national Democratic Party politicians for the ocupantes. The Puelmas retained ownership, and the numerous campesinos were never settled on land they claimed was public. However, the legal and political campaigns to restore San Ignacio de Pemehue's 130,000 cuadras to the state, combined with the ocupantes' persistent refusal to abandon the land, had an impact. By the early 1920s Francisco Puelma Castillo's heirs had begun to either sell or lease the estates they had inherited from their father, the surest way to avoid being enmeshed in the simmering social conflicts in southern Chile, so far from their homes in Santiago, and the easiest way to wring some money out of their inheritance.

Nonetheless, the conflicts over the status of San Ignacio, going back to Puelma Castillo's lease of the three lots, the settlement of ocupantes and inquilinos within San Ignacio's borders and their attempted eviction, culminating in the 1916 legal case, and the political campaign in congress led by congressmen like Irarrázaval and Torrealba would shape a renewed movement to restore San Ignacio to the state and settle it with ocupantes and inquilinos. The historical narrative developed by Fernández and his fellow ocupantes in their civil case in 1916 and Torrealba's detailed description of the origins of San Ignacio would constitute the template for a new attempt to wrest control of the Puelma estates in 1928, this time by a union, the Sindicato Agrícola Lonquimay. Armed with the well-documented history of San Ignacio's fraudulent expansion and supported at the local and national levels by the Democratic Party, the union would renew efforts to have the state expropriate San Ignacio and resettle the hacienda's five estates with their ocupantes and inquilinos. The Puelma Tupper family's struggle with campesinos and the Democratic Party would continue well into the 1930s.

The Bunster Family and Challenges to Property Rights on Guayalí and Ralco

Further north in Alto Bío Bío another prominent landowning family confronted similar challenges to their property rights. The family of Luis Martín Bunster held titles to two large estates in the region, Guayalí and Ralco, that totaled well over fifty thousand hectares. Bunster's property, which bordered San Ignacio de Pemehue, included part of the valuable Nitrito Valley, which had belonged originally to Lot D, auctioned by the state as a lease in 1893. Whereas the Puelma family battled a rural population composed largely of Chilean campesinos, many repatriated from Argentina, the Bunsters encountered their most serious antagonists among the region's Pehuenche communities. In 1934 a number of Pehuenches belonging to the Ralco community, including the community's lonko, Ignacio Maripi, joined the insurrection that swept the region. A major target of the 1934 rebellion was the Bunster family's Guayalí estate, to which the Ralco community had claimed historic rights, along with the neighboring Ralco estate. As was the case of nonindigenous Chilean campesinos, during the decades leading up to 1934 Ralco frequently went to court and appealed to regional officials and governments in Santiago to grant them legal titles to their land and restore land usurped by neighboring large estates. The community viewed indigenous law and the institutions established to regulate the settlement of Mapuches in reducciones, including the office of *protector de indios*, as key resources in their struggles with the Bunsters' Guayalí and Ralco haciendas.

The Bunsters' titles to Ralco (and probably Guayalí) were, if anything, even more fraudulent than those held by the Puelmas to San Ignacio de Pemehue. They dated to March and April 1881, when Rafael Anguita, a former mayor of the city of Los Ángeles, purchased land just north of the Biobío River from a number of indígenas in three separate sales in Mulchén. In the first deed, eleven indígenas, who expressed themselves through an interpreter, sold him a vaguely defined piece of land in La Laja for $1,500 pesos. In the second, seven indígenas, also through an interpreter, sold land in Ralco for $250 pesos. And, in the third, a group of indígenas, again through an interpreter, sold their land in Ralco for $350 pesos. In the case of Guayalí, Martín Bunster purchased the land that would constitute the estate from four caciques in 1882. An Indian Court judge (Juez Titular de Indios) in Victoria, Gustavo Bisquertt Susarte, made a powerful case during the 1930s that these land sales were fraudulent and that members of the region's indigenous communities held legal rights to the Bunsters' alleged property.[33]

Bisquertt noted that even though the land lay north of the Biobío River in La Laja, it was still part of what was known as indigenous territory. While landowners like the Bunsters contended that indigenous law did not apply north of the Biobío, Bisquertt argued compellingly that nowhere in the original 1866 law on indigenous settlement was the Biobío specified as a northern boundary of indigenous territory.[34] He pointed out that the foundational indigenous laws of 1852, 1853, and 1866 did not specify any borders to indigenous territory; rather, the law established that indigenous territory was defined as the place inhabited by indigenous people. In addition, La Laja had been part of the original province of Arauco, giving further weight to the argument that the region was considered to be part of the Araucanía and was thus indigenous territory. In fact, he asserted, the government commission in charge of settling indigenous people on reducciones had established three Pehuenche communities in La Laja with legal titles, or Títulos de Merced (land grant titles), thereby recognizing La Laja as indigenous territory.

The point was crucial because the prohibitions on the alienation of indigenous land established in laws in 1852, 1853, and 1866 were, therefore, applicable to La Laja. The 1866 law on indigenous settlement had established the position of protector de indios. Rather than the intendant and governor, the protector de indios had to represent the communities in land sales, contracts, or rentals and approve all legal transactions. No indigenous protector had been present during the 1881 land sales in Alto Bío Bío. In addition, the sellers had to either have legally registered titles to the land they sold, which the twenty-three indígenas did not have, or demonstrate material possession of the thirty-nine thousand hectares of the Ralco estate. Bisquertt made a convincing case that the twenty-three persons could not have had material possession of this vast stretch of land. None of the deeds stated that they held exclusive material possession of or even lived on the land that would become the Ralco estate. In fact, it appeared that at least three of the twenty-three indígenas lived at some distance from Ralco, near Mulchén. Finally, none of the twenty-three were referred to as caciques in the deeds. The 1866 law conferred all property rights to indigenous communities' caciques, or lonkos, who were to represent communities in land sales as well as in other commercial and legal transactions.[35]

In 1938, when Bisquertt issued his finding, he made one final argument against the Bunster family's rights to Ralco: neither they nor the estate's original owner, Rafael Anguita, had been able to establish material possession of the thirty-nine thousand hectares, whereas the members of the Ralco community had demonstrated uninterrupted material possession as required by the 1866 law. In fact, most damning in legal terms, leaving aside the blatantly fraudulent 1881 land sales, was the fact that the Ralco community had occupied land on the Ralco estate for decades, resisting all efforts to evict them, and that neither the Anguita family nor the Bunsters had established material possession of the fundo. In May 1886, for example, five years after he purchased the land in Ralco, Anguita died, leaving Ralco to his heir Octavio Anguita. At that point, the enormous estate had only twenty-four mares, one bull, and seven cows. That is, Anguita had introduced basically no improvements on the land, which could be used only for pasturing livestock. Anguita, like the Puelmas, had clearly viewed his purchase of land in Ralco as an investment in the southern frontier's dynamic real estate market and, while investing little or nothing in his property, had sat back and watched its value increase exponentially following the "pacification of the Araucanía."[36]

Like the Puelma properties, Anguita's Ralco estate was not unoccupied. At least 250 members of the Ralco community claimed the land. In 1890 Octavio Anguita went to court in Los Ángeles to initiate a complaint against the "cacique indígena Lepimán and others," who were, he stated, "disturbing his possession" of Ralco. Lepimán and others in his community countered with a complaint of their own against Anguita, introducing into evidence the testimony of twenty-one witnesses, presumably members of the Ralco community. Anguita also had witnesses, most prominently Martín Bryan Bunster and his son Luis Martín Bunster, owners of the neighboring Guayalí fundo. Although there is less information about this sale, it is probable that Bunster's purchase followed the same general procedure as Anguita's: an utterly fraudulent sale of an enormous property by indígenas with no demonstrable legal property rights and without the legally required intervention of the indigenous protector to represent the indígenas in the sale. Guayalí, like Ralco, lay on land claimed by the region's Pehuenche communities. In 1882 Martín Bryan Bunster purchased Guayalí from four Mapuche caciques, and his title to the estate was registered in La Laja's Conservador de Bienes Raíces.[37] Both of these sales coincided with the military push into the mountain valleys of Alto Bío Bío between 1880 and 1883 and the final defeat of Pehuenche groups.

In 1892, a decade after his purchase of the Ralco estate, Anguita went to court to request that members of the Ralco community be expelled from his property. A troop of gendarmes traveled to Alto Bío Bío and evicted the indígenas, but this was an apparently ineffective measure since the *lanzados* returned and continued to occupy land within the estate's borders. Anguita seems not to have pursued any further action and left his estate relatively abandoned, presumably content to sit back and watch property values rise. In 1908 members of the Ralco community sent a petition to the government requesting that they be legally settled on their land in Ralco and granted a Título de Merced, which they had never received, to the land they had occupied for generations. The indigenous settlement commission charged a surveyor, Enrique Evans, with the job of designating the community's location and establishing its title. However, Evans soon ran into obstacles presented by Héctor Anguita, Rafael Anguita's son. On 4 March 1908 Héctor Anguita sent a telegram to Evans in Nueva Imperial, telling him that he had instructions "to prevent any settlement [of indígenas]." The telegram contained an implicit warning: Evans shouldn't take the trouble of making a pointless trip all the way to Alto Bío Bío. The warning evidently worked because the Ralco community never received a title to its land, and no surveyor ever demarcated its boundaries. Anguita's ability to prevent the settlement of an indigenous community on land he claimed was consistent with landowners' actions to undermine the activities of the indigenous settlement commission elsewhere in Alto Bío Bío. In 1901, for example, wealthy landowners who had purchased leases of pasture in the region prevented "with force" a surveyor sent to settle a number of Pehuenche communities on titled reducciones. The landowners eventually obtained an order from the office of the lands inspectorate suspending the settlement of Pehuenche communities in Alto Bío Bío altogether.[38]

Octavio Anguita must have been eager to prevent the Ralco community's settlement in a titled reducción because he was getting ready to sell his Ralco estate. In 1909 he sold Ralco to Luis Martín Bunster for $40,000 pesos, roughly seven times the price in real pesos his father had paid for the property. The contract between the two parties freed Anguita from the responsibility of evicting the "indios who live [on Ralco]." Members of the Ralco community continued to reside within the borders of the estate for twenty-eight years following its original purchase. It appears that after 1892, Anguita had made little effort to evict them.

Luis Martín Bunster was a prominent local resident. He owned the neighboring Guayalí estate and had served as a land assessor in the region and a witness on behalf of Anguita in his conflicts with the Ralco community. Bunster was the son of Martín Bryan Bunster and nephew of José Bunster, members of a distinguished Valparaíso British merchant family. José Bunster had been a pioneering investor in southern property during the 1850s and had seen his initial investments lost during the 1859 Mapuche uprising, becoming then a vocal advocate of the military conquest of the Araucanía. In 1862 he had followed the military push southward, returned to Angol, and initiated the formation of a family empire of southern estates, grain mills, a railroad, and the region's first bank, the Banco Bunster. Members of the Bunster family held large properties throughout southern Chile.

Luis Martín Bunster pursued the eviction of the Ralco community from his new property far more energetically than Anguita had. In December 1910 he went to court to request that police expel Ralco's members from the Ralco estate, but his petition was denied. He then went to the appeals court in Concepción, which upheld the decision on 6 April 1911. Members of the Ralco community continued to occupy thousands of hectares they claimed in a permanent state of *rebeldía*, as one Indian Court put it in 1912, still without title to the land and in legal limbo.[39] On the one hand, the government refused to survey and grant them a Título de Merced. On the other, it also declined to authorize their eviction from an estate with recognized deeds.

In 1912 Benicio and Ignacio Maripi, lonkos of the five-hundred-member Ralco community, along with the lonkos of the Queuco, Manuel Pavian, Trapa-Trapa, Antonio Canio, Malla, Antonio Marihuan, and Callaqui communities, sent a number of petitions to the lands ministry. They argued that they and their ancestors had been born and raised in the high-altitude valleys bordered by the Biobío and Queuco Rivers and the Andes cordillera, but that since 1900 they had been "systematically dispossessed" of the most fertile land for pasture and crops by "our wealthy neighbors who today occupy an elevated social position. . . . [T]oday we are left only with sterile mountain land where our cattle have little pasture, and we have been forced to find our sustenance in the forests' piñones." The petition continued:

> The dispossession has arrived at such an extreme, your excellency, that it is enough for a wealthy person to take any indige-

nous person to a notary paying him an insignificant sum of money so that they take our names and sell our territories and soon the land is taken from us. This is demonstrated in the numerous deeds that exist in Los Ángeles, Angol, Temuco etc. of sales made in this way and made in favor of the gentlemen already mentioned.

On numerous occasions we have presented petitions to be settled, but until today we have achieved nothing. Over the recent years we have traveled to the capital to present our demands, but very little or, rather, nothing has been done for us. In fact, upon returning to our homes we are persecuted and sometimes brutally mistreated by the agents of these aforementioned gentlemen.

Among the landowners denounced by the Pehuenche lonkos was Luis Martín Bunster.[40]

The lonkos' petitions were rejected. As Luis Risopatrón, the lands and colonization minister, argued, much of the land they demanded was titled to private landowners. Risopatrón also affirmed landowners' legal arguments that Maripi and the members of the Ralco community were Argentines, not Chileans, who had fled the Argentine army during the Campaign of the Desert and taken refuge in Alto Bío Bío. As Argentines they were not entitled to be settled on reducciones. The accusation that the Pehuenche communities of Alto Bío Bío were nomads who could not demonstrate permanent occupation of their land as required by indigenous law and, moreover, were not Chilean but Argentine was a long-standing argument employed by landowners who had leased pasture in the mountains and who sought to expel the Pehuenche communities settled there.

Nonetheless, Ignacio Maripi and other members of the Ralco community persisted in their efforts to be settled legally on their land in Ralco and remained within the estate's borders. In 1919, for example, members of the community met with the intendant of Bío-Bío province to advise him that Ignacio Maripi "had been named cacique of the reducción." This was notable for two reasons. First, they described their community as a reducción, even though they had never been settled and never received a Título de Merced. Second, they described Maripi as the community's cacique so that he could serve as their legal representative as it engaged in legal proceedings to acquire a title.[41] As a reducción with a cacique, they conformed to the requirements established in indigenous law to be settled and granted a title.

The members of Ralco probably wanted the state's formal recognition of Maripi as cacique because their conflict with Luis Martín Bunster was back in court in Concepción. Seven years after his initial legal failures Bunster had returned to court seeking the Ralco community's expulsion from the estate. In his brief to the court, Bunster had referred to Maripi as "the indígena Maripe" in an effort to deny Maripi's status as cacique, and the community's status as a reducción. Rather than *mocetones*, or commoners, the other community members were, he maintained, Maripi's servants and family members.[42] However, the community now enjoyed support from a variety of parties, including a Franciscan missionary, Ángel Saavedra, who served as its advocate in petitions to the state.[43] The seventy families that composed the community had a lawyer whom Saavedra had arranged for to represent them in their legal battles over Ralco. A list of members of the Ralco community involved in the lawsuit included names of at least two people later detained for participating in the 1934 revolt, Ignacio Maripi and Segundo Piñaleo, as well as a number of people with the same last names of detainees, probably family members of future rebels: Levi, Pellao, and Maripi.

The community's lawyer made many of the same legal arguments later developed by the Juez de Indios Bisquertt. First, he demonstrated that the original sale of Ralco to Anguita in 1881 was fraudulent because the indígenas who sold the alleged property located in Laja and Los Ángeles resided in Mulchén and therefore could not demonstrate that they occupied or had dominion of the land in question. Nor were the indígenas or their interpreters known to the scribe who registered the sale, and in these cases the law dictated that the indígenas needed witnesses who could testify to their identity. According to the lawyer, the members of Ralco not only took no part in the sale but also had no idea that the sale had occurred. They thus continued their occupation of Ralco for over thirty years, demonstrating their legal dominion over the property; the foundational 1866 indigenous property law required only one year of permanent occupation. And, he contended, even though the community lacked a Título de Merced, the legal authorities continually referred to Ralco as a reducción and to Ignacio Maripi as the community's cacique, in effect recognizing Ralco's legal status as a reducción.[44]

Three years later the conflict with Luis Martín Bunster remained unresolved. The community had still not received a land title, but Bunster had been unable to dislodge them from Ralco. In December 1922 three lonkos from Alto Bío Bío's Pehuenche communities traveled to Santiago to petition President Arturo Alessandri to intervene on their behalf and protect their land from being taken over by Luis Martín Bunster. The lonkos laid claim to both of Bunster's estates in Alto Bío Bío, Guayalí and Ralco. While in the capital they met with the editors of the newspaper *Las Últimas Noticias*. They denounced Bunster's "abuses and theft" of their land. Mainuquilias Raiman, Manuel Lepeman, and Ignacio Maripi told the newspaper that "there is a señor named Martín Bunster, and he wants to take from us the small pieces of land that remain ours in Ralco, land that belonged to the cacique General Quellillanca, who founded Cancura, Huequén, Mulchén, and the towns of Los Ángeles, Angol, and Temuco." According to the lonkos, Quellillanca, "the most glorious" of Ralco's caciques, was Ignacio Maripi's grandfather. He had been a soldier for fifty years as well as *cacique general de Ralco*, and "he left us an established nobility that we still respect." They came, they said, to speak with "*nuestra altísima mercé* [our highest worship], our President, to ask for help since we now are Chilean, *señor*, pure Chileans." The lonkos emphasized their Chilean identity to stress their loyalty to the Chilean state and to fend off accusations that they were nomads from Argentina who had only recently settled on the Chilean side of the Andes cordillera. "We are the owners of Ralco, Lepoy, and Guayalí, which are in the cordillera, in the province of Bío Bío," they continued. But their efforts to receive a title to their land had been frustrated: "We have been here ten days, and we haven't been able to get anything, we are treated with bad will. It appears that they have forgotten the legacy of the gift of our valor [to Chile]. We have brought 300 pesos, the earnings of an entire year and we have spent it all already" (on food and lodging, it appears). They left the newspaper office "in the hope that they would be heard," leaving behind "a trace of misery, a smell of defeat, of implacable persecution."[45]

Two weeks later *Las Últimas Noticias* published Bunster's version of the conflict. To avoid continual problems he obtained lands for the indígenas to settle, but they refused to leave their land in Ralco. He then ceded land, he said, within the borders of the Ralco fundo "so as not to proceed violently with them or leave them without land, proceeding humanely despite the fact that they had no right to receive land that belonged to him, which the courts had denied them many years before." According to Bunster, the Ralco community had been instigated by agents external to the community, possibly the missionary Saavedra, to continue petitioning "to have their possessions inside the fundo belonging to Sr Bunster recognized." Bunster's patience had finally worn thin, and he had gone back to court "to put an end to this situation." Bunster was only trying, he claimed, "to obtain lands that were occupied by indígenas the first time in a completely irregular and abusive way, and that have been improved and cleared with the constant labor of many years by one of the most progressive agriculturalists in the south." Ralco's value had increased appreciably and would make the estate "a rich prize for the indígenas and the agents who instigate them if they could appeal to other rights than having occupied [the land] during some years against the will of the landowner."[46]

Despite Bunster's legal efforts to have the Ralco community expelled, community members continued throughout the 1920s to occupy land within the estate's borders. In addition, Ignacio Maripi kept up his efforts on behalf of the Ralco community. In 1924, for example, he visited a public school for boys in the town of Los Ángeles, accompanied by the head of the Lautaro regiment. His goal was to ask the school director for materials so that he could install a school for araucanos in Ralco. The petition was authorized by the school's director, and teachers furnished Maripi with reading primers, books, and chalkboards.[47] A year later Maripi and a number of other Pehuenches from Alto Bío Bío traveled to Los Ángeles to get legal permission to hold a *nguillatún*, a religious ceremony.[48] Maripi and Ralco clearly viewed the state as an important interlocutor and resource for the community.

As was the case with the conflict over San Ignacio de Pemehue, the struggle between Bunster and the Ralco community continued to simmer during the 1920s. Despite Ralco's small size and isolated location, the community had risen to national prominence. It had engaged in legal proceedings in the city of Concepción and found its cause aired by Franciscan missionaries and the local and national press. By the late 1920s Ralco's lonkos had engaged in an unceasing struggle to gain title to their land. They had petitioned the government repeatedly but unsuccessfully to send surveyors to map their community and grant them a Título de Merced. They had gone to court and to the newspapers. When the Sindicato Agrícola Lonquimay initiated its campaign to appropriate and settle San Ignacio, Ignacio Maripi and other members of Ralco as well as members of neighboring Pehuenche communities joined the union and organized union councils of their own. The community and the union had a common enemy, the Bunster family, and a common goal: to acquire land claimed by Alto Bío Bío's haciendas.

CHAPTER THREE
The *Inquilinos* Organize
Rural Labor and Social Unrest in Southern Chile

O N 20 APRIL 1928 inquilinos and ocupantes on San Ignacio de Pemehue's five estates organized a union, the Sindicato Agrícola Lonquimay, "in order to take advantage of the rights and benefits provided by recent [social and colonization] legislation." The union would, its leaders said, "promote the economic, moral, and intellectual improvement of its members and the general progress of this region." The union's official stamp was inscribed with three words: "populate, produce, and civilize." The language rang with the ideals of nineteenth-century Latin American liberalism, but the union also had a few concrete goals: found agricultural cooperatives on public land; introduce cattle and sheep from Argentina free of tariffs; and build seven rural schools and two farm boarding schools. The union identified its members as coming from diverse social backgrounds: property owners (*propietarios*) and rural workers (obreros campesinos), colonos and ocupantes nacionales. Many of the sindicato's original organizers identified with Chile's Democratic Party, and they stamped the party's ideology on the union's program.[1]

The union's close ties to the Democratic Party were understandable. Artisans, miners, and middle-class urban sectors had organized the party in 1887. Until one of the leaders of its left wing, the typographer Luis

Emilio Recabarren, left the party and founded the Partido Obrero Socialista (Socialist Workers Party, or POS) in 1912, it had been the major voice in Chile for the "liberation ... of the people," as its founding document stated. Democrats distinguished themselves from anarchists and the POS, which became the Chilean Communist Party in 1922, during the first decades of the twentieth century by seeking basic social and legal reforms through participation in the political system. The Democratic Party elected members to congress and worked for a number of labor reforms, including workers' compensation, regulation of child labor, labor inspectors in workplaces, a ten-hour workday, a Sunday day of rest, an end to payment with tokens and the monopoly held by pulperías over commerce in mining districts, and social insurance. Unlike the POS and anarchists, the Democrats attempted to exercise their influence by establishing alliances with other parties, including the more oligarchic Liberal Party and middle-class Radical Party.[2]

Democrats were critical of projects intended to people Chile's southern territories with European immigrants. They advocated instead "national colonization" with Chilean laborers.[3] In 1903 the party resolved to promote "national colonization and the [importation of] foreign livestock," two planks of the Sindicato Agrícola Lonquimay's initial program. That year a Democratic Party leader reported that national colonization had been a special concern of the party's bloc in congress. Democrats put before congress legislation on national colonization and traveled to the frontier region to study the problem of Chilean ocupantes and aspiring colonos. The Democrats also petitioned the government to end the policy of public land auctions, which had dispossessed thousands of ocupantes and led to the formation of large estates in the south. Malaquías Concha, one of the party's founders, argued that national colonization would "inculcate in the people ideas of order and respect for property rights, love of family, and will contribute notably to civilization, raising the moral level of the masses, and, more than anything, will put an end to social conflicts ... since the sons of this country will be able to acquire a piece of land to cultivate."[4] As in the case of the Puelma properties, Democratic Party congressmen throughout the south worked to represent the interests of rural laborers in their conflicts with large estates and colonization concessions contracted to bring European immigrants to southern Chile.

The Sindicato Agrícola Lonquimay quickly organized councils, or *consejos*, on estates in the region. These were not strictly workers' councils given that they organized a diverse rural population with a tangle of social identities. Some union members were inquilinos, some ocupantes and aspiring colonos, whom the union often referred to as *pobladores* (residents) on the estates, many all four at once. The councils mimicked the Communist Party–led national labor federation, the FOCH, which likewise organized local labor councils. In its early years, however, the Sindicato Agrícola Lonquimay had no ties to the national union.[5] In fact, in all its petitions and publications not once did the leaders of the sindicato refer to the FOCH. They had organized a union, but it is unclear how the union leaders on the five Puelma estates viewed unions further north in Chile's ports, cities, and mining areas with their militant traditions of revolutionary strikes and ties to leftist parties. The Sindicato Agrícola Lonquimay proposed a different path toward progress, one rooted in the Democratic Party's proposals for colonization and cooperativism on southern public land.

From its inception the Sindicato Agrícola Lonquimay defined itself as both a union, organized to represent rural workers' interests, and a cooperative whose goal was to settle public land, with its members organized in colonies. These dual identities reflected the union's diverse membership and Alto Bío Bío's complicated social realities. The sindicato's leaders drew on new labor legislation passed in 1924 to build one of Chile's earliest, most important rural unions. But they also hoped to take advantage of colonization laws that had been on the books since the late nineteenth century and that had been expanded during the late 1920s to settle their members on estate and public land as colonos. The program of the sindicato was devoted to improving conditions for workers on the region's estates and to settling the Puelma properties, which they deemed public land, with their members organized in a cooperative.

The key organizers of the union were Juan Segundo Leiva Tapia, a schoolteacher who had studied French and Spanish in Argentina and completed a couple of years of law school at the University of Chile, and Bruno and Jorge Ackermann, German immigrants and local merchants. Leiva Tapia's father, Juan Segundo Leiva Ramos, had been born in Argentina and was orphaned young while his parents were living in Chile. Despite his family's Argentine origins, Leiva Ramos had been raised in Chile. He built a successful livestock business in Neuquén, Argentina, and traded stock between Argentina's western province and southern Chile. Leiva Tapia, who was born in Neuquén like his father, moved to Chile as a child and then returned to Argentina to study at the

University of Córdoba. He returned to Chile once more to study law in Santiago but never finished.[6] Instead, he returned to Alto Bío Bío with the goal of building the region's first public schools. He also began to organize rural laborers to colonize public land.[7]

Bruno and Jorge Ackermann owned a pulpería neighboring Francisco Puelma Tupper's El Rahue estate. They sold goods to both inquilinos and colonos in the region. The Ackermanns joined Leiva Tapia in organizing the union because they understood that colonization of the Puelma estates with smallholders would help their business. As Harry Fahrenkrog Reinhold, who worked in the Ackermanns' pulpería, related in his memoirs of the rebellion, "If the lands remained in the hands of the Puelmas, the region's population would never grow, but if the fundos were colonized it would increase, and the greater the population, the more commerce." According to Fahrenkrog, the Ackermanns' ties to the region's estate laborers, who purchased provisions at their store, facilitated the work of organizing the union, whose members were initially "inquilinos from the Puelma fundos."[8] Leiva Tapia and the Ackermann brothers enjoyed the support of nearby Curacautín's newspaper *El Comercio* and its editor Froilán Rivera.

A 1929 report from the Sindicato Agrícola Lonquimay's directorate to Cautín's intendant made clear union leaders' goal of taking advantage of both the 1924 social laws and recent legislation promoting colonization in southern Chile. The *dirigentes* noted that they were sending the founding constitution of their union to the Departamento de Bienestar (Welfare Department) in Temuco to be legally registered. At this point, the union's members numbered more than three hundred. They informed the intendant that they had organized "at the heart of our institution the Lonquimay Agricultural Cooperative No. 1 with a starting capital of 273,400 pesos divided into 1,317 shares [*acciones*] to buy land in this region for our members."[9] The union's directors had written the constitution of this agricultural cooperative according to the dictates of the recent 1929 Agricultural Cooperatives Law (Law No. 4531) and registered it with the Civil Registry. This action constituted the union as a colonization society dedicated to organizing a cooperative of its members on either public land or estate land expropriated or purchased by the state.

But the Sindicato Agrícola Lonquimay maintained its identity as a labor organization. It had established in its union hall in Lonquimay both a Bolsa de Trabajo (labor exchange) to help its members find work and a Libro de Reclamos, where its members could register "the abuses that are committed daily against the pobladores on all the *grandes fundos*."[10] In effect, the sindicato held a dual legal status as both a union and a cooperative society and promoted a variety of programs, from representing the interests of estate workers to organizing the diverse rural population in a cooperative of colonos, many of them former inquilinos. Union leaders proposed that the cooperative be organized on public land and land belonging to the Puelmas' San Ignacio.

By the 1920s Francisco Puelma Castillo's children had chosen to deal with their inheritances in different ways. Probably in response to the ongoing challenges to their property rights from both the state and ocupantes/inquilinos, as well as their properties' isolation and distance from Santiago and relative lack of profitability, they had already chosen to sell or lease four of San Ignacio de Pemehue's five estates. Only Francisco Puelma Tupper retained possession of the estate he inherited, El Rahue, though he left it in charge of an administrator, José Saavedra, who had managed the estate since 1894. In 1920 Manuel Puelma sold the Lolco estate to a French citizen, Juan Bautista Olhagaray, for $505,000 pesos. In 1924 Olhagaray founded a commercial society, and ownership of the estate was now shared with two other French immigrants, Juan Bautista Charó and Juan Cadet Olhagaray. While Puelma had used Lolco to pasture livestock, the estate's primary use appears to have been as collateral for loans. He had already taken out two mortgages on the property at the time of its sale, one with the Banco Hipotecario de Chile for $120,000 pesos and the other with the Banco de Chile for $80,000. Meanwhile, the Villucura estate had been leased to Juan Antonio Orrego, who had married Teresa Puelma Tupper, and Sara Navarro Puelma, the widow of Guillermo Puelma Tupper, had leased the Chilpaco estate to José Miguel Gutiérrez. Rosa Puelma de Rodríguez had sought to follow the same path with the Ránquil estate. In 1924 she leased the property to a French resident of Argentina, Gaston Rambeaux, with the understanding that he would pay rent as well as make payments toward the eventual purchase of the estate. Rambeaux left an administrator and business partner in charge, José Paz, of Spanish nationality.[11]

Leiva Tapia and the Ackermanns appear to have been familiar with the history of the Puelma family's struggles to exercise their property rights over San Ignacio de Pemehue. They had detailed knowledge of the history of the hacienda's fraudulent expansion, which had been narrated in Roque Fernández's petitions and presented to congress by Senator Zenón Torrealba. They understood as well that the estates' history of legally dubious titles made them ripe for expropriation and colonization. By the late 1920s San Ignacio's estates, with the exception of Lolco, were run by administrators or had been rented out. The Puelmas resided in Santiago and exercised little personal control over their properties. A strong case could be made that the estates could be restored to the state and their land distributed to the region's ocupantes and inquilinos. The Sindicato Agrícola Lonquimay's leaders proposed that the government employ colonization laws to expropriate the Puelmas' San Ignacio and settle the five estates with their inquilinos in colonies organized as cooperatives.

Inquilinaje in Southern Chile

The Sindicato Agrícola was not alone in organizing rural laborers in southern Chile. During the 1920s inquilinos and ocupantes organized unions, colonization societies, and agricultural cooperatives throughout the region. As on the Puelma estates, inquilinos often claimed estate land, which they deemed to be public, and demanded titles to their small plots as colonos. They invoked these rights on the basis of their material possession, which was demonstrated by the improvements they had made, like clearing forests, planting crops, and building fences. Ocupantes settled on estate land as squatters, hoping to win titles to small plots of land. The formal legal terms "inquilino," "ocupante," and "colono" disguised a complicated social landscape. Many colonos and ocupantes were also inquilinos who claimed estate land as their own and who regarded their patrones' property rights as being illegitimate. In not a few cases inquilinos simply refused to follow their patrones' orders and worked their small plots as if they were their own, converting themselves into both squatter ocupantes and, in the legal language of the day, "aspiring colonos." Frontier land was public, they argued, and the estates where they lived and labored had been formed by fraud.[12]

As in central Chile, in the south large estates had built a monopoly over land and employed a permanent labor force of inquilinos who exchanged their labor and the labor of their household members for the right to work small plots of land on estates. During seasons of high labor demand landowners supplemented their inquilino labor force by hiring workers from a large population of landless, migrant seasonal laborers known as gañanes.[13] Unlike in central Chile, in Alto Bío Bío many inquilinos owned their own livestock, which they pastured on estate lands. This gave them a measure of autonomy that their counterparts further north did not enjoy. Landowners also gave inquilinos small plots of two or three cuadras to cultivate wheat and garden crops. In exchange, they were obligated to put one member of their household at the disposal of the estate to do the work of *mejoras* (improvements) and caring for the estate's livestock (this inquilino was known as *obligado*, or required). Some inquilinos in the south also entered mediería arrangements with their patrones, working estate land on shares, usually with the obligation of selling their crops to the landowners. As on estates in central Chile, inquilinos were often required to purchase supplies and food at pulperías at inflated prices. By the late 1920s many inquilinos in Alto Bío Bío were paid wages in addition to the right to work a plot of land, but by the time payday rolled around, usually after harvests were in, they had accumulated so much debt at pulperías that they received no pay at all.[14]

The Puelma and Bunster estates were largely devoted to raising livestock, although their owners also installed sawmills to take advantage of the abundant forests in the Andes cordillera. In his memoirs of life in the region and account of the rebellion, Harry Fahrenkrog Reinhold recalled that each inquilino was permitted to pasture his own cattle on the Puelmas' extensive lands and was allotted a small plot of two or three cuadras to cultivate wheat. Once a year, the estates' absentee owners arrived to oversee the two-week rodeos in which the livestock were corralled and separated into groups for fattening, slaughter, and breeding. Inquilinos herded the animals into pens and did the work of branding and castrating. Groups of animals were driven to different areas for veranada summer pasture according to the capacity of the mountain valleys to support the grazing herds. While lower land was preserved for the invernada winter pasture, the high-altitude valleys of the cordillera supplied cattle *mallines* (wetland meadows) and *coironales* (thatch grass on mountain hillsides), quilas, and piñones. Piñones also served the local campesino population as an important alternative to wheat when they were ground into flour. The Puelmas, like other landowners, provided their laborers access to small plots to cultivate crops as well as to different ecological niches, veranadas and invernadas, meadows and forests, where they could collect forest products and pasture their livestock.[15]

As in central Chile, gender shaped these social arrangements. By the late 1920s official government sources in southern Chile reflected a society in which inquilinos were identified as men who entered into contracts with their patrones, representing their children, wives, and other female members of their households. A glance at labor contracts, censuses, and the labor courts demonstrates that Alto Bío Bío's inquilinos were uniformly understood to be male. Only male inquilinos went to labor courts in Los Ángeles or filed complaints with labor inspectors. Censuses of Alto Bío Bío's laborers taken in 1934, leading up to the Ránquil rebellion, identified only men as inquilinos and ocupantes.[16]

Government officials consistently identified female campesinas by their supposed role tending the household rather than their labor in the agricultural economy. In the list of fifty-six detained campesinos following the rebellion's suppression, for example, only male campesinos were described in terms of their labor position or their landownership. Twelve were identified by the term *agricultor*. These were former inquilinos who for the most part had occupied plots on Ránquil but still did not possess legal titles to their land. Twenty-two prisoners, including all the detained Ralco Pehuenches, were identified as gañanes, seasonal or part-time laborers on the region's estates. Nine men were identified as miners. The three women imprisoned for their part in the movement, Margarita Ramírez, her daughter Sofía Cisternas, and Clementina Sagredo, were all described only as housewives or, in the formal legal language of the time, as dedicated to the tasks or labor appropriate to their sex, or *labores del sexo*, an abbreviation of *labores propias de su sexo*.[17] No matter what work campesinas did in and outside the household in Alto Bío Bío's fields and forests, their social identity was reduced in the government's eyes to the tasks appropriate to their gender, that is, work inside the home.

Certain jobs on Alto Bío Bío's estates were the unique preserve of men. These included shepherd (*campañista*) and the activities associated with bringing livestock down from mountain valley pasture for the annual rodeo and slaughter. But the line dividing the household and the fields was blurry; women joined their families in many agricultural activities, although their labor went unrecognized in government sources. Male inquilinos, while subordinated to their patrones, controlled and relied on the labor of their wives and children. This reproduced within the world of the large estates the gendered social order prescribed in colonization law since the nineteenth century: male colonos received land rights as heads of households with children and through their labor introducing improvements in frontier land. This labor always included the rarely recognized work of their wives and children. Campesina women performed the essential reproductive labor of childcare, cooking, cleaning, and tending small garden plots on estates, but they also harvested crops, tended livestock, and sheared sheep.

In her 1965 recollections of labor as a member of an inquilino family, Emelina Sagredo, who was active in the rebellion and whose two older brothers were leaders of the Sindicato Agrícola Lonquimay, emphasizes the work that went into harvesting crops, work performed by both men and women. She recounts that her entire household, which was originally from Santa Bárbara and was headed by her older brothers, worked on estates in Alto Bío Bío bringing in harvests, tending livestock, and shearing sheep. Indeed, women not only sheared the sheep but also cleaned and combed the wool, preparing it for spinning: "At home there was always work for women: the men went out to plant and we helped with the harvest. We had to tend the young animals so we could eat them during the winter, pigs, hens, turkeys, everything. In October, we sheared the sheep and they gave us wool. We washed the wool in pans at the side of estuaries . . . right there we made the fires to heat the water. Then you clean it . . . you comb it by hand and you make little balls of wool for spinning. . . . There was also the work of milling corn." She recalled also that when she was young her mother worked on shares with the region's indigenous Pehuenche communities harvesting wheat.[18] Sagredo also narrated vividly the women's work of collecting piñones in high-altitude valleys and grinding them into a flour that sustained their families: "We collected piñones in April, we went into the cordillera to collect piñones, luckily they didn't charge us even if they were on estates. . . . We went on horseback and in carts, but the cart remained far [from the tree stands], we had to carry the piñones in sacks on our shoulders or on horses." Women then took charge of grinding and cooking the piñones in large cauldrons.

Women worked hard, beginning at a young age, cooking, cleaning, and taking care of children. Sagredo recalled that in her family the men on estates were inquilinos who were *obligados*—required to labor for the estates' patrones—but the women could work freely. However, in exchange they were required to provide reproductive labor, especially cooking and childcare. She noted that as young girls, female members of her large household had to care for one sibling: "My mother told us you have to take care of this sibling as *obligación*." By using the word "obligación," her mother drew an explicit analogy between the work required of male family members by the estates and the work done in childcare performed by girls. As Sagredo remembered, "We had to keep the [younger children] clean, mend their clothes, take care of everything for them." In addition, even as girls they prepared the food and *mate* for the family. This work, she noted, was unceasing: "One could never take time off [*faltar*]."

Women's subordination within campesino households was reflected in widespread domestic violence. As Sagredo recalled, "In the countryside all men hit women, because they are women, or for little things, for not having a piece of clothing mended." Sagredo was quite clear that she chose never to marry, despite having romantic attachments during her life, because living with her brothers protected her from male violence and because, in her words, "[I] didn't want to become a slave." By refusing to marry, she implies, she avoided the burden of having children at an early age; she was able to exert some control over her reproductive life. Her view of campesina women's lives in Alto Bío Bío's cordillera was shaped by her understanding that women, their work, and their sexuality were always subordinated to male authority, often exercised through violence, within campesino households. Most female campesinas in Alto Bío Bío, like Emelina Sagredo and her sisters, lived in households headed by males where authority rested with their fathers, husbands, or brothers. While they contributed vital labor to the household economy, their rights to land within the borders of estates as members of inquilino families or as ocupantes hoping to be settled as colonos derived from the patriarchal authority, codified in the land and labor laws, held by male heads of households.

In Alto Bío Bío many of the more paternalist dimensions of labor control present on estates in central Chile were absent. Estates rarely had chapels, clinics, or schools, though they often had pulperías. By the 1920s pulperías on both the Puelma and Bunster estates were owned and managed not by landowners but by local merchants who were often European immigrants, like the Ackermann brothers, further attenuating the relationship between the landowners and their workers. This reflected estate owners' absence. Most landowners in the region, including the Bunsters and Puelmas, resided elsewhere, leaving their estates to managers, and visited their estates only rarely. In his memoirs of life in the region during the early 1930s, Harry Fahrenkrog Reinhold recalled that once a year the estates' absentee owners arrived to oversee two-week rodeos.[19]

While many contemporary commentators on the 1934 rebellion, including Fahrenkrog, recalled with nostalgia the peaceful nature of labor relations on estates in Alto Bío Bío, it appears that inquilinos lived and labored in conditions that would have eroded any effort at paternalist labor management. In 1928 Curacautín's *El Comercio* described how the region's inquilinos worked fourteen-hour days and were provided only meager rations and miserable lodging, often a one-room hut made of wood and straw for an entire family. Many inquilinos were paid only once a year, presumably as a tactic for keeping them dependent on and tied to the estate. Many never received their pay in money because they had become indebted at pulperías, where they purchased provisions at inflated prices. If inquilinos complained about working conditions or prices at the pulpería, they were threatened with eviction. In addition, they were required to sell their livestock and harvests to the estate owners, who pushed down prices, in exchange for the right to cultivate crops and pasture livestock on estate land.[20]

In southern Chile, landowners backed by local authorities bolstered workers' ties of dependence with coercion and violence.[21] Frequently local officials, judges, and the carabineros operated as landowners' agents in establishing discipline on fundos. In distant frontier areas like Alto Bío Bío, estate managers often served as the local political and judicial authorities, occupying the positions of local judge and government *subdelegado*. In some cases local officials installed pickets of carabineros on estates for security and discipline. During the early 1930s regional newspapers and military courts recorded a number of cases of landowner violence, supported by carabineros, which was employed to discipline laborers. For example, in May 1934, at the height of rural unrest in the south, *El Diario Austral* headed an article "Medieval tortures were revived in order to kill a poor inquilino." The article described the torture and execution of an inquilino who had been accused by a landowner of stealing sheep.[22] During this period military courts heard a number of cases of carabineros accused of detaining inquilinos and jornaleros at estate owners' behest. The cases suggest that the employment of carabineros as instruments of landowners' authority was not uncommon in the south.[23] In one 1934 case, a laborer testified that "because of a calumny against me [for stealing a lamb] by my patrón ... I was detained by carabineros who locked me in a storehouse [on the hacienda]."[24] Similarly, in 1932 Cautín's intendant reported to the police prefect that a mediero on the Quilongo estate had complained to his office that his patrón frequently punished his inquilinos "by placing irons on their legs, and, what is even more serious, they do this with the knowledge of the carabinero corporal."[25]

Landowners' use of violence to impose labor discipline had its roots in the southern frontier's unsettled social relations. Inquilinaje in southern Chile lacked the stability it enjoyed well into the twentieth century in central Chile. Absentee estate owners like the Puelmas and Bunsters left their properties in the charge of mayordomos. As George McBride noted in his 1936 study of Chile, "Where laborers live on large farms they bear little of the traditional relation to the patron that exists in central Chile."[26] Inquilinos and their families had only shallow roots on estates, unlike inquilinos in central Chile, where generations of workers might remain on one estate. Southern Chile's inquilinos often labored not for a lifetime but for shorter-term stints, at times moving from estate to estate, settling on public land, or migrating to Argentina. Frequently inquilinos' children did not remain on the estates where their parents were employed. In a 1921 study of colonization in Chile published by the American Geographical Society, Mark Jefferson observed that "the inquilinos do not suffice to gather the harvest. There is always lack of hands for that. So the landlords have always clamored for help, but only two months in the year. The sons of inquilinos may drift to the city ... but there are few factories, and there is little need for hands. Many go to the Argentine, both to the southern region and near Mendoza. The lot of the landless Chilean is very hard. He cannot find work in a country that has always encouraged and aided immigration."[27]

In addition to migrating across the cordillera to Argentina, rural laborers in Alto Bío Bío in the 1920s migrated to the north of Chile, drawn by advances paid by northern nitrate companies' *enganche* (hook) system. These workers composed part of Chile's large transient labor force of miners and gañanes who migrated from the countryside to the northern mines and back. In Bío-Bío province this pattern of labor migration posed an obstacle to production on rural estates. In 1924, for example, the Los Ángeles paper *El Siglo de Los Ángeles* described the serious problems confronting agriculturalists in the region, the most troubling of which was "the lack of laborers caused by the continual enganches of workers for the nitrate zone." The paper noted that the acreage put under cultivation in Bío-Bío had been restricted by the lack of available laborers. The situation had become so serious that landowners from Bío-Bío petitioned the minister of agriculture to prevent enganches to the north.[28] Similarly, in 1929 Cautín's intendant complained of a labor shortage "prejudicial to the landowners" caused by "the announcement of labor recruitment [enganche] for the north."[29] Curacautín's *El Comercio* described landowners' continued dependence on enganches to recruit inquilinos from outside the region with advances but ascribed their difficulty in building a permanent labor force to the miserable labor and living conditions on estates.[30]

Censuses of workers on the Bunsters' Guayalí estate from the early 1930s provide a useful portrait of Alto Bío Bío's impermanent agricultural labor force. A 1934 survey of fifty-four inquilinos and ocupantes on the estate found that nineteen had lived and worked on Guayalí for more than ten years and ten between five and ten years. Twenty-five, however, were more recent arrivals, having entered into inquilinaje agreements with Bunster within the last five years. More than half the inquilinos had lived and labored on the estate for ten years or less. Only six had been born on Guayalí to inquilino families.[31] Given that Guayalí had been carved out as privately held property during the 1880s and that its putative owners had only begun to invest in production, introducing livestock and laborers and erecting fences and buildings, during the first decade of the twentieth century, these figures are not surprising. In addition, because pasturing livestock required a relatively small labor force, few estates in Alto Bío Bío's cordillera would have had large permanent inquilino populations.

The Sagredo family, which settled as inquilino–medieros on Guayalí, is a good representation of rural laborers' mobility in the region. The family of eight siblings (four women and four men) came from the town of Santa Bárbara east of Los Ángeles. One of the brothers, Simón, traveled to Argentina with his children and found work tending livestock on the region's estancias. As his sister Emelina narrated, because there was no available land he returned to the Chilean side of the cordillera. Another brother, named Benito, who like Simón would become a leader in the Sindicato Agrícola Lonquimay, traveled first to the Lota coal mines near the city of Concepción and then moved to the nitrate zone in the north, where he found work in Arica. The siblings settled on Guayalí with their families as inquilino–medieros during the late 1920s and early 1930s. They had heard that land in the Nitrito Valley was public and that a colonization cooperative was going to settle the fertile valley, despite the fact that the Bunster family had appropriated and titled the land. Although they arrived in Nitrito as the Bunsters' inquilinos, they intended to acquire the land where they built homes and settled. The inquilino contract served as a means of establishing themselves on land they believed would be designated by the state for colonization. Like many other laborers in Alto Bío Bío, Benito and Simón Sagredo viewed their jobs as inquilinos as a tool for acquiring land and winning titles from the government as colonos. Both Sagredo brothers brought with them experience with left-wing politics. According to Emelina Sagredo, Benito worked with the FOCH and Communist Party in Lota and Arica, while

Simón received a "political education" while working on ranches in Argentina.[32]

The Sagredos' use of inquilinaje to acquire public land claimed by a privately held estate was the flip side of a traditional landowner practice of installing inquilinos on public land and then using their material occupation to demonstrate property rights. Throughout southern Chile land speculators and estate owners employed inquilinos to do the difficult labor of clearing forest and cultivating putatively unoccupied land to which they then petitioned for titles based on their material possession. Inquilinos' value lay both in their labor and their presence on the land, which established their patrones' material occupation, demonstrated by the improvements they had introduced, even when the supposed landowner lived not on the property but in a neighboring town or city or as far away as Santiago.[33]

Southern landowners also employed inquilinaje as a tool for appropriating the land of ocupante and colono smallholders and Mapuche communities. A common method used by landowners for dispossessing campesino smallholders was to claim that ocupantes and colonos were actually their inquilinos and to initiate judicial proceedings to gain title to their land. In 1931, for example, a Communist Party deputy, Abraham Quevedo, described in congress the various methods estate owners used to appropriate ocupantes' small plots. One such method, which harkened back to nineteenth-century appropriations of Mapuche land, was fictitious debt, in which a complicit debtor used ocupantes' land as collateral for a loan from an associate who provided the loan. Frequently impoverished and illiterate ocupantes, like Mapuche communities, had few resources with which to contest the placing of liens on their land in court. In addition, Quevedo described how land usurpers throughout southern frontier territory employed fictitious inquilinaje contracts in which they described ocupantes of public land as inquilinos, paying witnesses and going to court to claim the ocupantes' small plots and fold them into their estates.[34]

In 1936 the Democratic Party deputy Oscar Casanova similarly denounced the negligence of government surveyors employed by the lands measurement office in measuring and titling small plots in southern territory. He observed that when conflicts between "modest persons who occupy small plots" (ocupantes) and the owners of estates arose surveyors invariably reported that the ocupantes were the inquilinos of the large landowners, even when there was no proof of the "relation between worker and patrón, no proof of contract, or the conditions of the labor arrangement that would constitute a contract." In this way, he argued, lawyers and surveyors in the land measurement office had helped to make legitimate the titles of immense properties, "damaging the interests of the state and hundreds of modest families who have occupied for years small plots on these large fundos." Ocupantes had settled on their plots, he noted, in the belief that they lay on public land: "They occupied small stretches of virgin forest, they put all their labor into conquering the jungle and making the land cultivable, and then, after working thirty or more years, their rights to the land are not recognized in favor of the *latifundistas* [owners of large estates]." This is why, he noted, there had been "so many expulsions of poor ocupantes throughout the south."[35]

At times, aspiring colonos and ocupantes who occupied small plots of public land entered into inquilinaje contracts with neighboring estates to either gain access to more land to cultivate crops or pasture livestock or even to earn a small wage. In these cases estate owners could then appropriate ocupantes' plots by going to court or to the office of the lands inspectorate where they employed the labor contract as evidence that the ocupantes' land belonged to their estates. In 1939 a lands and colonization directorate report echoed Casanova in assailing large landowners' use of inquilinaje contracts to appropriate ocupantes' land. The report noted that "it is not enough ... to have contracts of inquilinaje with ocupantes who do not know how to sign their names and who by use of their thumb prints authorize a labor contract whose content and consequence they do not know and who are then expelled maliciously [from their land]." According to the report, illiterate ocupantes frequently signed inquilinaje contracts with neighboring estates in exchange for both small sums of money and the promise that they would receive title to their plots. Estate owners then used the inquilinaje contract to gain title to ocupantes' plots, acquiring at once their labor and their land.[36]

Landowners' use of inquilinaje labor arrangements to appropriate both unoccupied public land and land settled by ocupantes, colonos, and Mapuche communities meant that labor relations on southern estates were far less stable than in central Chile. Inquilinos were often former ocupantes or colonos who claimed property rights to public land folded into estates by invoking colonization laws. Rural laborers, both Mapuche and Chilean, nourished an understanding that they had earned rights to public land because they, not the estate owners, had done the work of clearing forest and planting crops, or, in the case of Mapuche communities, they had occupied the land since "time immemorial."[37] In addition, during the late 1920s and early 1930s a number of rural laborers signed inquilinaje and mediería contracts as a means to occupy estate land. As was the case with the Sagredo family, the goal was to establish possession of small plots on estate land and then petition for titles as colonos. This was especially true on estates perceived to be lying on public land, like the Bunsters' Guayalí and Ralco and the five fundos that composed San Ignacio de Pemehue. In a number of cases, inquilino-ocupantes like the Sagredos organized cooperatives and unions to claim estate land for its workers. This represented an inversion of large landowners' and speculators' well-tried strategy of contracting inquilinos to settle on public frontier land, which they then claimed as their own due to the improvements made by their laborers.

"The Lion of Tarapacá" and Social Reform, 1924–25

By the 1920s inquilinos' and ocupantes' understanding that they had been expelled unjustly from public land or that they enjoyed rights to both public and estate land based on their material occupation and labor introducing *mejoras* was reinforced by new political movements for social reform. These included state policies designed to redress the abuses that had occurred during the frontier's colonization. Throughout southern Chile campesinos organized colonization cooperatives and unions, invaded and squatted on estate land, went on strike to demand improved working conditions, and engaged in open conflicts with the authorities that often erupted into violence. Rural laborers not infrequently took up arms and confronted carabineros in pitched battles.

Arturo Alessandri's election to the presidency in 1920 instigated a wave of rural unrest in southern Chile. Alessandri, known as the Lion of Tarapacá, the northern nitrate-producing province he represented in the senate for the Liberal Party, led a populist political campaign in response to the economic and social dislocations caused by World War I and the postwar recession. Famous for his fiery rhetoric denouncing the traditional elite as "the gilded canalla" (swine), he sought to mobilize northern nitrate miners and workers, his "querida chusma" (beloved rabble). They were to form a base of electoral support, in competition with the POS and FOCH, behind a program of basic social and labor reforms. Once in power, Alessandri's Liberal Alliance government of the Radical and Democratic parties and sectors of the Liberal Party met with obstacles in congress to implementing its program of reforms. Only after an intervention by midlevel military officers led by Carlos Ibáñez and Marmaduke Grove did congress pass legislation putting a package of "social laws" promoted by Alessandri in place. The 1924 social laws, administered by a new bureaucracy of labor inspectors and labor courts, legalized unions and the right to strike, required labor contracts, and institutionalized state regulation of working conditions, collective bargaining, and arbitration of labor conflicts. Employers and workers were required to make social security payments, and employers to maintain a book recording such payments. Yet, as Brian Loveman notes, labor laws and courts did not explicitly include rural workers in their jurisdiction, and estate owners were not required to have contracts with their laborers.[38]

The contentious politics of implementing new social laws during the early 1920s, which were essentially passed by congress under pressure from reformist military officers like Ibáñez and Grove, coincided with debates over the status of southern properties and colonization. As the historian Fabián Almonacid notes, the fact that many southern properties held uncertain titles meant that landowners had difficulty acquiring mortgages on their properties through the Caja de Crédito Hipotecario. The bank imposed a new restrictive policy in 1920 of giving out loans only for properties that had been granted titles by the state or whose titles had been registered before 1866. The restrictions on acquiring mortgages generated a movement among southern landowners to push new legislation through congress or have the president issue a decree-law on the Constitution of Southern Property that would establish a special tribunal to determine property owners' rights on the basis of their material occupation and investments in improvements. In October 1925, shortly after Alessandri had gone into exile in response to Ibáñez's accumulation of power in his government, a new decree-law on colonization met some of southern property owners' demands to have their property rights recognized in law.[39] It was tempered, however, by a clause in a new 1925 constitution pushed through congress by Alessandri months earlier that established property's "social function," thus limiting the absolute reign of individual private property rights and establishing a constitutional basis for agrarian reform. In the 1925 debates about the constitution Alessandri had argued for a new "scientific" and "modern" understanding of property rights: "One could say that in fact the concept of property as a subjective right disappears to be replaced by the concept of property as a social function."[40]

While the push for new legislation on southern property came from landowners, the hope inspired by the 1925 colonization law and constitution breathed fire into a movement of landless laborers to gain access to plots either of public land or land lying within privately held estates. In 1925 *El Diario Austral* in Temuco reported that "almost all the inquilinos on estates in this region have joined *ligas agrarias*" (agrarian leagues). Unlike rural unions in central Chile that might have negotiated for improved working conditions and better pay, inquilinos' ligas in Cautín province sought titles to the land laborers occupied on estates. Inquilinos paid quotas to the organizations in the hope that they could obtain their own plots by "appropriating the lands of the patrón." *El Diario Austral* reported there had been "numerous cases of conflicts of this nature between inquilinos and patrones, many of which are moving through the courts."[41] The Sindicato Agrícola Lonquimay would follow the model established by these agrarian leagues. Members paid quotas or dues to the union, which were understood to go toward the purchase of plots of land on the estates where they resided and labored.

Cautín's agrarian leagues reflected a broader movement of inquilinos and ocupantes to appropriate estate land. In one typical case, ocupantes took possession of land that had been granted to the colonization company Sociedad Nueva Italia. Like other concessions, Nueva Italia had agreed to respect the rights of possession of ocupantes and indígenas within the boundaries of its enormous properties. However, Nueva Italia attempted to expel the campesinos both by force and by inducing them to sign inquilinaje contracts. The ocupantes in turn put up their own resistance to the dominion of Nueva Italia. In February 1925 a government commission, including an indigenous protector and a surveyor employed by the lands inspectorate office, traveled to Capitán Pastene to investigate the petitions of both indigenous and Chilean ocupantes of land belonging to the Nueva Italia concession. At the same time, the agricultural ministry requested that the interior ministry authorize a force of ten carabineros to quell "the effervescence that exists today among the ocupantes."[42] Later that year the lands and colonization directorate sent a telegram to the lands and colonization ministry reporting that it was necessary "to take urgent measures with the people who, without any right, are exploiting the forests that belong to Señor Ricci [Nueva Italia's concessionaire]." The telegram requested that carabineros be put at the disposal of the government forester overseeing Nueva Italia's logging operations. Months later, Ricci sent a telegram to the government protesting that the carabineros had been withdrawn and that Nueva Italia's inquilinos were claiming the estate's land as their own.

The inquilinos-ocupantes and Nueva Italia reached an agreement that stipulated the former would stop extracting wood from the estate's forests in exchange for a commitment by the government to settle them on two lots it purchased from Ricci. The compact appears to have been short-lived. In November 1925 the ocupantes continued to transport their crops, firewood, and charcoal to local markets in defiance of both landowner and state authority. The lands minister requested once again that the interior minister send twenty carabineros to evict the ocupantes-inquilinos from Nueva Italia's land. By the following month things had gotten so out of hand that the lands ministry received a telegram from a representative of the "ocupantes nacionales" petitioning the government to order Ricci to halt his abuses of them in order to prevent a tragedy. "They will," the telegram notified, "defend their rights energetically with firearms."[43]

Ocupantes' resort to arms was a response to the violence the Chilean state employed to resolve conflicts between poor campesinos and wealthy landowners in the south. In 1926 the Communist Party deputy Ramón Sepúlveda Leal denounced a typical case of carabineros' repression of a group of ocupantes who were engaged in a conflict with Santiago Wood in Loncoche over land they believed to be public. Five years earlier the ocupantes had settled on and cleared land claimed by Wood. Wood accused the ocupantes of being "a group of communists" who had invaded his private property. Sepúlveda traveled to Loncoche and found that carabineros, as was common in southern Chile, had acted on Wood's behalf and detained fourteen of the ocupantes. They had also burned the ocupantes' huts to the ground with their tools and belongings inside, a frequent method of dispossessing poor campesinos in southern Chile. They had beaten the ocupantes, also not uncommon in the south. The Democratic Party and the FOCH may have been involved in either organizing or supporting the ocupantes, as the carabineros, in the same locale and at the same time, arrested and beat a FOCH union leader and Democratic Party militant, charging him with assault.[44]

The Ibáñez Regime and Land Reform in the South

In 1927 Carlos Ibáñez, one of the officers who had led the 1924 military intervention and then a coup leading to Alessandri's resignation and exile, ran for president and was elected in a contest defined by rampant fraud. After Alessandri had returned to the presidency from a brief exile, Ibáñez had served as his interior and war minister. When Alessandri resigned the presidency for a second time, in 1925, Ibáñez served as interior minister and then vice president in a puppet government. While he ran as an independent candidate, critical of the traditional political class, Ibáñez received enthusiastic support from the Democratic Party, which was led by his brother, Javier Ibáñez del Campo, between 1927 and 1932. Ibáñez quickly accumulated dictatorial powers and established an authoritarian regime. He cemented his rule by cracking down on political opponents. Ibáñez used the police to infiltrate opposition political groups, especially the Communist Party, which suffered severe repression under his rule, and leftist unions affiliated with the FOCH. In addition, he sent political dissidents to prison camps and into internal and external exile. Like Alessandri before him, Ibáñez called on the armed forces to crush workers' strikes.

But Ibáñez was also a corporatist who sought to modernize both the state and economy, while wrenching power from Chile's traditional ruling elite. He wielded his expanded presidential powers in cooperation with a compliant congress to implement key social reforms, including the creation of a labor code in 1931, which brought together the 1924 social laws. The code extended rights elaborated in the earlier labor laws to rural laborers, most importantly the right to unionize and obligatory labor contracts. It also increased the presence of labor inspectors and courts in the countryside.[45] In February 1928 the Ibáñez regime passed a new Southern Property Law (Ley No. 4301 Sobre la Constitución de la Propiedad Austral) designed to establish a stable property regime and resolve the multitude of lawsuits and land conflicts in southern Chile. The law required that occupants of southern land produce titles and cadastral maps of their putative properties in order to demonstrate their rights to definitive titles. One of the law's goals was to guarantee that claims to public land in southern Chile "did not damage the interests of the state." The law reflected the Ibáñez regime's efforts to restore to the state public land that had been appropriated through fraud by large estates. According to a report by a new Ministry of Development (Ministerio de Fomento) established under Ibañez, the law would allow the state "to establish what lands belong to it and what lands belong to private parties, and to form a cadastral map on a solid and certain basis."[46]

Another 1928 development ministry report noted that the Southern Property Law was passed in order to regularize the regime of property in the south. This action was in response to "a movement of opinion generated by the landowners of the southern zone who were alarmed because credit institutions did not extend their benefits to properties whose titles were considered vitiated by prohibitive regulations ... and because the courts did not fully recognize the legality of titles to the immense majority of lands located [in the south]."[47] Like the 1925 colonization law, the Southern Property Law responded to landowners' interest in legitimating their titles. But, unlike the 1925 law, it permitted the state to distribute land occupied and cultivated before 1 January 1921 to *ocupantes*, drawing on the national colonization laws passed in the late 1890s and early 1900s. The goal was to increase production and build a large number of small agricultural properties, "thus combating pernicious social doctrines."[48] To Cautín's intendant, the law's ultimate goal of creating a population of smallholders out of the mass of agricultural laborers who had cleared forests and cultivated fields was "a social ideal in agreement with the government's goals." In the south especially, he declared, rural laborers' "perseverance and hard personal sacrifice, struggling with the climate, the isolation, and the forests, are deserving of the support and special protection of the government."[49]

In a striking statement of the government's intention to employ the Southern Property Law to subdivide large estates, Cautín's intendant reported to Ibáñez's development minister that "in Cautín province, the State will expropriate all land used for speculation, land that is not exploited and whose owners simply are awaiting capitalists who will pay what they ask." This situation, he underlined, was common among "all the owners of concessions of public lands." Perhaps most radically, the intendant remarked that many estates of more than three thousand hectares throughout the province were underexploited and held as instruments of speculation. According to the intendant, these large properties throughout Cautín would be expropriated and subdivided and their lots put on public auction.[50]

In December 1928 the Ibáñez government buttressed the Southern Property Law by creating the Caja de Colonización Agrícola (Agricultural Colonization Bank) to organize and administer agricultural colonies of smallholders on public land, to purchase and subdivide large estates, and distribute the land to both foreign and national *colonos*. The law establishing the bank gave the president the power to expropriate properties larger than five hundred hectares not intensively cultivated in order to found agricultural colonies.[51] The following month the government approved an Agricultural Cooperatives Law, which instituted a legal framework for establishing cooperatives of smallholders on public land and privately held land purchased or expropriated by the Agricultural

Colonization Bank. Curacautín's *El Comercio* editorialized that together the two laws would break the chains "binding ninety-five percent of the Chilean population that live in misery and a restricted economic situation." In a typically gendered image of male colonos domesticating nature that reflected the new rights accorded to campesinos, the paper celebrated a future in which Chile's fields would be populated with "innumerable smallholders, each with his own parcel, extracting from the prodigious mother earth her fruit in abundance. ... Goodbye poverty, goodbye misery!" Chile would once again be an exporter of a "superabundance of cereals owing to the labor of the Chilean worker who loves his *patria*."[52] The patriotic work of making Alto Bío Bío's frontier wilderness productive was to be the labor of the male campesino head of household.

The southern property, agricultural colonization bank, and agricultural cooperatives laws offered campesinos throughout southern Chile a set of potential legal instruments to claim both public land and plots on large estates. In addition, despite his authoritarian rule Ibáñez appeared less willing than other governments to employ carabineros to back the owners of large properties in the south. Instead, he expressed hostility to landowners who had accumulated extensive holdings at public auctions or as concessions from the state and announced his support for the rights of both inquilinos and ocupantes. In 1927 Ibáñez dictated that all courts and regional government officials south of the Biobío River, including intendants and governors, receive his interior minister's authorization before they sent carabineros to evict ocupantes from their land.[53] In 1929 the interior minister repeated Ibáñez's instructions to Cautín's intendant. He told the intendant that the government had information "that for some time there have been evictions [of small ocupantes] from their lands." He ordered the intendant to remind local officials of the president's instructions that "for no reason will [government officials] allow the police to be employed to dislodge the small ocupantes from their land without express orders from the President of the Republic."[54]

The presence of a more sympathetic president in the Palacio de La Moneda (the presidential palace also known as La Moneda) created an opening for rural workers, organized at times in unions and cooperatives, to invade, occupy, and squat on large extensions of land, asserting that they held rights based on their material occupation. They had cleared forests, made the soil productive, and contributed to national progress by incorporating the undomesticated territories of the frontier into the civilized national community. Whether inquilinos or ocupantes or both, they viewed estate land as public and invoked rights to be settled as colonos nacionales.

In an example of the hope inspired by Ibáñez's regime and new colonization legislation, in 1927 a large number of ocupantes on land within Luis Silva Rivas's Llaima colonization concession wrote the recently elected president to praise his government and its plans to implement a new southern property law. They had heard that "the government intends to cancel all the land concessions ... that haven't fulfilled their contracts or that are not legally constituted." The ocupantes, many of whom, Silva Rivas held, were his inquilinos, argued that the landowner had never fulfilled his end of the colonization contract, which required him to settle European immigrants on the concession's land, and should forfeit his property. They underlined that the concessionaire had not only accumulated tens of thousands of hectares of valuable frontier land originally intended for European immigrant colonos, but also had failed to fulfill the stipulations in his contract with the state that he respect the rights of the numerous Mapuche and Chilean ocupantes within the concession's boundaries. Rather than Silva Rivas's inquilinos, they declared, they were ocupantes whose rights to be settled as colonos should now be recognized under the Southern Property Law.[55]

Two years later Amelia Herrera, a widow and owner of the Santa Amelia fundo in Pitrufquén, went to the office of the governor of Villarrica to denounce an open rebellion by her inquilinos. The governor, accompanied by a representative for Herrera and a carabinero, traveled to the estate to investigate. When they arrived, the governor reported, they found sixty inquilinos, men and women, meeting in a state of "half-drunkenness." According to Santa Amelia's administrator, the workers had been organized by one Edmundo Vergara, who had informed them that he would initiate proceedings with the development ministry to allow them to obtain titles to their huts and parcels of land on the estate as colonos. The workers had given Vergara money to fund the legal formalities in Santiago.[56] The governor informed the rebellious inquilinos that they had to "recognize as their patrón the Sociedad Nacional Bosques y Maderas," a large logging company to which Herrera had rented the estate. In exchange they would be allowed to extract wood from the forests as long as they paid the company a share. That is, the inquilinos had to work as medieros, on shares, with the company but could remain on their land.[57]

Throughout the south, landowners complained of outside agitators who, like Vergara, incited inquilinos to appropriate their patrones' land. In 1929 the development ministry reported that in Cautín, "motivated by the Southern Property Law, a number of people have dedicated themselves to introducing propaganda among the inquilinos on estates to convince them that said law concedes them property rights to the land they work."[58] In a typical case, Felipe Santiago Smith, who resided in Valparaíso, petitioned the intendancy in Cautín to send carabineros to Cunco, where "some of the inquilinos on his Nueva Escocia estate pretend that the estate is public and have rebeled against its administrator ... in such a way that it is impossible to continue with agricultural production."[59] Further north near Cañete, Abelino Grandón, an inquilino on the Chau-Chau fundo, petitioned the government for help because the landowner had evicted him and a number of other inquilinos. Three carabineros, following the orders of the governor of Lebu, had enforced the eviction, leaving the workers abandoned by the side of the road. Apparently, Chau-Chau's inquilinos were part of a larger movement of workers in Lebu who had resisted their patrones' authority. A government surveyor investigated Grandón's petition and reported to the regional lands measurement office in Angol that Grandón was "one of the many rebellious inquilinos [*inquilinos sublevados*] in this region."[60]

The movement of inquilinos and ocupantes to claim estate land reached further south to Llanquihue and Chiloé province, whose intendant wrote the lands and colonization minister in 1929 describing "the absolute necessity of authorizing representatives of the government to proceed energetically with all those individuals who, ... as simple inquilinos, have transformed themselves into the owners of their patrones' lands, becoming *inquilinos alzados* [rebellious inquilinos]." According to the intendant, in a number of cases laborers had "taken by force the lands of whose owners they were simply inquilinos or empleados."[61] That same year the newspaper *El Llanquihue* reported that "for some time now we have heard with alarm that in this region men with subversive ideas have infiltrated the mind of the peaceful worker with their false doctrines." The paper expressed its "energetic protest against the unjust abuses committed by the rebellious inquilinaje and ocupantes who have no right to legally constituted private property."[62] Similarly, the Ministry of Southern Property reported that on a number of estates around Osorno "the inquilinos ... oppose their patrón, whom they had respected and recognized until yesterday, calling themselves ocupantes of public lands."[63]

Southern landowners likewise confronted land invasions by squatter *ocupantes* who often petitioned the state to be settled as *colonos* on the small plots they occupied. In 1928 the owner of the San Juan de Trovolhue *fundo* in Cautín wrote the intendant that "lately, with the implementation of the laws on the Constitution of Southern Property ... my *fundo*, along with a number of other *fundos* in the region, has been invaded by a considerable number of alleged *ocupantes* and *indígenas* who are trying to take possession of my *fundo* without any right."[64] Cautín's intendant received a similar petition from the owners of the Las Ñiochas estate in Imperial, who denounced a land invasion by "numerous groups of *indígenas*" as well as "some Chilean individuals." In both cases the *ocupantes* argued that the land they had settled on, cleared, and cultivated was public, not private, property.[65] In Bío-Bío province police stationed in Los Ángeles reported in 1931 that twenty-five *ocupantes* had organized a "colonization cooperative" and invaded an estate and distributed its land among themselves, refusing "to obey the *fundo*'s *patrones*."[66] The police report implies that, more than a land invasion by outsiders, the *ocupantes* may have been *inquilinos* who had rebelled against their *patrón* and refused to recognize either his demands for labor or his property rights.

Inquilinos' understanding that they enjoyed new rights under the social and colonization laws passed since 1924 also led to numerous labor conflicts on southern estates. In 1930, for example, the owner of the Long-Long estate reported to the Cautín intendancy that a group of *inquilinos* was preventing "the normal development of labor in the fields" and "maintaining an active campaign of agitation on the estate." These workers, he said, "do not show the consideration and respect that they owe to the *patrón* and labor inspector."[67] According to police reports, the *inquilinos* had protested low salaries as well as an order from the landowner that no worker could leave or enter the estate without his authorization. Similarly, in 1929 Pedro Soto sent a telegram to the intendancy asking for the support of carabineros to quell a workers' movement on his estate near Temuco. A group of "*inquilinos* on my estate," he wrote, "have instigated my servants [*servidumbre*] to insubordination." The workers had demanded wage hikes and gone on strike.[68] In this case as in others it is revealing that the landowner viewed his estate laborers as subordinates who owed him loyalty. *Servidumbre* carries the connotation of dependent servant or serf.

In a typical case of the labor unrest sweeping Cautín province during the late 1920s, Alfredo Lacourt informed the province's intendancy that Nemesio Guiñez, an *ocupante* on a plot of public land neighboring his

Colico estate, was preaching "communist ideas against order, work, the authorities, and patrones, helping indebted inquilinos abandon the estate at night [while] ignoring their debts." A police report backed Lacourt, noting that the workers who had fled had been "enganchados" (recruited with advances). Guiñez had, Lacourt said, incited them to abandon the estate under cover of night, promising they could settle on nearby public land as ocupantes and work for themselves. In this case, the proximity of public land allowed the inquilinos to escape the debts they had contracted with their patrón and petition to be settled on small plots as colonos.[69]

Rural workers organized movements to improve working conditions on estates throughout Bío-Bío province during this period. In February 1929, for example, the Los Ángeles daily *El Siglo* described the spread of labor unrest and communism on the region's fundos. Local authorities informed the paper that the province had witnessed a number of "communist or subversive" actions in which "a few audacious or bad elements, taking advantage of their *compañeros*, who are generally campesinos or ignorant, induce them to protest that their daily wages are too small and to protest the food rations [provided by patrones], or any insignificant issue, making them frequently abandon their work, doing serious damage to industry and agriculture, especially during the harvests." The intendancy ordered carabineros to travel to a number of Bío-Bío's estates to investigate cases where they had received denunciations of purportedly communist-inspired labor actions by agricultural workers.[70]

In a case that closely approximates that of the Puelmas' San Ignacio de Pemehue, in 1928, the same year as the Sindicato Agrícola Lonquimay began organizing laborers in Alto Bío Bío, ocupantes on the Pellahuén estate in Traiguén organized a union, the Sindicato Blanco de Obreros, to defend their rights to be settled as colonos within the borders of the estate.[71] A large number of ocupantes began to hold meetings led by a group of organizers who, according to a public prosecutor, "incited them to rebellion ... in the sense that they should not recognize the rights of the Banco Chileno Garantizador de Valores or of those who had bought land on Pellahuén [from the bank], inciting them to even use violence." Many of the ocupantes had either arrived with their parents as children or had been born on Pellahuén and had lived there for more than three decades. When the Banco Chileno Garantizador had taken ownership of the property in 1927 because the estate's owner had failed to make his mortgage payments, they had stayed on as renters (arrendatarios). But during union assemblies, they said, the union leaders informed them that the estate was public and that they could be settled as colonos. The ocupantes nurtured the hope that they would be settled as colonos and rejected a proposed solution that they remain on the estate as medieros, working the land on shares with its new owners.

In 1926 the interior minister had given instructions authorizing the use of carabineros to expel ocupantes from Pellahuén.[72] In response, the Democratic Party deputy Héctor Álvarez put forward legislation declaring Pellahuén's expropriation to be in the public interest (*utilidad pública*) so that its land could be distributed to more than eight hundred families of ocupantes and indígenas who resided within the estate's borders. But Álvarez's efforts failed. Instead, the Banco Garantizador de Valores took control of Pellahuén and petitioned the government to order carabineros to accompany a surveyor sent to measure the estate. The governor of Traiguén reported that the ocupantes opposed the measurement, which they viewed as a prelude to their expulsion.[73] In February 1927 Carlos Ibáñez, then interior minister, gave strict orders that carabineros not be used to evict the ocupantes from Pellahuén. Ibáñez worked out an arrangement in which the ocupantes agreed to recognize the bank as Pellahuén's owner in exchange for remaining on the land as arrendatorios. Ibáñez declared that the government "was working to guarantee the rights acquired by the ocupantes by working on their land and contributing to true progress."[74]

Ibáñez's actions in support of the ocupantes raised their expectations that once in power his government would settle them on their land as colonos. According to Arturo Belmar's wife, the ocupantes organized their union to petition the Ibáñez government to expropriate Pellahuén "so it could be sold to the actual ocupantes who are members of the Sindicato Blanco." Belmar informed the ocupantes that no one could evict them and that they should oppose any efforts to dislodge them from their land by violent means (*medios violentos*). Other leaders of the ocupantes' movement held meetings at which they collected money to fund a legal suit seeking titles to their land and government recognition that Pellahuén was public land.[75]

The Sindicato Blanco was not the first union organized on Pellahuén. As early as 1906, years before labor legislation legalized unions in Chile, workers on the estate had organized a union, the Sindicato Pellahuén, and demanded titles to plots on the fundo's land, which they claimed had been acquired by their patrones via fraud. In this case, as in the case of the Sindicato Blanco and the Sindicato Agrícola Lonquimay, the union was organized as an instrument for claiming estate land. In fact, Pellahuén's organization as a privately held estate followed closely San Ignacio's history of fraudulent expansion. In 1884 Esteban Freire had purchased the property from an indígena and then quickly sold his new estate in 1889 to Jervasio Alarcón. Over the years, Pellahuén, like the Puelma family's San Ignacio de Pemehue, expanded exponentially from approximately twenty thousand hectares in 1889 to sixty-one thousand hectares in 1905. During a legal battle with the state over Pellahuén's borders, Alarcón hired Alberto Larenas to survey and map the estate as he engaged in a lengthy legal battle with the state over his property titles. And in a striking parallel with the history of the Puelmas' San Ignacio hacienda, Agustín Baeza, the general lands inspector, brokered a deal in 1902 to resolve the legal dispute between Alarcón and the state, recognizing the legitimacy of Alarcón's deeds just as he had recognized the Puelmas' deeds the year before.

In yet another example of the rampant fraud that lay behind the formation of large estates in the south, Baeza, shortly after signing the agreement in which the state recognized Pellahuén's titles, left his position as lands inspector and became the president of a newly organized public company organized by Alarcón that owned Pellahuén, the Sociedad Agrícola Pellahuén. Nonetheless, despite these machinations, Pellahuén's ocupantes remained on their land, resisting various efforts to evict them and, in 1906, organized the Sindicato Pellahuén. In 1913 their conflict with Alarcón erupted in what the Conservative Party deputy Emilio Claro described in congress as a "true battle" between police sent to evict the ocupantes "and an enormous group of men, women and children." The ocupantes, he said, "irrigated Pellahuén's soil with their blood."[76]

When ocupantes and inquilinos on both San Ignacio's five fundos and Pellahuén organized unions in 1928 with the goal of colonizing the estates where they lived and labored, they drew on long histories of well-documented landowner and government fraud. They also built on long histories of conflict defined by lengthy litigation over dubious property titles and punctuated by episodes of violence. Despite carabineros' efforts to evict the campesino squatters from Pellahuén and San Ignacio, they remained on their land and turned to new social and colonization laws passed after 1924 to try to win land titles from the government. It is notable that the ocupantes organized unions to make their claims to be settled as colonos. This speaks to the power of the 1924 labor laws even in these remote, isolated regions of southern frontier territory to galvanize a sense of legal rights and organizational possibility among the rural poor. The Pellahuén and Lonquimay unions also reflected a new political context. Ocupantes and inquilinos throughout the south viewed the Ibáñez regime as sympathetic to their cause.

In 1930, for example, the interior ministry reported on the "violent occupations by individuals who claim rights to land" belonging to the Compañía Valdivia's Toltén ranching and logging estate in Cautín province.[77] President Ibáñez lent his support to Toltén's ocupantes. He sent to the intendant a transcription of a telegram from the campesinos. In it they denounced "abuses against our persons by the director of the Compañía Valdivia, señor Eugenio Claro, who burned our houses accompanied by more than seventy men. We colonos, ocupantes of these lands, number thirty, all poor and without resources to defend ourselves." Ibáñez requested that the intendant send carabineros not to defend the estate's property rights but to safeguard the ocupantes: "I insist that it is indispensable to give the greatest security [*garantías*] to the ocupantes."[78] For the first time a president used his power to direct regional officials and the armed forces to protect the property rights not of large landowners or logging and ranching enterprises but of poor ocupantes. As much as the new laws designed to settle frontier territory with smallholders, Ibáñez's use of the power of the presidency on behalf of campesinos inspired hope among southern Chile's rural laboring classes. Finally, they might secure legal titles to their small plots of land, whether they squatted as ocupantes or worked as inquilinos or both.

CHAPTER FOUR

Populism in the Countryside
*The Sindicato Agrícola Lonquimay and
Carlos Ibáñez*

IN DECEMBER 1928 JUAN Segundo Leiva Tapia traveled to Santiago to petition the government for support of the Sindicato Agrícola Lonquimay. Upon his arrival he requested and received a meeting with President Carlos Ibáñez, marking the first time in Chilean history an occupant of the Palacio de La Moneda received a union leader in his office. "You are Leiva?" Ibáñez asked in a friendly manner, extending his hand. "Yes, your Excellency," Leiva Tapia replied, "and I have come to give you greetings in the name of the Sindicato Agrícola Lonquimay." Atlas in hand, Ibáñez then proceeded to ask Leiva Tapia detailed questions about Alto Bío Bío's geography and forest resources. The president next turned to the union, asking when it had been organized and how many members it had. After Leiva described the union's organization, Ibáñez said, "All right, have a seat and tell me what it is that you are asking for." Leiva read the union's statutes, concluding with its slogan and founding principles, "To populate, produce, and civilize," then petitioned the president for "protection from the State." "To populate the region," Leiva continued, "the Sindicato Agrícola Lonquimay needs land; that land exists in the Alto Bío Bío region, where a public reserve has lately been established, despite numerous colonos and *ocupantes de suelos* (occupants of the land) having lived there for many years since the founding of the Lonquimay colony." The union's goal was to settle the newly organized Alto Bío Bío forest reserve with its members.[1]

Leiva presented Ibáñez with a detailed map of the terrain he himself had drawn. After examining the map, Ibáñez summed up his position: "I have the best intentions to help the colonos, ocupantes, and, in general, the agricultural producers." On the subject of the reserve, he declared, "I will procure a solution favorable to your aspirations with the Minister [of Development]." But Leiva Tapia persisted in outlining the union's demands: "Second point, your excellency, the union wishes to exploit with its members livestock on the land we are petitioning for. We would bring from Argentina, through the Caja Agraria, 2,000 sheep." "That is very noble," Ibáñez responded, "and I will help you with that with the Caja [de Colonización Agrícola]." Leiva Tapia then laid out the union's third request: "We need, Excellency, to educate our children, who are numerous, since the region is large and since in the winter it snows intensively, we can't bring them to Lonquimay." Once again the president gave Leiva Tapia assurances of his personal support: "Ok, you, who are a teacher, are going to study the population, and you are going to tell me where and what kind of school we can found."

Leiva Tapia thanked the president and got ready to leave. But Ibáñez stopped him, asking him about how carabineros and government authorities in Alto Bío Bío acted, "the condition of indígenas, inquilinos and rural workers," commerce, the region's agricultural production, and, finally, the situation created for colonos by land auctions that had been done "capriciously" in previous years. Leiva Tapia reported that he responded to Ibáñez's inquiries truthfully, but "intentionally keeping quiet about and forgetting many things," since, he noted, "it is not my character to bother anybody." He offered only a brief explanation: "The local slander coming from the almost feudal local regime that a few señores have exercised over the laboring classes made me stay quiet." Leiva Tapia moderated his language and even the union's goals in his meeting with Ibáñez. Not once did he mention the Puelmas or Bunsters or their enormous estates. Ibáñez himself staked out a more radical position, denouncing the "capricious land auctions" that had led to the formation of enormous estates and expressing both hostility to the landowning elite and interest in the condition of rural laborers and indígenas.

Ibáñez left Leiva Tapia with a pledge to the members of the Sindicato Agrícola Lonquimay: "Tell your members, the colonos and ocupantes of that Zone, that I will not provide public forces to dislodge them. In any case, it is necessary to punish the bad faith of those [who acquired land at auction]." This represented an extraordinary moment in Chilean history. For the first time a president had addressed directly the leader of a rural union and expressed his personal support for poor campesinos, while denouncing large landowners. Ibáñez's rousing populist language struck a chord with Leiva Tapia, who described the president in glowing terms to *El Comercio:* "The illustrious leader of the Chilean people, the *excelentísimo* Señor Carlos Ibáñez del Campo, is a true father of the Patria who thinks like us and sincerely aspires to make his country a great Nation, progressive and civilized, fulfilling an ideal that we also have proposed: populate, produce, civilize."[2] The Agrarian Cooperatives and Colonies Law passed later that year only confirmed the union's faith in Ibáñez and the promise of land reform in southern Chile.

At this point, the union's members and directorate came from all walks of life. They included local merchants and professionals as well as inquilinos, ocupantes, colonos, and members of Pehuenche communities. As a sign of its inclusive membership, when the union held a meeting in April 1929, a year after its founding, it did so in Lonquimay's church, with the support of the local priest. In attendance were "the authorities and most respectable residents of Lonquimay and Cura Cautín."[3] The location of the union in Lonquimay spoke to the support and direction the labor organization received from urban middling sectors, who may have shared an antagonism to the region's absentee landowners, the Puelmas and Bunsters. Local merchants had little to fear from the union's organizing campaigns on Alto Bío Bío's large estates or its goal of settling public land in the region. Rather, the union's program, if implemented, would bring a mutually beneficial prosperity to the region: rural schools, a large population of colono smallholders, a train linking Lonquimay to Curacautín—a project promised Leiva Tapia by Ibáñez—, and peaceful social relations. Above all, increased agricultural production on subdivided estates promised a general increase in the standard of living for all of Lonquimay's residents. The landowners, on the other hand, lived far away in Santiago. To Lonquimay's residents their enormous estates must have represented an obstacle to the economic progress of the town and region, even an impediment to the region's integration into the nation, a precarious situation reflected by the lack of public schools and roads.

The union leaders' ideological perspective is discernible in letters and reports written by Leiva Tapia. In a 1929 editorial published in *El Comercio,* he applauded Ibáñez's efforts to build a state-directed labor relations system that would ensure both workers' rights and harmonious social relations between workers and patrones. The organization of both workers and employers in unions, he argued, would produce harmony and agreement as well as "social peace." Rather than the language of class conflict, Leiva Tapia drew on the corporatist ideas that influenced Ibáñez and the commission he had appointed to draw up a new labor code.[4]

The Sindicato Agrícola Lonquimay's leaders also promoted cooperativism, a form of collective social and economic organization that could overcome the limits of individual landownership on small parcels in the frontier. "Integrated cooperativism" would resolve the problems inherent in national colonization laws and the experience of settlement thus far in the frontier region. When colonos received land and titles they often lacked the resources to make their land productive and after a few years sold their small plots to neighboring large estates. Carving out arable land from the dense forests or rocky mountain soil could take years, and most colonos could not afford to wait that long for their harvests. Southern soil, once cleared of forest and underbrush, usually through cutting and burning, produced only a few cycles of harvests before it lost its nutrients. Without a system of extensive rotation, the forest would not be allowed to grow back and the soil to recover. Harvests dwindled, soil eroded, and plots lost their ability to produce sufficient crops. Impoverished colonos then sold their plots to large estates, which employed the decimated soil in pasturing cattle, letting their livestock feed on the underbrush and wild bamboo that quickly invaded land cleared of forest. A cooperative could use a more extensive and rationally planned form of agriculture and livestock rearing.[5] Well into 1931 cooperativism constituted the cornerstone of the union's ideology. In April of that year the union held an assembly of around two hundred of its members in Quilleime, with speeches from union leaders like Leiva Tapia and Manuel Astroza, the union president. Froilán Rivera, the editor of *El Comercio*, gave a lengthy talk on consumers' and producers' cooperatives: "The assembly member Rivera, it appears, has a true vocation for these economic matters," the paper observed. "The simple way in which he developed his thesis made it easily understood by all the members, theories that they received with the most enthusiastic applause."[6]

Following his meeting with Ibáñez, Leiva Tapia dedicated his energy to the commission of the president to develop a plan for a network of public schools in Alto Bío Bío. In April 1929 he issued a lengthy report about education in the region. Chilean children in Alto Bío Bío had no schools, and so, following long-standing routes of migration, they traveled through mountain passes to cross into Argentina to attend school there. The neighboring country had established rural schools just across the border from Lonquimay and instituted obligatory primary school education, a model, Leiva Tapia believed, for Chile. He noted the Argentine influence on the Chilean children in Alto Bío Bío: they spoke with marked Argentine accents as well as with the Argentines' "prudent and correct behavior," and they had the "accent of free men." Leiva Tapia urged the government to follow the Argentine example.[7]

As well as working on Ibáñez's charge to build rural schools, Leiva Tapia took to heart the president's pledge that he would never authorize force to evict ocupantes from their land. The Sindicato Agrícola Lonquimay became a vociferous defender of ocupantes' land rights throughout Alto Bío Bío. The same month he submitted his report on schools Leiva Tapia sent a petition to the intendant of Cautín province and the governors of Victoria and Mulchén protesting the violent expulsion and harassment of ocupantes from Ránquil and El Rahue, the two estates the union hoped to settle with its members in a colonization cooperative. According to Leiva Tapia, the evictions had begun following the dictation of the Southern Property Law. Commissions of inquilinos and ocupantes had traveled to Santiago to denounce the abuses committed by the Puelmas as well as by Lonquimay's subdelegate, José Paz, the administrator of the Ránquil estate.[8]

Reaching Santiago from this isolated corner of the Andes cordillera would not have been easy. It would have taken days on foot or horseback to get to the nearest town and railroad station. Travel to Santiago meant both making a difficult journey and taking a leap of faith. The ocupantes and inquilinos must have believed that a government sympathetic to their plight and open to their demands occupied La Moneda. Their long trips to Santiago spoke to the weight of Ibáñez's words, especially his promises to guarantee the rights of ocupantes and "laboring classes" in southern Chile, as well as the hopes kindled by the Southern Property and Agrarian Colonies and Colonization laws.

Despite Leiva Tapia's favorable reception in La Moneda, the Puelmas succeeded in obtaining recognition of their estates' titles in an August 1929 decree by the Ministry of Development (Decreto Número 3,871, 14 August 1929) under the Southern Property Law without any study of San Ignacio's titles or borders. Armed with this decree, the Puelmas continued to evict inquilinos and ocupantes from El Rahue and

Ránquil, targeting members of the Sindicato Agrícola Lonquimay. The union denounced "the abuses and violations of rights that they are committing on the Puelma estates against the pobladores there because they belong to our Institution, evicting them and thus appropriating their improvements and harvests, or preventing them from cultivating."⁹ Union leaders sent an urgent telegram to Santiago asking the government "to prevent the violent expulsion" of the would-be colonos ordered by judges in Mulchén and Lautaro. They also requested that the government survey San Ignacio de Pemehue and settle union members on land expropriated from the estate by the Caja de Colonización Agrícola. They had, they said, organized a colonization cooperative within the union, the Ránquil-Rahue Cooperative.¹⁰

It seems the Puelmas and Bunsters had the support of local government officials hostile to the sindicato. The union leadership accused Lonquimay's subdelegate of refusing to obey "the orders of the supreme Government" by not recognizing either the union or its right to hold meetings. The subdelegate defended himself by noting that the union had been "telling people that Rahue and other estates are public property" and that its denunciations of his actions were "made only to harass the authorities."¹¹ However, the governor of Victoria supported the union's right to hold meetings, overriding the subdelegate and the hostility of the local carabineros, who had tried to prevent a union assembly. Bruno Ackermann traveled to Victoria to thank the governor personally and invite him to attend a union meeting in their "modest local in Villa Portales" in Lonquimay.¹²

Personal appeals to higher authorities, from the president to his regional governor, appeared to bear fruit for the union. Perhaps most important, also in September 1929 Leiva Tapia wrote to President Ibáñez notifying him that the head of the welfare department in Cautín had refused to register the Sindicato Agrícola Lonquimay because agricultural workers' unions were not covered by the 1924 labor laws. Leiva Tapia explained to the president that this was precisely why the government needed to pass a law legalizing campesino unions. Ibáñez sent his response to Leiva Tapia by telegram, informing him that he had officiated the union's legal recognition since "if the law does not regulate these organizations, neither does it prohibit them."¹³ Indeed, the issue of campesino unions had been pushed by Ibáñez's intendant for Cautín province. In December 1927 the intendant wrote in Temuco's *El Diario Austral* about the importance of incorporating rural workers into the national labor relations system. He intended to request that Ibáñez dictate agrarian labor legislation that would regulate relations between workers and landowners on rural estates.[14]

Well before Ibáñez promulgated by decree the corporatist 1931 labor code, he extended key provisions of labor and social security laws into the countryside. As early as 1927 the government's social insurance and labor bureaucracy had begun to intervene in rural labor relations in Cautín province. That year, for example, Cautín's welfare office investigated widespread conflicts over wages between estate owners and their medieros and jornaleros. Inspectors from the welfare secretariat visited various fundos and interviewed workers and landowners, collecting information about workers' pay, lodging, and food rations. Inspectors noted that customarily landowners did not pay their workers, whether seasonal workers or sharecroppers, until the end of the harvest season. Until then, workers received from their patrones small advances in the form of provisions, clothing, and money. By the time harvest seasons concluded, however, workers' debts often exceeded what they were owed, and they left their jobs without being paid at all. As the inspectors observed, when the workers received no pay after the harvests were in, they would go to Temuco's welfare office "to demand justice."[15]

The weight of the 1924 social laws and the shifting political climate allowed rural workers to view labor inspectors and the social welfare office as a resource in their conflicts with landowners. An example of rural workers' sense of their new rights was a 1930 conflict between inquilinos and their patrón on an estate near Temuco. In this case, the administrator of the fundo complained to the police that a group of inquilinos had petitioned for an increase in pay for transporting wood by cart from forest stands to sawmills. When the estate's administrator rejected the petition, the inquilinos "threatened him, saying that they would present a complaint to the Social Welfare Office in Temuco."[16] With the Ibáñez government in power, inquilinos had a new sense of labor rights and protections

In 1928 Ibáñez himself toured Bío-Bío province as part of a campaign to promote the use of the new obligatory social security system (*seguro obligatorio*) requiring employer contributions on fundos employing agricultural workers. Labor inspectors reviewed the social insurance books (*libretas*) of agricultural workers on a number of fundos to make sure landowners were up to date with their payments. In addition, Temuco's labor inspector called in sixty-five landowners to his office to collect their workers' libretas and check to see that they had paid social security taxes. If they had not, they would be subjected to fines. Included on the list of landowners called into the labor inspector's office was the Bunster family with its twenty-eight inquilinos.[17] By 1928 landowners in Alto Bío Bío could no longer act with complete autonomy. They were increasingly bound by labor laws and the presence of the state social insurance and labor bureaucracy. Government officials staffing welfare offices and labor inspectorates now treated agricultural laborers as workers and patrones as employers, both subject to the social legislation passed between 1924 and 1928.

In 1931 the inspector for the social security office (Caja de Seguro Obligatorio) denounced a number of landowners in Bío-Bío province for failing to keep their workers' libretas up to date. The inspector imposed fines on a number of these landowners for not following Law 4054: "All fundos that have only some of their workers insured, openly mocking the Law [4054] and whose books are not up to date on their payments," the inspector noted, would be similarly fined in the future.[18] Another report noted that labor inspectors in Bío-Bío province were visiting fundos to make sure that landowners were making payments to the Caja de Seguro Obligatorio. Among the fundos listed as failing to follow Law 4054 in 1931 was Ránquil.[19]

In September 1929 Ibáñez had personally intervened to have a reluctant local Welfare Office register the Sindicato Agrícola Lonquimay. The president sent Cautín's intendant a telegram saying he had information that the welfare office in Temuco had refused to register the sindicato as a legal union. "Since there is nothing in the law that expressly prohibits the existence of this kind of union [an agricultural laborers' union]," he wrote, "you will order the welfare office to reconsider the resolution it adopted and proceed to register the union cited above."[20] Ibáñez also sent a telegram noting that he had heard that local officials had not only refused to cooperate with workers who were organizing unions under the established labor law, but also opposed unionization, "thus removing the only guarantee of social justice now and in the future." He ordered his intendants and governors to make certain all public officials acted in tune with the government's interest in promoting legal unions, even rural unions, consistent with the labor laws.[21]

Two months later Ibáñez wrote the intendant that "according to information in my power in Lonquimay and Alto Bío-Bío there is no respect for the rights of the campesinos and inquilinos on the estates, and free transit [on roads] is cut off." Ibáñez described labor relations on the estates as being defined by "the violation of labor laws and the abuse of the most fundamental rights of man."[22] The government gave strict orders to the carabineros that "pobladores and inquilinos on the estates be guaranteed their rights of free transit on public roads, especially near Lonquimay," a right, it appears, that had been violated systematically by landowners, backed by carabineros.[23] As he had before, Ibáñez stood fast by his promise that he would not permit carabineros to evict campesinos from Alto Bío Bío's estates. He instructed Cautín's intendant to "impart clear and final orders to the carabineros that they must end arbitrary arrests and that nobody should be dislodged from their land while the government, following the Southern Property Law, resolves definitively where justice lies in this situation." The president also appointed Leiva Tapia, "an inspired and patriotic man," subdelegate, replacing the official who had been antagonistic toward the union, and denounced the exploitative conditions on Lonquimay's estates. In part, Ibáñez's support for Leiva Tapia, the ocupante smallholders, and the Sindicato Agrícola Lonquimay was driven by his hostility to estate owners who had acquired land fraudulently and thereby impeded his ultimate goal of increasing the Chilean population in the cordillera along the border with Argentina.[24]

In addition to throwing his support to the Sindicato Agrícola Lonquimay and endorsing the extension of existing labor legislation into the southern countryside, Ibáñez issued orders to provincial authorities to prevent campesinos' exploitation by merchants (*comerciantes*) and company stores on estates (pulperías). In 1930 he sent a telegram to Cautín's intendant stating that he had information about "the true exploitation of inquilinos and smallholder agriculturalists by some unscrupulous merchants." According to the president, rural laborers and smallholders sold their crops "en verde" (in advance, before the harvest) for usurious prices or in exchange for alcoholic beverages or articles of basic necessity. Merchants afforded rural laborers small credits in return for putting up their livestock as collateral and then used the debt to appropriate the livestock. Ibáñez instructed Cautín's intendant to tell provincial and local officials that the government intended to crack down with an "iron fist" on "the crime of usury."[25]

It is not difficult to imagine how Ibáñez's efforts on behalf of rural laborers would have been received in Alto Bío Bío. The president had made a direct assault on landowners' and merchants' control of territory, transit, and commerce in the region. He had argued, in effect, that the

1924 labor laws applied to the rural workers on estates, regulating and restricting estate owners' treatment of their laborers. For the first time a Chilean president had denounced estate owners directly for violating labor laws as well as workers' "fundamental rights of man." He had even traveled to Bío-Bío province to make sure local officials implemented new social insurance laws.

Bolstered by Ibáñez's support, the Sindicato Agrícola Lonquimay expanded its organizing drive throughout 1929 and 1930. In September 1929 Eugenio Ossa Lynch, representing Francisco Puelma Tupper, went to the Ministry of Development to denounce a "true uprising [*sublevación*] among the inquilinos and empleados" on El Rahue. "The attitude of said inquilinos and empleados is based on the right they believe they have to be settled according to the Law on the Constitution of Southern Property on the land where they live and that they believe is public." The instigator of the movement, according to Ossa Lynch, was a man named Benjamín Cáceres, who lived in Lonquimay. The sindicato, Ossa Lynch declared, "is trying to appropriate the lands belonging to the Puelma Tupper family."[26] By the spring of 1929 the union had organized a union council on Guayalí as well. One of the union leaders, Simón Sagredo, was employed as an inquilino on the Bunster estate. On 15 October 1929 the undersecretary of the interior sent a telegram to Cautín's intendant to ask what measures he had taken "to restrict the subversive activities of inquilinos who are badly advised by Cáceres and other agitators." "The Minister," he wrote, "has been informed of new sublevaciones of inquilinos on the Ránquil and Luayale [Guayalí] fundos."[27]

The leaders of the Sindicato Agrícola Lonquimay told a different story. In a letter to the governor of Victoria, they requested protection against the abuses and outrages committed against union members on the El Rahue, Ránquil, Chilpaco, Villucura, Lolco, and Guayalí estates "for the crime of having joined our Society." A number of the union members held that workers on the six estates had been subject to abuses and attempted evictions for the sole fact of having joined the union. They wrote the president too, noting that since 1929 expulsions and abuses of the estates' residents had increased and were threatening to produce serious consequences. They asked that the government intervene to stay violent evictions ordered by judges in Mulchén and Lautaro and remeasure San Ignacio de Pemehue's borders. In addition, they stated that they were appealing to the Ley de Colonización by organizing the Ránquil-Rahue Cooperative.[28]

The union leaders flipped the landowners' accusation that they were disrupting the social order on its head, arguing that "it is not the pobladores here who have incited revolt but the administrators and those in charge of the Puelmas' estates who have incited the people to revolt with their repeated acts of hostility designed to force them to abandon their possessions and to steal their *adelantos* [improvements] and crops." The union leaders' language was significant. Poblador implied residence; they had literally "peopled" the inhospitable mountain borderlands, as opposed to both wealthy absentee landowners like the Puelmas and foreign-born but resident landowners like Olhagaray and Charó. In addition, poblador elided differences in social position between inquilinos and ocupantes, foregrounding the fact that, as much as they were inquilinos, they composed the region's population. They were residents with rights based on material occupation of their land.

The union leaders described the long history of violent land expulsions and bloody massacres that had driven tens of thousands of Chilean laborers across the cordillera to Argentina during the first decades of the century: "We don't want to repeat here the massacres that are registered in our legendary history. We do not want to once again experience the horrible acts that were carried out on this land against our ancestors: fires, violent expulsions, and long caravans of refugees crossing the Chilean–Argentine Andes. These memories live in the memories of today's children of this land." They invoked the corporatist ideals of the recent social and agrarian legislation, emphasizing that organizing rural laborers in unions and cooperatives would produce social discipline while promoting agricultural development. Thanks to the Sindicato Agrícola Lonquimay, the union leaders contended, there were "defined orientations, unity, and criteria, and up to a certain point discipline and order among the majority of our members." Rather than seek conflict, the union wished "to solve the agrarian problem in our region peacefully, following our social and agrarian laws the best we can." But to do this, the union leaders pointed out, they needed the support of the authorities. Thus far they had received support from La Moneda, but local and regional officials continued to side with the Puelmas and Bunsters.

In October 1929, for example, the governor of Victoria reported that Juan Segundo Leiva Tapia had disseminated "subversive propaganda among the inquilinos of the Rahue, Villa[u]cura, Lolco, Chilpaz[c]o, and Ránquil estates making the inquilinos believe that the lands they occupy are public and that they have the right to occupy them, the result of which is that they do not obey their patrones." Lonquimay's subdelegate and carabineros had filed complaints against Leiva Tapia in the court in Lautaro for his "disruptive and subversive actions." He had been arrested, though by the time he was appointed subdelegate he had been released from jail.[29] In late 1929, despite his appointment as subdelegate, Leiva Tapia still faced charges in Lautaro of engaging in subversive activities and disturbing the public order. Lautaro's governor had initiated a case against him, as well as other leaders of the Sindicato Agrícola Lonquimay, for introducing themselves onto the region's estates and "seducing the inquilinos, telling them that the lands are public and that they can appropriate them."[30]

Almost all government officials, save Ibáñez, viewed Leiva Tapia as a subversive who belonged in jail rather than in local government. Ibáñez's interior minister, for example, telegrammed Cautín's intendant that he had received serious complaints about "the conduct of Lonquimay's subdelegate, who is abusing his position to harass among others the owners of the Lolco fundo owned by the French firm Olhagaray y Charó."[31] In December 1929 Olhagaray y Charó had denounced the new subdelegate, who, they said, had "provoked ocupantes to abuse and harass the company" on the Lolco estate.[32] The minister instructed the intendant to notify Leiva Tapia that he should end "this policy of abuse that the Government does not accept" and remarked that he had advocated removing Leiva Tapia from his position for a long time.[33] Ibáñez's support was insufficient, as in February 1930 the governor of Victoria replaced Leiva Tapia as subdelegado with the carabinero officer Francisco Espinosa Orrego.[34]

Some of the Sindicato Agrícola Lonquimay's other leaders also faced criminal charges. The governor of Mulchén levied charges of "illicit association" against Benjamín Cáceres, a worker on El Rahue and union leader. Cáceres was arrested and placed in "preventive custody." His alleged crime was organizing rural laborers in an illegal association, the Sindicato Agrícola Lonquimay. According to the police, Cáceres and one José Quilondrán "dedicate themselves to subversive activities disturbing public order and threatening private property and the peace of the region, organizing meetings on the fundos, inciting the inquilinos to rise up against their patrones, telling them they themselves have the powers of government to distribute all the lands as a gift from his excellency the President of the Republic." The police described Quilondrán and Cáceres as "agitators of the inquilinos on the fundos."[35] However, the union's registration with the local welfare office, overriding the opposition of both the governor and the intendant, made it impossible for the local judge, governor, and police to keep Cáceres in jail.[36] In an expression of his support for the union and mincing no words with his reluctant regional officials, Carlos Ibáñez telegrammed Cautín's intendant, instructing him "to place Benjamín Cáceres, whose imprisonment according to information in my power was arbitrary, in immediate freedom."[37]

The Balance of Power Begins to Shift

In response to the ongoing confrontation with the Puelmas and Bunsters the union presented an exhaustively researched study of the titles to the Puelma estates, prepared by Bruno Ackermann, to the intendant of Cautín province, which was read in the House of Deputies by the Democratic Party deputy Manuel Navarrete on 30 October 1929. Ackermann began his review of the history of the estates' titles with a reiteration of the Sindicato Agrícola Lonquimay's program to settle the region's mountain borderlands by restoring two hundred thousand hectares of estate land to the state. "I am certain that on the excess of land that could become property of the State," he said, "citizens brought from the heights of the cordillera" could be settled in colonies organized in cooperatives. Ackermann asked the government to suspend the decree issued earlier that year legitimizing the titles to the Puelma estates.[38]

Ackermann then proceeded to lay out the long, convoluted history of the titles to the five estates that had composed the San Ignacio de Pemehue hacienda. His detailed narrative hewed close to the legal brief brought in 1916 by Roque Fernández and the case made in congress by Zenón Torrealba in 1919. Ackermann likely had either followed the previous court case, as well as Fernández's and the other ocupantes' lengthy conflict with the Puelmas and Torrealba's efforts to expropriate the estates, or had learned the history from regional Democratic Party leaders. Froilán Rivera, the editor of the Curacautín newspaper *El Comercio*, a supporter of the Sindicato Agrícola Lonquimay, was a Democrat and may have transmitted the history to Ackermann and Leiva Tapia.

Ackermann began his brief with José María Rodríguez's sale of "4,000 cuadras in the subdelegation of Mulchén to Cornelio Saavedra" and continued with Saavedra's and Bulnes Pinto's sales of the lots that would become San Ignacio to Francisco Puelma Castillo in 1881. In spite of the property boundaries described in the deeds from these sales, he observed, San Ignacio had grown to hundreds of thousands of hectares. Along with the original titles, Ackermann marshalled Puelma Castillo's 1889 leases of pasture to prove that the "colonos in Alto Bío Bío occupy public land." As the claimants in the 1916 case had similarly argued, he pointed out that when the leases expired in 1896 and the lands inspectorate was ordered to take possession of the land to settle repatriated Chilean campesinos from Argentina, Francisco Puelma Castillo's heirs had refused to restore the land to the state. Ackermann made the same argument articulated by Roque Fernández in 1916: by "having taken [the land] in rental contracts of March 1 1889, Sr, Puelma Castillo recognized the state as the only owner and possessor of these lands."

Ackermann also reprised what had been a centerpiece of the 1916 legal case. When Elisa Tupper de Puelma died in 1896, Eliodoro Yáñez, the family's legal representative, contracted Alberto Larenas to survey San Ignacio and divide the property into plots among her heirs. As Ackermann noted, "In this manner the Tupper Puelma y Cía has symbolically appeared as the owner of this land that is the exclusive property of the State and occupied in large part by colonos *chilenos* who claim rights based on their consistent labor, bringing value [to the land] with their individual and collective work with their families." Ackermann also described the 1901 agreement between the state and the Puelmas, with Yáñez representing the Puelma Tupper family and Agustíin Baeza the state. The 1901 arrangement, he observed, constituted "an obvious fraud."

Ackermann and the other union leaders sent a telegram to Santiago requesting that a government commission investigate the Puelma properties. This commission would include a delegate from the government, a delegate from the patrones, a delegate from the *diputados obreros* (workers' deputies), and a delegate from the Sindicato Agrícola Lonquimay. A recently appointed government commission composed of the intendant and a public prosecutor was not, they said, "a guarantee for the *clase obrera campesina*." That commission had refused to investigate the pobladores' rights based on occupation, abuses they had received from the Bunsters and Puelmas, or prior forcible expulsions. The commission members had also "declared themselves openly against the *sindicato clase campesina organizada*." As a result, twenty families on the Puelma estates had been given eviction notices.[39]

The telegram marked a shift in language from Ackermann's description of the union members as ocupantes-colonos and colonos chilenos. The union's telegram rang with the language of class, whether it was "clase campesina," or "clase obrera campesina." The union referred to its members literally in class terms. "Obrera campesina" could refer to a whole gamut of labor positions, from day laborer to seasonal worker to estate laborer, but in collapsing these social identities the union implied that these various types of agricultural workers all constituted a class, the clase campesina, whatever the obreros campesinos' relationship to their patrones. Lonquimay's rural poor were workers, now organized in a union and subject to the reigning social and labor laws. *Obrerista* ("workerist") language of class pushed the union's less political and less ideological claims to speak for ocupantes and colonos, its commitments to colonization and cooperativism, in a more radical direction. Inquilinos and ocupantes belonged to the clase obrera campesina, a politicized identity that reflected the growing radicalization of sectors of the Sindicato Agrícola Lonquimay and its leaders.

The different forms of address in Ackermann's petition and in the union's telegram reflected two strains of politics within the Sindicato Agrícola Lonquimay's leadership. Ackermann, a merchant, viewed the union members as actual or future colonos, smallholders who would be organized in an agricultural cooperative. Other union leaders, among them probably Leiva Tapia—who had, as noted above, employed class language in his December 1928 account of his meeting with Ibáñez, denouncing the "feudal local regime" and its exploitation of "the laboring classes"—viewed the union members as belonging to a class of obreros-campesinos. The union was, after all, a union, not simply a colonization cooperative. Leiva Tapia's loyalty to Ibáñez and Ibáñez's support for the union leader make it highly unlikely that he was at this time a member of the decimated Communist Party. But the class language in the telegram reflects both an *obrerista* view of rural society that would have jibed with Ibáñez's corporatism and a Marxist view of social organization that might explain how Leiva Tapia and other union leaders would later make the ideological journey from supporting Ibáñez to supporting the Communist Party, from *obrerismo* to revolution.[40]

In response to the union's petitions, in late 1929 the director of the Lands Department, Ernesto Maldonado, recommended a review of the 1929 decree recognizing the Puelmas' titles in order to avoid "the serious consequences the decree ... would create for the peace of the ocupantes and their families."[41] On 27 March 1930 Ibáñez issued a new decree that named a commission to study the question of the Puelma estates' borders and the rights of the many ocupantes located in the region.[42] The government intended to review the 14 August 1929 decree because the Puelma estates had many ocupantes who claimed that "they occupy not private property but public land to which they claim rights under the Southern Property Law." The decree declared forthrightly that the borders fixed in the 1901 deal between Agustín Baeza and Eliodoro Yáñez did not correspond to the borders in the original 1863 sale from Nahuel to Rodríguez or the borders established in the subsequent land sales to Saavedra and Bulnes Pinto and then to Puelma Castillo. There was, the decree stated, following Ackermann's detailed history, sufficient evidence that the borders established in 1901 included "lands recognized as public by Francisco Puelma Castillo, who had rented them for six years and then continued occupying them without any title."

The new decree revoked that of 1929 and named a commission, led by Ernesto Maldonado, whose mandate was to determine the original borders of Francisco Puelma Castillo's property and the rights of ocupantes to public land as well as to survey "the other land to which [the ocupantes] believe they have a right." In addition, the decree charged the panel with drawing up a blueprint of a town (*pueblo*) in Alto Bío Bío, with administrative and judicial authorities, public welfare services, schools, a civil registry, police, and a telegraph and post office "to bring the benefits of civilization to the region."[43]

Leiva Tapia's alliance with Ibáñez had borne fruit, despite the fact that he had been removed from his position as subdelegate after only a few months. In response to his study of the educational needs of the local population, the government had begun to build eleven schools in Alto Bío Bío. It had initiated the founding of a town in the Nitrito Valley, which would give the government an official presence, since a municipal government would be the first state institution in Alto Bío Bió, north of Lonquimay. Leiva Tapia reported that the development ministry, employing a report prepared by the Sindicato Agrícola Lonquimay, had initiated studies of how to build a colony on six thousand hectares within the Alto Bío Bío forest reserve. And Ibáñez's commission was examining the titles of the region's estates and would soon release a report on the status of the "150,000 hectares usurped from the state."[44]

The union's increased power was consecrated the following July, when Cautín's intendant nominated candidates who would "represent the *elemento obrero*" (workers) to be appointed by the government to positions in city councils, *juntas de vecinos*, throughout the province. This measure was part of the Ibáñez government's corporatist strategy of integrating workers and their organizations into the state apparatus, both through unions and by appointing workers or representatives of workers' organizations to positions of local political power. In Curacautín the intendant proposed Froilán Rivera, the editor of *El Comercio* and a leader in the Sindicato Agrícola Lonquimay. He noted that Rivera, a barber and journalist, "enjoys prestige in the locality and has ties to the elementos obreros." Most important, he had demonstrated in his articles that he was an "ardent supporter of the government." In Lonquimay the intendant proposed keeping Juan Evangelista Molina Villar, who had been previously named to the position, as a member of the Junta de Vecinos, representing the region's workers. The intendant described Molina as a "modest agriculturalist who works his own land and is a member of the Sindicato Agrícola Lonquimay."[45] At this point, membership in the union signified loyalty to Ibáñez. The government viewed the sindicato as a conduit between Ibáñez and the region's elemento obrero and also as a useful tool for prying once public land out of the hands of Alto Bío Bío's regional oligarchy and settling it with industrious Chilean colonos.

The relationship between Ibáñez and the Sindicato Agrícola Lonquimay had been consolidated in January 1930, when Leiva Tapia had been named to the regional committee of the Confederación Republicana de Acción Cívica (CRAC) in the town of Victoria.[46] The CRAC was a political organization established to channel electoral support from legal workers' organizations to the Ibáñez regime and bypass traditional political parties. As part of its populist and corporatist project, the Ibáñez regime was able to pass an electoral law that gave the CRAC fourteen seats in the House of Deputies and one in the senate. These would be divided equally between obreros (blue-collar workers) and empleados (white-collar workers) and give workers' organizations a quota of representation in congress.[47] Leiva Tapia's incorporation into the CRAC reflected the close ties between the country's largest union of agricultural workers and Carlos Ibáñez.

The Sindicato Agrícola Lonquimay's growing power emboldened workers on the Bunster and Puelma estates to rebel against landowner authority and claim the plots they occupied as their own. In April 1930 the Bunster family sent a telegram to the interior ministry denouncing an organized "foco comunista" (communist cell) in Alto Bío Bío, which was "disguised as the Sindicato Agrícola Lonquimay." The communist foco was, the Bunsters said, trying to extend its operations to their Guayalí estate. The Bunsters charged that inquilinos, supported by the union, had "refused to obey the orders of the landowners and a picket of carabineros" sent to enforce discipline. "The inquilinos," the Bunsters complained, "took control of an *invernada* pasture, depriving 3,000 head of livestock, who will die of hunger during the winter, of their pasture." The inquilinos had introduced their own livestock onto the invernada. The Bunster family petitioned the government to act decisively to protect "life, property and hacienda threatened by the work of communists who have invaded the province."[48] Francisco Vial, the Bunsters' legal representative, also petitioned the government for support, denouncing "the serious situation in the region created by the Communist propaganda of a handful of people who have dedicated themselves to stirring up the inquilinos, who before were peaceful [*tranquilos*], to revolt so that all agricultural labor is now paralyzed."[49] At this point, the sindicato had a directorate that included a Pehuenche, Eloi Nahuelcheo, who most likely was from one of the communities that had engaged in lengthy conflicts with the Bunsters.[50]

In response to the Bunsters' denunciations, a group of nine carabineros traveled to Guayalí, where they found that a number of the estate's inquilinos had joined the Sindicato Agrícola Lonquimay. The carabineros interviewed Gonzalo Bunster, who informed them that he believed his life was in imminent danger. He had received "personal communications" that indicated that his inquilinos had threatened him. Bunster also stated that he could not get any of the inquilinos who had joined the union to work, despite the fact that as inquilinos they were obligated to have one person from each of their households permanently at his disposal.[51] Bunster further complained that the inquilinos Simón Sagredo, José del C. Vega, Daniel Alegría, Pascual Torres, Juan Pino, Manuel Pacheco, Domingo Carrasco, Antonio Cárdenas, Pablo Ortíz, Prudencio Salazar, and Lisandro Baeza had been notified by the judge in Los Ángeles to abandon the estate. But, he continued, "up to today they have not yet done this. On the contrary, they are actually cultivating the land as if it were their own."[52]

The carabineros then sought out the inquilinos but were able to interview only two, Manuel Segundo Pacheco Sepúlveda and Juan Pablo Ortíz, whom they found planting wheat. The pair stated that "they were working on their own and that they had nothing to do with Señor Bunster because the land was public property and they had no obligation whatsoever to work for him." Bunster had tried to have the carabineros force "the inquilino Pacheco" "to leave his job" on the estate since he was planting crops without Bunster's permission, but they had strict instructions from the intendancy not to evict any of the estate's ocupantes and to limit their activities to investigating the facts on the ground. This must have been quite frustrating for Bunster, who would have been accustomed to employing carabineros as an instrument of his rule over his inquilino labor force. Nonetheless, to guarantee Bunster's personal security, they installed a picket of two carabineros at Los Guindos, the location of the landowner's big houses on Guayalí.[53]

Alto Bío Bío's fundos were locked in something of a stalemate. The Ibáñez government had refused to order carabineros to expel rebellious ocupantes and inquilinos from the Bunster and Puelma estates. The Bunsters' inquilinos continued to work land on the estate as if it were their own and claim colono status. Inquilinos on the Puelma properties similarly disobeyed their patrones' orders and, with the support of the union, petitioned for the expropriation and redistribution of the estates' land. But local carabineros had acted to support the Bunsters by stationing a picket on Guayalí, and regional officials continued to view the Sindicato Agrícola Lonquimay as a source of subversion and social disorder. All eyes now turned to the government commissioners, whose findings would determine the future of the Puelma and Bunster estates and that of their workers.

CHAPTER FIVE

Agrarian Reform Arrives in Alto Bío Bío

IN APRIL 1930 THE commission named by Ibáñez to investigate the Puelmas' titles to San Ignacio de Pemehue traveled to Alto Bío Bío, spending days traversing territory that stretched from Mulchén to the Pemehue cordillera. They were accompanied by a surveyor and a forest guard. One night they stayed in houses on the Lolco estate. This was no surprise because government officials had always found comfortable lodging in the landowners' big houses. But this was no ordinary trip. The following day the commissioners boarded a launch to cross the Biobío River. They were met by 425 men (the absence of women was not unusual) organized in their union councils in "proper formation" with a Chilean flag waving above them. The union members welcomed the government officials with a rousing salute: "Long live Chile! Long live President Ibáñez! Long live the government commission!" After ceremonies and speeches, the commissioners accompanied the union leaders Juan Segundo Leiva Tapia, Jorge Ackermann, and Benjamín Cáceres to the campesinos' future town, which they had named Santa Graciela. Then, on a plain in the Nitrito Valley where the town square would lie, surrounded by *lleuques* (Chilean plum yew, or *Prumnopitys andina*), cypresses, and apple trees, a photographer snapped pictures of the visiting dignitaries and the union's councils.[1]

Later, the union leaders met with Ernesto Maldonado, a meeting at which representatives of the region's estate-owning families were also present. A lengthy discussion of Santa Graciela's layout and the design of the town's houses ensued, with union members proposing modern libraries and workshops for the new municipality. The town would also have a police station, post office, a social welfare office that would offer aid to mothers, the elderly, and children, and a consumers' cooperative. Instead of taverns, it would have a theater with modern art. The union leaders asked that the small woods remaining in the valley be conserved as part of a public park. Maldonado agreed to the union leaders' proposals and ordered his surveyor to plan a town with a one-hundred-hectare radius to accommodate the large population of future colonos.[2]

And this brought Maldonado to a key matter, a subject of terminology that lay at the heart of the land and labor conflicts sweeping southern Chile. One can infer from the union leaders' description of the meeting that the landowners' representatives, including Gonzalo Bunster, had made a point they would hammer home again and again. These were no ocupantes, hoping to settle and civilize untamed, public frontier wilderness. The members of the union were not prospective settler colonos, but inquilinos who owed their patrones their labor and obedience and who had no rights to the land, even if they had worked it for years. Maldonado met the question of whether the residents of the large estates were ocupantes or inquilinos head on. If the estates' land turned out to belong to the state, he told the assembled parties, then they were ocupantes. If the commission's study found that the land was private property with legitimate titles, then they were inquilinos "whose situation would depend on the landowner."[3] This, in a nutshell, was the conflict that had been roiling social relations in southern Chile for years. Were laborers inquilinos residing on estate land who owed obedience to their patrones or ocupantes of public land who held rights to be settled as colonos?

During the meeting with Maldonado and the landowners' representatives, the union leaders pointed out that Gonzalo Bunster had complained that "his people" had changed a great deal and that the Sindicato Agrícola Lonquimay had made them "subversive." The union leaders responded that the true subversive was Bunster since he disrupted peaceful social relations by behaving abusively toward his workers. The union, they argued, was a force of social discipline and harmony: "Above all, we love social peace and order." And, they pointed out, Bunster and the other landowners were alarmed because the old feudal order was crumbling around them because "they confuse respect with humiliation, duty with the forced obligations of the slave." To the landowners, they argued, "the worker doesn't exist in the true sense of the word, but rather is a man-beast who pays tribute to his master with all his labor in exchange for a crust of bread, like an ox or a horse."[4]

This last point spoke to the rapidly changing state of labor relations on the region's estates. The union leaders pointed out that in the past, workers were "servants with no rights, only duties." But now, with the labor reforms of 1924, it was widely recognized that the worker had both obligations and rights. This, the union leaders declared, was what had "alarmed these señores hacendados." Nonetheless, in denouncing the hacendados' abuse and exploitation of their workers, they implicitly recognized that their union's members were inquilinos as well as ocupantes and aspiring colonos.[5] In fact, the union leaders defined the members both as ocupantes or pobladores and as agricultural workers or obreros campesinos. They appealed to the 1924 labor legislation as well as to the recent colonization laws to limit patrones' power over both land and labor.

Maldonado was able to forge a treaty between the two parties, although it was short-lived. Gonzalo Bunster, representing the landowners, and Simón Sagredo, representing the obreros, as they called themselves, hammered out a deal to keep the peace while the commission went about its business of examining the properties' boundaries and deeds. The pobladores, another term they used to describe themselves, would return to work to keep agricultural production in the region going under conditions that had prevailed prior to the Southern Property Law. Workers would receive two cuadras for cultivating crops, pasture for fifty head of adult livestock and twenty head of young livestock, and a salary of one peso a day. Each inquilino family would be required to provide one person to work on the hacienda. The same arrangement was worked out with the owner of the Lolco estate, Juan Bautista Charó, the following day. This was a classic labor arrangement characteristic of inquilinaje throughout the south, and it made it clear that, for the moment, the union's members remained inquilinos and the landowners patrones.[6] Maldonado reiterated Ibáñez's pledge that under his rule he would allow no evictions of ocupantes; for the time being, whether inquilinos or ocupantes, the laborers organized in the Sindicato Agrícola Lonquimay could remain on their land.[7]

In late May 1930 the union held a large assembly of its councils at which it hosted a number of visiting dignitaries, including Mario Gerlach, the labor inspectorate's local social welfare secretary and labor inspector, Lonquimay's mayor, Augusto Schweitzer, and his wife, Ema Torres de Schweitzer, and the region's judge (*juez de subdelegación*), Julio Morales. As the labor inspector traveled to Lonquimay across the extensive Pehuenco plateau at twelve hundred meters above sea level under a torrential freezing rain he was escorted by one hundred horsemen, members of the El Rahue estate's union council.[8] The assembly says a great deal about both the union's ideology and the extension of the state-directed labor apparatus into the southern countryside in 1930. Leiva Tapia and Jorge Ackermann began the meeting by going over the union's books and accounting with the labor inspector. They then presented a brief history of the union and its "educational, moral, and economic" projects in the service of the public good. Gerlach followed with a brief history of labor unionism in Chile and the government's goal "that all workers in Chile associate and cooperate [in unions]." He congratulated the "obreros-campesinos" on having understood the importance of union organization and for having founded "the first agricultural union in the republic and the largest union in Cautín province." This was something of an exaggeration but nonetheless suggested the national significance of the Sindicato Agrícola Lonquimay's organizing efforts among agricultural laborers in the southern cordillera.

Following Gerlach, Leiva Tapia read Ibáñez's circular titled "Labor Legislation Creates Social Harmony and Economic Equilibrium," in which the president laid out his vision of a corporatist labor relations system. Using prolabor, populist language, Ibáñez argued that "today unions have become true cooperatives of will and energy directed toward the progress and welfare of the workers ... the true engines driving national prosperity and the dignity of the people." Unions integrated workers into the economy and society, promoting both social order and progress. It would appear that Leiva Tapia and the other leaders of the sindicato shared Ibáñez's corporatist ideology, in part because it affirmed the legitimacy and legal status of their union. As Gerlach pointed out, the Sindicato Agrícola Lonquimay marked an important first step toward extending the 1924 social laws to rural workers. The Ibáñez government viewed Alto Bío Bío as a place where it could initiate a series of reforms, expropriating large estates, organizing colonos' cooperatives on public land, and building rural unions, measures that were impossible in central Chile.

Chile's First Agrarian Reform

After two months the government commission headed by Maldonado presented a report favorable to the Sindicato Agrícola Lonquimay that resulted in a new government decree.[9] The report was definitive: "The commission was able to establish incontrovertibly, by using maps and documentation from the period, that the actual borders of the Villucura, Lolco, Ránquil, Chilpaco, and El Rahue estates, do not lie within the borders in the original deeds but outside of them." It also found that the 9 December 1901 deed altered the original borders of the estates, "depriving the State of enormous extensions of land." Nonetheless, the officials responded favorably to the Puelma family's arguments that they enjoyed property rights based on their years of material possession and the improvements they had made on the estates. The report stated that "Francisco Puelma Castillo's heirs have worked, made productive, and introduced improvements on part of the land they claim."[10]

The commission extended this argument to the Lolco estate, which had been sold to Charó and Olhagaray: "The actual owners bought this land [Lolco] in good faith and cultivated it, having invested large amounts of capital and executed considerable works, like bridges, canals, roads, fences, houses for inquilinos etc. and, moreover, have followed the Ley de Seguro Obrero." It was the government's policy "to reward effort and individual labor in order to obtain the maximum productivity of its soil ... placing on the land the productive elements which could be considered the most apt and with greatest right to colonize the land belonging to the State." For these reasons the owners of Lolco were to be given special consideration. The report contrasted the advances made by Olhagaray and Charó with the relative neglect and abandon on the four Puelma estates.

Because the only foundation for the Puelmas' land claims lay in the history of their occupation and investments in their putative property, the commission added a detailed analysis and description of the estates. Very much like the reports produced by Chile's agrarian reform agency (CORA) during the 1960s and 1970s, when it investigated conditions on estates to assess whether they were eligible for expropriation, that of the commission detailed the use and management of the land as well as social conditions on the five properties. The report provided detailed accounts of production, exploitation of resources like meadows and forests, and inventories of the estate owners' investments, including plantings of forage, trees, and crops, irrigation canals, roads, bridges, and fences. In addition, much like the later CORA reports, it examined workers' conditions, detailing whether the landowners followed the existing "social legislation," especially paying social security taxes, furnishing decent housing, and signing legally required contracts with their workers. Alto Bío Bío would be the place where the Chilean state initiated the administrative apparatus and legal protocols employed decades later during Chile's agrarian reform. The procedures for establishing both property rights and the state's right to expropriate private property for redistribution to its workers would begin with the government commission's report on the Puelma estates.

The commission report provided a history of the estates' deeds going back to the original sale of a "campo eriazo" (an empty or abandoned land) from Nahuel to José María Rodríguez. It noted that although maps created in the 1890s, including the 1894 map, gave the estate's northern border as the Mulchén River from its confluence with the Agua de los Padres estuary, until its origin, the original 1863 deed did not give the Mulchén as a boundary. Referring to the Mulchén River, the deed gave the river only as a point where the western border formed by the Lirque and Llollanco estuaries ended. The commission concluded that the Mulchén was not then, as had been widely assumed in numerous recountings, San Ignacio de Pemehue's northern border.

The commission found that the eastern border, defined as the Andes cordillera in the 1863 and 1874 deeds, was also in doubt. In the earlier deed, José María Rodríguez sold to Manuel Bulnes Pinto the fundo with the following borders: to the south the Agua de los Padres estuary following its course to the east until its beginning and from here to the Andes cordillera. Seven years later, Bulnes Pinto sold the easternmost lot of his Santa Elena hacienda to Puelma Castillo. The deed for this sale also stated that the eastern border of the property was formed by the cordillera. The commission determined that "The cordilleras to which the deeds refer can only be that cordillera where the Renaico River begins." As the original 1863 deed put it, the southern border followed "this same path until it hits the Renaico River, following the Puelche River until it hits the Cordillera." The Renaico River had its origin in the Pemehue cordillera, the commission reasoned, and thus had to be the cordillera referred to in the deeds. San Ignacio de Pemehue could not extend eastward beyond the Pemehue cordillera.

Finally, in reviewing the sale of four thousand cuadras made by José María Rodríguez to Cornelio Saavedra, the commission found that the deed gave specific borders: on the south, the Renaico River from its origin to the Chanco valley, to the Coronado Fort and land belonging to cacique Manquelipe; on the west, a fence that ran from the Chanco valley to the confluence of the Lirque and Agua de los Padres estuaries; on the north, the Agua de los Padres estuary; and from the origins of this estuary a straight line to the cordillera, leaving between it and the Renaico River a width of thirty cuadras in its entire longitude until reaching the cordillera. This meant, the report noted, that the land extended thirty cuadras to the Pemehue cordillera. In effect, all the land claimed by the Puelmas as belonging to San Ignacio east of the Pemehue cordillera to the border separating Chile and Argentina and south of the Renaico River was public.

Having established the true borders of both the Santa Elena and San Ignacio haciendas, the panel of officials concluded that the total size of the properties sold by Rodríguez to Bulnes Pinto and Saavedra was 40,365 hectares, which left "an enormous margin to be considered as excess." Almost the entirety of the Puelmas' estates, more than 130,000 hectares, in Alto Bío Bío lay on public land. The commission determined that the auctions of various lots to Puelma Castillo in 1889 were of public land, as had been contended by various parties for decades. The Puelmas' argument that the land was not public but had been included in the original sales was based on Larenas's study from 1893. But, the officials pointed out, the Puelmas did not include Larenas's study in their petitions in 1929–30, and the commission, despite searching in various archives, could not find it either. The only actual surveyor's report the commissioners were able to locate in government archives was Larenas's 1896 survey of San Ignacio de Pemehue, which had been commissioned by the Puelmas. The commission also located a 5 May 1897 letter from Larenas to Eliodoro Yáñez, the family's legal representative, describing the commission he received from the Puelma family and from the Banco Hipotecario de Valparaíso. This suggests that during the 1890s the Puelma heirs had taken out a mortgage on their enormous property in southern Chile. In general, the commission found that Larenas's survey of San Ignacio de Pemehue was of dubious value since the 1893 government-sponsored report had vanished, and the survey he had produced in 1896 had been made while he was on the Puelmas' payroll.

The commission performed an extensive investigation into the history of San Ignacio's eastern border, which was given in different documents as the massif central of the Andes cordillera and the international border dividing Chile and Argentina. Often these were conflated. A key turning point in the history of the Puelma estates' expansion came in the 1890s during diplomatic negotiations between the two countries over the border in the Andes cordillera. In 1898 Diego Barros Arana, representing Chile, and Francisco Moreno, representing Argentina, worked out an agreement that moved the international border eastward, drawing a line between the Cerro Copahue and the Paso Llaima and vitiating earlier agreements that had made the Andes massif central the border. Moreno had argued that according to an 1881 treaty the massif central, not the smaller mountain chains to the east, was the established border. However, this border effectively divided the Biobío River. Barros Arana argued successfully for drawing the border to the east, and when Moreno finally agreed, the new treaty left the entire upper valley of the Biobío River, including the river's headwaters, in Chilean hands.

As the commission pointed out, the Puelma family's contention that their properties' eastern limits were defined by the Chile–Argentina border ignored this history. The commission's report demonstrated that the deeds gave the massif central, not the more recent and further eastern border with Argentina, as the property's boundary. The commission conducted a detailed history of land sales and transfers of indigenous property and demonstrated that legislation over the decades made it clear that the borders of "indigenous territory" acquired during the "pacification of the Araucanía," gave the eastern border as "the massif central of the Cordillera de los Andes, where rivers like the Malleco, Biobío, Renaico have their origins." The commission pointed out that the Pemehue cordillera was the major cordillera in the massif central and the place where the Malleco River was born. A long legislative history bolstered the commission's finding that when the original estate was purchased during the sales of the 1860s, 1870s, and 1880s, the eastern border of indigenous and then Chilean territory was understood to be the massif central of the Andes cordillera. When the border with Argentina had shifted to the east in 1898, the Puelmas had simply expanded the borders of their estates eastward as well.

Because the commission found that the five fundos that composed San Ignacio Pemehue were not located within the borders laid out in the original deeds, the legal status of the estates' laborers and ocupantes had to be defined. The question of whether they were inquilinos or were ocupantes with the right to be settled on the estates as colonos remained open. The commission's first finding appeared to be detrimental to the

Sindicato Agrícola Lonquimay. After studying the different estates' account books, which had records of payments to workers and the jobs they performed, taking an inventory of the age and scope of improvements on the estates, and interviewing ocupantes-inquilinos, the first serious government study of the estates' pobladores, the commission concluded that "on none of these fundos have there been ocupantes. On these properties there are only families whose heads have arrived as empleados or inquilinos of the people who, as either renters or owners, have been in possession of these 178,000 hectares of land." The commission noted further that "some of those who call themselves ocupantes, when questioned by us, did not deny having arrived at the places they occupy today as inquilinos or empleados." Others told the officials they had settled on the estates as workers "but that they were convinced they were working on land that sooner or later would be recognized as public." These ocupantes-inquilinos had contracted with the estates as inquilinos but with the goal of eventually "obtaining titles to the pieces of land they occupied" as part of their labor contracts.

All the campesinos who lived and labored on the estates belonged to families whose male heads worked as inquilinos or empleados. The commission's survey of the estates' workers reaffirmed a central feature of campesino life in Alto Bío Bío: labor on estates was organized through male inquilinos' contracts with landowner patrones and the subordination of their wives, children, and other family members' labor. Notably, none of the estates' workers were single men; like colonos, they invariably settled on estates with their families, whose labor was essential to both their work for the estates and to the reproduction of the household economy.

None of this appeared to bolster the claims of the union members since as inquilinos they exercised few rights and implicitly recognized their patrones' authority over their land and labor. Nonetheless, the fact that the land they occupied was public meant there were two competing claims to public land, the putative estate owners' and the ocupantes-inquilinos', both based on rights rooted in material occupation. It fell to the commission to decide whose rights should prevail. In the past, the state had almost always supported estate owners in these situations, even if the land was public and despite its commitment to repatriating the thirty thousand Chileans in Argentina and settling them as colonos throughout southern Chile. Now, however, a government more sympathetic to southern Chile's rural poor was in power.

The first sign of a change in agrarian policy in southern Chile was the Ibáñez government's approach to unions of rural workers. Government officials like the intendant of Cautín had urged extending labor legislation to the countryside, and Ibáñez himself had implicitly recognized that there was no reason labor laws could not apply in the rural sector. In addition, his secretary of welfare and labor inspector had told the members of the Sindicato Agrícola Lonquimay that incorporating themselves into the state-directed labor relations system through unionization was the best route to achieving social and economic progress. Now, the commission detailed the history of the sindicato and described it not as a subversive or communist foco, inciting inquilinos to rebellion, but as a force for progress and social order. In fact, the commission cited the organization of the ocupantes-inquilinos in disciplined union councils as evidence in the union's favor. It recounted the union's early goal of settling its members on the Alto Bío Bío forest reserve and the government's rejection of this proposal because "it was not viewed as being in the interest of the state to use this land for colonization since it was not appropriate for agricultural production." The union then continued organizing its members "to settle them on lands they viewed as public and that had conditions for efficient and remunerative production." Here, the commission indicated key criteria that bolstered the union's case for having rights to the estate land: the land was public, and they had plans to exploit it efficiently and profitably. The report observed approvingly that "the union is perfectly organized on each of the estates, Rahue, Chilpaco, Lolco, Ránquil, Villucura, through delegates with their respective *mesas directivas* [leaderships], who control the acts of their members on each one of these estates." This institutionalized labor organization spoke in favor of the ocupantes-inquilinos: they were respectable citizens incorporated into the state labor relations apparatus who were working for the progress of their isolated region.

The commission proceeded to describe each of San Ignacio de Pemehue's five estates, beginning with the northernmost, 51,600-hectare Villucura. Like all fundos in the region, the estate was dedicated to raising livestock and was divided into low-altitude invernadas and high-altitude veranadas. Over the years, Villucura's owners had built a road running through the whole property all the way to Mulchén. The road was in fairly bad shape, the commission observed, really appropriate only for driving cattle. In line with the government policy on building roads in the region, it remarked that a public road connecting Villucura to

Mulchén was necessary since free transit on the road depended on the estate's owners' good will. The Puelmas had built other privately owned roads to transport their livestock, linking Villucura to the international road to Argentina and to Curacautín, Los Ángeles, and Santa Bárbara.

The report included a detailed inventory of other improvements made by the Puelmas over the years: 237 cuadras of fencing enclosing meadows, 5 small bridges, and a 60-meter bridge crossing the Lolco River. In addition, they had built a house for the estate's mayordomo, but, as absentee landowners, no owner's "big house." There were 9 huts made of logs for inquilinos. The estate possessed 2,500 cows during summer and 1,500 in winter as well as 800 sheep. The commission was unimpressed by these minimal investments in Villucura's productivity. The report noted that little had been done to improve the natural conditions for raising livestock, like introducing exotic species of pasture and building irrigation canals. This state of affairs contrasted sharply with the neighboring Lolco estate, where "the cultural improvements make manifest how initiative and labor can transform the zones of the cordillera thought to be of minor importance to national production into true emporiums of wealth for the future."

The report appended a detailed study of social conditions on Villucura. First and foremost, it observed that all the residents of the estate, whether they called themselves ocupantes or inquilinos, had originally been inquilinos or empleados. In total, Villucura had twenty-eight inquilinos, who exchanged their labor for rights to pasture twelve to fifteen adult animals and up to twenty young animals (for empleados) and up to ten adult and up to twenty young animals (for inquilinos) on the estate's invernadas and veranadas. The workers also received a cuadra of land they could cultivate, assigned to them by the hacienda. In addition, they had the possibility of cultivating more land on shares (*a medias*) with the estate, with the mayordomo's authorization and oversight. The workers had followed this arrangement "until recently, submitting to the conditions and rules established on the hacienda." None of the workers received a wage.

About half of these workers had arrived in Villucura in the mid-1920s, but several had worked on the estate for well over a decade, one since 1911. Most had been fired in 1929 for refusing to work and for disseminating "active propaganda." The inquilinos had supposedly been instigated by the Sindicato Agrícola Lonquimay, which convinced them they could obtain titles to the plots granted them by the estate. Others were fired for "being contrary to the established order on the hacienda and insulting the mayordomo" or simply for "not obeying orders." Nonetheless, Villucura's dismissed inquilinos had remained on the land they occupied on the estate in flagrant disobedience of their patrones' orders. As on the Bunsters' Guayalí, the estate's administrator had attempted to evict rebellious inquilinos who were working with the union but with little success; the inquilinos continued to work the land as if it were their own, claiming to be ocupantes.

Villucura's relative abandon and isolation, reflected in its owners' absence and the limited improvements they had introduced, allowed its workers to simply disobey the estate's mayordomo and claim the land as their own. Yet in March 1930 they had all signed a document in which they recognized they were "the hacienda's inquilinos" and agreed to leave the estate. At the time of the commission's investigation none had done so. Despite accusations about communist focos and subversive or anarchist propaganda, the commission found after questioning them that "these are good, sober, hardworking people." All agreed to return to work while the commission elaborated its report.

The 41,791-hectare Lolco estate stood in marked contrast to Villucura. When the estate was assessed in 1924, it held a value of $695,000 pesos. The commission found that most of this value came from improvements introduced by Olhagaray and Charó between 1920 and 1924. The firm had taken "maximum advantage of the soils at their disposal," introducing herds of livestock, planting fodder of exotic species (*pasto ovillo* or European cat grass and clover), cultivating 3,200 *quintales* (320,000 kilograms) of wheat, and building canals to irrigate their meadows. While native grasses and plants, largely *coirón*, *junquillo*, and *quila*, made for seasonal pasture, well-irrigated fields of clover and cat grass allowed for a permanent supply of fodder for the estate's herds. To help expand their pasture, Olhagaray and Charó had constructed 15 canals of "true importance," irrigating 434 hectares, an area they planned to duplicate in the near future. Lolco's French owners had brought in sawmills to produce wood from the estate's forests of *roble*, *raulí*, and *coigüe* with which they had built houses, warehouses, and fences. Like Villucura, Lolco had a number of internal roads, and roads connecting the estate to Mulchén, Santa Bárbara, and Curacautín, which were only passable on horseback. Olhagaray and Charó had also built an impressive forty-kilometer road connecting the estate to the public road between Curacautín and Lonquimay, making it possible to reach the owners' houses by automobile. In addition, they had built numerous bridges over canals, estuaries, and ravines. The estate had 410 cuadras of fences, including 115 cuadras of wire fences.

Lolco's relative modernity was marked by the construction of a 1,500-meter-long canal that drove a hydroelectric turbine. The turbine powered a sawmill and provided electricity to the estate's big houses as well as to warehouses and stables where livestock found refuge during the hard winter months. The company had built numerous buildings, including a large house for the administration, a barracks for carabineros, a school for 70–80 children, and 8 houses for inquilinos. The commission praised the new workers' housing as hygienic and comfortable, in distinct contrast with the old huts (*rucas*) for inquilinos on the other fundos, which were made of logs and "where the inquilinos live in a state of absolute abandonment." The firm had also planted orchards of fruit trees and was experimenting with foresting with other species. At the time of the commission's report, the estate had 2,491 cows, 191 horses, 2,337 sheep, and 292 goats and was assessed at $723,261 pesos. Over the decade Olhagaray and Charó owned Lolco, the estate had increased its workforce from 6 to 44, a sign of its growth and modernization. To the commission, Lolco was a model of what the "effort and labor of man can accomplish" and stood in marked contrast to estates owned by Chilean agriculturalists (the Puelmas) "who manage their fundos by correspondence and whose absenteeism is the cause of the failures they constantly suffer, which force them to go to the government every time a real or apparent crisis threatens their interests." Here, the commission clearly referred to labor difficulties and workers' efforts to claim estate land.

The situation on the 37,623-hectare Ránquil fundo was, perhaps, the worst in the commission's eyes. Ránquil's Spanish administrator and Lonquimay's former subdelegate, José Paz, had escaped to Argentina after facing arrest and criminal charges for engaging in the contraband livestock trade, leaving the estate abandoned. He had also fled debts he had contracted with Chile's Caja Agraria, from which he had purchased a large number of livestock. Informed of what had happened, Gastón Rambeaux, Ránquil's French renter, traveled to Chile from Argentina to meet with Rosa Puelma. He tried to get out of his contract to buy Ránquil, using as his excuse the fact that he couldn't exercise dominion over the property because of its rebellious inquilinos. Like many landowners who purchased southern estates, he had inherited a difficult social conflict with his estate's laborers. Rambeaux offered to pay an indemnification of one hundred thousand pesos to void the contract to purchase the estate, but Rosa Puelma's lawyer rejected the offer, leaving the estate's status in legal limbo and the land to its inquilinos. Rosa Puelma's dominion over her property was tenuous at best. Her former inquilinos could claim with a certain justification property rights based on material possession.

The commission noted the lack of planning and order on Ránquil, which was in "a complete state of abandonment." It described improvements that dated back to Rosa Puelma's administration, but these were meager: a small administration house in decent condition, a storehouse and kitchen in an annex, a warehouse for storing machinery in bad condition, and a stable in equally bad condition. The officials saw an abandoned orchard of apple trees and former garden as well as a number of fences that had been knocked down or burned. On the plus side, there was a good network of roads and a forty-meter bridge over the Ránquil River. The commission provided a list of thirty-nine inquilinos, including a number who would later participate in the 1934 rebellion. They now had their run of the place, working the land as if it were their own. In addition, the commission heard reports that people from neighboring estates and Lonquimay had settled on Ránquil after it had been abandoned by Paz eight months earlier.

Francisco Puelma Tupper's 28,000-hectare El Rahue estate, contiguous with Ránquil, was in comparatively better shape, though its conditions paled next to those on Lolco. Puelma Tupper, like Rosa Puelma, was an absentee owner whose main residence was in Santiago. El Rahue was not a prosperous estate. It held fewer livestock than that of some of its neighbors, only 980 cows, 127 horses, and 28 mules. Its workers alone possessed a considerable number of animals: 129 horses and mules, 183 cows, 1,333 sheep, 499 goats, and 36 pigs, suggesting that their livestock was at the heart of the estate's production. The estate had only 19 inquilinos and empleados. Improvements included some wire fences and two fields of cultivated fodder, probably of exotic species, irrigated by a 69-cuadra canal. Puelma Tupper had built 11 houses for El Rahue's inquilinos and 7 for its empleados, as well as a network of roads.

As on Villucura, a number of El Rahue's workers had stopped obeying the estate's owner and manager and, supported by the union, claimed the estate land as their own under the Southern Property Law. One inquilino had worked on El Rahue since 1918, but in 1928 "had refused to fulfill his obligations." Manuel Astroza, who would become president of the Sindicato Agrícola Lonquimay, was an inquilino on El Rahue and had also stopped working for Puelma Tupper. Similarly, Manuel Ovalle, an inquilino since 1911, stopped obeying orders in 1929; Cipriano Jara, hired as an inquilino in 1927, stopped working in 1930; Ramón Parra, hired as an inquilino in 1928, halted his labor the following year; and Galindo Quilodrán, also an inquilino and a recent arrival in 1925, was fired in 1928 "for not fulfilling his obligations." Like the other recalcitrant inquilinos, Quilodrán refused to leave the estate, remaining with his livestock on land he had been granted as part of his labor contract.

Sara Navarro Puelma had rented the 19,739-hectare Chilpaco estate to José Miguel Gutiérrez and then to José Paz. Chilpaco too was in a relatively undeveloped state. Gutiérrez had left it in the hands of an administrator, and Paz had abandoned his position, leaving the estate, like Ránquil, without management. Chilpaco had only 12 inquilinos and empleados, among them notably Ismael Cartes, who had arrived three years before. Cartes would later become one of the leaders of the 1934 rebellion. The estate possessed 1,500 sheep, 400 cows, and 6 horses. In general, the committee reported, all of its buildings were in bad condition. As on Villucura, the estate's inquilinos lived in huts made of logs. The commissioners were left with the impression that Chilpaco "had been abandoned for a long time."

The panel's descriptions of the Puelma estates made it clear that the family had invested little in developing the property inherited from Francisco Puelma Castillo. The neglect of the estates stood as evidence in favor of the Sindicato Agrícola Lonquimay's petitions that they be expropriated and settled with their inquilinos and ocupantes. Equally damning to the Puelmas' case for their property rights were the dismal social conditions on the estates. Inquilinos lived in a state of abandonment, and labor relations had deteriorated to the point that workers refused to follow the landowners' orders or respect their property rights. On all four estates inquilinos worked the land as if it were their own. While the commission's finding that all the pobladores on the estates were inquilinos appeared prejudicial to the Sindicato Agrícola Lonquimay's cause, its description of the lamentable state of the properties' management and social conditions strengthened the case that they could be expropriated and settled with their workers.

The commission had also been charged with surveying a location for a new town and, after studying the region and listening to the recommendations of the Sindicato Agrícola Lonquimay, it decided that the Nitrito Valley would be the ideal place. Nitrito lay at 780 meters above sea level with fertile land watered by the Nitrito estuary. Sheltered by tall chains of hills, Nitrito's climate was relatively benign and snowfalls short during the winter. And, there had been a previous settlement there, a town and fort established in 1882 by the military engineer Martín Drouilly. When the commissioners traveled to Nitrito they were accompanied by members of the Sindicato Agrícola Lonquimay and received by 350 "pobladores" of the region's estates who petitioned to have the new town located in the valley. The commission ordered that a survey of Nitrito be performed to lay out the blueprint for the town.

The commission report resulted in a decree repealing that of 1929 that had recognized the Puelma family's titles to the five estates composing San Ignacio de Pemehue.[11] However, despite the commission's finding that almost the entirety of the estates' land lay outside the borders of the original deeds, the decree recognized as valid the deeds held by Francisco Puelma Tupper, Rosa Puelma Tupper, Juan Antonio Orrego, Sara Navarro Puelma, and the Sociedad Olhagaray y Charó, to a total of 139,362 hectares. In an unprecedented victory for rural laborers, however, the decree expropriated 30,000 hectares of land "to resolve the problem of land in Alto Bío Bío and to leave a public reserve to later settle the pobladores." Following this decree, the land measurement office determined that the 30,000 would be carved out of the Ránquil estate where a new colony would be established.[12]

The Puelma family did not appeal this decree to the Ministry of Lands and Colonization within the six months established by law, probably because Ránquil had become something of a headache, and they were satisfied with receiving an indemnification from the government for an estate they had been unable to sell. Nor did the Puelmas make any other kind of administrative or legal appeal to block the decree.[13] Only one month later the government issued a second decree, expropriating 4,000 hectares of the Bunsters' Guayalí fundo, in response to petitions from the Sindicato Agrícola Lonquimay. The decree recognized the validity of the Bunsters' title to Guayalí, including the 22,860 hectares that fell under the Southern Property Law (the rest of the 60,000-hectare property it found were further north and not affected by the law). But it expropriated 4,000 of these hectares "to provide a solution to the land problem in the region, settling the pobladores whom the government views as having rights." As in the case of the Ránquil estate, the lands measurement office would determine the exact location of the 4,000 hectares, but the pobladores had already settled in the Nitrito Valley and demanded the land they occupied from the government.[14]

While the commission investigating San Ignacio de Pemehue's borders had not dealt with Guayalí or Ralco, the organization of a union on Guayalí and persistent conflicts between the estate's laborers and the Bunsters drove the government to expropriate the four thousand hectares. The government decree was also a response to a petition from Luis Martín Bunster's widow, Celmira Gómez Bunster, who had asked that the state recognize Guayalí's borders and title following the commission's finding that none of the Puelma estates had legitimate boundaries. Apparently alarmed by the roiling social conflict on Guayalí, the commission's report, and the decree expropriating most of Ránquil, Gómez Bunster had sought to have the government recognize her property rights.

The land measurement office and land inspectorate found that Guayalí's titles, like the Puelma titles, had problems. However, as in the case of the Puelma estates, expropriation of the entire estate would have been a radical move. The government sought a compromise that would leave most of Guayalí's land in the Bunsters' hands. It noted that the family of Luis Martín Bunster had exploited Guayalí productively and introduced improvements on the twenty-two thousand hectares. The family had maintained its possession of the property for more than ten years, and "the policy of the current government is to reward labor and individual effort with the goal of increasing public and private wealth, and to place on the land the elements that cultivate it, and who should be considered the most apt and with greatest rights, to colonize the state's land." Thus despite the deficiencies of Guayalí's title, the decree recognized the legitimacy of the Bunsters' property rights, with the exception of the four thousand hectares on which it would settle the pobladores—who were, in fact, Guayalí's inquilinos—as colonos.[15]

The Puelma and Bunster estates were not the only properties in which the Ibáñez government intervened. In 1930 the southern property ministry reviewed the Pellahuén fundo's titles and found that a long history of fraud had accompanied the estate's original sales and expansion over the years. In July of that year it issued a decree declaring the Banco Garantizador de Valor's titles to 42,600 hectares of the estate invalid.[16] As in the case of San Ignacio, the state had tried to recuperate much of Pellahuén, which it defined as public land, since the late 1890s in a variety of lawsuits. And as in the case of the Puelma estates, Pellahuén was occupied by a large population of campesinos who had been defined over the years as the estate's laborers and arrendatarios. Government surveyors began settling Pellahuén's ocupantes as colonos with titles to their small plots.

The Ibáñez government had found that both the Puelma and Bunster families' titles to their many thousands of hectares were illegitimate and could be restored to the state. But in both cases the government dictated the expropriation of mere fractions of their properties to resolve conflicts with ocupantes and inquilinos. The expropriations were small measures, but, as in the case of the Pellahuén estate, they represented first steps toward a more full-blown agrarian reform by meeting the demands of inquilinos and ocupantes to be settled on estate land as colonos and by reaffirming the state's dominion over southern property.

During the spring of 1930 the union worked with the government to develop a plan for the colonization of Ránquil and the Nitrito Valley. In November the Sindicato Agrícola Lonquimay sent a committee to Santiago to meet with the development minister, this time armed with a carefully elaborated proposal for how to implement the decree of 31 July 1930. The union president, Manuel Astroza Dávila, Juan Segundo Leiva Tapia, and a new member of the union leadership, José Galindo Quilodrán Ibáñez, met with the minister to discuss the "definitive solution to the land problem in Alto Bío Bío." The minister welcomed them warmly and heard their petition, which included a remeasurement of San Ignacio de Pemehue and the application of the Southern Property Law to the entire hacienda. Fueled by their success in gaining most of Ránquil, the union now set its sights on all five of San Ignacio's fundos. The minister asked for all the antecedents and then cited them at a meeting with Ernesto Maldonado the next afternoon. He informed the union leaders that he would meet with President Ibáñez to discuss the subject.

In the second meeting the next day the minister, accompanied by Maldonado, spoke to the union leaders directly, and the news was not what they had hoped for. The government intended to modify the decree of 31 July for reasons of "moral and political order," and begged them not to insist and to be content with the 4,000 hectares in Nitrito and Llanquén and 7,625 hectares more that the state would buy them in Ránquil, together with the 30,000 hectares belonging to the new colony. But the government was disposed to back the union in every initiative it took to expropriate through the Caja de Colonización the bordering land that they deemed necessary to increase the size of the new colony. In total, the land granted to the new Alto Bío Bío colony would include 41,625 hectares in Ránquil, Nitrito, and Llanquén.[17]

In a subsequent meeting on 26 September, 1930, the union leaders met with Maldonado to discuss the subject of invernadas and veranadas. The lands and colonization director proposed that the high-altitude veranadas on the new colony be shared as a commons "in the Swiss or Norse style" and thus remain public property. The union leaders disagreed, maintaining that not all the new colonos would have the same number of animals and there would be no incentive to introduce improvements in the summer pasture. The resistance reflected a tension between government officials' interest in imposing state management of national resources like forests and high-altitude meadows, as well as collective forms of landownership on colonies, and campesinos' desires for individual parcels. It also says something about the ideology of the union and its campesino members in 1930. Rather than seek a restoration of commonly held land or community control over resources like land, forests, meadows, and water as commons, they worked to establish individual ownership of both invernadas and veranadas with smallholders organized in cooperatives. The campesinos aspired to individual, not collective or communal, landownership, with titles received from the state as colonos.

In the end Maldonado conceded that the union could draw up a plan for parceling and distributing the land on the new colony, a plan that the Minister of Southern Property would study and then introduce as a special law in congress. The union itself would receive three parcels in Nitrito, Troyo, and Colonia Ránquil where it would have schools and services for its members. Finally, Maldonado agreed that it would be up to the union to decide who had rights to be settled as colonos and to oversee the distribution of individual parcels. The government would establish free transit on the network of roads in the region that were necessary for the colony's economic viability, connect Ránquil and Nitrito to the national postal and telegraph network, and establish a town or pueblo in Nitrito. Maldonado repeated that the Ibáñez government would halt all evictions from the estates until the new colony was organized and prevent any changes in labor conditions that "constituted harassment." Until the definitive expropriation and redistribution of land, the future colonos were, in the eyes of the government, still inquilinos.[18] But the government would prevent landowners' retaliation and efforts to evict inquilinos and ocupantes from the estates.

In December 1930 union leaders traveled to Santiago once again to meet with Maldonado and the Minister of Southern Property. As before, the meetings went well. Their plan for the new colony was approved, and

Maldonado gave the union leaders an official blueprint of the now-parceled Ránquil colony to take back to Lonquimay. In addition, two surveyors were appointed to travel to Alto Bío Bío to oversee the process of installing the new colonos, 110 families drawn from the union membership, all of whom had been pobladores on the "old fundo San Ignacio de Pemehue."[19]

In a meeting with the southern property minister, the union leaders received a provisional commitment from the government to expropriate the El Rahue, Guayalí, and Chilpaco estates to build new colonies. The Caja de Colonización Agrícola would negotiate a price for the properties with their owners. The minister suggested that they meet with the director of the bank to study the estates' acquisition. The director instructed them in the legal procedures they needed to go through to have the bank acquire the estates and redistribute the land to colonos. In a very promising vein, the bank director told the union leaders they should prepare a list of future colonos who would acquire parcels. He would appoint a surveyor to work with the union on drawing up plans for subdividing the estates.[20]

The Sindicato Agrícola Lonquimay attempted to translate its success in acquiring estate land on which to settle its members into supporting the local Pehuenche communities in their struggles with the Bunster family. As noted earlier, by 1930 the union had organized councils in Ralco, Guayalí, Queco, and Lolco, all estates with a number of Pehuenche laborers and all estates with land claimed by the region's Pehuenche communities. Most important, one of the Ralco community's lonkos, Ignacio Maripi, built an alliance with the union, a development that represented a critical resource in Ralco's long-standing struggles to gain a Título de Merced and recognition of the community's land rights on the Ralco, Guayalí, and Lolco estates. In late 1930 Maripi and Leiva Tapia met with the Minister of Southern Property in Santiago to request a title to land Ralco had occupied "from time immemorial." The minister asked for more background information and promised that upon receiving it his office would respond to their petition.[21]

By the early 1930s members of the Ralco community along with Chilean ocupantes, numbering roughly 550 together, had occupied an invernada of 11,493 hectares, which they claimed was public land, on the Bunsters' Ralco estate.[22] Like many of the conflicts between large landowners and peasants on the frontier during the 1920s and 1930s, Ralco's confrontation with the Bunsters included "Chilean" ocupantes as well. In fact, as government censuses reflected, Chilean and Mapuche campesinos both occupied land on the Ralco estate and engaged in bitter conflicts with the Bunster family. Thus Ralco's lonkos petitioned the state to settle the community with a Título de Merced but also defended the rights of the neighboring "poor Chileans" who were also squatting on estate land and claimed the status of colonos. A few years after the Ránquil rebellion, the Ralco community petitioned the Ministry of Lands and Colonization for support in their continuing conflict with the Bunster family: "We declare that we occupy the lands in Ralco from time immemorial, since our ancestors were the first to populate [the region]. ... And now we ask that the supreme government take interest in us, send us a surveyor to determine the borders of our reducción, respecting the rights that the poor Chileans may have who occupy the place on public lands that neighbors our possession, excepting the representatives of the Bunster Gómez family who have always abused us and now are trying to take our land from us."[23] Members of the Ralco community worked on neighboring estates, probably in the company of "poor Chileans." Like many of these Chilean laborers, they also resided in the borderlands between estate and public land and viewed estate owners' property rights as illegitimate.

In addition, landless rural laborers at times went to work on shares with Mapuche communities during harvest season. Emelina Sagredo remembered that she had "known Mapuches from the day I was born" because her mother "worked with a reducción de indios harvesting wheat" on shares as a mediero.[24] The Sagredo family inhabited a world in which ties of labor and geography crossed over the barriers of ethnicity separating the Chilean and indigenous rural poor. Nonetheless, Pehuenche communities like Ralco drew on a different understanding of their property rights, one derived from the existing indigenous law rather than the national colonization laws invoked by rural laborers like the Sagredos. Pehuenche communities claimed land on the basis of their history of occupation from time immemorial. They cited indigenous law, as Ralco had done over the years in its litigation with the Bunster family.

A cornerstone of Ibáñez's reforms in southern Chile was a 1927 law directed at breaking up and privatizing land held communally by Mapuche communities granted Títulos de Merced since the late nineteenth century. The law posed a threat to Mapuche communities' precarious control of lands threatened by the encroachment of large estates and, in Alto Bío Bío, logging and ranching interests. However, for not a few communities the law on the division of indigenous communities represented an opportunity. These communities had been invented as fictions, colonial-style reducciones that from the very beginning suffered from land scarcity. Most communities were granted land insufficient to support their members, and most almost immediately confronted threats to their land rights from neighboring estates. The new law, while certainly an effort to push Mapuches and their land into the market, gave some communities a tool for acquiring public land and expanding their members' individual holdings. The law was also a legal means of protecting land held through the Título de Merced in legally recognized individual property titles, a new legal instrument to defend Mapuche land from being stolen.[25] Unlike many Mapuche communities, Ralco had never been granted a Título de Merced. Its status as a community thus had no legal standing. The land reforms introduced by the Ibáñez regime did not pose a threat to Ralco's dominion over communally held land. Moreover, Ignacio Maripi viewed an alliance with Leiva Tapia and the Sindicato Agrícola Lonquimay as a means for the community to finally gain legal title to land occupied by Ralco for generations.

In January 1931 the Sindicato Agrícola Lonquimay's "numerous councils" from El Rahue, Ránquil, Lolco, Guayalí, Ralco, and Queco gathered in a general assembly to hear Leiva Tapia's report on the union leaders' meetings in Santiago over the previous months. They also came together to inaugurate the Ránquil colony in Troyo, initiating the measurement of parcels by the commission of surveyors presided over by Joaquín Oyarzún. Five hundred people attended the meeting. The union's councils had expanded to include estates and land outside the San Ignacio de Pemehue hacienda. Ralco and Queuco were the names both of estates and Pehuenche communities. The union now included councils organized among the local Pehuenche population as well as among the region's Chilean rural laborers, targeting three new estates for colonization: Ralco, Queuco, and Guayalí.[26]

The union assembly, as was customary, flew the Chilean flag at the head of each "disciplined formation" of its councils, including women and children, and concluded with expressions of patriotism and thanks to Ibáñez, "the most correct and accomplished gentleman, the man who feels in his own flesh the misery of the poor," whom they viewed as "the most patriotic Chilean who has sat in the seat of the presidency." "In a word," the union leaders concluded, directing themselves directly to Ibáñez, "the people would give their lives for your Excellency's health and well-being."[27]

The success of the union's alliance with Ibáñez was consolidated five months later when the government issued a decree-law expropriating the entirety of the Bunsters' Guayalí estate, leaving aside four thousand hectares for the founding of a town (Decreto con Fuerza de Ley No 258, 20 May 1931). The decree authorized the president to expropriate Guayalí in the public interest (*utilidad pública*). According to the Bunster family's representatives, the government had been pressured by "a number of individuals, ex-inquilinos evicted from the fundo because they were subversives, led by Juan Leiva Tapia." These rebellious inquilinos had "once again coerced the government, ... which dictated the decree ... that authorized the expropriation of the entire fundo." According to the Bunster family, Leiva Tapia, used this new decree to direct the settlement of the expropriated Guayalí with aspiring colonos, including the estate's former inquilinos. The ocupantes then took control of the Bunsters' land, "breaking down fences, appropriating livestock, and, in a word, acting like owners and lords [*señores*]." This revolt culminated a process that had begun in 1929 when a number of Bunster's inquilinos had refused to follow their patrón's orders, instead working estate land as if it were their own. In early 1932 the Bunster family's representative noted that "the depredations committed [by the former inquilinos] and the paralyzing of work on the fundo for two years meant the loss of many thousands of pesos to the Bunster family."[28]

Following the decree giving the president the power to expropriate Guayalí, the Bunster family continued to pepper the government with complaints about its former inquilinos' occupation of the estate. In May 1931 carabineros, accompanied by a surveyor, traveled to Guayalí to investigate the Bunsters' claims that "twenty families from Queco and other locations had taken possession of Guayalí." They found that six agricultural workers (*trabajadores*), "induced by the Secretary General of Alto Bío Bío's Sindicato Agrícola Lonquimay, don Juan Leiva Tapia," had settled on the estate without the Bunsters' authorization.[29] Among the six was Albino Acuña, a former inquilino who had been an *antigua vivente* (longtime resident) on the estate and who had begun planting land in Nitrito on his own. Two workers from the neighboring Lolco estate, Erasmo Baeza and Manuel Sandoval, had left Lolco and settled on Guayalí with their livestock. Both had begun to plant crops on share with established "antiguos ocupantes" without the administration's authorization. Another one of the men had come from Queco, settled in Nitrito with his sheep and goats, and begun planting crops on shares with Simón

Sagredo and Carlos Sánchez. Similarly, Víctor Rojas had come from Villucura to settle on land on Guayalí. Finally, Juan Rosa Cofré was brought to Guayalí by Leiva Tapia, he said, from the Ralco estate and had settled on a plot that he considered his because of his rights as a union member (*sindicalista*). The carabineros stationed on Guayalí had not acted to prevent the land occupations because they had been placed there, they reported, only to protect the estate's big houses.[30]

These police reports suggest a number of developments in social relations on the region's estates. First, empowered by the Ibáñez government's legislation and political support, the Sindicato Agrícola Lonquimay had expanded its activities to include a number of estates outside the Puelmas' original five properties where it had established councils. Second, the union had received support in Santiago for the expropriation of Guayalí. As a result, both inquilinos who had lived and labored on the estate for a number of years and ocupantes, often laborers on neighboring estates like Villucura, Lolco, and Ralco, had recently settled on small plots within the estate's borders and worked the land as if it were their own. They understood that membership in the union made them eligible to receive parcels of land on estates targeted by the government for expropriation. That is to say, they believed that as sindicalistas who had paid union dues they had the right to be settled as colonos on public land.

The Sindicato Agrícola Lonquimay consolidated its influence in Alto Bío Bío in July 1931, when it helped establish a regional labor organization, the Comité Social Obrero de Curacautín. The organization reflected the sindicato's continued identification as a workers' organization, a union whose members were obreros as well as campesinos. The Comité Social Obrero included Curacautín's Manuel Rodríguez Sharpshooting Club, Agricultural and Industrial Cooperative, and the local branch of the Democratic Party, all institutions that would have had urban middle- as well as working-class members. The comité's vice president, Manuel Astroza, and its secretary general, Leiva Tapia, were, respectively, president and secretary general of the Sindicato Agrícola Lonquimay. In mid-1931 the union continued to count on its alliance with the Democratic Party and to work to represent a multiclass coalition drawn from both the region's towns and countryside.[31]

In June 1931, as Chile reeled from the global economic crisis that had thrown tens of thousands of miners and urban workers into unemployment, some housed in temporary hostels in Santiago while others traveled the country in search of work, the union celebrated its new colony in Ránquil, its name now changed from Santa Graciela to 23 de Enero. To the union's leaders their new colony constituted a possible solution to the starvation that beat at so many Chilean doors. Surveyors had begun parceling the colony's thirty-seven thousand hectares the previous summer and settling the campesino residents (*vecinos*). Many of the new colonos had already planted crops, and now, as winter approached, the union reported that they had cultivated four hundred cuadras, which, when harvested, would produce twelve thousand quintales of wheat. The 23 de Enero colony would consume most of the fruits of its labor but would have a surplus of seventy-five hundred quintales, which it could sell. All the colony needed, the union leaders argued, was the "smallholder with his pair of oxen, plow, tools, seeds, strong arms, and the will to make the earth produce." And if there was no money to purchase their wheat, they would simply exchange their harvests for other goods, "product for product." The colony was a model for an agrarian reform that could reignite agricultural production and bring prosperity to the Chilean countryside, eliminating starvation and unemployment.[32]

CHAPTER SIX

The Fall of Ibáñez and Political Radicalization in Southern Chile

IN APRIL 1931, TWO months before public protests and a military coup would remove him from power, Carlos Ibáñez dictated an order instructing carabineros to arrest "individuals who attempt to subvert the public order." As he confronted Chile's deepening economic crisis and increasingly militant movement of ocupantes and inquilinos to appropriate estate land in southern Chile, Ibáñez turned from his corporatist positions on rural social relations to the repressive techniques of rule that had established political order during his dictatorship. Los Ángeles's *El Siglo* reported that the president's order came in response "to a number of cases that have been produced recently in different towns, in which individuals and groups have invaded fundos violently, taking control of their land." According to Ibáñez, any threat to private property would be dealt with by carabineros. "Disruptive elements" who occupied land on fundos would be handed over to the courts.[1]

The global economic crisis triggered by the 1929 crash of the stock market in the United States had a devastating effect on the Chilean economy. The northern nitrate industry collapsed, leaving Chile without a source of foreign earnings and unable to service its external debt. As sources of revenue and credit dried up, the government slashed public spending, including the wages of public employees and military salaries. After the First World War the nitrate export economy had experienced a steady decline in the face of growing European production of synthetic nitrates. The Great Depression dealt a death blow to the industry that had driven the Chilean economy since the 1870s. Armies of unemployed workers and miners migrated from the north to central and southern cities looking for work, including to the city of Temuco, many housed in state-run hostels (*albergues*).² By 1931 Chile had become the country in the Americas most deeply impacted by the global recession. Levels of imports and exports dropped to historic lows, the financial sector contracted as United States banks shut off the spigot of credit, and unemployment and wage cuts hit the urban working- and middle-classes hard. In July 1931 associations of university students, white-collar workers, and professionals engaged in a strike to demand an end to dictatorship. Facing opposition from across the political spectrum, Ibáñez resigned and went into exile in Argentina.³

Ibáñez's interior minister, Juan Esteban Montero of the Radical Party, assumed the powers of the presidency and called for elections. In September he stepped down to campaign for the upcoming elections, leaving the presidency in the hands of his interior minister and fellow Radical, Manuel Trucco. As Montero prepared to hand over power to Trucco, a revolt at naval bases in Coquimbo and Talcahuano erupted. The naval mutiny or rebellion, as it was referred to, began as a response to pay cuts in the armed forces but quickly expanded to include radical demands, including agrarian reform, a public works project for the unemployed, protection for domestic industries, and a "social revolution."⁴ Neither the Comintern nor the Communist Party participated in organizing the naval rebellion, but both the Communist Party and the FOCH gave their support to the movement, organizing solidarity strikes in Concepción, Santiago, and Valparaíso and sending FOCH delegations to support the mutineers. In Concepción, unemployed workers joined the insurrection. As the radicalized movement expanded and confronted government repression, its leaders declared their solidarity with both the FOCH and the Communist Party.⁵

The naval rebellion came to play a role in both the anticommunist and Communist Party imaginaries. The traditional political parties described the rebellion incorrectly as a mutiny fomented by the Communist Party, which had allegedly infiltrated squadrons in Coquimbo and Talcahuano. For its part, the Communist Party exaggerated its role in organizing the uprising. Despite its failure to follow through on its project of assuming the direction of the rebellion, party leaders viewed the *marineros'* (sailors') movement as a sign of the potential in Chile for an imminent revolutionary insurrection.[6] More generally, the naval rebellion reflected the crisis of the Chilean state and political order brought on by the fall of the Ibáñez dictatorship and the Great Depression as well as by the emergence of radical new possibilities for revolutionary change. After 1931 the Communist Party reemerged in public life following years of repression under Ibáñez and a new Trotskyist leftist party, the Communist Left (Izquierda Comunista), grouped together former anarchists and communists.

During these months of political turmoil the Sindicato Agrícola Lonquimay maintained its support for the institutional stability and reform of southern property relations represented first by Ibáñez and then by Montero. In October Juan Segundo Leiva Tapia, representing the sindicato, endorsed Montero's presidential candidacy in an open letter published in *El Mercurio*. That the nation's most important newspaper, which enjoyed deep ties to Chile's landed and financial oligarchy, published the union's letter indicates the prominence the sindicato had attained at the national level. Leiva Tapia argued that the union had to place its "regional and institutional interests" before its "merely theoretical ideals." The union had already made real two planks of its program: its "nascent colony in Alto Bío Bío" and its "agricultural labor organization." To build on these successes it required "peace, tranquility, and justice from wherever it comes." Leiva Tapia viewed Montero as representing continuity with the Ibáñez regime, despite whatever theoretical, that is, ideological, objections he and the union leadership might have to his candidacy. In a letter to the union's members published in *El Diario Austral*, Leiva Tapia endorsed Montero, whom he had known when he was his professor at the University of Chile law school and who was, he said, "the best friend of his youth." He noted that many leftists would view him as "a traitor, coward, and sellout" for endorsing the Radical and not pushing the union members to launch themselves into "the revolutionary storm."[7]

Montero drew on the support of the oligarchic Liberal and Conservative parties as well as his own Radical Party, while his major opponent in the elections, Arturo Alessandri, represented the Democratic Party as well as dissident sectors of the Liberal and Radical parties. Given the role of Democrats in organizing and leading the Sindicato Agrícola Lonquimay, the union's support of Montero would have required making the difficult decision of abandoning its former political ally in favor of the continuity offered by Montero's candidacy.[8] In 1931 Leiva Tapia identified himself as a leftist but did not align with the Communist Party or support the party's candidate in the 1931 elections, Elías Lafertte. Rather than pursue his "theoretical ideals," he hewed to a pragmatic strategy of working with the social reformist governments in power to win estate land for the union and its members.

In November 1931 Montero defeated Alessandri. Once in office, he sought to restore political stability and basic political freedoms. He also began his brief time in government with a commitment to economic orthodoxy. However, the economic crisis ruled out a return to liberal economic policies designed to stimulate growth via mining exports and foreign credit and investment. During his months in power Montero returned increasingly to Ibáñez's nationalist and corporatist policies, including protective tariffs and price controls on basic goods.[9] In southern Chile, Montero's government maintained the status quo, without following through on the Ibáñez government's commitment to expand colonization and extend labor laws into the countryside.

Despite the Sindicato Agrícola Lonquimay's backing of Montero, the union's efforts to colonize the Puelma estates were largely thwarted. Ránquil's recently settled colonos continued to occupy their plots, but they still awaited legal titles while the government negotiated the amount Rosa Puelma would be indemnified for the expropriation of her property. The redistribution of land in the Nitrito Valley to Guayalí's ocupantes-inquilinos was also stalled, as were the plans to build the 23 de Enero municipality. And although the leaders of the sindicato had received the go-ahead from Ibáñez's ministers to develop plans to colonize the other Puelma properties, the now-bankrupt government showed little inclination to purchase the estates and distribute their land to the campesino ocupantes.

On 16 December 1931 the governor of Victoria met with Froilán Rivera, now the Sindicato Agrícola Lonquimay's *consejero* (adviser), as well as Leiva Tapia, its general secretary, and Pedro Rivera, the treasurer. The union leaders told the governor that a government commission from the "southern property office" (Ernesto Maldonado's commission) had settled Ránquil's 37,000 hectares with 130 colono families. An additional 40 families had occupied land on Ránquil without government permission, probably induced by the government's expropriation of the estate. In the Nitrito Valley 80 families continued to occupy 4,000 hectares lying on the Bunsters' Guayalí estate. The union, which now had over 436 members, had been registered by the welfare secretary in 1931 and the provincial labor inspectorate in Temuco in 1929. Union members paid an initial fee of $5 pesos and annual dues of $24 pesos, though these had been recently reduced to $12 pesos. The president of the union was Manuel Astroza Dávila.

The union leaders intended their report to the governor to demonstrate that they had followed the requisite legal procedures in registering their organization with the labor authorities. They presented the Sindicato Agrícola Lonquimay as a legally recognized union that had helped establish a colony in Alto Bío Bío. Rather than a source of subversion, it had been an instrument of social order and progress. That the former inquilinos had settled on estate land with their families, as heads of household, further signified their social respectability and their eligibility to receive titles to their plots as colonos under the prevailing colonization laws. However, the governor's report on the meeting revealed both the changing political circumstances and local officials' persistent antagonism to the union. The governor informed the lands and colonization minister that the union leaders had engaged in "destructive acts." They had "incited the inquilinaje on the estates of the cordillera to disobey their patrones under the pretext that they have usurped public lands." Union leaders, he reported, had led inquilinos to believe that "since they live on this land they will have their rights recognized as ocupantes of public lands and will have the option for free titles." "Thus incited," according to the governor, "the inquilinaje has begun to reject the patrones' rights, refusing to obey them, which has brought the complete disorganization of agricultural labor in an extensive area."[10]

Victoria's governor attached a 26 December 1931 report on the Sindicato Agrícola Lonquimay by Lonquimay's labor inspector. According to the labor inspector, the union members were only the instruments of Juan Segundo Leiva Tapia, who, through extortion and violence, had coerced them to join and pay union dues. Leiva Tapia ruled "in this distant cordillera" because he had "a year or two of law school, has legal knowledge, and a facility for making speeches." The inspector marshalled evidence from testimony he had taken from the region's workers. Some of these workers were, in actuality, the administrator and foreman on the Bunsters' Guayalí estate, Víctor Vergara and Froilán Labrín Díaz, who testified that Leiva Tapia and Simón Sagredo, "the president of the Sindicato de Guayalí [that is, the Sindicato Agrícola Lonquimay's council on Guayalí]," had attempted to coerce them with threats of physical violence into joining the union and paying large fees in exchange for the promise of a piece of land when the estate was expropriated. Vergara complained to the labor inspector that because he had refused to join the union "he has been continually harassed and ... the people [inquilinos] do not obey him and mock him and his orders are never followed in any way."[11]

Meanwhile, Lonquimay's subdelegate denounced the union leaders as "fanatical and communist" ("gente muy exaltada y comunista") in his report. He included testimony from a longtime resident of the region who called the union leaders "bad elements, communists." They had incited "the people, who were until today peaceful and hardworking" and who were now sublevados. The fundos' workers, he said, "don't obey anybody and live in an independent Chile, under nobody's authority."[12] Such descriptions represented two consistent themes in the local authorities' and landowners' characterization of southern Chile's social unrest. First, outside agitators, often described as communists, had roiled up otherwise peaceful and hardworking laborers, inciting them to disobey their patrones and occupy privately held estate land as if it belonged to them. And second, these agitators, some of whom led unions and colonization cooperatives, were swindlers who extorted money from credulous inquilinos and ocupantes by inducing them to pay them money in the form of quotas, which would then purportedly be used to purchase plots on either public or private property.

Without Ibáñez in power the Sindicato Agrícola Lonquimay could expect little support from the new regime in Santiago. However, Montero's government lasted only six months. On 4 June 1932 Marmaduke Grove, one of the officers who, with Ibáñez, had intervened to force congress to pass Alessandri's social reforms in 1924, led a military coup against Montero. Grove had been deported to Argentina in 1929 and then been sent into internal exile in 1931 for his efforts to organize opposition to the Ibáñez dictatorship. Now he established a Socialist Republic, governed by a junta composed of General Arturo Puga, Eugenio Matte, like Grove a former opponent of Ibáñez who had been sent into internal exile during the dictatorship, and Carlos Dávila, a journalist and Ibáñez's former ambassador to the United States. With Grove as the de facto head of the junta, the government issued decrees designed to build a socialist economy and courted support from both the Communist Party and Trotskyist socialist groups. Grove decreed, among other things, the collectivization of agriculture, expanded price controls, and the nationalization of industries, including foreign-owned mines.[13]

The Socialist Republic lasted twelve days. Dávila engineered a new coup against the socialist junta, sending Marmaduke Grove once more into internal exile. Dávila incorporated fellow civilian supporters of Ibáñez into his government and maintained Ibáñez-era corporatist policies designed to expand state intervention in the economy and society. But now, as during the twelve-day Socialist Republic, the government's commitment to socialism was backed by key sectors of the military. Dávila imagined a state-directed transition to a socialist economy without any mobilization from below. As Paul Drake notes, to Dávila "socialism" meant "state capitalism," an eschewal of the liberal principles which had guided economic policy until the Great Depression and an embrace of state intervention to promote capitalist economic development.[14] Following in Ibáñez's footsteps, Dávila's government banned the Communist Party once again and cracked down on leftist unions. In addition, as the head of a government whose major backing came from the military, Dávila implemented through a decree-law (no. 50) an Internal Security of the State Law, which considered "as an enemy of the Republic" any persons "who propagate or foment by word of mouth or in writing doctrines that advocate the destruction of the social order or the political order of the State through violent means." The law also made it a crime to "promote, instigate, or sustain strikes that violate existing legal provisions."[15] Dávila asserted that "Socialism is not disorder but control. ... [It] does not mobilize the masses in order to launch them into ruinous violence but seeks to guide them and to assure them justice and well-being."[16]

As the economic crisis deepened and social unrest spread during 1932, Dávila relied increasingly on the military for political support and the internal security decree-law to establish order. After he'd been in power for one hundred days, however, the armed forces removed him and named General Bartolomé Blanche as provisional president. In the face of civilian and regional military protests and revolts, Blanche resigned and elections were held in October, the first step toward the restoration of civilian rule. Arturo Alessandri, who had run unsuccessfully against Montero in 1931, defeated a crowded group of rivals that included, once again, the Communist Party's Elías Lafertte as well as Marmaduke Grove. Alessandri conducted his 1932 campaign without the populist rhetoric that had characterized his political campaigns in the 1910s and 1920s. He courted support from the Conservative and Liberal parties by emphasizing that restoration of civilian government would lead to neither social disorder nor the eruption of the leftist parties into the political arena. Instead, he insisted that Chile needed "a strong government" and that if he were elected "there will be order and discipline in all social hierarchies, whatever the costs and regardless of whoever is hurt."[17] During Alessandri's first months in power, the government cracked down on the Communist Party–led teachers' federation and arrested eighty members of the Communist Party, including Deputy José Vega Díaz, with the support of the traditional parties in congress. The Alessandri regime would represent not rupture but continuity with traditions of authoritarian politics in Chile, including during the Ibáñez government; now, however, Alessandri governed with the support of the Radical, Conservative, and Liberal parties and the guise of a multiparty democracy.[18]

The political turmoil in Santiago between August 1931 and October 1932, including military coups, provisional presidents, and the Socialist Republic, exacerbated conflicts on the ground in southern Chile, affording rural laborers an opportunity to occupy and claim land. Rural laborers were emboldened by both Ibáñez-era laws and the political opening created by the fall of Ibáñez's authoritarian regime. Socialist and revolutionary options, driven underground by Ibáñez, reemerged and offered ocupantes and inquilinos glimpses of new political possibilities. Meanwhile, Chilean governments increasingly solved conflicts over land and labor by sending in the carabineros. Campesinos frequently met violence with violence. The south's reputation as Chile's wild west appeared to be borne out in a wave of fierce clashes between carabineros and rural laborers. Many of these conflicts had brewed for decades but now took on a more urgent and radical cast.

In March 1932, for example, two hundred people met in a forest belonging to Luis Silva Ricci, the owner of the Nueva Italia colonization concession. The meeting was organized by local Democratic Party leaders from Las Sauces, Pellahuén, and Lumaco who, as a police report recorded, spoke about "the government's actions, unemployment, poverty, giving away the country's wealth to foreigners, and the right to property." One of the prominent local Democrats "incited those present," many of whom were apparently estate laborers, "to disobey their patrones, emphasizing that everyone had the same right to the land."[19] Six months later, in September 1932, a *poblada* (mob) of more than one thousand *indios* invaded land claimed by the El Budi company. Temuco's *El Diario Austral* described the members of the region's indigenous communities as ocupantes armed with revolvers, carbines, knives, and other heavier weapons. The paper reported that they were "armed and disposed to confront whoever tries to evict them."[20] A carabinero "who spoke *mapuche*" was charged with exhorting them to abandon the estate, which they had "taken by force." His negotiations with the Mapuches were unsuccessful, and the land occupation continued for several weeks. At that point the Budi company received a court order authorizing the eviction of "the indígenas who had occupied a large piece of land on the [Budi] fundo." A company of twelve carabineros traveled to Budi, expelled the Mapuche ocupantes, and then destroyed their *ramadas* (huts made of branches).[21]

Budi and the land that had belonged to Silva Ricci had been colonization concessions. Their property had been the subject of dispute by local Mapuche communities and ocupantes for decades. But similar land conflicts also roiled privately owned estates. In July 1932 the district judge and the municipal government of Pucón denounced the actions of one José Miguel Reyes, who had incited "the arbitrary ocupantes of land belonging to third parties." Reyes was a man with "very advanced and subversive ideas" who had found in Pucón "a vast field of action for his communist ideas and his pernicious actions against the established order ... among the squatters on public land, whom he incited against the legitimate owners with spilling blood and with arms if necessary." The region had been shaken by "a movement of a large number of aspiring colonos." The ocupante land invaders had transgressed the authority of the lands and colonization department by ignoring its orders and introducing themselves on privately held property. Ocupantes had "effected true assaults on land held for a long time by private parties."[22]

The following month forty laborers repatriated from Argentina, accompanied by their families, invaded land on Percy Compton's Llafenco hacienda in Pucón, Villarrica. Compton, a British citizen who resided in Valparaíso, had left the estate in the hands of an administrator. The ocupantes were "convinced that no government authority could expel them from the lands they occupy," which they claimed were public. They built huts and disrupted work on the estate. When carabineros were sent to reestablish order, the ocupantes allegedly attacked them, stating that there was now a "communist regime" in power and that "only dead" would they leave their land. The ocupantes were armed with axes, knives, and one carbine. A number of landowners from the region had seen land on their fundos similarly occupied and petitioned the regional intendancy to have carabineros expel the so-called assailants. The governor of Villarrica himself accompanied carabineros to Pucón in order to dislodge the ocupantes.[23]

Amid the political turmoil of September 1932 *El Diario Austral* described how "because of the change of government, the [invasion of Llafenco] repeated itself, but now with seventy individuals who invaded land belonging to the [Compton] company."[24] The paper reported that Llafenco was only one among a number of southern estates confronting armed occupation. In one case, two thousand people, "many of them armed," had occupied land belonging to the Sociedad Agrícola y Ganadera Toltén, built huts, and prepared the land for planting. The regional government ordered forty carabineros from Pitrufquén to evict the ocupantes.[25] In November 1932 the governor of Villarrica denounced the "alarming situation" created by "abuses of private property" and "armed land usurpations" in the Pucón-Toltén-Villarrica region. "Criminal and bloody conflicts" had swept the region. Ocupantes had invaded "even legally constituted [private] property" and ignored "altogether the authorities, who lack the resources to combat this fever of armed usurpations."[26] The next month the lands and colonization directorate reported that in the Pucón-Villarrica region a group of ocupantes armed with revolvers, axes, and knives had prevented a surveyor from measuring land, "having occupied these lands without any right and with brute force." The report noted that the "aspiring colonos" distributed land in Pucón among themselves, "without respecting in any way the corresponding [government] authority and adopting all kinds of abuses and violence."[27]

Challenges to estate owners' property rights extended further north into Alto Bío Bío. On Bunster's Guayalí estate, things had gotten so out of hand that, the landowner claimed, a group of thirty-two of his inquilinos sublevados, armed with sticks, axes, and spades, had assaulted him when he was traveling to Guayalí from Los Ángeles and demanded that he give them five hundred pesos he had. According to Bunster, the principal assailants were Simón Sagredo and his sons, Juan Pablo Ortíz and his sons, Abraham Peña, Albino Acuña and his son, Atanasio Peña, and Modesto Acuña. They had forced him to sign a paper stating that he had given them the money voluntarily.[28] Cautín's intendant transmitted Bunster's denunciations to the government in Santiago and observed that the inquilinos' rebellious opposition to their patrón's authority had been simmering for a long time: "These inquilinos, because of the misguided preaching of unhealthy elements, believe they have the right to occupy land on the fundo, which they say is public because the government dictated a decree of expropriation signed by President Ibáñez."[29] The governor provided similar context, underlining the blurry boundaries between the ocupantes and inquilinos who had joined the Sindicato Agrícola Lonquimay. According to the governor, unions had been organized by "inquilinos on a number of estates in the cordillera and by ocupantes of small plots of public land, many of them inquilinos of the Guayalí estate belonging to the señores Bunster." The government had not yet selected the four thousand hectares to settle the campesinos, which had created "a delicate and difficult situation to put it mildly ... since the inquilinos resist obeying their patrones and occupy the land without any authorization." In addition, the governor noted disapprovingly, "the union leaders have ideas that are frankly antisocial (*disociador*)."[30]

The inquilinos' story of their conflict with Bunster differed. The subdelegate and police interviewed a number of union members and ocupantes on the four thousand hectares in the Nitrito Valley set aside for colonization by the Ibáñez regime. According to the ocupantes/inquilinos, Gonzalo Bunster had gone on a customary tour of the Guayalí estate accompanied by a private guard, which included his brother and four or five other men. On 8 December they arrived at what the campesinos referred to as the *reserva fiscal* (public reserve) in the Nitrito Valley. Bunster and his guard began by savagely killing some of their livestock. They then proceeded to tear down fences protecting the campesinos' vegetable gardens. Bunster attempted to get a number of campesinos to leave the houses they had built in Nitrito: "With his private guard he makes all kinds of threats and has even said that as long as there is a Bunster he will stubbornly confront them [*salir con su porfía*] and expel the actual ocupantes and take control of the Reserva Fiscal." The union members pointed out that the district judge was the administrator employed by Bunster on Guayalí, Víctor Vergara, and that the local carabineros received subventions from him (the carabineros said Bunster furnished them with horses and pasture as well as lodging for the picket stationed on Guayalí). They also noted the history of violence against their group. The year before, Bunster had beaten the inquilino Albino Acuña and evicted him and his family from their house. This was an act of retaliation, as Acuña had earlier brought charges in the local court against Bunster for "violating the domicile of his daughter."[31]

A Lonquimay carabineros' report confirmed much of this but added further details. Bunster and his group had specifically targeted Albino Acuña, attacking him "with blows, knocking him to the ground and leaving him with wounds on his face." The assault was likely punishment for Acuña's audacity in challenging Bunster's authority in court. Fifteen or twenty of Acuña's neighbors, upon learning of the assault, confronted Bunster. The Bunster party was armed with revolvers while the ocupantes had only sticks, rocks, and axes. The large group of campesinos intended to detain Bunster and deliver him to the carabineros in Lonquimay, but in the end, "so that he wouldn't get mixed up in these affairs," Bunster paid them a sum of five hundred pesos to indemnify Acuña for his wounds. In a sign of the inquilinos' abiding commitment to legal procedure, they demanded that he sign a receipt for the payment.[32]

Whether an act of banditry or an organized response to landowner violence, the Guayalí inquilinos' confrontation with Bunster reflected the turbulent state of land and labor relations on Alto Bío Bío's estates during a time of great political uncertainty. The patrón could no longer do what he wished on land he considered his property. Nor could he exercise his customary authority over his inquilino labor force. Bunster may have been accustomed to resorting to beatings to exercise discipline on his estate and using force to evict inquilinos from their homes, but his laborers, emboldened by changes in the political climate and organized in the Sindicato Agrícola Lonquimay, now confronted him with a sense of collective purpose and empowerment.

Shortly after the confrontation with Bunster, the Sindicato Agrícola Lonquimay established ties with the Communist Party–led FOCH. In February 1933 the FOCH declared that it had organized in Curacautín a Consejo de Oficios Varios with more than one hundred workers and campesinos. The Consejo de Oficios Varios maintained "close contact with the Sindicato Agrario de Lonquimay, which has numerous consejos of Colonos and Ocupantes de Tierras." The consejos had "formed campesino guards to defend themselves from the usurpers of land ... the evil concessionaires Bunster and Puelma."[33] Notably, the FOCH newspaper *Justicia* saw the Puelmas and Bunsters not as landowners but as concessionaires who had leased public land from the state. They, not the campesinos, had usurped public land by claiming it as their private property. That the Sindicato Agrícola Lonquimay's estate consejos had formed defense committees reflected their increased militancy in response to the harassment and violence employed by landowners like Gonzalo Bunster to evict disobedient ocupantes and inquilinos from their estates. The union's ties to the FOCH represented both the increased presence of the national labor organization in the southern countryside and the growing radicalization of a sector of the local union's leadership.

Because of political repression, FOCH consejos had remained dormant in southern towns like Victoria. But following Ibáñez's resignation they sprang back to life. As early as August 1931 workers reorganized the FOCH's Consejo Federal de Oficios Varios in Victoria with the assistance of a FOCH delegate from Temuco. *El Diario Austral* reported that union members had suffered all kinds of persecution under Ibáñez.[34] After the Ibáñez regime's fall, the FOCH organized consejos in southern towns from Los Ángeles and Victoria to Curacautín, giving the national labor union a presence in the southern countryside and, in Alto Bío Bío, strengthened its ties to the Sindicato Agrícola Lonquimay's estate councils. By early 1933 Leiva Tapia, the Sagredos, and other local union leaders had begun to move away from their alliance with the Democratic Party and support for legal social reform to the revolutionary politics of the FOCH. In February 1933 Leiva Tapia attended a national FOCH congress as a delegate from the sindicato.

The Sindicato Agrícola Lonquimay's turn to the left can be explained in three ways. First, the end of the Ibáñez regime allowed for an efflorescence of revolutionary socialist and communist parties and the reemergence of the FOCH in the labor movement, making socialism part of the political vocabulary and ideological toolkit of the times. Key sectors of the military, as the naval rebellion and Grove's Socialist Republic indicated, also supported revolutionary socialist solutions to the economic crisis that gripped the country after 1929. The global economic crisis led to the collapse of traditional political arrangements and the bankruptcy of liberal economic ideology. Even a conventional figure like the Radical Carlos Dávila articulated a rhetorical commitment to socialism, and the Liberal Party used the phrase in its 1932 program. As Elías Lafertte, secretary general of the FOCH and Communist Party leader, recalled in his memoirs, "Everyone spoke a great deal about socialism. Everyone, even Alessandri, spoke of the need for state socialism. ... For some this meant one thing, for others something very different, but everywhere you heard the word 'socialism.' "[35]

Second, Alessandri's election in 1932 brought to power a figure who had been the principal adversary and rival of Ibáñez, the union's major ally and supporter. The Democratic Party's support for Alessandri in the 1932 campaign would certainly have weakened its influence among some of the union leadership. In fact, as the union's early history demonstrated, its alliance with Ibáñez was more important than any political or ideological support for the Democrats. When the Democrats threw in their lot with Alessandri at the national level, they would have alienated themselves from union leaders like Leiva Tapia who had been loyal supporters of Ibáñez. Third, the weakness of the Chilean state, crippled by the global economic crisis and shaken by increasingly turbulent political divisions and by the rise of military movements like the naval rebellion and the Socialist Republic, dovetailed with increasingly violent confrontations over land and labor in the southern countryside. As ocupantes and inquilinos battled estate owners and carabineros during 1932, it would not have been hard for them to see a revolutionary insurrection and a socialist state as both possible and imminent.

The Alessandri government adopted a two-pronged approach to the escalating social conflict in southern Chile. On the one hand, the government pushed forward new legislation on colonization designed to expand the existing southern property and national colonization laws. Like the governments before it, Alessandri's second administration looked to Chile's southern frontier to implement an agrarian reform that would absorb the large population of floating urban and rural unemployed workers while modernizing agricultural production by breaking up large estates. On the other, Alessandri intensified the coercive crackdown initiated during Ibáñez's last days in power on the movements of inquilinos and ocupantes to colonize both public and privately held estate land.

In a sign that the new government intended to put an end once and for all to land occupations Alessandri sent his lands minister, Carlos Henríquez Argomedo, to tour the south. Henríquez's mandate was to investigate and resolve major conflicts over land in southern Chile. The fact-finding mission had been instigated in part by a recent wave of expulsions of ocupantes and colonos.[36] The minister met with members of Mapuche communities, ocupantes, and aspiring colonos, at times in crowds numbering in the hundreds, in Temuco, Puerto Domínguez, Llaima (the site of the Silva Rivas concession), Pucón, Allipén, Capitán Pastene, Selva Oscura, Nueva Italia, and Traiguén. In Capitán Pastene, Henríquez was greeted by hundreds of ocupantes waving Chilean flags and heard the petitions of commissions from the region's indigenous communities, including members of the Huaiquivil reducción, which was engaged in a long-standing conflict with the Nueva Italia colonization concession. The minister promised to increase the size of the Huaiquivil reducción but also pledged "to defend the property rights of sr. Ricci," whose estates had suffered a series of "invasions and land occupations."[37]

In Budi, Henríquez found that neighboring indigenous reducciones had pushed their borders onto the company's estate. In late 1932 Budi had expelled members of Mapuche communities who had occupied land claimed by the enormous former concession. The company razed thirty huts, leaving five hundred people indigent, as a petition for support to the Cautín intendancy put it.[38] The minister and his advisers reviewed the estate's titles and boundaries and found them fixed and indisputable. He then met with the indígenas who were "convinced to withdraw."[39] As in Capitán Pastene, Henríquez lent the government's support to Budi's property rights in its conflicts with Mapuche communities.

The minister and his advisers then moved on to Toltén to visit the Sociedad Toltén, whose five fundos, San Roque, Camaguey, Machitún, Los Mapuches, and Santa Elena, had been invaded by hundreds of aspiring colonos and their families. The campesinos occupied ten thousand of the company's fifteen thousand hectares, which they had distributed among themselves.[40] They destroyed fences everywhere where gates were chained so that they could enter and leave by the public roads. They also appropriated a considerable number of livestock and built huts among the company's wheat fields. The ocupantes had organized a cooperative with nine hundred members. In Camaguey, they claimed a large quantity of valuable forest as their property and stated forthrightly that they planned to find a *contratista* to mill and sell the wood.[41] In October 1932 the Toltén Company had begun expelling both Chilean and Mapuche ocupantes.[42] With the lands minister's arrival in the region, the company won the government's backing. In January 1933 the intendancy ordered carabineros to expel the ocupantes.[43]

In Nueva Italia, Budi, and Toltén, the Alessandri government supplied carabineros to back estates' property rights over the claims of Mapuche communities and ocupantes. In March 1933 Alessandri sent instructions to all intendants and governors to put an end to land invasions in the south. The government ordered carabineros to dislodge and arrest people who had invaded private and public land, allegedly instigated by professional agitators. *El Diario Austral* reported that the government crackdown had been caused by disruptions in the region's agricultural production: "In the southern region, agricultural production suffers disturbances, especially the plantings. These individuals violate property rights and disturb public order."[44]

The government's shift in policy was, in part, a response to pressure from estate owners. In March 1933 landowners held a large meeting in

Angol to hear the report of a commission that had traveled to Santiago to discuss the situation of southern agriculture. The agriculturalists denounced "the usurpation of private properties by inquilinos and medieros on the region's estates, who, encouraged by a few professional agitators, refuse to recognize the authority and rights of the patrón with the false pretext that they are occupying public lands." According to the landowners, inquilinos and medieros, "violently resist accepting the conditions that they agreed to with their patrones."[45] The governor of the department of Angol echoed the landowners when he wrote the intendancy of Bío-Bío in Los Ángeles that "in this department there are numerous fundos occupied by individuals who call themselves colonos and who are nothing more than inquilinos and medieros rebeldes, who, having served the owners of these fundos for four or five years, have declared themselves the owners of considerable extensions of lands, instigated by professional agitators to rebel against their patrones, who make them believe that the land they occupy is public." The governor's office had denounced several of these supposed agitators to the local police, and they had been arrested.[46]

Southern landowners found a receptive audience in the Alessandri government. The interior minister wrote to the intendant of Cautín noting the "serious problems produced by the acts of [land] invasion." The minister, echoing the landowners, remarked that "in the southern region, agricultural labor is suffering disturbances, and in some parts, the harvests, already begun, will be very difficult for this reason." These land usurpers violated "the right to private property" and disrupted "the public order." The minister instructed the intendant to send carabineros to expel rebellious inquilinos and ocupantes from southern estates and to work with the Servicio de Investigaciones (the Chilean equivalent of the FBI) to investigate the "instigators" and "professional agitators" who provoked land usurpations.[47]

Among those agitators targeted for arrest figured Juan Segundo Leiva Tapia. In March 1933 the Communist Party named a commission to attend an international conference of the Communist Confederación Sindical Latino Americana in Montevideo, Uruguay. It speaks to Leiva Tapia's rise within the ranks of the FOCH and his importance to the party that he was named to the commission to travel to the conference along with prominent party and FOCH leaders like Elías Lafertte. At the time of the Montevideo conference, both Lafertte and Leiva Tapia faced arrest warrants, the latter probably for his activities as an agitator of Alto

Bío Bío's inquilinos, and had gone into hiding.⁴⁸ Nevertheless, they made the trip across the cordillera to Argentina clandestinely. Once in Uruguay, they were arrested and expelled.⁴⁹ Upon his arrival back in Chile, Leiva Tapia was detained and sent into internal exile for six months on the islands of Guaytecas and Chiloé, according to him because of his membership in the FOCH and his attendance as a FOCH delegate at the Montevideo conference.⁵⁰

There is no evidence that Leiva Tapia was, at this point, a Communist, despite the many accusations of landowners and political officials in Alto Bío Bío. Lafertte, one of the party's central leaders, does not describe him in his memoirs as a member of the party. Rather, he notes only that Leiva Tapia was a local labor leader whom he encountered for the first time at the February 1933 FOCH congress, where Leiva Tapia appeared as a delegate representing the Sindicato Agrícola Lonquimay. According to Lafertte, Leiva Tapia was a "representative of agricultural settlers [colonos agrícolas] in Lonquimay" who "argued admirably and spoke with logic and at the same time with passion."⁵¹ Leiva Tapia had affiliated the Sindicato Agrícola Lonquimay with the FOCH, but none of the declassified Comintern archives or party publications mention him or the sindicato. While the party chose Leiva Tapia to join the delegation to the Montevideo conference because of his high profile as a FOCH delegate representing an important union of agricultural laborers, membership in the party would not have been a requisite. As the historian Olga Ulianova notes, the party would also have chosen "fellow travelers" and people sympathetic to the party.⁵² Leiva Tapia himself described his arrest and internal exile as owing to his joining the FOCH, distancing himself from accusations that he was a communist militant.⁵³ Nonetheless, he now articulated a far more radical political posture aligned with the positions of the Communist Party than he had in 1931 when he supported Montero's presidential candidacy.

Alessandri's 1932 election has often been heralded as restoring Chile's tradition of civilian rule and inaugurating four decades of uninterrupted multiparty democracy. While the military did return to the barracks after almost a decade of frequent coups, Alessandri's new government maintained many of Chile's authoritarian political practices. As Lafertte's and Leiva Tapia's deportation to distant parts of Chile demonstrate, Alessandri continued the Ibáñez-era policy of detaining political opponents from the Left, often sending them into internal exile. Alessandri, like Dávila before him, used the internal security of the state law to crack down on both the Trotskyist and Stalinist Communist parties as well as on leftist unions. In addition, he asked for and received from congress extraordinary powers that gave the executive dictatorial powers to suspend the "rights to individual freedom, freedom of expression, freedom of assembly, and the privacy of the home."[54]

To Alessandri´s opponents on the left, the president's embrace of the paramilitary Republican Militias represented the true authoritarian character of his regime. The militias had been formed during the Dávila government almost immediately after the fall of Grove's twelve-day Socialist Republic. They were formed as an armed civilian response of the upper and middle classes to both social unrest and military uprisings. But paramilitary organizations had a long genealogy going back to at least the first decade of the twentieth century, when nationalist and xenophobic Patriotic Leagues were organized in northern Chile. The leagues were part of a movement to purge the provinces of Tarapacá and Antofagasta, conquered from Bolivia and Peru during the War of the Pacific, of their Bolivian and Peruvian residents. The Patriotic Leagues were used as well by employers and the government to combat northern Chile's radical socialist workers' movements.[55] After the 1925 military coup led by Carlos Ibáñez and Marmaduke Grove, upper-class groups organized civil guards as a counterweight to the military in the name of protecting civilian rule.[56] The associations of university students, doctors, and engineers that organized protests against Ibáñez in 1931 also organized civil guards to protect against military intervention in politics. After the naval mutiny of 1931 these same sectors organized civil guards to protect the social order and private property from the threat posed by a popular working-class movement, the FOCH, and the Communist Party.[57]

During his first two years back in office, Alessandri embraced the Republican Militias, to which his government supplied arms, to offset sectors of the military sympathetic to either Ibáñez or the revolutionary left, including factions supportive of Grove and socialism or the Communist Party. In addition, Alessandri viewed the militias as an important tool for quelling popular mobilization.[58] While the militias claimed their purpose was to support the constitutional order in response to military interventions, their roots in White or Civil Guards and upper- and middle-class membership made them instruments of repression in the eyes of much of labor and the left.[59] To the president's political opponents on the left, his support of the militias and use of extraordinary powers reflected the authoritarian, antipopular character of his regime.

The Alessandri administration proved itself to be no friend of the Sindicato Agrícola Lonquimay. The distribution of land to the ocupantes on the Guayalí estate was stalled.[60] On Ránquil the ocupantes remained on the land but were unable to receive titles to their lots in the new colony because the government could not establish "a just indemnification for the damages to its legitimate owner, doña Rosa Puelma v. de Rodríguez, with the object of her ceding all rights to the state." In addition, Alessandri's lands minister asked the Consejo de Defensa Fiscal to review the decrees issued by the Ibáñez government expropriating Ránquil and redistributing its land to its inquilinos. On 5 June 1933 the consejo issued a finding in a memo to the lands minister in which it determined that decrees No. 265 of 27 March 1930, No. 1730 of 31 July 1930, and No. 1693 of 13 March 1931 of the former Ministry of Southern Property were invalid and that decree 3,871 of 14 August 1929, which had recognized the validity of the Puelmas' titles, should be restored as the law.[61] Alessandri's lands and colonization minister issued a report on 5 June 1933 stating that the Ibáñez regime decrees were illegal, although he did not support the eviction of the inquilino-ocupantes.[62]

In late November 1933 the Alessandri government also began to undo the decree-laws issued under Ibáñez granting land to laborers on the Guayalí estate. On 24 November 1933 the lands and colonization ministry issued a new decree to attempt to put an end to the conflict over Guayalí (No. 4834). The decree reviewed the history of the Ibáñez government's actions to resolve conflicts between the Bunster family and Guayalí's inquilinos and ocupantes, especially the August 1930 decree (No. 2243) that extracted 4,000 of the estate's 22,886 hectares to resolve land conflicts in the region and the May 1931 Decree Law (No. 258), which had declared the entire estate to be of utilidad pública and authorized the president to expropriate it. The new decree announced that because of lack of funds "the government does not intend to make use of the powers of expropriation conferred on it" by Decree No. 258. Decree No. 4834 did not revoke the 1930 decree and reaffirmed that the government would settle the pobladores—including in that term "the inquilinos and ocupantes who refuse to recognize the dominion of the Bunster estate"— on 4,000 hectares carved out of Guayalí. Members of the Bunster family had stated that they would accept this resolution to the land conflict.[63] The negotiations between the Bunsters and the government included the government's concession that the 4,000 hectares would not be located in the Nitrito Valley, the place originally selected by the Ibáñez government for the Santa Graciela–23 de Enero colony. Instead, they would lie in Llanquén, a high-altitude, rocky location further up the cordillera useful only for pasturing livestock during the summer.

The Alessandri government clearly intended to reverse the steps taken by the Ibáñez regime to resolve land conflicts in Alto Bío Bío. More generally, the government revised Ibáñez's policy of refusing to authorize the use of carabineros to expel ocupantes and rebellious inquilinos from large estates. In one typical case from March 1933 Cautín's intendant ordered a troop composed of a captain, two other officers, and thirty-four carabineros to dislodge, "employing armed force if necessary," the campesinos who had occupied land, planted crops, and built houses on an estate belonging to Percy Compton in Villarrica.[64] In a similar case Felipe Santiago Smith went to the Cautín intendancy to complain that some of the inquilinos on his Nueva Escocia fundo in Cunco, "instigated by third parties," had rebelled against the estate's administrator, claiming that the estate lay on public land. The inquilinos had made it impossible for the estate "to continue its agricultural production." The intendant ordered carabineros to notify these *inquilinos alzados* (rebellious inquilinos) that they had to recognize Smith as the estate's owner. If they failed to do so, carabineros would evict them by force.[65]

However, widespread social upheaval in southern Chile could not be resolved solely through repression. The Alessandri government sought to complement its crackdown on land occupations with an expansion of existing colonization laws. Like its predecessors, the government viewed colonization in the south as a crucial response to the economic dislocations caused by the Great Depression. A colonization commission composed of the agricultural minister, the chair of the congressional agricultural commission, and the director of the Caja de Colonización Agrícola elaborated a project for national colonization and the subdivision of frontier land, which it delivered to the president and congress. The new colonization law, the commission report argued, was of vital national consequence: it "will produce the economic recovery of the country and internal peace." Colonization would both increase agricultural production and put the army of Chile's unemployed to work in the southern countryside.[66]

The new colonization scheme proposed two forms of land redistribution. First, unemployed obreros and inquilinos on estates that were purchased or expropriated would be settled on collectively owned property administered by the Caja de Colonización. Second, unemployed empleados (urban white-collar workers) would be given individual *parcelas*. Empleados would make an initial down payment to the Caja de Colonización, but the bank could exempt empleados from the payment if they were unemployed. They would earn definitive titles to their plots after three years of agricultural labor. *Parceleros* on an expropriated or purchased property would form cooperatives, sharing the use and ownership of agricultural machinery, seeds, and other elements of agricultural production. After the first three years, these colonos would make payments as stipulated by the existing colonization laws.[67] In early February 1934 Alessandri sent a bill to congress requesting $10 million pesos for the Caja de Colonización Agrícola to purchase southern estates and settle them with colonos. The bill also expanded the president's power to expropriate southern properties.[68]

As a sign of the government's interest in resolving social conflict with more than police power, the Alessandri government worked to purchase and settle the Toltén Company's five estates with hundreds of recalcitrant ocupantes. In early 1933 the lands and colonization minister ordered that forcible evictions from Toltén be suspended.[69] Consonant with the government's new policy, the Central Socialista de Colonización, which had the support of congressional members from the Radical and Democratic parties, mediated the conflict between the company and the ocupantes.[70] In March 1934 the central worked to resettle two hundred colonos and ocupantes who had been thrown off their land and had their huts and harvests reduced to ashes by the Compañía Ganadera y Agrícola Toltén. The ocupantes had demanded that they be settled as colonos on the company's land, invoking the Southern Property Law. An agreement was reached in which the Caja de Colonización Agrícola agreed to purchase thirteen thousand hectars on the estate and settle the ocupantes there. The only problem was that congress refused to go along with the scheme and vote the funds needed for the purchase. The ocupantes were once again evicted from Toltén.[71] They then proceeded to organize another movement to take back the estate, holding secret meetings in hidden valleys covered by the company's forest, on the run from the private police force hired to guard the forests. As the Socialist Party's *La Opinión* reported, the ocupantes "had the goal of engaging the company's police force, which would have provoked a bloody struggle."[72]

The conflagration was averted when the president of the Central Socialista de Colonización, Juan de Dios Moraga, negotiated an arrangement between the lands ministry, the ocupantes, and the Toltén Company. Moraga spoke to a meeting of 350 ocupantes about the agreement. The speech was translated by "the indígena Segundo Colil Jiménez in the aboriginal language." The presence of both Chilean and Mapuche ocupantes meant too that the indigenous protector was brought in to help broker the deal.[73] In April 1934 a commission of surveyors traveled to Toltén to survey the 15,000 hectares that the government intended to purchase from the Compañía Agrícola Toltén.[74] *El Diario Austral* wrote that the government's colonization plan in Toltén amounted to an "agrarian reform." This was the phrase, the paper noted sympathetically, that a number of European countries used to describe "the most important development in the social-economic-agricultural sphere." The paper saw agrarian reform in Europe as a "neutralizer of social ferment" and a means to ending "anarchy."[75] Alessandri's colonization program would similarly end the social turmoil sweeping the southern countryside.

In early May 1934 the lands and colonization minister traveled to Temuco to supervise the implementation of the government's agrarian policy. On this occasion *El Diario Austral* advocated the subdivision of large estates since "the small property owner who feels his own future linked to the fertility of the soil he exploits loves order and does not attend assemblies or organize mutinies in response to the subversive and utopian preachings of political adventurers." Colonization and agrarian reform would, in addition, absorb "the large armies of unemployed ... and remove them from socially disruptive politics." To *El Diario Austral*, "The acquisition of the fundo belonging to the Compañía Agrícola Toltén constitutes the first step in an effective colonization plan." The paper expressed its hope that other southern fundos would soon be purchased and subdivided: "The country demands it with urgency."[76]

The Alessandri government planned to initiate the colonization program in Cautín province by acquiring three large haciendas, Toltén, Nueva Italia, and Ránquil, subdividing them and distributing plots to their ocupantes. The colonization of the three estates would serve as a template for agrarian reform in southern Chile.[77] Ránquil's former inquilinos and ocupantes now had reason to hope that they would at last receive legal titles to their land on Rosa Puelma's former estate. The resolution of the conflict between ocupantes and the Toltén Company demonstrated the possibilities of colonization law and Alessandri's agrarian policy. The fact that the government was willing to intervene to avoid a bloody battle with campesinos and apply the colonization laws to settle them on the plots they occupied while indemnifying the company for its losses pointed toward the possible resolution of other land conflicts throughout the south, including in Alto Bío Bío.

The politics of colonization and agrarian reform shaped tensions between the Central Socialista de Colonización and the Alessandri government on one side and the Communist Party and FOCH, with their small but growing network of unions and campesino organizations throughout the south, on the other. In November 1933 the central held an assembly in Temuco. Among the 350 delegates were deputies and senators from the Radical, Democratic, and *ibañicista* (pro-Ibáñez) Agrarian parties. Also present were Temuco's mayor and representatives of government agencies, including the Caja de Colonización Agrícola, the lands directorate, and the social welfare secretariat. The colonization central represented political forces at odds with the Communist Party and the FOCH: Democrats, Radicals, and *ibañicistas* as well as the Alessandri government itself. Nonetheless, one of the central's directors made a lengthy speech to the assembly about Chile's agrarian history in which he underlined the central's goal of making "socialization of the land a national aspiration."[78]

At the opening of the assembly, Juan Segundo Leiva Tapia, described by the police as "the communist delegate from the Sindicato Obreros y Campesinos de Lonquimay, y Alto Bío Bío," took the floor and denounced the central executive committee for attempting to restrict the freedom of speech of the group he represented. Leiva Tapia proposed a vote that all present be given time to speak, "especially obreros and campesinos," and that the assembly's organizers name a campesino to be head of the executive committee. The union leader went on to critique Alessandri's colonization law as insufficient to meet campesinos' demands for land. At this moment the Communist Marcos Carrasco, as he was identified by the police, shouted from the gallery, "Death to the dog Alessandri." In response, the Democratic Party deputy Arturo Huenchullán took the floor to refute Leiva Tapia. Huenchullán asserted that the central and assembly were vital to passing and perfecting the new colonization law being debated at that moment in the senate. The law "would be of enormous benefit to the *campesinado* (peasantry) and the country's economic and social health."[79]

The Central Socialista de Colonización viewed Alessandri's colonization legislation as holding the best promise of meeting rural laborers' demands for land. The job of the central, its organizers believed, was to push Alessandri to fix deficiencies in the legislation working its way through congress. The assembly voted to petition the government to suspend all evictions of ocupantes and indígenas, resurvey land concessions and distribute all land recuperated by the state to colono smallholders, and make changes to the colonization law to benefit poor campesinos, including expanding the government's powers of expropriation.[80]

The many speeches included one by Manuel Aburto Panguilef, the director of the Federación Araucana. Panguilef had emerged during the 1920s as the leader of a movement in defense of Mapuche communities. He opposed the subdivision and privatization of Mapuche land and advocated the restoration of Mapuche religious and cultural practices as well as the formation of an autonomous Araucanian Republic. Nonetheless, the *parlamentos* organized by Aburto Panguilef's Federación Araucana included delegates from the Communist and Democratic parties, and the federación had ties to the FOCH.[81] By 1933, however, Aburto Panguilef had broken with the Communist Party and cast his lot with Alessandri, with whom he had met in La Moneda. In his speech to the colonization central, he denounced Leiva Tapia and the Communists at the assembly for being insolent (*atrevidos*) and criticized their attacks on Alessandri, declaring that "the Araucanian race" supported the government's initiatives and the activities of the central. He expressed his hope that "the indígenas' aspirations will be heard by the president."[82] While Aburto Panguilef and the Federación Araucana embraced the ethnonationalist project of building an Araucanian Republic, in sync with Soviet and Comintern policies on building independent soviet republics of ethnic minorities, by the early 1930s they had split with the Communist Party. Panguilef's denunciation of Leiva Tapia and the other Communists present at the conference made clear too that, unlike Ralco and Ignacio Maripi, he had no ties to the Sindicato Agrícola Lonquimay and rejected its increasingly revolutionary politics, choosing instead to work with the Alessandri regime.

Leiva Tapia rejected this conciliatory approach. When he was eventually allowed to take the podium, "to great acclaim from a number of Communists," he denounced the government's colonization project as a fraud and a lie designed by the "bourgeois and reactionary government" to "exploit and enslave" campesinos and obreros. Rather than respond to the aspirations of those who worked the land, he told the assembly, the colonization law handed over southern land to foreign capitalists and Chilean oligarchs. During his speech, Leiva Tapia's "communist followers" created a climate of disorder, launching stones at members of the executive board and throwing "communist leaflets" from the balcony. When Deputy Huenchullán tried to restore order, Leiva Tapia's followers interrupted him, shouting, "death to the assassin and bandit Alessandri," "it is necessary to kill the thief," and "down with the vulture." Finally, carabineros arrived and threw out the "disruptive Communists."[83]

The degree to which competition with Alessandri shaped the Communist Party's strategies and tactics in the countryside was made clear in Leiva Tapia's and the other Communists' hostility to the government's colonization policy. Alessandri's agrarian policy was, the party held, "demagogic ... rich in promises and poor in practical policies." At base, the party contended, Alessandri refused to dismantle or even regulate the latifundium that dominated landownership and agricultural production. Alessandri's policies of reducing taxes on property owners and lifting restrictions on food prices favored landowners, not the rural poor. To compensate, the "crafty old man" was trying to deceive workers, speaking to them of "agrarian reform and subdivision of property."[84] To the party, Alessandri's agrarian reform was really just the colonization of public lands with unemployed workers, many of them urban empleados. Alessandri had stated in the announcement of his colonization law that "we will expropriate, following the Law, all those properties that, during a determined period, have not produced crops, owing either to the laziness or incapacity of their owners." The president had requested $100 million pesos from congress to purchase estates that would be subdivided and settled with colonos. The Communist Party judged that the major beneficiaries of this policy would be landowners, who could sell their large properties to the state for their declared value. They would then recuperate their land after it had been cultivated by colonos who were unable to make the required payments to the Caja de Colonización Agrícola for their parcels. The state needed not only to expropriate the land but also to equip colonos with farm machinery, credit, and tools. History had shown that without state support and access to credit colonos were often forced to sell their small plots to large estates.[85]

In September 1933 the Communist Party's regional committee in Concepción printed a leaflet to commemorate the second anniversary of the naval rebellion. The pamphlet described how workers in Talcahuano, Santiago, and Valparaíso had gone on strike to support the marineros and declared that the Communist Party "immediately supported the insurrection and tried to expand the movement through an effective alliance of the marineros, *soldados*, obreros, and campesinos." For the party "the marineros' movement" was "the greatest realized over the past years in Latin America." The pamphlet attacked the repression of the movement in which, it alleged without evidence and with typical hyperbole, "hundreds of marineros were vilely assassinated."[86]

One of the party's major concerns was the Republican Militias, which it viewed as paramilitary shock troops preparing the way for fascism. And they compared the labor legislation introduced in 1931, especially the board established under Ibáñez to arbitrate labor conflicts, the Junta de Arbitración y Conciliación, to fascist institutions designed to undermine working-class movements. The party called for the dissolution of the Republican Militias, an end to the laws that gave "extraordinary powers" to the executive and the "anti-worker laws dictated by Ibáñez, Montero, Dávila, Blanche, and Alessandri," and the freeing of jailed political dissidents, including "Astorga, Labraña, Lafferte, Leiva, and Ilozca and all the workers and carabineros imprisoned for social political crimes."[87] It is notable that Juan Segundo Leiva Tapia figured in the Communist Party's list of dissidents detained by the Alessandri regime and sent into internal exile.

The Communist Party's antipathy for Alessandri—"the butcher," "the massacrer," "the tyrant," in short, the *canalla*—was in part a response to the violent repression of workers' movements in the nitrate mines of San Gregorio (1921) and La Coruña (1925) and to Alessandri's crackdown on party militants.[88] But the party also reviled Alessandri because he posed serious competition for its working-class base. The Lion of Tarapacá's populism and the social reformist legislation he helped push through congress posed a challenge to the party's revolutionary program. During the 1920s this competition between, as the historians Julio Pinto and Verónica Valdivia put it, the Communist Party's "revolución proletaria" and Alessandri's "querida chusma" played out in the northern nitrate fields among miners and port workers.[89] By the 1930s Alessandri's populist social reformism, including his rhetorical commitment to expropriating unproductive estates and redistributing their land, also posed a challenge to the party's efforts to organize in the countryside. With the northern mines in the throes of a protracted crisis and the dispersal of former mine workers throughout the country, the focus of social conflict moved southward during the early 1930s with the unemployed miners themselves. Whereas the nitrate mines and northern ports had been the site of the party's most effectual organizing during the first decades of the century, by the 1930s it had turned to the countryside as a vital arena of struggle. Juan Segundo Leiva Tapia's inclusion as a FOCH delegate to the labor conference in Montevideo reflected the significance of the countryside and Chile's largest union of agricultural laborers to the ongoing competition between Alessandri and the Left to win the hearts and minds of Chilean workers.

CHAPTER SEVEN

Expulsion from the Nitrito Valley

Toward the end of 1933 the Alessandri government took definitive action to crack down on the Sindicato Agrícola Lonquimay. In part, the move was a general response to the wave of rural unrest sweeping southern Chile. But Alessandri's intervention in Alto Bío Bío was also a reaction to the Sindicato Agrícola Lonquimay's growing radicalization. By late 1933 members of the union leadership had moved left. Union leaders like Juan Segundo Leiva Tapia and Simón and Benito Sagredo aligned their politics with the FOCH and Chile's Communist Party, displacing more moderate and Democratic Party–identified figures like the Ackermann brothers, the local merchants who had been key participants in the union leadership since 1928, and Manuel Astroza, the union president.

In January 1934 a commission of surveyors traveled to Lonquimay to redraw the boundaries of the land granted to the ocupantes and inquilinos on Guayalí. Their goal was to move the campesinos out of the Nitrito Valley invernadas to high-altitude Llanquén. They were accompanied by a carabinero from Temuco who joined the two carabineros already stationed on Guayalí.[1] Upon his arrival, the head of the commission, the surveyor Arturo Fernández Correa, reported that "today almost none of the inquilinos obey the orders of the Bunster family and are working their small plots of land as they wish inside the above-mentioned estate."[2] Fernández called a number of Guayalí's rebellious inquilinos to Los Guindos, where the estate's big houses and picket of carabineros were located. He intended to assign them plots on the four thousand hectares in Llanquén.[3]

The surveyor's initial efforts to supervise the inquilinos-ocupantes' removal from the Nitrito Valley were unsuccessful. Upon his arrival in Guayalí he received a formal petition from the "antiguos ocupantes who worked before as inquilinos on the Guayalí fundo." They asked that the plots in the Nitrito Valley granted them by the Ibáñez government be expanded to one hundred hectares, as established in Alessandri's colonization legislation.[4] Many of the estate's former inquilinos stated that "they would not leave the places where they were." Fernández then informed them he would get a court order to evict those who did not agree to move to Llanquén and that they would lose their rights to settle within the four thousand high-altitude hectares.[5] Following this threat, most agreed, but there were some cabecillas, among them Juan Pablo Ortíz, Modesto Acuña, and Lindor Sagredo, who tried to convince the other inquilinos that the commission headed by Fernández did not have the power to evict them from Nitrito. Ortíz and Acuña were antiguos ocupantes who had lived and worked on Guayalí as inquilinos, respectively, since 1916 and 1906.[6] Fernández requested that these ringleaders be cited to appear at the intendancy to reinforce his authority in the face of the "subversive campaign they have been organizing."[7] If they did not appear, he notified them, they would be declared *rebeldes* and expelled from the estate by force. The list of those cited was long and included a number of people who months later participated in the Ránquil rebellion, most notably members of the Ortíz, Acuña Sandoval, Lagos, and Sagredo families.

Nonetheless, Fernández was able to get a number of the fundo's workers to sign documents in which they recognized the Bunsters' property rights and agreed to follow the landowners' orders as inquilinos. Sixteen of the twenty-one inquilinos and empleados who signed the document did so with thumbprints. On the patrones' side, the documents were signed by Guayalí's administrator, Víctor Vergara, the estate's foreman (*capataz*), Froilán Labrín, and the manager (mayordomo) Segundo Ramos; and for the government, representatives of the carabineros and Arturo Fernández. The Bunster family's legal representative, Vial Friere, also signed the documents.[8] Fernández then set up camp, accompanied by a fellow surveyor named Aguilera, so that he could subdivide the four thousand hectares in Llanquén. In total, twenty-nine inquilinos agreed to be settled in Llanquén. Twenty or so inquilinos and empleados agreed to stay on, recognize the Bunsters' property rights, and follow their orders. This left twenty-five who did neither and were therefore required to leave Guayalí.[9]

A conflict emerged between inquilinos who had lived and worked on Guayalí for more than ten years and who petitioned to receive one hundred hectares per family and those who were more recent arrivals "who had introduced themselves by force" on the estate and were not inquilinos but ocupantes. The long-standing inquilinos believed they had the right to more land than the ocupantes. In fact, the lists of the estate's workers included nineteen who had lived and worked on Guayalí for more than ten years and ten between five and ten years. Twenty-five were more recent arrivals, having been either contracted as inquilinos or simply settled within the estate's borders as ocupantes within the last five years. Among recent arrivals were figures like Benito and Simón Sagredo, who had been inquilinos on Guayalí for about six years. In the end, of the fifty-four people who were being expelled from Guayalí, Fernández found that only thirty-two had rights to be settled, having had possession of their land since before Decree No. 2243 of 2 August 1930, in which the state reserved the four thousand hectares to settle ocupantes and inquilinos. The rest had either settled as ocupantes or signed inquilinaje contracts within the last three years.

A census of the Guayalí inquilinos and ocupantes who held land rights revealed the gendered organization of property rights codified in colonization laws. Almost every campesino, whether former inquilino or ocupante, with rights to be settled as a colono was a male head of household. Most were married, a few widowed. All had children. There were five exceptions, women who were granted rights to plots on the four thousand hectares; all five were widows with children who inherited their property rights from their deceased husbands. Typical of these women who stood to be granted plots as colonos was sixty-five-year-old Delicia Muñoz, "widow of Vidal," as she was identified in the census. Muñoz had nine children and lived with her son-in-law on Guayalí, where she had been a resident for twenty-four years, undoubtedly as a member of an inquilino family. Despite having lived in a male-headed household, she held property associated with agricultural labor, which she would bring with her to her new plot: two oxen, four milking cows, six dry cows, one steer, four horses, six sheep, two pigs, two carts, two plows, one chain, two axes, and one hoe. Like all the campesinos surveyed, including inquilinos like the Sagredos, Muñoz possessed her own livestock and tools and thus a certain independence from Guayalí's patrón. This was the case of Margarita Ramírez as well, a widow and female head of household who acquired rights to be settled as a colono with her livestock and agricultural implements on Ránquil. Ramírez would later be one of the handful of women who joined the rebellion.

While a large number of the campesinos surveyed by Fernández were identified as inquilinos or former inquilinos, not a single widow was identified by labor position, whether inquilino, gañan, or obrero agrícola. Their only social identity for the government surveyor was their status as widow of a colono or ocupante. If settling land and improving the property were conditions for acquiring legal titles and colono status, only men's labor was recognized by government officials. Thus when the women's husbands died, their property rights derived from their status as inquilinos' or ocupantes' widows, not their own labor or land rights.[10]

The subordination of female campesinas' labor to male heads of household and its elision in official documents were visible in the organization of both the Sindicato Agrícola Lonquimay and the Nitrito Colonos Committee. When inquilinos occupied estate land and claimed it as their own, they did so as families. That is, in Alto Bío Bío, as throughout southern Chile, inquilinos and ocupantes invaded or occupied estate land not as individuals, but as households. Women joined their husbands in these actions to appropriate estate land, but none of the leaders of the campesino organizations were women. Male heads of household represented Alto Bío Bío's campesinos to the state in their many meetings with government officials and, organized in union councils and local committees, in their struggles with the region's landowners.

On 1 February 1934 Fernández ordered the rebellious (male) inquilinos and ocupantes to come to his camp, where he would allocate their plots in Llanquén. The campesinos appeared to understand that the surveyor's instructions had no teeth because not one of those designated to be removed from Nitrito showed up. Fernández notified them that they had to appear the following week and that if they didn't he would inform the lands ministry. He directed them to suspend work on the land they occupied. When this threat bore little result, the surveyor informed the lands directorate by telegraph. He returned to his camp on 14 February with orders from the directorate: "Tell the ocupantes and inquilinos that if they don't present themselves to receive assigned plots by February 20, they will lose their rights to be settled [as colonos]." The majority of the workers were busy with their harvests, and only two signed documents certifying that they would receive plots in Llanquén.[11]

Meanwhile, a committee of campesinos from Nitrito traveled to Santiago and met with President Alessandri, the second time a president had received rural laborers from Alto Bío Bío in La Moneda. The committee asked that he intervene to prevent the eviction of the fifty-four families from Guayalí. As during the Ibáñez regime, the committee received support from Democratic Party congressmen. Party leaders met with Alessandri, accompanied by Pedro Rivera Muñoz, who attended the meeting "representing 240 colono families in Alto Bío Bío, to ask that fifty families not be thrown off their land." Alessandri eschewed the rousing populist language Leiva Tapia had encountered when he met with Ibáñez in 1928. The president made no assurances he would prevent the campesinos' eviction from Nitrito, but he did promise them he would look into the situation with his lands minister.[12]

The Nitrito colonos' meeting with Alessandri took place in the heated climate of debate about the new colonization law. The law under consideration in congress now gave the president the power to purchase and subdivide southern estates where there had been "questions of social order before 1 July 1933" and distribute small plots to ocupantes who would be organized in cooperatives.[13] It also gave the president the power to expropriate fundos by decree in the name of utilidad pública to provide the Caja de Colonización Agrícola land on which it would organize colonies of agricultural laborers. Shortly after his meeting with the aspiring colonos from Alto Bío Bío, Alessandri requested that congress provide $10 million pesos to the bank, three million of which would be employed to resolve "social conflicts" over land. On 19 February 1934 the House of Deputies passed Law No. 3420 authorizing the president to spend $3 million pesos to acquire fundos in the region governed by the Southern Property Law, "with the goal of settling ... the ocupantes of said properties who have material possession of the land."[14]

Perhaps because the ocupantes on Guayalí held on to the hope that the new colonization law being negotiated between Alessandri and congress would finally result in the long-delayed purchase of the estate, they refused to follow Fernández's instructions to abandon their land in the Nitrito Valley. Rumors reached the surveyor that the ocupantes Simón Sagredo, Juan Pablo Ortíz, and Modesto Acuña—all of whom would play leadership roles in the rebellion—were going to the houses of the Guayalí inquilinos, "counseling them that they should stay where they were." Fernández requested that Cautín's intendant intervene to expel the ocupantes-inquilinos. On 13 February the three leaders of the

Nitrito colonos committee were informed that they had to present themselves at the intendancy in Temuco. The intendancy imparted orders that the Nitrito inquilinos-ocupantes move to Llanquén within forty-eight hours. The instructions to the carabineros were clear: "If they put up resistance, they will be forcibly evicted."[15] But this measure backfired. Simón Sagredo simply refused to go, and Modesto Acuña and Juan Pablo Ortíz returned from the meeting in Temuco even more "fired up" (*exaltados*) since the authorities had taken no measures against them.[16] The spirit of resistance spread. A frustrated Fernández reported that those inquilinos on the Guayalí fundo who had accepted settlement on the four thousand hectares in Llanquén refused to move and continued to work on the land they occupied: "The only measure left to take and which will have results," he concluded, "is *lanzamiento* [eviction]."[17]

A week later a lieutenant at the head of twelve carabineros arrived at Fernández's camp from Lonquimay, following the orders of the Cautín intendancy. The carabineros gave the *pobladores sublevados* forty-eight hours to move to their plots in Llanquén. The aspiring colonos then sent telegraphs to President Alessandri, and the officer informed the intendancy that the eviction would produce serious social disorder. As a result, the eviction notice was suspended while the government in Santiago decided what course to pursue. When the carabineros arrived, eleven campesinos had signed documents (*actas de entrega*) in which they agreed to accept plots in Llanquén and abandon their land in the Nitrito Valley. But once the eviction order was suspended and the carabineros had returned to Lonquimay, the pobladores reassumed their "subversive and bellicose attitude."[18] On 4 March Fernández met with the intendant in Temuco, who informed him that he had received instructions from the president and interior minister to take no measures without an "exact and definitive order" from the government in Santiago. It appears that the major stumbling block was the Bunster family's refusal to sell land from Guayalí in the Nitrito Valley to the Caja de Colonización Agrícola. Fernández then returned to Lonquimay and began an assessment of Ránquil in order to calculate how much Rosa Puelma should be reimbursed for the expropriation of Ránquil.[19]

On 13 March Fernández sent a telegram to the intendancy denouncing abuses committed by the campesinos, whom he described as sublevados, and requested that a pair of carabineros be sent to maintain order on the Guayalí estate.[20] That day Cautín's intendant received instructions from the interior minister that he could proceed to order the evictions from Guayalí and settle the rebellious ocupantes in Llanquén. A surveyor working with Fernández proceeded to inform the ocupantes that they had to move by March 15.[21] A number continued to resist, offering different explanations for their refusal to move out of the Nitrito Valley. Gregorio Vidal Muñoz, for example, did not agree with the boundaries of his assigned plot and wanted them altered and expanded. According to the surveyor, Vidal was only looking for a pretext to delay moving and was really waiting for the results of meetings that union leaders were holding in Santiago with government officials, hoping to stave off the imminent evictions. Similarly, Domingo Díaz Norambuena told the surveyor Aguilar that after he heard discussions in a union assembly, he had changed his mind and wanted to continue to stay on his land with the other rebeldes, since they had news that they were going to get some results from the meetings in Santiago. A group of seven aspiring colonos stated that they were just beginning to harvest their crops and needed more time before moving out of the valley. The surveyor confirmed that the harvests were late that year because of bad weather but concluded that the ocupantes were using this as a pretext for delaying the move to Llanquén while they awaited news from Santiago. Union leaders had "promised them land on the best parts of the fundo Guayalí [in the Nitrito Valley] as long as they didn't accept plots [in Llanquén]."[22]

On 21 March the interior minister sent another telegram to Cautín's intendant authorizing him to employ carabineros to proceed with evictions of the recalcitrant campesinos. The intendant agreed to place carabineros at the disposal of Fernández, who would direct the evictions.[23] That same day, however, the Democratic Party senator Artemio Gutiérrez and Deputy Arturo Huenchullán sent an urgent telegram to the intendancy in Temuco. Juan Pablo Ortíz had told them that Alessandri and his lands minister had promised the campesinos that there would be no evictions and that the government would purchase the Guayalí estate in order to bring the conflict to a peaceful end.[24] This new political intervention led to something of a stalemate. Apparently the intendant refrained from ordering the evictions and, in frustration, Fernández requested that he be permitted to return to Santiago.

In the meantime, Arturo Huenchullán traveled to the south, hoping to resolve the conflict on the ground, while Artemio Gutiérrez remained in Santiago, where he attempted to negotiate a settlement between the government, the Bunster family, and the aspiring colonos. The Bunsters were willing to cede four thousand hectares in rocky Llanquén but persevered in their refusal to relinquish land in the Nitrito Valley. In the end, Gutiérrez's intervention bore little fruit, and, according to Huenchullán, the government had to respect the Bunster family's property rights and evict the ocupantes and their families from Nitrito.[25]

The Bunster family did not follow the Puelmas' path of recognizing the expropriation of their estate and accepting indemnification from the government. Rosa Puelma resided in Santiago and rarely if ever visited the estate she had inherited from her father. She had rented the estate for a number of years to Gastón Rambeaux and then engaged in lengthy litigation with her renter, while encountering major conflicts with Rambeaux's administrator, José Paz. The Bunsters, on the other hand, visited their estate regularly and resided in the nearby town of Los Ángeles. As Gonzalo Bunster's conflict with his inquilino Albino Acuña demonstrated, Guayalí's owner had personal relationships, often conflictive and violent to be sure, with his workers and exercised his authority over his property and workers in person during visits to the estate, even if he left the day-to-day management in the hands of the administrator, Víctor Vergara. As the long-standing conflicts with both neighboring Pehuenche communities and estate laborers made clear, the Bunsters had no intention of giving up their claims to the Ralco and Guayalí estates. And the Alessandri government appeared to have little interest in moving against a powerful southern landowning family. Perhaps this had something to do with politics as well. Alessandri had appointed a member of the Bunster family, Mario Bunster, to be intendant of Cautín, cementing ties between the president and one of southern Chile's most prominent families.

On 26 March Fernández received a telegram from the lands directorate ordering him to remain in Alto Bío Bío because the interior minister had imparted new and final orders to the intendant to come to a definitive solution to the situation of the ocupantes in Guayalí. The intendant had received orders to proceed with the evictions, and on 1 April Fernández arrived at his camp accompanied by a captain from Victoria and lieutenant from Lonquimay at the head of a force of twenty-five carabineros "to fulfill orders given by the interior minister."[26] On 2 April Fernández once again notified the pobladores sublevados that they had to move immediately. Now, however, he was backed by carabineros and the interior minister's orders. Of fifty-four families, thirty now accepted plots in Llanquén. Seven families asked to be settled in the Ránquil colony, seventeen said they did not want to receive plots because they were leaving to work in neighboring "fields and towns" but would stay temporarily in Llanquén.[27]

A last-ditch effort by Arturo Huenchullán failed to sway Alessandri from following through with the eviction. On 3 April the deputy telegrammed the president to alert him that the "eviction order being implemented by thirty carabineros is causing alarm in the entire region. . . . Fifty and more families will remain on the public road in the middle of the cordillera's hard winter." "It is probable," he warned Alessandri, "that there will be deaths like in San Gregorio," a reference to the infamous 1921 massacre of protesting nitrate miners during Alessandri's first government.[28] Despite this appeal to the president, carabineros proceeded to expel the remaining ocupantes in Nitrito from their land, burning their small huts and, according to the ocupantes, appropriating their provisions and tools. On 7 April the carabineros informed the intendancy that they had gone to Lonquimay and implemented the eviction order "dictated by the Supreme Government against the ocupantes of the Guayalí estate." The carabineros also arrested Simón and Benito Sagredo, whom they referred to as "two subversive individuals," for resisting the carabineros' actions and for being Communists.[29] The carabineros reported that when they were following government orders to expel the ocupantes from Guayalí, the Sagredos opposed their actions and incited the other ocupantes to resist using any means they could.[30] A picket of nine carabineros remained on Guayalí to prevent any of the campesinos from returning to occupy land within the estate.[31]

The Sagredo brothers were detained for a number of reasons. They had instigated the local population to oppose the resettlement in Llanquén to be sure. But the crime cited in carabineros' reports was their alleged work as communist agitators in inciting the local population to revolt against the state. The carabineros obtained some evidence to back these accusations. In one of the Sagredo brothers' homes they found a pamphlet from the 1932 plenary session of the executive committee of the Chilean Communist Party titled "The Great Battles to Come" (Hacia los Grandes Combates). The pamphlet appeared to show that the Sagredo brothers at this point were supporters of and possibly militants in the Communist Party.[32] According to the carabineros' report, Simón Sagredo was a "recognized communist element," a leader of the Nitrito ocupantes who had incited inquilinos to disobey the government with his "continuous subversive preaching." He was also a leader of the Sindicato Agrícola Lonquimay.

The Communist Party pamphlet might help explain both the position of the party and the ways in which the party's platform informed the thinking of the rebellion's leaders. "Hacia los Grandes Combates" was a searing attack on the Alessandri government and Chile's devastating poverty and unemployment. It began by denouncing Alessandri's agrarian and colonization policy for "condemning to death thousands of unemployed people, agricultural workers, with the swindle of selling them parcels of uncultivable land, condemning vast sectors of campesinos to ruin." This section of the pamphlet was underlined in pen, suggesting that it represented a key position for Sagredo. In fact, the Communist Party's attack on Alessandri's colonization law echoed Leiva Tapia's denunciation of the policy at the congress of the Socialist Colonization Central the prior November, reflecting both a radical critique of the law's limitations and the party's view of Alessandri and his limited social reforms as a threat to its organizing efforts in the countryside.

The pamphlet also decried the Alessandri government's use of repression and violence. It attacked in personal terms Alessandri's resort to the Internal State Security Law promulgated by Dávila (Decree Law No. 50) to crush workers' liberties and repress hundreds of working-class leaders as well as the activities of the Republican Militias, "white guards" which were preparing "to attack the starving and rebellious people." According to the Communist Party, Alessandri had made it clear with his support of the militias and repression of labor and the Left that Chilean democracy was a farce. The party called for the dismantling of the Republican Militias, the organization of workers' self-defense pickets, and an end to the array of repressive laws implemented by both Ibáñez and Alessandri, which violated the freedoms of association and the press as well as the right to strike.

While the Sagredo brothers were under arrest, an event occurred that foreshadowed things to come. When the carabineros went to detain Simón Sagredo, he pulled out a revolver and attempted to open fire on them. The carabineros said that the trigger stuck and Sagredo failed to get a shot off. Sagredo's account differed. He had pointed his gun at the carabineros but only to "meter cuco" (scare them) since the gun didn't work. Whichever version is true, it certainly says something about social relations in Alto Bío Bío. A former inquilino on the Guayalí fundo, who now squatted on land within the estate and was a leader of the Sindicato Agrícola Lonquimay, went about challenging landowner authority, disobeying the public authorities, and threatening carabineros with a pistol.[33]

Included as evidence was a letter Simón Sagredo gave to the carabineros addressed to "the *jefe de carabineros* who expelled the colonos from Nitrito." Sagredo began the letter by noting that the "Nitrito colonos" had not been heard in their many petitions. As "Chileans and men," he declared, "we will defend our homes that are now threatened ... with our blood and at the cost of our lives. We are also sons of this country called Chile, and we prefer to die rather than starve on those rocky, inhospitable lands where the government has sent us to settle, handing over our cultivated land to the millionaire landowners." The letter was signed by the Nitrito Colonos Defense Committee.[34]

Sagredo's language revealed codes of masculine honor that shaped campesinos' relationship to landownership. He invoked his rights as a male head of household and male citizen, a son of the nation, to claim public land.[35] In part, his appeal to masculine dignity and citizenship rights was rooted in colonization laws implemented since the nineteenth century. Consistent with the agrarian legislation of the time, Sagredo, like other campesinos, understood landownership and the rights of colonos to settle on public land as due to men who were heads of families. Thus the Sagredo brothers represented both their children and their sisters in their claims to be settled in the Nitrito Valley as colonos. Similarly, the other leaders of the Nitrito colonos' committee, men like Modesto Acuña and Juan Pablo Ortíz, were heads of household.

Despite the carabineros' report, the Victoria court ordered the Sagredos released on 12 April since there was not enough evidence to support preventive detention. And on 16 May the court found that there was insufficient basis to back the charge of subverting the public order. Free from prison, the Sagredos continued organizing the Nitrito ocupantes to resist their forced removal to Llanquén. Perhaps they were animated now even more by the abuse they had suffered while detained. In the barracks on Guayalí the carabineros had hung the Sagredo brothers from a beam by their wrists and beaten them; when they were released, they could not even move their arms to dress themselves. When carabineros went to detain them, they also beat the Sagredo brothers' sister Emelina with a saber. She remembered that: "I saw them taking [Benito and Simón] away on horses and I shouted at them: 'Bandit, why are you taking my brothers away?' And the *paco* [cop] took out a *charrasca* [blade], like a long sabre that they use, and hit me in the back ... with the flat side. Later I wanted to go help them because I heard that they had hung them all night by their wrists from a beam with a hard strap, those they use for lassos, in the Bunsters' *calabozo* [cell]." Like other landowners in Chile, the Bunsters appear to have had their own cell or guardroom where they detained disobedient inquilinos.[36]

Earlier, the Sagredos had helped to organize the Nitrito Colonos Defense Committee, which bore the stamp of the Communist Party. They were aided by the teacher who ran a school for Pehuenches in Ralco, Luis Muñoz, who, when he was arrested during the rebellion, had "subversive *proclamas* (manifestos)" signed by the Nitrito Colonos Defense Committee that had been circulating in Alto Bío Bío's fundos.[37] One proclama, titled "Manifesto of the Nitrito Colonos to the Region's Campesinos, Obreros, and Indígenas," reproduced faithfully Communist Party rhetoric and positions calling for energetic opposition to landowners and the state. The manifesto began by describing how the colonos had been expelled from Nitrito by the "government of Arturo Alessandri, which starves and massacres obreros and campesinos." Carabineros had sacked and set fire to their huts (*chozas*), "committing every kind of abuse against us and our defenseless women." The pamphlet elaborated on how the bloodthirsty carabinero who had led the violent eviction, Captain Fierro, had beaten workers in the Las Raíces tunnel and imprisoned the Sagredo brothers, who had also been savagely beaten (the pamphlet was evidently printed after the Sagredos' release and before the revolt). It was not uncommon for disobedient laborers to suffer physical abuse at the hands of landowners and carabineros. During the rebellion the Sagredos cited the harsh punishment they had received after their arrest as a symptom of the violence campesinos faced during their eviction from the Nitrito Valley.

The Communist Party pamphlet then followed the party's ideological line, denouncing the actions of "social democratic" Democratic Party politicians in the region. It stated that Artemio Gutiérrez and "el indio Huenchullán" had deceived the Nitrito ocupantes-colonos when they promised that they would not be evicted and urged them to accept Alessandri's assurances. It described "the anguishing situation in which we now find ourselves, 63 families of colonos, on 25 hectares of land [each] high up in the cordillera without land apt for cultivation or pasture for our livestock, since snow covers all the sparse grasses. Our food, which consists of the seeds which we had saved for planting, will run out, and the animals, with which we cultivate the land, will die for lack of pasture, and we will die for lack of food, shelter, and clothing in the cold and harsh winter." Thousands of workers in Lonquimay's gold placer mines were also "dying from hunger and cold, living in the open air and in huts made of branches."

The manifesto asserted, as had the Sagredos, that the Alessandri government had appropriated lands which they had made productive with their labor and handed them over to the "bandit Gonzalo Bunster." This charge was repeated: Alessandri had increased the number of carabineros in the region in order to help Bunster appropriate their land and livestock; the Bunsters and their agents were "land thieves who sack and kill defenseless campesinos." With its denunciation of the ways in which Alessandri had sold Chile out to "gringo imperialists, the national bourgeoisie, and feudal landlords," its attacks on social democrats, and its denunciation of the violent repression made concrete in the paramilitary Republican Militias, the manifesto's rhetoric mirrored that of the Communist Party. Its rousing call to action also rang with party rhetoric: "In the face of all these injustices we make a fervent call to all campesinos, obreros, and indios, to unite with iron strength in the Federación Obrera de Chile or in Committees of Campesinos and Indios to fight for the reconquest of our land, which has been usurped. . . . Let's struggle for the organizations of Soviets of Obreros, Campesinos, and Indios, the only way to obtain the free enjoyment of the land, for bread and liberty."[38]

Luis Muñoz had a second proclama when he was arrested, this one issued by the regional committee of the Communist Party in Concepción. This manifesto was titled "In Defense of the Alto Bío Bío Colonos" and was addressed to the "Worker, Campesino and Indio Comrades." It exhorted them to prevent "the pillaging and dispossession of the workers, campesinos, and indios."[39] It would appear that much of the language from the Nitrito colonos' manifesto was taken directly from this manifesto, including a denunciation of how Alessandri, "the massacrer of San Gregorio and La Coruña, has razed with blood and fire the huts of the Nitrito colonos." The proclama likewise related, with a strong dose of hyperbole, that Captain Fierro, "the bloodhound of the landowners," had "beaten barbarically the colonos Simón and Benito Sagredo and shot and beaten with sticks the rest of the colonos." The manifesto listed a series of violent dispossessions of ocupantes-colonos, including in Pellahuén and Toltén, noting the "repetition of these criminal evictions in Ralco and other sectors, condemning to death by hunger and cold hundreds of campesino families." It demanded the restoration of the Nitrito ocupantes' land and called on them to organize committees of campesinos and unions of inquilinos and obreros agrícolas. Notably, it did not call for armed resistance or an armed insurrection.

The forced displacement of the Nitrito colonos out of the valley to Llanquén was the last straw for many of the campesinos who had worked for years to be settled on land in Alto Bío Bío they considered public. As Simón Sagredo noted in his letter, the aspiring colonos were prepared to defend their land by all means necessary, even by spilling their blood. The land reforms introduced under Ibáñez, especially the Southern Property Law, and Ibáñez's commitment to extending labor laws to the countryside and permitting the unionization of rural workers, raised southern campesinos' expectations that estate land would be expropriated and redistributed to inquilinos and ocupantes. These measures had, in the spirit of the Ibáñez regime's corporatist ideology, been intended to establish social peace and order as well as modernization in the countryside. Instead, by raising and then, ultimately, frustrating campesinos' hopes for meaningful changes in land and labor relations in southern Chile, these reforms only pushed rural workers to pursue both armed and unarmed collective action in defense of land they considered either public or their own because of the years of labor they had invested in making it productive. In addition, given that a number of the Sindicato Agrícola Lonquimay's leaders, including Leiva Tapia and the Sagredo brothers, were now allied with the FOCH and Communist Party, the party's rhetoric and ideology established a framework for interpreting the Alessandri government as illegitimate. Furthermore, they encouraged the organizing of self-defense committees to oppose the repressive government and its paramilitary Republican Militias as well as a president who had presided over some of the most infamous massacres of workers in Chilean history.

On 13 May 1934 complementary elections for the House of Deputies were held in Bío-Bío province. Juan Segundo Leiva Tapia ran for the seat as a candidate of the Communist Party, coming in last behind candidates from the Socialist and Democratic parties as well as the eventual Radical Party winner.[40] Leiva Tapia was now clearly a party member and pursued the party's dual strategy of running candidates in elections while preparing grassroots mobilizations in strikes and land invasions with the ultimate goal of installing a government of soviets. Perhaps Leiva Tapia's defeat in the elections propelled him along the insurrectionary path. Regardless, campesinos' increasing militancy on the ground found formal political expression in the ideological move of figures like Leiva Tapia, the Sagredos, and the Sindicato Agrícola Lonquimay away from the Democratic Party to the Communist Party and their increasing inclination to challenge the Alessandri government's repressive measures with an insurrection from below.

A more local cause rooted in southern Chile's agrarian social relations pushed rural laborers to revolt in Alto Bío Bío. As a number of the Nitrito campesinos noted, when Fernández, supported by carabineros, attempted to move them from the Nitrito Valley to Llanquén, they had not had time to harvest their crops. If they abandoned their land, they would lose many months of labor as well as the basis of their subsistence. Simón Sagredo made this explicit in his letter when he stated forthrightly that in the move they would be handing over cultivated land to the millionaire landowners. In fact, the timing of the eviction is critical. April was the autumn harvest season. The Nitrito campesinos stood to lose not only their land to Bunster but also their crops. In a 1972 interview in the Communist Party publication *Ramona* commemorating the rebellion, Emelina Sagredo recalled:

> I was thirty-three at the time. We were 200 smallholders [*hijueleros*], those who barely survived on that impoverished soil. It was then that the Government gave us some forested land. We had to clear it with axes.... It was a year of good harvests. The wheat, the alfalfa, the rice grew like never before. We didn't have enough sacks for so much grain. We had never seen little plants and seedlings with so many buds. The grasses grew tall and juicy. It was because these were newly [cleared and cultivated] lands. And the ewes gave birth to three [lambs at once], and we had chickens.

There may be an element of nostalgia and exaggeration in this recollection, but these sentiments are worth underlining because they demonstrate that campesinos recalled the time before the rebellion, the years when they had cleared and cultivated their own land in the belief that the government would reward them with titles, as prosperous. To former inquilinos, the harvests must have been especially sweet because they belonged only to them: there was no landowner to extract a share, no landowner to appropriate their labor.[41]

Emelina Sagredo remembered that "just as the land began to produce, they evicted us. The guilty party was Gonzalo Bunster. He was the owner of the whole region. He couldn't be satisfied that the newly cleared land was in our hands, and he began to use his influence in the capital. And the butcher in La Moneda gave him what he pleased. It all passed into Bunster's hands." Sagredo's narrative highlights a sequence of events that were not commented on after the rebellion. It is not insignificant that a large segment of the interview deals with memories of how hard she and the other campesinos had labored to clear and plant land in the Nitrito Valley and how Gonzalo Bunster had moved in once their crops had been cultivated.

In the same issue of *Ramona* cited above, Ismael Cartes, one of the leaders of the revolt and a former inquilino on the Chilpaco estate who later settled on Ránquil, recalled in vivid detail the campesinos' stolen harvests and lamented the loss of their labor: "All our work remained behind there. The land cleared of forests and rocks, leveled, plowed, tilled ... and fertilized. We had prepared the soil for many years of cultivation, and they didn't even let us finish the first year." As Cartes recalled further,

> We left and moved up to higher, unoccupied rocky lands. They were poor soils, hard, rocky, we called the place *El Matadero*. It was the middle of April, and the first snow had begun to fall. We suffered a great deal. The cold bit bitterly. *El diablazo*. We were going to be buried in the snow until September. The forage we brought began to run out. The livestock became skinny. So we began to work the mountain soil. It was hard, like the devil. The plows couldn't break the soil. The oxen broke their backs pulling them. Our provisions became scarce and we began to starve. So we went up the mountain. Up high, a tree grows. We call it the Pehuén ... the Araucaria pine. It's a great tree that produces fruit, the piñones. That was the only thing we had to eat.

Bunster was not only staking property rights and asserting the legitimacy of his land titles. The timing of the campesinos' eviction suggests he was also acting to take their harvests and land, which now was valuable because it had been recently cleared and cultivated. The inquilinos and ocupantes saw Bunster not only stealing land granted them by the Ibáñez regime: he was also appropriating their crops and the labor they had invested in making the four thousand hectares in the Nitrito Valley productive.[42]

In fact, the developments in Alto Bío Bío conformed to a social dynamic that had increasingly defined land and labor relations on the frontier. Landowners contracted with inquilinos and medieros to clear and plant land on their estates and then expelled their laborers, effectively claiming ownership of their harvests, either of crops cultivated on shares (a medias) or of crops planted on plots granted to inquilinos in exchange for their labor on the estates. Many of the Sindicato Agrícola Lonquimay's petitions involved landowners' appropriation of inquilinos' improvements and harvests, basically the years of labor they had invested in making the tough Andean terrain cultivable. As early as 1929, for example, the union had denounced "the abuses and violations of rights that they are committing on the Puelma estates against the residents there because they belong to our Institution, evicting them and thus appropriating their improvements and harvests or preventing them from cultivating."[43]

During the late 1920s and early 1930s, as the labor authorities extended their reach into the remote mountain regions of Alto Bío Bío, a number of inquilinos and medieros went to labor courts in the city of Los Ángeles to complain about their treatment at the hands of their patrones.[44] As part of the 1931 labor code, the Ibáñez regime had expanded the system of labor courts introduced in 1927 to bolster the authority of labor inspectors, implement the new labor laws, and adjudicate conflicts between workers and employers.[45] The cases in the labor court reflect the development of the state-directed corporatist labor relations system introduced in 1924–25, as the Ibáñez regime initiated efforts to regulate labor and living conditions on rural estates as well as in urban areas. The very existence of the labor court cases in Los Ángeles speaks to the state's penetration of a rural society in which estate owners had held unchallenged power for generations. The cases also indicate that even in frontier regions like Alto Bío Bío rural workers had an increasing sense of rights and capacity to challenge estate owners' authority over land and labor.

A typical case was that of José Contreras, who took the landowner he worked for, Gustavo Neuman, to the labor court in Los Ángeles in January 1932. Contreras defined himself as an agricultural worker (obrero agrícola) who resided in the town of Los Ángeles. He had been contracted as an inquilino by Neuman to work on his Pallilhue estate. The verbal contract determined that Contreras would be paid a wage of one peso per day, plus regalías, which consisted of shares of the harvests he produced (making him as much a mediero as inquilino). Contreras had cultivated potatoes and corn on the estate, estimating that his harvests would be forty sacks of each, half of which were his and half of which belonged to Neuman, according to their agreement. He had followed Neuman's orders for a year, beginning in January 1931. However, before he could complete the harvest Neuman expelled him from the estate and appropriated his crops. In addition, Neuman had failed to keep his social security *libreta* up to date, paying taxes only until August 1931. Contreras's recourse to the labor authorities was successful, and both parties agreed that he would remain as an inquilino-mediero until after the harvest in April. Contreras, who was illiterate, signed the agreement brokered by the court with his thumbprint.[46] A similar suit was brought by the obrero agrícola Pedro María Arévalo, who went to court to demand restitution because a landowner, Meces Medis, with whom he had signed a mediería contract, had evicted him from his estate in May 1932 after he had worked there for six months. Medis owed him money, Arévalo claimed, for the harvests of wheat and oats he had produced and that Medis had appropriated without providing Arévalo his shares.[47]

Baldomero Jara Jara, an inquilino on the Campamento fundo brought a similar case against his patrón, Benjamín Carrasco, before the Los Ángeles labor court in 1932. He had worked for Carrasco for three years. According to their verbal contract, he was to receive one peso a day in wages, a cuadra of land to work on his own, and seeds and tools in exchange for his labor on the estate. In November 1931 Carrasco had fired Jara without any justifiable cause and retaken the cuadra of land he had cultivated for three years. In firing Jara, Carrasco was able to appropriate, without compensation, half a cuadra of wheat his inquilino had cultivated as well as the other half, which had been prepared for planting garden crops (*chacra*). Like other inquilinos, Jara would have both used his crops for his family's subsistence and marketed them locally or sold them to his patrón. Jara requested indemnification of $1,400 pesos (800 for the wheat and 600 for the chacra). The case was resolved before the labor authorities when Carrasco agreed to let Jara harvest his wheat and Jara agreed to follow Carrasco's orders, continuing his labor as his inquilino during the harvest for a wage of one peso a day. Jara also agreed to repay Carrasco a $40 peso debt (probably an advance payment for Jara's future harvest) and return wheat seeds Carrasco had given him.[48]

Landowners' practice of expelling inquilinos, medieros, and ocupantes before they could harvest their crops became so notorious that in early 1934 it sparked debate in congress over the pressing need to pass Alessandri's colonization law. In February 1934 the Democratic Party deputy Oscar Chanks Camus stated that in the region he represented, which included Traiguén, Victoria, and Lautaro, landowners were evicting a large number of laborers from their estates before they could harvest their crops. This was not a new practice but "happened every year." According to Chanks, generation after generation of laborers on the Pellahuén estate had lost their harvests when the property's wealthy absentee landowners arrived with armed men in Traiguén just before harvest time to expel ocupantes and steal their crops. The Democratic Party deputy Juan de Dios Ampuero denounced the expulsion of twenty-seven ocupantes just as they were ready to harvest their crops on the Cancha Rayada estate in Llanquihue. They had lost the crops they had "cultivated with so much labor and effort and with so much sacrifice" and had been "thrown onto the road into ruin."[49]

There is no concrete evidence that the Alessandri government ordered the Nitrito campesinos' eviction in order to allow the Bunster family to steal their harvests. However, the campesinos experienced the eviction not only as loss of land but also as appropriation of their crops and labor. Such abuse would become a defining dynamic during the revolt. When the Ránquil rebels assaulted estates and pulperías, they understood their actions as recuperation of goods stolen from them, their crops, tools, and other possessions, during the expulsion from the Nitrito Valley. In addition, they would have seen the carabineros' actions on behalf of the Bunsters as belonging to a broader social dynamic in which landowners frequently defrauded their inquilino and mediero laborers of land they had cleared and cultivated and their rightfully earned share of crops waiting to be harvested. Nor would the campesinos have experienced the violence that accompanied the eviction as unusual. Carabineros and landowners frequently burned campesinos' huts and appropriated their possessions during evictions. They often beat the campesinos at patrones' behest as well.

This time, however, conditions had changed. These were not defenseless laborers without the resources to confront landowner violence. They had organized a union with councils on estates throughout the region. The union had successfully represented their interests, and they had won the right to establish colonies on the Guayalí and Ránquil estates. In addition, they had organized self-defense committees and built alliances with the national labor federation, the FOCH, as well as with Democratic Party congressmen like Huenchullán and Gutiérrez. They now confronted both the state and the region's landowners with the strength of a labor organization five hundred strong that enjoyed national political support.

The campesinos were also armed with a sense of rights imparted by the labor and colonization laws as well as by the Ibáñez government's commitment to expropriating estates in the name of modernizing agricultural production and settling colonos on frontier land in southern Chile. The circulation of the terms "socialist," "agrarian reform," and the "socialization of landownership" emanating from the Alessandri government and sectors of the Liberal Party, as well as from the Radical, Democratic, and Agrarian parties, also added ideological fuel to the campesinos' drive to colonize Alto Bío Bío's haciendas. If even *El Diario Austral* could declare its enthusiastic support for agrarian reform, then surely the Sindicato Agrícola Lonquimay's goal of expropriating the Puelma and Bunster estates was not a stretch.

Finally, as Juan Segundo Leiva Tapia, the Sagredos, and other members of the Sindicato Agrícola Lonquimay's leadership moved to the left and aligned themselves with the FOCH and Communist Party, the party's rhetoric of an imminent insurrection to overthrow the Alessandri government backed by sectors of the military dovetailed with widespread land conflicts throughout southern Chile. Campesinos' increasingly violent challenges to both landowners' property rights and the authority of the state in the south appeared to Leiva Tapia and the other members of the union's leftist leadership to promise social revolution from below as a real possibility. This was a revolution that the Sindicato Agrícola Lonquimay was prepared to initiate in Alto Bío Bío, where, they imagined, isolated by winter storms from the rest of Chile, they would be protected from the state's repressive apparatus. The events of the past three years, from the naval mutiny to the Socialist Republic, had taught them that their revolutionary spark would ignite insurrections across Chile, from south to north.

CHAPTER EIGHT

"All You See Is Yours"
The Sindicato Agrícola Lonquimay's Road to Revolution

AT NIGHTFALL ON 21 June 1934 news arrived in Lonquimay that *impresos subversivos* (subversive manifestos) were circulating in the region's fields, towns, gold placer mines, and camps housing workers building the Las Raíces tunnel. The manifestos contained insults directed at "His Excellency [Arturo Alessandri] the President of the Republic," the Democratic Party congressmen Arturo Huenchullán and Artemio Gutiérrez, and carabineros. Rumors spread through Lonquimay and Alto Bío Bío that the colonos and miners in Ránquil, along with workers from the Las Juntas and Pedregoso gold placer mines, were preparing an uprising in Guayalí, Nitrito, and Lolco that would spread south through Ránquil, Rahue, the placer mines, and the Las Raíces tunnel. Rebellious workers were said to be preparing to sweep down from the north and sack Lonquimay. The date fixed for the uprising was winter's first great snowfall, which would block the mountain passes to Lonquimay, denying carabineros access to the region.[1]

Lonquimay's subdelegate, Augusto Schweitzer, asked the officer in charge of the town's police station, Lieutenant Luis Cabrera Urrutia, to investigate the reports, and on 22 June Cabrera sent a pair of carabineros to Ránquil.[2] Around the same time, an inquilino on one of the region's estates handed over twenty-three copies of the manifesto, and Cabrera spent 24 and 25 June questioning him. He sent the manifestos to his commanders and requested a warrant to apprehend "the individuals who distributed the manifestos."[3]

While rumors of an imminent insurrection swirled, eighty-six workers in the Las Juntas gold placers held an assembly to demand that the mine concessionaire provide them food. A letter from Lonquimay's leading citizens to the region's intendant noted that "given the existing alarm," the miners' assembly "was taken as an act of rebellion." Reports of the assembly arrived in Lonquimay on 22 June, when a committee of three workers came to town to meet with the state mine inspector, Humberto Carrasco. Carrasco informed Cabrera that the miners' meeting did not have a "subversive character." Rather, because winter weather made work in the placers impossible, the miners had been forced to ask the concessionaire for food on credit. They had come to Lonquimay to petition the inspector to exercise his influence with the concessionaire. After two days of meetings, Carrasco was able to obtain provisional food assistance for the miners. Nonetheless, public alarm grew. Lonquimay's leading citizens asked Schweitzer to call a meeting of the town's residents and public employees with the object of adopting some measures to prevent "terrorist attacks that were rumored to be in preparation." They agreed to ask the government to send twenty carabineros "to protect the town and private interests from the threats implied in the existing rumors about the sacking of Lonquimay by campesinos and mine workers."[4]

Lonquimay's leading citizens regarded workers in the region's gold placer mines (*lavadores de oro*) as posing as much of a threat to social order as the leaders of the Sindicato Agrícola Lonquimay. In 1931–32 the Ibáñez and Montero governments had initiated a Campaign for Gold, whose objective was to acquire precious reserves for the national treasury as prices of copper and nitrates plummeted on the world market. The government's effort to stimulate gold production took on greater urgency during the Socialist Republic and then during the government of Arturo Alessandri as Chile confronted insolvency. After 1932 the government provided concessions and licensed private entrepreneurs to install gold panning operations, while guaranteeing a fixed market and price for the gold they produced. At the same time, the government sought to settle thousands of unemployed workers in mining camps, where they would supply inexpensive labor for gold-panning operations.[5] While in some regions the state exploited gold directly, in others, like Alto Bío Bío, small, independent contractors were given concessions to work gold placers in exchange for a commitment to contract unemployed workers and sell their gold to the state agency in charge of gold mining. The government paid for the costs of transporting unemployed workers to the placers, gave them tools and equipment, and paid concessionaires subsidies. In some cases, concessionaires were required to establish pulperías, where their workers could purchase provisions.[6]

By 1933 gold placer mines employed thirty-one thousand workers throughout Chile.[7] A number of small gold concessions dotted the Andes cordillera in Alto Bío Bió, including within the borders of the Ránquil and Guayalí estates. Workers in the placers labored for low wages and lived in rudimentary huts in the mountains without plumbing and exposed to the elements, often sleeping on nothing more than piles of straw.[8] Curacautín's *El Comercio* published a report about miners near Lonquimay who lived in caves carved into the banks of the rivers where they labored without adequate clothing and food. Miners, like agricultural workers, were forced to buy provisions or exchange gold for food at local pulperías at extremely high prices. The placers were, the paper editorialized, a "human *matadero*" (slaughterhouse) where disease was rampant.[9] In at least two cases in Lonquimay, pulpería owners on estates were also gold-placer concessionaires whose workers exchanged their gold for goods. José Frau and Juan Zolezzi, the latter an Italian immigrant, both initiated gold-panning operations as concessions from the state and established pulperías in Troyo on the Ránquil estate.

To Lonquimay's leading citizens, miners represented the socially disruptive force of the unemployed and transient as well as northern Chile's long history of militant labor activism. Antonio Ortíz Palma is a good example of the miners who engaged in the rebellion. Ortíz Palma was thirty years old and illiterate. He was originally from Santiago but had worked in the north and was, he said, a member of the Socialist Party of Antofagasta. Ortíz Palma testified that on 16 April 1934 he was working in the gold placers in Lonquimay that were in charge of the concessionaire Juan Zolezzi. While he was at work a colono named González arrived and told his work gang (*cuadrilla*) that soon the social revolution would erupt and that the workers in the placer mines needed to organize. Shortly after this meeting he attended two meetings held in *ranchos* (huts) and led by the "agitator colono González and the secretary of the Sindicato de Mineros."[10] By 1934 workers in the gold placers, most of them from the north, had organized a union.

As the economic crisis deepened, it appears that ocupantes and colonos, many of them former inquilinos, also worked in Alto Bío Bío's placers, exchanging their gold for food at the local pulperías. At a time of bitter poverty, the rivers' gold kept both unemployed workers from the north and the region's obreros agrícolas alive. One description of Ránquil recounted how the members of the new colony devoted themselves to panning for gold and contraband to sustain themselves.[11] This introduced a new dynamic in Alto Bío Bío's social relations. By 1933–34 the region's working poor had come to rely increasingly on the placers for their survival and on the pulperías where they sold their gold. As they confronted starvation during harsh winter months when panning for gold was impossible, they came to view the pulperías as the immediate cause of their misery.

The other source of fear felt by Lonquimay's residents stemmed from the hundreds of workers employed in building the Las Raíces tunnel through the cordillera, which would connect the region, isolated on the eastern slopes of the Andes, to Curacautín and the rest of Chile. The government had initiated work on the tunnel as a public works project to produce jobs for the unemployed. Hundreds of workers, like many of the miners panning for gold, came from the north. As in the gold placers, the FOCH sent organizers to the rough camps housing the tunnel's workers. In late 1933 the FOCH publication *Justicia* reported optimistically on the possibilities for organizing a union among the tunnel's two hundred workers.[12] Police reports would later indicate that communist delegates had held meetings with the workers and distributed "subversive manifestos" in the workers' camps. In early April 1934 Cautín's intendant reported that eight hundred workers had engaged in a strike, demanding wage increases and the dismissal of a mayordomo and capataz general. Despite the workers' reportedly peaceful and respectful behavior, the intendant sent fifty carabineros to the tunnel to put an end to the strike. The company in charge of building the tunnel then fired many workers and expelled them from the camps.[13] Nonetheless, FOCH organizing in the Boca Sur camp fueled rumors that the tunnel's workers were going to join agricultural laborers and miners in a broad insurrectionary movement.

As the rebellion unfolded during the last week of June, *El Diario Austral* reported that carabineros had established that days before the rebellion "two delegates from the Federación Obrera de Chile and one delegate from the Ránquil rebels [*facciosos de Ránquil*], affiliated with the Communist Party, met with the workers of Boca Sur." The police reported that these delegates "incited the workers to revolt and asked that when the revolt broke out they mutiny and cut off access to the carabineros who would come as reinforcements."[14] Perhaps because of the repression of the strike, however, workers from Las Raíces played no role in the rebellion, and carabineros were able to move through the tunnel toward Lonquimay.

On 27 June Cabrera sent two carabineros to Ránquil to investigate and arrest "the individuals who had distributed subversive manifestos insulting His Excellency the president and carabineros days before." The two carabineros returned to Lonquimay at four in the morning the next day and informed Cabrera that they had been told by a resident of Ránquil that the previous day "a large group of individuals armed with carbines, revolvers, shotguns, fire arms, and clubs ... assaulted the pulperías belonging to Bruno Ackermann, Juan Zolezzi, and José Frau Pujol, the first located in the ford of the Bio Bío River in Ránquil, the other two in the place called Troyo." In addition, they reported that "the *asaltantes* had assassinated srs. Zolezzi, Alfonso Zañartu, and Pedro Acuña Lobos, the former two partners in the Zolezzi pulpería and the latter an employee in the Frau pulpería."[15]

Cabrera immediately ordered his entire force of eleven men to get ready to confront the *revoltosos* (rebels) and block their march toward Lonquimay. Before departing, Cabrera conferred full police powers upon subdelegate Schweitzer, authorizing him to organize the defense of Lonquimay and to recruit "trustworthy people" into a civilian militia, a Guardia Blanca (White Guard). Within a few hours the militia numbered about forty members, all chosen from Lonquimay's most select citizens. The intendant of Cautín later gave the White Guard formal authority to exercise police powers in Lonquimay.[16] Lonquimay residents had already organized a Republican Militia. These paramilitary organizations prepared to defend the town against an attack by "the subversive movement."[17]

The Communist Party and Preparations for Rebellion

Ample evidence shows that Communist Party militants played a role in organizing and leading the insurrection. Following the rebellion's repression, a number of prisoners testified that FOCH and Communist Party delegates from Concepción had been traveling around the region, sowing the seeds of insurrection. Two prisoners detained after the revolt testified, for example, that during the days before the rebellion two communist delegates had traveled to Alto Bío Bío, where they distributed manifestos and celebrated meetings in Quilleime and Troyo. The delegates had spread "revolutionary propaganda in Alto Bío Bío, especially in Ránquil and Llanquén." The informants told the police that the communist delegates had convinced people that a revolt was possible because carabineros "wouldn't come since they would be busy fighting a revolt that had broken out throughout Chile."[18] A police report established, on the basis of information obtained from other detainees, that two Communists, "un tal Alarcón" (one Alarcón) and José Emiliano Balboa, had come from Concepción along with two other unidentified individuals to direct the movement.[19] *El Diario Austral* reported that the "agitador máximo" (leading agitator) Alarcón had "continuously made trips from Lota to Lonquimay, meeting with Leiva."[20]

Alarcón appears often in the testimony of prisoners detained after the rebellion. They describe him as a delegate from the Lota coal mines near Concepción, a Communist, and a leader of the movement. Alarcón's presence and his revolutionary discourse at the union assembly that triggered the rebellion indicate the role played by the FOCH or the Communist Party's regional committee or both in the coal mining region of Concepción in organizing the rebellion. After the rebellion was repressed, police arrested three "subversives" who were alleged to have been organizing a "revolutionary strike" in the Lota and Coronel coal mines. The plan, as given in a police report, was for the movement to also take over the carabineros' barracks in Lota and Arauco. One of the three detainees, Manuel Hernández, had in his possession "manifestos that provoked sedition" and had been in contact with Juan Segundo Leiva Tapia.[21] It is difficult to know how much value to assign to this police account. But it is likely the Communist Party's manifestos were indeed circulating in Lota given the party's presence among coal miners and in the city of Concepción. Added to reports of Alarcón's role in organizing the rebellion, the specific claim that one of the three Lota "subversives" had been in contact with Leiva Tapia is certainly plausible.

The figure of José Emiliano Balboa is more complicated and reflects the government's and the press's tendency to lump all radical social activists together as communists regardless of their political orientation. Balboa, a blacksmith who worked on the San Ramón estate near Loncopangue, was detained for participating in the revolt. He testified that he had worked on San Ramón for ten years and had been a member of the Democratic Party since 1925. His involvement in the revolt began when he attended a union assembly in Quilleime led by Simón Sagredo, Juan Segundo Leiva Tapia, and "one Alarcón, a delegate from Lota." Balboa's social profile differed slightly from the agricultural laborers who composed the bulk of the Sindicato Agrícola Lonquimay's membership. As a blacksmith, he was a skilled worker, but like inquilinos he resided on and was employed by a large estate. San Ramón lay about 172 miles by road north of Lonquimay, south of Los Ángeles. That a worker on a Loncopangue estate was an active member of the union is a sign of the Sindicato Agrícola Lonquimay's influence throughout Alto Bío Bío. Balboa's militancy in the Democratic Party indicated that the party continued to exercise influence on the union's politics well into 1934.[22]

Other figures detained following the revolt were, however, members of the Communist Party. One of them was Higinio Godoy, a forty-year-old shoemaker and native of Concepción who was living in Boca Sur.[23] After being released from detention, Godoy confessed to having been in charge of distributing subversive manifestos in violation of the Internal Security of the State Law (Decree-Law No. 50) implemented during the Dávila regime.[24] In his confession, he said that he had been distributing manifestos printed by "subversive presses" throughout the region. The manifestos incited workers to revolt and engage in strikes as the best means of implanting a government of workers, campesinos, and soldiers.[25] Godoy probably printed and distributed the manifestos found by carabineros in the possession of Luis Muñoz and the Sagredos, both the manifestos of the Nitrito Colonos Defense Committeee and the Concepción Regional Committee of the Communist Party.

Godoy, as Olga Ulianova notes, was an important figure in the Communist Party. While both the police and *El Diario Austral* referred to him as Reginio or Remigio Godoy, Ulianova points out that the Godoy detained after the revolt for printing and distributing "impresos subversivos" was, in fact, Higinio Godoy, who appears frequently in the declassified documentation of the Comintern.[26] For a brief period in 1930, before the entire committee was arrested by the Ibáñez regime, he had been secretary general of the party's central committee. In 1932, having been released from prison, he headed the executive council of the FOCH. That a distinguished party and FOCH leader like Godoy had been in Boca Sur speaks to the presence of Communist Party leadership in, at a minimum, engaging in ideological work, printing and distributing "impresos subversivos" among agricultural laborers, miners, and workers in the Las Raíces tunnel.

Ulianova views Godoy's arrest as evidence of the Communist Party leadership's role in the revolt. However, the details of his detention demonstrate only the party's attempt to organize workers in Alto Bío Bío, not its role in either planning or leading the revolt. It is telling that the Temuco appellate court chose not to charge Godoy for any of the crimes committed during the revolt or for taking part in or leading the revolt. He was charged only with distributing subversive manifestos. The manifestos' rhetoric was indeed revolutionary and an expression of the Communist Party's ideological line, including denunciations of Alessandri and "social democratic" Democratic Party congressmen. None of them, however, promoted an armed insurrection, other than the exhortation to campesinos, indígenas, and obreros to engage in strikes and organize unions, self-defense committees, and soviets. That Godoy was not in attendance at the meeting that launched the rebellion, was never identified by witnesses as one of the rebellion's organizers, and was never charged for crimes related to the revolt indicates that he probably played no role in the movement's planning. Rather, his presence in Boca Sur and on the list of detainees suggests he was engaged in political work in the region, drawn there not only by the organizing possibilities presented by the large groups of workers in the Las Raíces tunnel and the gold placer mines but also by ties that had been established between the FOCH and the Sindicato Agrícola Lonquimay the previous year. In fact, Godoy's evident absence in the planning of the rebellion suggests that the Communist Party's national leadership played no role in directing or organizing the revolutionary insurrection.

The evidence does demonstrate that local leaders like Alarcón, the Sagredos, and Leiva Tapia as well as FOCH delegates had organized workers in the El Raíces tunnel, the region's gold placer mines, and on the Puelma and Bunster estates in an insurrectionary movement. They had contacts who, if not Communist Party militants, certainly had ties to the party. Among these was Luis Muñoz, the teacher who ran a "school for indios," as it was often described, in Ralco. Muñoz was arrested after the revolt, as noted above, in possession of Communist Party proclamas. Although he did not face charges for participating in the revolt, a number of prisoners testified that he circulated the proclamas and held meetings with Leiva Tapia, Alarcón, and the Sagredos during the months leading up to it. A local union leader named Astudillo was also active in the FOCH and probably in the Communist Party, attending and addressing the June 1934 FOCH congress as a delegate from Alto Bío Bío and meeting with the Sagredos, Leiva Tapia, Alarcón, and Muñoz, among others, in the month preceding the rebellion.

A denunciation to the police made by Constancio Cortés, a concessionaire of the Polón gold placers in Lonquimay's cordillera, vividly depicts these meetings. On 7 June, Cortés reported, he sent his son and one of his workers to the home of Luis Mendes near the Mayay estuary to purchase wheat and flour. Because of a landslide triggered by heavy rain and snowfall they were unable to return home and lodged in Mendes's house. That night "two Communists" met with a number of "indios" in Mendes's house. Cortés stated that he had known that Juan Segundo Leiva Tapia and Benito and Simón Sagredo had had various meetings before in Mendes's house. According to Cortés's son, one of the Communists, named Astudillo, told the group they had come to arrive at an agreement with the other compañeros, Leiva Tapia, the Sagredos, and others who were in Lepoi, Guayalí, Nitrito, and Ránquil, and they distributed *volantes* (fliers).[27] Many of the volantes, Cortés said, had been found among the "indios Trepay y Maya, who had been given them by the same two Communists."[28]

At the meeting in Luis Mendes's house, the two Communists, probably Alarcón and certainly Astudillo, told the others that "in four or five days they would be fighting for the Communist Party that was going to declare civil war on the President of the Republic, and that the redistribution of the lands was coming." They also said they were leaving on 8 June early in the morning for the "house of the teacher Luis Muñoz who has a school for indios in Lepoi." They planned to meet the following day in Contraco and then move on to Nitrito, where they were going to meet with Leiva Tapia, Benito, Simón, and Juan Sagredo, and others to form a committee and plan a "death blow to the administrators of Guayalí and Ránquil, Lolco, Villucura, Lonquimai." According to Cortés, the two Communists said they had cabecillas in "Lonquimai, Túnel Las Raíces, Curacautín, Victoria, Temuco, Concepción, Valdivia, Los Ángeles, Santa Bárbara, Mulchén, Nacimiento, Angol, Purén, and Cañete," a network of southern towns.[29]

Muñoz's role in organizing the rebellion was confirmed by other witnesses. After the rebellion ended, carabineros detained José del Cármen Vega Tapia "for being one of the authors of the seditious uprising in Alto Bío Bío." Vega Tapia was a gañan, domiciled in Lepoy on or neighboring the Bunsters' Ralco estate. Workers on Ralco and the Santa Ema estate close by had informed the police that Vega was a leader of the rebellion and was hiding in Muñoz's home in Lepoy. They had heard that Vega, Segundo Hermosilla, and others had held meetings to plan the rebellion in Muñoz's home.[30] For his part, Vega denied the charges. He had lived and worked on Guayalí until April when, with other workers, he was expelled and removed to Llanquén. He had decided to go to Santa Bárbara, where he had been born, since Llanquén proved inhospitable. En route, however, "at the request of professor Muñoz, who lives among the indios, I stayed in this place [Ralco]."[31]

Cortés's account was echoed by miners detained following the rebellion. Antonio Ortíz Palma told police "they were preparing this movement in May led by Leiva Tapia. ... Leiva Tapia had the mission of traveling around the pueblos and especially the haciendas sowing communism."[32] Similarly, Adolfo Sánchez Salazar, who was arrested with Ortíz Palma and worked in a pulpería serving the gold placers in Llanquén on the Guayalí estate, told police that "they [Juan Pablo Ortíz and the Sagredo brothers] had been saying for a month that there would be a general revolution in the whole country and that when it broke out in the center of the country, those in the cordillera had to rise up and kill all the bourgeoisie, *turcos*, and *gringos* to reconquer our land, taking advantage of the fact that carabineros wouldn't be able to arrive at our region because they would be busy defending the president in the center of the country." Sánchez Salazar testified that "they held meetings in Ránquil and Troyo during good weather and in a shed in Quilleime during bad weather."[33]

Ortíz's and the Sagredos' rhetorical attacks on "turcos" and "gringos" point to an additional dynamic shaping social relations in Lonquimay. By the early 1930s Spanish and French immigrants had taken ownership or administration of estates like Ránquil, Contraco, and Lolco. German immigrants like Bruno and Jorge Ackermann and Italian immigrants like Juan Zolezzi engaged in trade and owned pulperías. And as the list of Lonquimay's merchants indicates, at least two Arab immigrants from the Middle East, the Siade brothers Pedro and Nicolás, also engaged in trade in the region. A growing timber industry in Curacautín and the regional trade in gold may have attracted European and Middle Eastern immigrant merchants to the region. The immigrants' presence added a degree of xenophobia to miners' and rural laborers' hatred of the landowning oligarchy represented by the Puelmas and Bunsters.

In the aftermath of the rebellion, agents from the Servicio de Investigaciones and carabineros cracked down on communist activists, invoking the 1932 Internal Security of the State Law that banned activities against the established order and the "propagation of destructive [*disolventes*] doctrines." In the town of Corral, near the city of Valdivia, an agent from investigaciones and a carabinero sergeant arrested Alberto Rodríguez Viscarra, originally from Arica in the north but now working in the Altos Hornos de Corral steel plant, and Carlos Humberto Rieloff Vargas, "a dangerous communist agitator" from Traiguén. The two Communist Party militants had in their possession a number of pamphlets, including "Tasks for Organizing Unions and Revolutionary Union Opposition," "Let's Create the Unity of All the Country's Workers to Struggle Against Hunger and Reaction," and "Against Hunger, Misery, and Unemployment."[34]

The pamphlets were accompanied by a handwritten draft of a document that sheds light on the role of regional Communist Party committees in the rebellion in Alto Bío Bío. On 1 July a "camarada delegado" from the party's regional committee in Concepción traveled to Valdivia to inform the party's local committee there of the events in Lonquimay. His narrative gives a glimpse of the Concepción regional committee's role in and understanding of the rebellion. "Last February," the delegate reported, "fifty-three *pequeños* campesinos [campesino smallholders] and inquilinos and indígenas were evicted from their properties, altogether 600 families thrown off their land by a carabinero lieutenant at the head of twenty-five carabineros, who burned down their houses, destroyed their harvests, and stole their provisions, depositing them in the storehouse of Víctor Vergara, mayordomo of the Ránquil fundo." The report demonstrated detailed knowledge of events on the ground despite a few glaring errors of fact. Especially revealing is the emphasis on the uprising's local causes, including landowners' appropriation of campesinos' provisions. The delegate, much like the campesinos themselves, stressed that the eviction constituted a theft of inquilinos' and ocupantes' goods as well as of their land.

The delegate from Concepción identified the extreme suffering of the campesinos who had been expelled from Nitrito as the immediate cause of the insurrection. "From March until this day," it noted, "the compañeros have suffered the most brutal consequences, having been thrown off their land, to the degree that they have not had enough to eat, and this is why they found themselves in urgent need of taking the Lonquimay valley, disposed to die fighting for the conquest of their lands rather than die of hunger, cornered in the cordillera." He described "[that,] happily, the compañeros in these days have recuperated some of their stolen provisions and believe they can support themselves with these provisions for three months, confronting their enemies, who haven't been able to find a pass into Lonquimay." This account underlined campesinos' understanding that in the act of rebellion they were only righting the moral scales, winning back what was rightfully theirs.

The report pointed to the role of the Communist Party's regional committees in the planning of the insurgency. The rebel leaders believed the uprising would spread throughout the south "because of *acuerdos* [agreements with Communist Party committees] in the provinces named above." The union leaders apparently presumed the rebellion would spark a national revolution that would be supported by factions sympathetic to the Communist Party in the navy and army. As the report detailed, "This *camarada delegado* informed us that they had sent delegates to different regions of the country and that with this movement of obreros campesinos they believe themselves to be one step from the revolution of workers, campesinos, soldiers, and sailors, and they say that they have elements in the navy." This account is further evidence that the Sindicato Agrícola Lonquimay's leaders had been in contact with FOCH or Communist Party committees or both in other southern towns, most important, as the report itself indicates, the party's regional committee in Concepción. The document echoed other descriptions of the rebellion's organization, which narrated how the movement's leaders believed that their revolutionary movement could sustain itself during the winter "by recuperating the provisions that had been stolen from the compañeros campesinos ... and that they could resist the attacks from carabineros because carabineros would be unable to reach the region."[35]

There is considerable corroboration, then, that, after the Nitrito campesinos' expulsion from Guayalí in April, Juan Segundo Leiva Tapia, Simón and Benito Sagredo, Juan Pablo Ortíz, Astudillo, Alarcón, and Luis Muñoz as well as other union leaders had spent the month of May meeting to plan an insurrection. Leiva Tapia, Astudillo, and the Sagredo brothers clearly had ties to both the FOCH and the Communist Party and were in communication with the regional branch of the party in Concepción, if not party leadership in Santiago. During the revolt, carabineros in Lonquimay took a prisoner who had messages in his poncho from Leiva Tapia. Under interrogation the prisoner confessed that his job was to send a telegram to certain party leaders in Concepción to let them know the insurrection had begun. *El Diario Austral* saw this confession as constituting irrefutable proof that "the movement did not only obey local causes but was the result of a plan devised by communist leaders."[36] The evidence appears to support *El Diario Austral*'s claim. However, it points to the role played by FOCH and Communist Party activists from Concepción, not the national party leadership.

While neither the Chilean Communist Party's national leadership nor the Comintern played a role in organizing the rebellion, the Comintern's promotion of agrarian and anti-imperialist revolution would have certainly influenced the Sindicato Agrícola Lonquimay's leaders' embrace of armed insurrection. In addition, the fiery rhetoric of Communist Party and FOCH leaders like Elías Lafertte and Carlos Contreras Labarca conveyed the message that workers and campesinos should organize revolutionary uprisings to bring down the Alessandri government. One can get a sense of the party leaders' language from their speeches at a FOCH Congreso de Unidad Sindical (Labor Unity Congress) in late June 1934, at which the six hundred members present elected a new presidium that included "delegates from Alto Bío Bío." Elías Lafertte told the assembled delegates that the FOCH congress was a key step in the "emancipation of the working class," that it "signified the most rebellious protest of the working class ... against the tyranny of the Alessandri government." The FOCH's ultimate goal, Lafertte told the assembly, was to establish "soviets of obreros, campesinos, soldiers, and sailors." Carlos Contreras Labarca echoed Lafertte in even stronger terms. Workers had not been defeated by Alessandri's repressive measures, he announced, but were still "on their feet, fighting for a government of soviets." The party leader denounced the miserable conditions in the gold placer mines, where thousands of workers were toiling on the brink of starvation: "The acts of president Alessandri against the working class have reached their pinnacle, since he is sending them to die of hunger and without any protection or support at all in the *lavaderos de oro*." Contreras Labarca ended his speech by exhorting "the revolutionary workers" to "avenge with blood all this injustice and cement an indissolvable unity to conquer power." Contreras Labarca's invocation of insurrection as an instrument of revenge against the violence and injustice imposed by Alessandri would surely have resonated with local leaders like the Sagredos, who had promised that their violent expulsion from the Nitrito Valley would be avenged with blood.[37]

Astudillo, described as a "delegate from Alto Bío Bío," addressed the FOCH congress in equally incendiary language, describing the miserable conditions of workers there and their "savage exploitation." He denounced the fact that "the assassin and massacring government was drowning in blood the just movement of campesinos in his region, who have done nothing other than resist being dispossessed of their lands. . . . This *canalla* and bloody Alessandri . . . a short while ago with Decree 4834 expelled into abandonment 61 families, 300 people, in order to recognize the rights of the *latifundistas* Gonzalo Bunster and Puelma." Astudillo called for workers to unite and "organize a great mass movement and then revolution that destroys forever this disgusting [*asquerosa*] oligarchy that governs us."

After the uprising in Alto Bío Bío erupted on 27 June, the FOCH assembly continued meeting. Astudillo once again addressed the delegates, pointing out the significance of the armed insurrection of Alto Bío Bío's campesinado "because it means that the *hambreador* [exploiter or starvation-provoking] and oppressive regime of the criminal Alessandri has made itself unbearable." He urged FOCH members to "engage in revolutionary propaganda and foment intense struggles, continuing strikes and uprisings to demonstrate to the tyrant that the working class is organized and disposed to fight until the end, that is to say, until the triumph of the agrarian anti-imperialist revolution, which will implant a government of soviets in Chile."[38] Astudillo's rhetoric reproduced faithfully the party's ideology of insurrection, which was to promote strikes, land occupations, and local uprisings, which would bring down the Alessandri regime and form the foundation of the organization of soviets of workers, campesinos, and indígenas.

Only Astudillo discussed campesinos' struggles in Alto Bío Bío. Party leaders like Lafertte and Contreras Labarca did not mention the bitter conflict there, where, even as they addressed the FOCH assembly, the Sindicato Agrícola Lonquimay's leaders were holding their final meetings to prepare an insurrection that would trigger, they hoped, a national revolution. In fact, it appears that FOCH and Communist Party leaders like Lafertte and Contreras Labarca and even Higinio Godoy were unaware of local preparations for an armed insurrection in Alto Bío Bío. Carlos Contreras Labarca later communicated to the Comintern in Moscow that the news of the uprising took the assembled FOCH delegates and Communist Party leaders by surprise.[39]

The first reports to the Comintern from its emissary "Horacio" in January 1935, six months after the rebellion, indicate that party militants organized the rebellion but were not following dictates from either Santiago or Moscow. Horacio critiqued a general tendency within the Chilean Communist Party in favor of insurrection. His communications reflected a moment of transition in the Comintern as it moved from the insurrectionary strategy of the "third period" to the Popular Front strategy of the post-1935 period. Horacio emphasized that the party should focus its work on strikes and movements for "immediate demands" as well as building a strong and unified labor movement.[40] He stressed that southern Chile was the region with the greatest social discontent and the highest level of organizing among campesinos. However, rather than describe the Ránquil rebellion or refer to the Sindicato Agrícola Lonquimay, Horacio focused on other unions and what he said were growing Mapuche organizations linked to the FOCH. He critiqued the "comrades and organizations" nationally and in Alto Bío Bío specifically "who take a truly revolutionary combative position" but who "forget the struggle for short-term political and economic demands . . . and they plan as the only program . . . armed insurrection." Apparently ignorant of the Sindicato Agrícola Lonquimay's history of organizing, Horacio argued that had there been a broader organization around immediate local demands, the Ránquil rebellion would have expanded beyond Alto Bío Bío.

Horacio's critique reveals the distance between Comintern policy and the union leadership's decision to pursue armed insurrection. Most important, it demonstrates the degree to which local Communists in Concepción, Lonquimay, and throughout the south may have acted with autonomy from the Comintern and the party's national leadership in Santiago. Horacio saw the party's long-term goal as insurrection, but local militants needed to focus their labor in the short term on organizing unions, strikes, and land occupations, which could then form the basis for local armed uprisings. More political, as opposed to military, preparation, Horacio contended, was necessary to prepare the terrain for insurrection.[41] In his interpretation, local party members had directed the insurrection in Lonquimay by following the mistaken strategy of pursuing armed insurrection as opposed to revolutionary strikes and land occupations.

Carlos Contreras Labarca's account of the rebellion confirms the view that the insurrection was planned and directed by leaders of the local party or FOCH or both. In a meeting of the Comintern's South American Secretariat, he described the party's central role in leading the rebellion: "In Lonquimay we had a revolutionary uprising of workers, campesinos and indígenas. They occupied, following a revolutionary path, large latifundios, haciendas, in the south. The Comintern directed this movement with the revolutionary unions of the FOCH."[42] Yet despite this fairly typical self-representation of the party as directing mass struggles, Contreras Labarca underlined the role of the FOCH and its "revolutionary unions" in the movement's organization. In addition, his only concrete reference to the Communist Party's role in preparing an armed insurrection was his version of how, after the rebellion began, Astudillo, whom he referred to as "a campesino from Lonquimay," "was speaking to the FOCH congress." The delegation from Lonquimay then proposed to the FOCH assembly that its unions organize "armed demonstrations, an uprising in the month of July." That is, while the party and FOCH had played a role in organizing unions among workers from diverse sectors in Alto Bío Bío, the push for a nationwide armed uprising came from Astudillo and the Alto Bío Bío delegates to the FOCH congress, not the party leaders who were taken by surprise by news of the revolt. Contreras Labarca claimed that the party had been able to introduce itself into the region months before, gaining "more than one hundred militants," and that "the FOCH ... was able to create in Lonquimay a strong union of agricultural workers." And he related how the party leadership worked in Lonquimay "to prevent the eviction of campesinos from their lands, to call for a common struggle and solidarity among all the campesinos and indígenas in this region." This political work did not, however, include planning an armed uprising.

Contreras Labarca reiterated the history of party manifestos circulating in the region and the organization of the Nitrito Valley's Colonos Defense Committee. Similarly, the party leader underscored that the party worked to organize workers in the gold placer mines, agricultural workers, workers in the timber industry, workers in Lonquimay and Nitrito, and "the indígenas of the region of Remoto [sic]," which were, he stated, "the forces we mobilized for the struggle for immediate demands of the masses, in defense of revolutionary slogans, putting forward the perspective of the revolutionary occupation of the land of the large landowners." These descriptions of the party's activities are consistent with other evidence, despite a few errors and discrepancies. Most notable in Contreras Labarca's narrative of the rebellion for the Comintern was his emphasis on party militants' local organizing among workers, miners, and indigenous communities in the region and his description of the Alto Bío Bío delegates' call for an armed uprising at the FOCH conference.

The Communist Party's *Bandera Roja* published a more detailed picture of the party's role in preparing the Ránquil rebellion in late July 1934. The paper printed a fairly accurate reading of the party's activities in Alto Bío Bío as well as a detailed history of land conflicts in the region going back to the nineteenth century. *Bandera Roja* wrote that, following the eviction of colonos from Nitrito, "the Sindicato Agrario Lonquimay, related fraternally to and directed and led by the Federación Obrera de Chile, launched the slogan of the formation of Committees of Colonos to struggle for the reconquest of their land in Nitrito, for the defense of their land in Ránquil and in other colonies, committees of indios to struggle for the restoration of their land usurped by estate owners." Directed by the FOCH, the union had also promoted the organization of "comités de lucha" (combat committees) among workers in the Las Raíces tunnel and in the gold placers "to obtain a better price for their gold, free medical attention, hygienic housing, and food assistance."[43]

Aside from exaggerating the degree to which the FOCH directed and led the Sindicato Agrícola Lonquimay and ignoring the union's organization during the Ibáñez regime and alliance with Ibáñez, *Bandera Roja*'s history was consistent with the evidence of FOCH organizing in Alto Bío Bío. Campesinos in Nitrito, led by the Sagredos, had formed a defense committee with the support of the FOCH and the party's Concepción regional committee. And Sánchez Salazar's testimony speaks to the presence of labor organizing and perhaps even a union among workers in the gold placer mines. Too, workers in the Las Raíces tunnel were definitely organized: they had engaged in a strike at the beginning of April, and Higinio Godoy had been operating in the workers' camps in Boca Sur, distributing his "subversive manifestos."

Unlike Horacio's and Contreras Labarca's reports to the Comintern, *Bandera Roja*'s more informed and detailed account highlighted that the Ránquil rebels' revolutionary movement flowed organically from local struggles. The paper contended that a local movement for immediate economic demands had led to the regional revolutionary insurrection: "The struggle for these demands, especially in Nitrito for the reconquest of their land, has driven the armed uprising of all of Lonquimay's obreros, campesinos, and indios, who for their own demands and in support of the Nitrito colonos have thrown themselves with revolutionary spirit into combat, giving this insurrectional movement a mass character." The paper made no mention of the central party leadership or Comintern, accentuating the insurrection's regional roots and the role of the FOCH.

The paper certainly exaggerated the alliance of the region's obreros, campesinos, and indigenous communities in the movement. For example, the Las Raíces tunnel workers did not join the rebellion, despite having engaged in a strike only weeks before. The paper claimed that the

Ralco community's involvement signaled the revolutionary consciousness of Chile's "indios," who were prepared to struggle for national liberation and an Araucanian Republic. More likely, however, is that members of the Ralco and other Pehuenche communities who took part in the rebellion, like their nonindigenous or Chilean campesino allies, struggled for the restoration of land usurped by large estates. This was a conflict that had endured for decades in Ralco and had taken the community through a number of alliances, including, finally, Ignacio Maripi's alliance with Leiva Tapia and the Sindicato Agrícola Lonquimay.

There is no evidence that Pehuenche communities joined the rebellion as part of broader ideological or political struggle for national ethnic territorial self-determination. Yet the paper's emphasis on the Pehuenche communities' participation is abetted by quite a bit of evidence. As noted above, members of these communities would have joined the union's councils on Queco, Ralco, Lolco, and other neighboring estates like Contraco that employed members of Pehuenche communities as laborers.[44] Furthermore, union leaders like Astudillo and Leiva Tapia had held meetings in Ralco during the month preceding the rebellion. Members of Ralco, including Ignacio Maripi and his son, took part in the rebellion and had worked with the Sindicato Agrícola Lonquimay since 1931 to win back land stolen by the Bunster family. There is good evidence that party militants had tried to organize in the region's Pehuenche communities, holding meetings and distributing Communist Party manifestos.

In the end, the decisions made by local union leaders like Leiva Tapia, the Sagredos, and Astudillo in Alto Bío Bío and Alarcón in Lota make sense not as part of a broader national plan designed by the party's central committee but as a regionally rooted revolutionary movement led by party or FOCH members who were neither in communication with nor adhered to the ideological line of the party leadership in Santiago, to say nothing of the Comintern's representatives in South America. Yet the party's ideological stance and revolutionary rhetoric provided a framework for interpreting the Alessandri regime as repressive and illegitimate and insurrection as a legitimate tool for bringing to power a government of obreros and campesinos. Certainly party leaders endorsed local insurrections based in strikes led by FOCH unions or in campesinos' occupation of haciendas. Party leaders' revolutionary rhetoric would have been interpreted on the ground by local union leaders like Leiva Tapia and the Sagredos, or by the party's regional committees in the south, as a call to armed revolution.

The Quilleime Assembly

The Ránquil rebellion began with an assembly of the Sindicato Agrícola Lonquimay in Quilleime, just south of Ránquil's gold placer mines in Troyo. Accounts of this assembly open a window into the union leaders' goals, strategy, and ideology. On 24, 25, and 26 June Leiva Tapia, the Sagredo brothers, Alarcón, and other union members like Juan Pablo Ortíz had begun traveling around the region's estates and gold placers, alerting workers to a meeting to be held the evening of June 26. The union had held meetings in this location before, so it came as no surprise to its members when they were called to a meeting to vote on a change in the union leadership. Miners detained after the insurrection described how Juan Segundo Leiva Tapia and Juan Pablo Ortíz had gone to the placers in late June to invite them to the meeting. Juan Orellana Barrera, a union member, testified that he was in Nitrito panning for gold at the end of June when Juan Pablo Ortíz (an inquilino and ocupante on Guayalí) invited him to attend the union assembly. He was told, he said, that the meeting was about a change in the union leadership.[45]

Campesinos too told of how Leiva Tapia, the Sagredo brothers, Alarcón, and other union members had invited them to the meeting. Florentino Pino Valdebenito had lived and worked on Ránquil since 1914, first as an inquilino, then an ocupante, and finally an aspiring colono on a fifty-hectare plot designated to him after the 1930 decree, to which, like the other Ránquil colonos, he had still not received a title. He testified that on 25 June Alarcón, Benito Sagredo, and a group of fifteen others arrived at his house and told him that the revolution had broken out all over Chile and that he should join it. They threatened him, he said, telling him that if he didn't join, "there was the river," that is, they would kill him and throw him into the river. The group stayed at his house, and the next day they all went to the Quilleime sheds. When they arrived in the morning they found forty people already assembled. By dusk their number had grown to eighty.[46]

Pablo Cisternas Ramírez, who had also settled in the Ránquil colony with his mother, Margarita Rámirez, and his brother Juan, related that on 26 June Juan Sebastián Lara invited him and Juan to the meeting in Quilleime. Having been born on the Lolco estate to an inquilino family, Cisternas now described himself as a gañan. He shared a home with his mother on her land in Ránquil but had worked and resided on Lolco since 1933.[47] As happened with Pino Valdebenito, a threat allegedly accompanied the invitation: Lara told the Cisternas Ramírez brothers that if they did not go to the union meeting, another "commission" would come for them. On 26 June, a little after midday, they arrived in Quilleime, where they found some two hundred men had assembled. Like many others, Cisternas Ramírez declared that he attended the meeting under threat and that he had heard that the meeting was called to change the union leadership.

Two things are notable in the testimony. First, almost all the prisoners detained after the insurrection declared that they had been summoned to the meeting under threat of violence. This may have been the case in some instances, but in others it served as a form of legal exculpation. In the case of Pablo Cisternas Ramírez, this narrative rings hollow. Cisternas's mother was close to Leiva Tapia, and she played a leadership role in the insurrection and in the union assembly in Quilleime. Leiva Tapia was a frequent visitor to Ramírez's home—some accounts had him living there during the six months leading up to the rebellion—even though Cisternas, who moved around the region working different jobs, said he did not see him there frequently. Nonetheless, given his mother's prominent role in the revolt as well as her relationship with Leiva Tapia, that it would have required threats to induce him to attend the meeting seems far-fetched.

Second, a common narrative, again elaborated as a form of exculpation by detained campesinos, was that people at the meeting had gone to Quilleime because they had been told that the aim of the assembly was to elect new union leadership. A typical iteration was the testimony of Arturo Pino Alegría. Pino Alegría was born on Guayalí to an inquilino family.[48] With other Guayalí inquilinos he had been forced to move from Nitrito to Llanquén. Pino Alegría attested that "before June 26 I had never heard of any kind of revolt, and only on that day Simón Sagredo came to get me at my house at six in the morning, and told me to come to a meeting of the Sindicato Agrícola to change the leadership. He said that if I didn't go, they would come to get me." In this and other cases the account might certainly have been true, but in others, as in the case of Cisternas Ramírez, who would certainly have been given a clear idea of the assembly's revolutionary goals from his mother or Leiva Tapia, it amounted to no more than a way of distancing the accused from identification with the movement's insurrectionary program.

During the afternoon the men who numbered forty at midday grew, some said, to eighty, then to two hundred, then to three hundred by nighttime. The meeting began with a vote on the change of union leadership, apparently to replace moderate union leaders like Manuel Astroza. Then Leiva Tapia, Simón Sagredo, and Alarcón addressed the assembly. According to Antonio Ortíz Palma, Leiva Tapia spoke first and said to the campesinos and miners, "*Camaradas*, the social revolution is approaching in Chile, and it is necessary that we ourselves begin it by providing an example. Communism must prevail in Chile because then all men will have what they need and will live better. With the present regime we have no future since we don't have what is indispensable [to survive]. Today, for example, the pulperías have closed their doors to our workers. They give you [food] but not enough to satisfy the hunger of your families. Rise up and struggle. Let's be the first spark of the rebellion." He then addressed the "indígenas" at the meeting: "You who work the soil are in need of land, and all you see is yours, so accompany us in this movement. I warn you that the first man who backs out will fall by the bullets of his own comrades."[49]

This account was more detailed than others but followed a common narrative found in a number of testimonies of prisoners detained after the rebellion. Another prisoner present in Quilleime said that Leiva Tapia told the assembly that "confidential news had arrived ... that all the regional branches of the Communist Party had been told to start revolutionary strikes in the entire country to implant the soviet regime in Chile and then industrial workers and campesinos would be happy since they would have all the facilities of the worker and campesino government for the general welfare and that the indígenas and colonos would all have their own land, because the land would pass over to the state. That the land was for those who made it productive." Leiva Tapia told the assembly that "the revolutionary spark would begin in this sector. If you don't have provisions, there is the pulpería, they are yours." He then incited those present to revolt and told them to attack the pulperías immediately to supply themselves with provisions and to resist the attacks of carabineros.[50]

In a similar version, José Emiliano Balboa Benítez told police that "Leiva Tapia said the country was in a moment of crisis and the only way to achieve the welfare of the working class was revolution, which was going to break out in the entire country." In addition, Simón Sagredo told the assembled sindicalistas that "no one could leave the meeting and there were three paths, with the patrón, with the *proletarios*, or death." Alarcón followed Sagredo and, according to Balboa Benítez, announced that "the revolution was a certainty, that they could kill him if this weren't true, that he couldn't lie because he represented 14,000 workers in Lota." Alarcón added that "sailors in Talcahuano were *adeptos de ellos* [loyal to the Communist Party], and that he knew this because he had attended a congress in Talcahuano in April." Alarcón went on to tell the assembly that they would have to begin the revolt on 27 June because on 30 June "the revolution would break out in the entire country."[51]

If one takes these various descriptions of the meeting in Quilleime together, a number of things stand out. Almost all those present concurred that Leiva Tapia, Sagredo, and Alarcón told the assembly that a national revolutionary strike and insurrection were imminent and that the campesinos in Alto Bío Bío would strike the first blow. Leiva Tapia and the Sagredos apparently intended for their movement to ignite a national revolution in coordination with Communist Party regional committees across the country. Counting as many as five hundred members and councils on at least seven estates, the Sindicato Agrícola Lonquimay was the largest rural union in Chile and the only one organized by region rather than estate. The union had spearheaded one of the first efforts to expand the 1924 social laws to cover rural laborers and, when Ibáñez was in power, one of the first experiments with agrarian reform by engineering the expropriation of Ránquil and Guayalí. The union's national importance was visible in the many meetings its leaders held with Ibáñez, his ministers, and members of congress between 1928 and 1931 and later with Alessandri and his ministers in 1933. Democratic Party congressmen had taken up the union's cause and represented its case to both Ibáñez and Alessandri and in congress.

As union leaders like Leiva Tapia turned to the left after the fall of the Ibáñez government, the Sindicato Agrícola Lonquimay held similar importance to the Communist Party. Free of the intense repression visited on the party by Ibáñez, the Communist Party began organizing unions in towns throughout southern Chile, including in nearby Los Ángeles. The sindicato's centrality to the Communist Party's and FOCH's campaigns to organize the countryside was reflected in Leiva Tapia's incorporation into the delegation chosen to attend the Montevideo conference alongside the party's most well-known leader, Elías Lafertte. Similarly, as Contreras Labarca's speech to the FOCH conference and *Bandera Roja*'s reporting show, the party made concerted efforts to organize former nitrate workers sent to the gold placer mines as well as Mapuche communities. Leiva Tapia and the Sagredos may well have seen themselves at the vanguard of a revolutionary movement in the Chilean countryside that included miners, workers, and indigenous communities as well as campesinos.

The goal of bringing down the government, in fact, was not completely unrealistic. During the previous three years Chile had experienced a number of military coups, local uprisings, and changes of government, including the twelve-day Socialist Republic. The 1931 naval revolt revealed that sectors of the military would support a revolution. Alarcón's statement that the "arsenal in Talcahuano," which had joined the naval revolt, would buttress the movement undoubtedly reinforced the belief that as the revolution spread from Alto Bío Bío key sectors in the armed forces would join it. Moreover, the Sindicato Agrícola Lonquimay did not act alone. Its leaders had been in conversation with regional party leaders in Lota, Concepción, Temuco, and Valdivia, if not party leaders in Santiago, who intended to help coordinate the rebellion in other parts of the country. Leiva Tapia, the Sagredos, and Alarcón viewed the revolt as part of a larger series of nationwide strikes and uprisings led by the Communist Party's regional committees in southern Chile.

In practical terms, Alto Bío Bío was an advantageous place to begin an insurrection. Winter snowfall isolated the region and would block access to carabineros, giving the revolutionaries all winter to exercise control over a sizable swathe of territory. As many accounts underscored, the revolt was timed to coincide with the year's first major snowfall. During the winter months the revolutionary army of campesinos and miners could provision themselves with supplies from the local pulperías. An additional benefit was that store owners had weapons. For a revolutionary movement armed almost entirely with sticks and knives, the pulperías' handful of rifles, pistols, and shotguns was vital.

Not everyone who attended the meeting supported Leiva Tapia's and the Sagredos' call to arms. Manuel Astroza, the union's former president, a Democrat and a longtime worker on the El Rahue estate who had settled in the Ránquil colony, spoke out against the uprising to those around him in the crowd. One detainee later testified that "Manuel Astroza Dávila wanted to speak, probably against the movement, since I heard him mutter, as the session opened and listened to his comment in opposition to the ideas they were disseminating, but the leaders didn't let him speak."[52] Astroza himself testified that "every time I spoke to Leiva Tapia he treated me like a defector and threw in my face that I didn't want to participate in the revolution."[53] Enough prisoners corroborated this account that Astroza was freed almost immediately following his detention.

Nearly every prisoner detained after the revolt said they had been unwilling participants, forced under threat of death to join the ranks of the rebellion. There was general agreement that Leiva Tapia and Simón Sagredo threatened to kill those who refused to rebel. If they didn't join the rebellion's ranks they would be killed and thrown into the Biobío River. Onofre Ortíz Salgado swore that Simón Sagredo said that "none of the people there could move, and if they didn't follow them they would be thrown into the river."[54] José Nieves Alegría Espinoza, born on the Ralco estate but since childhood a poblador on Ránquil as a member of an inquilino family, and then on seventy hectares his father had received in the Ránquil colony, affirmed that "the speakers said no one could leave the meeting or they would be killed."[55] He testified that they positioned people "armed with sticks, and many with knives, to guard the exits."[56]

The assembly in Quilleime is instructive as much for what it does not say as for what it does say about the ideas and ideology of the insurrectionary movement. Leiva Tapia's and Alarcón's revolutionary rhetoric bore the stamp of official Communist Party ideology. Their assurances that a revolutionary insurrection or general strike of workers and campesinos was imminent echoed a general Communist Party position during this period. But, as the Comintern's analysis of the movement's mistakes shows, Leiva Tapia, the Sagredos, and Alarcón deviated from the official party position, which emphasized focusing on immediate economic and political demands and deemphasized armed insurrection. Party rhetoric at both the national and regional levels promoted the organization of soviets of workers, campesinos, and indígenas, including the organization of an Araucanian Republic, but neither Leiva Tapia nor Alarcón referred to these concepts in their speeches. The two leaders told the union assembly only that overthrowing the despotic Alessandri regime via armed uprisings would improve conditions for "the working class" and "proletariat," addressing the violence and deprivation faced by workers, miners, and campesinos. The uprising would allow the rebels to make the fertile valleys monopolized by the Bunster and Puelma estates their own. The revolutionary movement would give land to "those who work the land" or to "those who make the land produce." Finally, in targeting the pulperías, Leiva Tapia assured the union members both that the provisions were rightfully theirs and that they could appropriate goods to supply the movement. This spoke to both campesinos' and miners' experience of the local pulperías as the immediate cause of their misery and exploitation as well as their understanding that landowners had consistently appropriated their improvements and harvests.

Leiva Tapia's speech to the assembly hewed close to the position he had adopted since the Sindicato Agrícola Lonquimay had established ties to the FOCH in early 1933. In an interview with *El Comercio* after his return from internal exile (*relegación*) in Melinka, Leiva Tapia denied that he was a Communist but discussed the importance of the FOCH. The union leader echoed party rhetoric, as he had at the socialist colonization congress in Temuco, in denouncing "foreign capitalism," the "feudal-bourgeois latifundio," and a regime which "strangles the working class in the countryside and city." But, as Ulianova notes, Leiva Tapia constructed his own analysis of Chile's agrarian problem, one that had little to do with any position adopted by the Communist Party. As in the Quilleime assembly, his basic philosophy was that the land was for those who worked it. In defending his ties to the FOCH, he argued that "the FOCH will not take land away from the campesinos. On the contrary, the FOCH works to give land to the true campesino, to him who works it." According to Leiva Tapia, on the basis of this principle, the FOCH would defend the interests of "the campesino obrero, the small ocupante and colono, the poor, medium-size, and even rich landowner who administers and cultivates their fundo as long as they are not an enemy of economic transformation." The union leader's position on support for wealthy landowners who made their properties productive and did not oppose the economic changes to be introduced by a revolution in no way iterated the Communist Party's focus on organizing unions and soviets of rural workers and destroying latifundia. Seven months before the revolt Leiva Tapia argued, in a departure from the party's position, that revolution meant not armed struggle but "a movement of opinion, a change in men's mentality."[57]

By June 1934 Leiva Tapia had moved from this position to supporting an armed insurrection that would trigger strikes and uprisings throughout the country. Yet his belief in distributing estate land "to those who work it" did not wane. To Leiva Tapia and in all likelihood to the campesinos who joined him, communism represented not collectivized agriculture, communal ownership of the land, or even the organization of soviets, which he never mentioned, but the expropriation of large estates and a government that would use its power to benefit campesinos and obreros and put an end to the repressive policies of the Alessandri regime. If Leiva Tapia and the rebellion's other leaders had an agrarian program, it was to break up large estates formed by fraud on public property and redistribute the land in small plots to the individual campesino families that worked it. If they had a political program, it consisted of promoting local uprisings that would win military support, bring down the Alessandri government, and destroy the political power wielded by the "disgusting oligarchy," as Astudillo referred to it. The union had worked since 1928 with the corporatist institutions and laws established since 1924 in alliance with the Democratic Party, but Alessandri's election and reversal of the Ibáñez-era decrees dictating the expropriation of Ránquil and Guayalí had demonstrated that this approach no longer worked.

The violent eviction of ocupantes from the Nitrito Valley in April 1934 and the failure of his May 1934 campaign for deputy appear to have triggered a change in Leiva Tapia's thinking. If in November 1933 he did not advocate armed insurrection, by June 1934 the futility of working through legal and political channels with the union's Democratic Party allies, combined with the Alessandri government's use of carabineros to expel union members from their land, had pushed Leiva Tapia, the Sagredos, Astudillo, and other union leaders to embrace an armed assault on the region's large estates. The Communist Party's policy of promoting insurrection to depose Alessandri and "avenge with blood" his acts of repression, as Contreras Labarca put it at the June 1934 FOCH congress, gave the union leaders both an ideological language for interpreting an armed uprising as a legitimate response to state violence and a vision of a real political possibility: a revolution from below to place in power a government sympathetic to campesinos, indígenas, and obreros.

CHAPTER NINE

Rebellion and Repression

AT DAYBREAK ON 27 June 1934, Leiva Tapia, the Sagredos, and Alarcón organized the assembled sindicalistas in Quilleime into groups led by "captains." They directed bands of thirty to forty men to take over the region's pulperías and estates as a prelude to a national revolution. The assembly divided into roughly two groups, one led by the Sagredos and the other by Leiva Tapia and Alarcón. While the immediate cause of the rebellion was ocupantes' April eviction from the Guayalí estate's land in the Nitrito Valley, a substantial number of the movement's participants were ocupantes and colonos who had settled on Ránquil and maintained possession of their small plots. Indeed, reducing the rebellion's origins mechanistically to ocupantes' violent eviction from Nitrito and the harsh conditions they confronted in Llanquén, as so many accounts in the press and congress later would do, overlooks the ties of solidarity that united inquilinos and ocupantes who were members of the Sindicato Agrícola Lonquimay in collective struggle with Alto Bío Bío's estates. A number of the ocupantes evicted from Nitrito had friends, family, or companions who had settled on Ránquil. And, once organized in the union, inquilinos and ocupantes throughout the region, not only those expelled from Nitrito, joined the rebellion inspired by the revolutionary promise that the estate land they worked would be theirs.

Because of the Sindicato Agrícola Lonquimay's victory in winning Ránquil's expropriation decree from the Ibáñez regime and establishing a colony with former inquilinos and ocupantes from the Chilpaco, El Rahue, and Ránquil estates, the group led by Leiva Tapia and Alarcón organized assaults not on estates but on the pulperías owned by immigrant merchants, where they exchanged gold from the local placers for goods. The rebels' plan was to take the region's pulperías, a ready supply of arms and provisions with which to withstand eventual attacks by carabineros and the long winter months during which the region remained isolated on the eastern slopes of the Andes. Leiva Tapia also directed groups of men to guard the Rahue and Ránquil bridges. The Sagredo brothers led a second group, many of them inquilinos and ocupantes from Lolco, Guayalí, and Contraco, including a number who had been expelled from Nitrito, to invade the estates and assault the carabineros stationed on Guayalí. They planned to provision themselves with goods from the estates' storehouses and appropriate estate land they hoped to settle as colono smallholders. At this point, few of the campesinos had firearms; most, including the captains, carried only sticks, knives, and the occasional machete.

Police reports and judicial records gave detailed accounts of what took place during the rebellion.[1] They also served as the basis for reporting in the regional and national press. These official reports focused on the criminal violence committed by the bands of rebels and ignored the political content of the movement's actions. In the press, the official rendering of an organized insurrection as the criminal actions of a mob was exaggerated in hyperbolic and almost entirely apocryphal descriptions of the violent abuses committed by the movement. A literal reading of the judicial and police records produces a narrative of the rebellion as an unplanned orgy of mob violence shaped by the state's tendency to lump all acts of violence by peasants together in the realm of ordinary crime.

However, by reading official sources as well as the record of campesinos' enunciations and actions "against the grain," in the words of Ranajit Guha, and paying close attention to the historical context in which both the state's counterinsurgency was deployed and the rebellion emerged it is possible to get some sense of how Alto Bío Bío's campesinos understood their movement. As Guha argues in his seminal work on colonial South Asia, during rebellions peasants "invest disparate attacks on property and person with new meaning and rephrase them as a part of a general discourse of rebellion." Whereas for the "official mind," that is, the police, judiciary, and government officials, acts of disobedience and resistance are viewed as crimes, to peasants the acts, when associated with a collective rebellion, hold a different meaning. They can signify, in the words of the historian Gilbert Joseph, "justifiable protest." During the Ránquil rebellion, what the law defined as common crimes acquired a different meaning in the eyes of campesinos, who understood their actions to be part of a broader collective movement to right past wrongs and usher in a new social order and revolutionary regime.[2]

The union leaders' speeches at the meeting in Quilleime made clear the rebellion's political and ideological context. The assembled campesinos would have been in no doubt that the movement was organized to initiate a national revolution and, more concretely, appropriate estate land and redistribute it to its inquilinos and ocupantes. In addition, Communist Party militants had held meetings with campesinos and miners throughout the region, organized the Nitrito Colonos Defense Committee, and distributed the infamous proclamas subversivas. However, it is likely that for many of Alto Bío Bío's campesinos who joined the rebellion, the Communist Party program of forming soviets and campesino self-defense committees as well as engaging in rebellion with the aim of bringing to power a revolutionary socialist government meant in practice righting the wrongs committed against them by carabineros, the owners of pulperías, and estate owners, overturning the basic social hierarchy, and settling the region's large estates as colono smallholders. Throughout the rebellion campesinos' actions reflected a determination to strip local elites and carabineros of their authority and to turn the social order on its head in the context of a broader national revolution that promised to place in power a government sympathetic to "the poor."

Only traces of women's part in the revolutionary movement remain. As noted above, of the sixty-two campesinos eventually detained in Temuco, only three were women: Margarita Ramírez, her daughter Sofiá Cisternas, and Clementina Sagredo. In addition, few of the prisoners described women's actions during the rebellion. Only Emelina Sagredo and Margarita Ramírez were described as having a role in the assaults on estates and sacking of pulperías. In general, other than Sagredo's participation, with her brothers, in an attack on carabineros, women's role appeared to be redistributing goods appropriated from pulperías, an extension of their responsibility for reproductive labor in campesino households. Most prisoners' testimony mentioned that Ramírez engaged in this activity. Sagredo remembered in 1965 that she and other women supported male campesinos who battled carabineros by handing out goods taken from pulperías to campesino families: "We distributed everything. I was among those who distributed goods. We gave cheese, butter, sugar to everyone. We were in groups of women. We also distributed cups, knives, spoons. . . . We had to have everything ready for the campesinos who went out to confront the carabineros, take care of them well. We corralled the rich people's livestock. The moment didn't last long, but we shared [the goods] well, we ate well. And we helped each other."[3] Women did not necessarily stay at home during the rebellion, but they mostly remained behind to distribute food to campesino families while their male relatives engaged in direct violence, leading the assaults on estates, pulperías, and carabineros.

The Assaults on Pulperías

According to the testimony of detained prisoners questioned during the judicial proceeding, early in the morning of 27 June one of the bands of men led by Florentino Pino Valdebenito and Juan Domingo Lagos headed for the Frau pulpería in Troyo. Pino Valdebenito had lived and worked as an inquilino since 1914 on Ránquil and settled on a plot in the Ránquil colony. The Lagos family had worked as estate laborers and also settled on Ránquil. Pino Valdebenito, Lagos, and their men were armed with sticks and knives. José Frau Pujol was in Lonquimay, where, like most pulpería owners, he had his primary residence. He had left his business in charge of his employee, Pedro Acuña Lobos. When they arrived, the group led by Pino Valdebenito and Lagos found Acuña and his wife, Delia Rosa Ortega Espinosa, drinking *mate*. Ortega Espinosa said four men led by Lagos entered the pulpería and asked Acuña about the price of gold. The conversation quickly turned into an argument. The workers complained that they were paid too little for the gold they extracted from the placer mines. They became increasingly angry with Acuña's response that it wasn't he who fixed the price of gold. Given that they planned to assault the pulpería, the men may have used the negotiation over gold prices to catch Acuña unawares.[4]

But the argument also hints at laborers' dissatisfaction with the prices they received for gold and their dependence on exchanging gold for provisions in the pulperías. A commission sent by the FOCH to Alto Bío Bío to investigate atrocities committed by carabineros during the repression located one cause of the rebellion in pulperías' inflated prices for basic food items like sugar, mate, beans, flour, and potatoes. The FOCH report noted agricultural workers' and miners' grievance that *pulperos* underpaid for gold and "stole a half a gram more for each [gram] they bought."[5] Emelina Sagredo likewise recalled that the pulperos paid very little for the gold campesinos extracted and charged inflated prices for basic goods. Campesinos' situation was often so desperate that they sold their crops to the pulperos for a low fixed price in advance of the harvest for whatever they could get and then received nothing at harvest time.[6] Thus, when the campesino rebels assaulted the pulperías, their actions were shaped by the understanding that they were righting the moral scales and exacting punishment for a persistent fraud that had driven many to hunger.

As the argument in the Frau pulpería escalated, two of the men, Cesáreo Quilondrán and Alegría, grabbed Acuña and tied him up. Acuña shouted to his wife to get the gun he kept under his pillow, but when she entered the bedroom one of the men held her hands while Lagos took the revolver from her. Then Ortega Espinosa saw "around thirty men" enter the pulpería, led by Florentino Pino Valdebenito. What the men did next reveals something about social relations in Alto Bío Bío. Employing an "imperious manner," Pino Valdebenito ordered Ortega Espinosa to give cigarettes and matches to his men, who then installed themselves in the kitchen and drank mate while they smoked. This was an inversion of the social hierarchy, a "world turned upside down."[7] The campesinos, sitting while being served, were now being brought cigarettes and mate by those who ran the pulpería, consuming precious luxuries when they could barely afford food for their families.[8]

Pino Valdebenito testified that when the larger group entered the pulpería he ordered his men to tie up Acuña. He also claimed that he prohibited the group from sacking the pulpería. Later in the morning, he said, he got an order from Leiva Tapia to kill Acuña, "with the warning that if I did not do it, Acuña and I would both be thrown into the Bio Bio River." He then gave Cesáreo Quilondrán a revolver, in all probability Acuña's gun, and ordered him to shoot Acuña, which he did. On his orders, he confessed, "Cesáreo Quilondrán, José Paillaleo, and José Merillán threw the cadaver into the Bio Bio River."[9] That two men with Mapuche names, most likely members of nearby Pehuenche communities, numbered in a group whose members mostly hailed from the Ránquil colony was a reflection of the ties of solidarity between indigenous and nonindigenous campesinos in their conflicts with Alto Bío Bío's haciendas.

Pino Valdebenito testified that to prevent Acuña's wife from witnessing his execution they took her away and locked her in a shed for about an hour. The group then sent her to the Zolezzi pulpería, about six hundred meters away, also in Troyo. He declared later that "nobody tried anything against señora Acuña." When Ortega Espinosa returned to the Frau pulpería the next day in the company of carabineros she saw that the revoltosos had stolen three suits, two white wool jerseys, shawls, a pair of men's shoes, four sheets, two pairs of underpants, three men's shirts, a lantern, six napkins, six forks, three porcelain jugs, two women's blouses, and a pair of glasses.[10]

Detailed lists of goods stolen by the rebels as described in police reports and in the testimony of pulpería employees and owners had two purposes. The lists served to establish the value of items lost during the rebellion. They also provided evidence to the police of a common crime: robbery or armed robbery. And, indeed, judging by a simple reading, the rebels engaged in theft and looting. But looked at from another angle, the list of goods stolen from pulperías may indicate something quite different. As historians like Henri Levebre, Georges Rudé, and Ranajit Guha have shown, looting was a common occurrence during peasant insurrections across the globe, but it rarely meant merely common theft for individual gain. In the case of the Ránquil rebels, acts of theft constituted a symbolic as well as a material assault. Porcelain jugs, glasses, and cloth napkins were emblems of class. The campesinos quite literally stripped these markers of social distinction from pulperos and landowners and appropriated them for themselves. To the authorities, the list of stolen items stood as an indictment of the rebellion as the common criminal actions of a mob. To the rebels, however, theft took on another meaning, much like smoking and consuming mate while being served by a pulpero's wife: a social inversion and seizure of goods whose value lay in their meaning as symbols of social status.[11]

Other witnesses did not confirm Pino Valdebenito's testimony that Leiva Tapia ordered Acuña's execution. Their testimony indicates that Leiva Tapia ordered the assaults on the pulperías but not the killing of pulperos. As Franklin Quezada Rogers, the appellate court judge assigned to investigate the rebellion, later concluded, the fact that Leiva Tapia arrived after Acuña's murder suggests that this was a decision made by the members of Pino Valdebenito's party. Why kill Acuña? The group of men may have harbored hatred over their exploitation by the pulpería. His murder was less part of the revolutionary strategy devised by the leaders than a reflection of the everyday tensions that shaped life and labor in Alto Bío Bío. It was animated by a sense of retribution, perhaps even punishment, for what workers perceived to be the unjust practice of overcharging for goods and underpaying for gold. Ultimately the killing may have been payback for denying them the provisions they desperately needed to weather the harsh winter months when panning for gold was impossible.

Meanwhile, on 27 June another band of men led by Onofre Ortíz Salgado, Juan Domingo Lagos, and Elías Lagos also went to Troyo to take the Zolezzi pulpería. Ortíz had worked as an inquilino on Contraco, where he had disagreements with his patrones, the Spanish immigrants José and Martín Gainza, who had rented the property from Juan Olhagaray. It appears that Olhagaray had carved Contraco out of the Lolco estate. Ortíz had moved to Llanquén to work on shares with Cesáreo Orrego, who also played a leadership role in the rebellion. According to Luisa Seguel, Zolezzi's wife, Ortíz, the Lagoses, and their men arrived at nine in the morning. Like the group in the Frau pulpería, they "pretended they wanted to buy goods and sell gold." Zolezzi had a pistol in his belt, but the men were able to take it from him. Witnesses testified that they took Zolezzi out to the patio and stabbed him to death.[12] When Zolezzi's partner, Alfonso Zañartu Rodríguez, intervened, he was also allegedly stabbed to death. The band took the pulpería's empleados, Blanca Aurora Orrego, Carlos Deramond, and Luis Aburto, prisoner and forced them to throw the cadavers into the Biobío River. The empleados went unharmed. Throughout the rebellion servants and employees who worked in the estates' big houses and in the pulperías were largely unscathed by violence.[13]

A police report noted that the group then robbed the pulpería of cash and goods, including a shawl, some cloth, thread, a pair of pants, two dresses, cigarettes, three pairs of underpants, three pairs of clogs, a pair of shoes, and other small items.[14] They handed the cash and goods to Leiva Tapia and Margarita Ramírez, who were in charge.[15] Onofre Ortíz also took a carbine from the pulpería, which he would later use in battles with carabineros. He confessed to the police that he had ordered Zollezi's death and had stabbed Zañartu. But, like Pino Valdebenito, he said he was following Leiva Tapia's orders.[16]

The account of the assault and murders contained in the police report and Onofre Ortíz's confession was contradicted by testimony from Zolezzi's wife and a servant, Blanca Aurora Orrego, who contested Ortíz's claim that Leiva Tapia had directed him to kill Zolezzi and Zañartu. Like a number of other witnesses, they told the court that Leiva

Tapia arrived when the bodies had already been thrown into the river.[17] On the other hand, the witnesses did concur that when Leiva Tapia arrived in the company of Margarita Ramírez, the two supervised the looting of the pulpería, and Ramírez oversaw the distribution of the store's provisions, including flour, mate, sugar, and cigarettes. Ramírez was also placed in charge of Zolezzi's and Acuña's wives.[18] When Delia Rosa Ortega Espinosa arrived from the Frau pulpería, she was locked in a bedroom where Carmen Luisa Seguel de Zolezzi was under guard but attended by her servant, Blanca Aurora Orrego. The three women were freed on 29 June when carabineros arrived in Troyo.[19]

Leiva Tapia's intent was evidently to protect the female members of the pulperías' households, including servants, by guarding them and placing them in the charge of Margarita Rámirez, who was still with them when carabineros freed the three women. There are also indications that Leiva Tapia and Ramírez attempted to control looting in the pulpería. Juan Orellana Barrera, who panned gold in Nitrito and attended the union assembly in Quilleime, attested that he took two hundred pesos, a shawl, and other items from the store. However, Leiva Tapia and Ramírez confiscated the goods and cash. The money, Leiva Tapia told Orellana Barrera, was to be used to send "a delegate outside the region," presumably in an effort to expand the revolutionary movement to other southern towns and estates.[20]

Early in the morning on 27 June Juan Segundo Leiva Tapia instructed Ismael Cartes, a former inquilino on the Chilpaco estate who had received a plot in the Ránquil colony, to join a group of men who were stationed at the bridge over the Ránquil River. According to Cartes's testimony, he rode on horseback and was armed only with a riding crop. While a large group of men remained at the Ránquil Bridge to prevent carabineros from crossing the river, Cartes led eleven men to join another group that had been assigned to guard the bridge over the Rahue River. The group led by Cartes came upon Baldovino Cid, who was panning for gold, and asked him for a goat to eat. While they were at Cid's house, Harry Fahrenkrog, "the gringo Enrique Fahrenkrog," in Cartes's words, arrived. Fahrenkrog, an immigrant from Canada whose family was originally from Germany, had been left in charge of the pulpería in El Rahue. The store belonged to Jorge and Bruno Ackermann, German immigrants themselves and among the original organizers of the Sindicato Agrícola Lonquimay. The store's owners were away, and the employee was in charge. Cartes hit Fahrenkrog in the head with his riding crop, and the group locked him in the kitchen. Ten more men from the Leiva Tapia group arrived at daybreak on 28 June. These individuals, among whom was José Paiñaleo, a Pehuenche, arrived on horseback with an order from Leiva Tapia to open the Ackermanns' pulpería. According to Cartes, they then took flour, mate, sugar, and cigarettes.[21]

Víctor Reyes Burgos, an "agricultor de Ránquil" with a ninety-five-hectare plot on the estate-turned-colony, had been a member of the Sindicato Agrícola Lonquimay. He described how, after riding on horseback with the group led by Cartes and Quilondrán and, armed with a stick, joining in on the attack at the Ackermanns' pulpería, he returned with the other men to the Ránquil Bridge when news arrived that carabineros were headed in that direction. They joined the groups of men who had assaulted the Frau and Zolezzi pulperías and the group of men that had been stationed there during the night. While most of the rebels defending the bridge were armed only with sticks, the movement had accumulated some firearms, enough to prevent the carabineros from crossing the Ránquil River. Fermín Quilodrán San Martín, who had lived since birth on Puelma Tupper's El Rahue estate and who had then settled as an aspiring colono on Ránquil after the decree expropriating the estate, told police he had spent the day of 27 June collecting a handful of firearms, including carbines and shotguns, to arm the men stationed at the Ránquil Bridge.[22]

Ismael Cartes's group had been informed that carabineros were on the way, so they headed for the Ránquil Bridge.[23] In a 1972 interview Cartes said, "I was given the responsibility of guarding the southern bank of the Ránquil River with eighty compañeros in front of the bridge made of tree trunks. We had to watch for the movement of troops, send messages, and, if the moment came, fight to the death to not let them cross." He recalled, "We had two Winchester carbines, half a dozen shotguns, those were our weapons."[24]

At six o'clock in the evening the eleven carabineros led by Cabrera arrived at the Ránquil Bridge. They saw that across the river the rebels had built palisades of rocks and sticks and dug trenches. Some had firearms but most were armed with sticks, hoes, and pitchforks. The rebels and carabineros exchanged fire. A group on horseback armed only with sticks and clubs charged toward the carabineros positioned on the other side of the bridge. The unequal balance of firepower favored the carabineros, who, despite being outnumbered, carried carbines. Ismael Cartes was on horseback, but before he could reach the carabineros he was wounded multiple times and lost his mount. When night fell the armed conflict ended with the carabineros still stationed on the other side of the river. A number of rebel combatants took advantage of the darkness to leave their positions and escape into the mountains. By morning the entire group of rebels had retreated into the interior of the region's estates, and the bridge was clear. The carabineros found eight campesinos dead on the other side of the bridge. They themselves had only limited casualties: two carabineros with gunshot wounds.[25]

Cabrera and his men then proceeded to Troyo, where they discovered the looting in the Zolezzi and Frau pulperías and heard reports of the deaths of Zolezzi, Zañartu, and Acuña.[26] Later it emerged that the rebels also had killed, "with a blow from a machete to the side of the head," Manuel Salas, the mayordomo on Ránquil and El Rahue.[27] Cabrera telegrammed the intendancy to request reinforcements. At this point he appears to have gathered a great deal of intelligence from detained rebels who had either been captured or had deserted following the battle at Ránquil Bridge.[28] Cabrera and his men then went in search of the Lagoses, Onofre Ortíz, and Leiva Tapia, whom sources had identified as the movement's leaders. Some captured rebels informed Cabrera that Juan Segundo Leiva Tapia was hiding in the Lagoses' house. The carabineros went to the house and opened fire until Leiva Tapia surrendered. They reported that they then took Leiva Tapia, who was bound, with them as they headed north toward Nitrito and Llanquén in pursuit of the groups of men who had assaulted the pulperías.[29]

The reinforcements requested by Cabrera were already on their way. On 28 June a detachment of forty-five to fifty carabineros led by Cautín's prefect, Commander Fernando Délano, left Temuco by a special train to Curacautín.[30] A plane was sent to survey the revoltosos' position and "atemorizarlos" (terrorize them). The survey proved futile because the pilot was unfamiliar with the region and got lost, an ineffective first foray into the use of aviation in counterinsurgency in the Chilean countryside. Meanwhile, Bío-Bío's prefect, Colonel Ramón Briones, had ordered carabineros to prevent rebels from descending on Mulchén and Santa Bárbara and to fence them in by sending reinforcements from those two towns.[31] By 29 June Lieutenant Robertson and eight men had gone to reinforce Cabrera in Ránquil and Captain Monreal had led twenty-six men to Troyo. Délano himself remained with twenty-five men at the head of the Las Raíces tunnel.[32]

During the afternoon and evening of 29 June the troops led by Cabrera and Robertson advanced from Ránquil toward Llanquén. The next day they arrived at the southern bank of the Llanquén River, where they were met with gunfire from a large group of campesinos positioned across the river. The combat lasted well into the evening, when the carabineros withdrew to Troyo to set up camp and pasture their horses. The rebels had, for the moment, stopped carabineros from crossing the Llanquén and moving northward toward Guayalí, Contraco, and Lolco.[33] As at the Ránquil Bridge, however, the battle favored the carabineros. None suffered casualties while a number of rebels were killed, including, according to police reports, Leiva Tapia, who allegedly died in the crossfire. In the morning the campesinos' bodies had disappeared. A police report claimed that the rebels had taken the corpses of their fallen comrades, including Leiva Tapia, and thrown them into the river.[34] None of these bodies were ever found.

The Assaults on Contraco, Guayalí, and Lolco

On 27 June two carabineros stationed on the Guayalí estate, Rafael Bascuñán Rodríguez and Raúl Montoya Villagrán, had left their barracks to investigate rumors of the union meeting in Quilleime and the manifestos circulating in the region. They headed straight for the Sagredos' home in Nitrito. They knew the Sagredos well, having only months before assisted in their detention and beating. As *El Diario Austral* put it, "They went there because they knew about the brothers' communist activities, and that they must have known what there was to know about the manifestos."[35]

As the group led by the Sagredos made its way toward Nitrito, the men came upon the two carabineros. The police related that Bascuñán and Montoya were assaulted "by a numerous group of armed individuals, from in front and behind, who pulled them from their horses, disarmed them, and killed them with their knives, stones, and clubs, taking off their uniforms and throwing their cadavers into the Bío-Bío River."[36] The police account and numerous others by detained prisoners maintained that Simón and Benito Sagredo, Juan Pablo Ortíz, Erasmo Baeza, and Emelina Sagredo were the "authors of the homicides." Other witnesses identified Juan Bautista Sagredo Valenzuela, "a colono from Ránquil," as one of the leaders in the confrontation with the two carabineros. A member of the group testified that "when we saw the carabineros, Simón Sagredo and Juan Bautista Sagredo Valenzuela went ahead on horseback and knocked Corporal Bascuñan to the ground, one with a stick he had and the other with the butt of a revolver." Montoya was also knocked off his horse. A group of men then beat the carabineros with sticks and allegedly stabbed them until they were dead. Emelina Sagredo, witnesses testified, stripped the carabineros of their uniforms and ordered Abraham Peña Campos to bury the uniforms. Their bodies were then thrown into the Biobío River.[37]

The group led by the Sagredos set up camp in Nitrito. The next day the Sagredo brothers divided the men into two groups. One band, led by Benito Sagredo, headed for Contraco.[38] As noted above, the property belonged to Juan Olhagaray, and he had rented it to the Spanish immigrants Martín and José Gainza.[39] Among the leaders of the group, which witnesses described as being composed of about eighty men, was Juan Pablo Ortíz, one of Guayalí's rebellious inquilinos. Ortíz had been active with the Sagredos in organizing the Nitrito Colonos Defense Committee and opposing the ocupantes' eviction from Nitrito. A number of witnesses identified Ortíz and Sagredo as the leaders of the attack on Contraco and "the revolutionary directorate."[40]

Adolfo Sánchez Salazar worked as an employee in a pulpería belonging to Adolfo Rubilar that served the gold placer mines within the borders of the Guayalí estate. He lived on Guayalí with his family and was taken prisoner by the group led by the Sagredos during the revolt. He joined the movement, he swore, as did many others, under threat of death. Sánchez Salazar depicted the group that assaulted Contraco as being composed of "forty mounted men, who went first, the rest on foot." The horsemen, he declared, "were armed with carbines, shotguns, and revolvers, the rest with clubs."[41] Other witnesses put the number in the group at sixty and testified that most of the men were armed with sticks and knives.[42]

When the Gainza brothers saw the group of rebels approaching, they shot at them from the windows of the house. Martín Gainza then barricaded himself in a bedroom, while José Gainza fled up a nearby hill armed with a revolver. A few men caught, disarmed, and bound him and then returned to the estate's big house. Meanwhile, Carmen León, "a colono from Llanquén," took an ax and began to knock down the door of the room where Martín Gainza had hidden, yelling "come out of there gringo swindler," and Marcos Hermosilla threatened to shoot through the door with a carbine. Martín Gainza surrendered, and Benito Sagredo tied him up and asked him for the keys to the estate's storehouse. Gainza gave Sagredo the keys, and his men took goods and a shotgun. Sánchez Salazar and other witnesses described how Juan Pablo Ortíz and Benito Sagredo distributed cheese and wheat to each inquilino family, the majority of whom were "indios" from neighboring Pehuenche communities. They also, Sánchez Salazar said, threatened the inquilinos, forcing them to join the movement.[43] Isidoro Piñaleo similarly testified that he and other workers on Contraco, "most of whom were indigenous," were forced to join the movement, being threatened with shotguns and revolvers.[44] At about midday Sagredo ordered one of the fundo's shepherds to bring a flock of sheep, and they butchered fourteen.[45] A police report asserted that the men also "dedicated themselves to looting the house, stealing clothing, bedclothes, tools, china, kitchen and dining utensils, cereals, firearms, cash, and livestock."[46]

The specific events in the assaults on Contraco, Lolco, and Guayalí provide some clues about the forces driving the rebellion. As in the case of the pulperías, a degree of personal animosity and vengeance shaped the rebels' violence. These were workers like Onofre Ortíz, who had had direct conflicts with the Gainzas, their patrones. As León's threat indicates, these conflicts were shaped both by workers' sense that their patrones were gringos and that exploitation on the estates constituted a fraud or injustice. Like the gringo pulperos, the Gainzas were "swindlers." The term carried the sense of a fundamental unfairness in social relations as well as workers' understanding that estate owners' property rights were illegitimate, rooted in the unjust usurpation of public land. Moreover, given carabineros' appropriation of the Nitrito ocupantes' goods and crops, the campesino rebels acted with the sense that they were recovering goods that were rightfully theirs.

The well-organized distribution of provisions to the estate's Pehuenche inquilinos reflects the rebellion's leaders' attempts to mobilize the region's indigenous communities, many of which supplied labor to the estates. Distributing food, as in the pulperías, met the basic needs of rural workers who suffered deprivation and hardship during the harsh winter months while making concrete the rebellion's revolutionary redistributionist promises. As in the case of the assaults on pulperías, the movement's leaders also intended estates' storehouses to supply the ranks of the rebellion during the winter months until a national revolution took place. Simón Sagredo, for example, ordered his brother Rosendo Sagredo to go to Contraco on the afternoon of the assault to guard the food in the storehouses, presumably to prevent looting.[47]

At four or five in the afternoon Benito Sagredo gave the order to return to Nitrito. Sánchez Salazar's declaration holds that before they left, Sagredo gave orders to the sentinels to kill the Gainzas and throw them into the river, "threatening them with death if they didn't do it."⁴⁸ During the night, the rebels made the Gainza brothers disappear ("les hiceron desaparecer"). The police attested that the Gainzas' cadavers had not been found, and they were presumed to have been executed and thrown into the Biobío River: "The empleada Lorenza Elena Sandoval Maldonado says she heard shots near the river and, wanting to bring breakfast to her patrones, found that they were no longer in the house."⁴⁹ It also appears that the band killed, "with blows to the head," Herminio Campos, described by town dignitaries as a "prestigious resident" of Lonquimay who was employed as mayordomo on Contraco.⁵⁰

The same day as the assault on Contraco, another group of men led by Simón Sagredo headed toward Guayalí. Their goal was to assault the barracks on the estate where carabineros had been stationed since 1930. When they arrived, the group of close to forty men found the carabinero Bernardo San Martín Calderón sleeping. They bound San Martín and forced him to wear clothing belonging to Víctor Vergara, the estate's manager, whom they also took prisoner. In this case, they literally stripped the carabinero of the authority represented by his uniform. They obtained from the barracks a carbine, ammunition, and food. According to a police report, they also assaulted the estate's big house, "robbing everything they could find," and sacked Víctor Vergara's house. They also took Vergara's horse, spurs, and poncho (*manta*). Vergara was an old enemy. He had represented the patrones of a number of estates as their property manager, and in this capacity had overseen evictions of inquilinos and ocupantes. The horse and spurs would certainly have been of use to the campesino rebels, but these goods can also be seen as symbols of Vergara's social power. Vergara now had to walk, bound, on foot without his *manta*, while his captors rode on horseback, a distinct inversion of the social order. When the Sagredos had been arrested, bound, and taken to the barracks on Guayalí, they had traveled on foot while the carabineros rode. Apparently, during the assault on Guayalí's houses there was a shootout with an estate foreman, Froilán Labrín, who suffered bullet and knife wounds. The men then returned to Nitrito, bringing San Martín and Víctor Vergara with them as prisoners.⁵¹

As in Contraco, in Guayalí they recruited around thirty-four inquilinos "by force." They also took with them forty cows and a number of horses as well as the foreman Teofilo Zapata and mayordomo Jorge Valderrama as prisoners.⁵² How did they force thirty-four workers to join their movement? Did they possess the necessary tools of coercion? Or did persuasion play a role? In this case, a party of maybe forty or fifty men, most unarmed, supposedly coerced thirty-four laborers to join their ranks. Perhaps they employed threats, but their capacity to force the inquilinos to join the movement was limited. Some willingness on the part of the inquilinos would have certainly been necessary, and since most came from Pehuenche communities that had long-standing conflicts with neighboring estate owners it is not difficult to see why they might have joined the rebellion for reasons other than the force employed by the rebel band.

As historians of other regions and periods have noted, "pressing" was a way of forging collective solidarity, pushing a perhaps reluctant minority to join peasant rebellions around the globe. Georges Rudé, for example, argues that in the case of nineteenth-century England, "an essential measure" of mobilizing agricultural laborers during rebellions was "to muster a sufficiently imposing force." Guha similarly notes that pressing during peasant insurrections amounted to a mixture of intimidation and persuasion; threats as an instrument to convince fellow peasants to join an insurrection were common in colonial India. Perhaps rather than "coercion," "intimidation" is the right word to characterize the Ránquil rebellion. Certainly the rebel bands employed persuasion by redistributing the estates' provisions to their inquilinos. But perhaps the leaders of the rebellion's major mode of both intimidation and persuasion was stripping carabineros and estate owners and managers of their authority and assuming the mantel of social and political power themselves. The campesino rebels displayed their new authority as a way of persuading perhaps otherwise reluctant estate laborers to join their ranks.[53] They appropriated carabineros' and landowners' symbols of social prestige and power: their horses, guns, clothing, fine goods, and weapons. To be sure, such impounding signified an inversion of the social hierarchy, but it was also a statement of authority. The rebels now wielded the power once held by landowners and carabineros. They backed their symbolic claims to authority with the assertion that their rebellion was part of a national movement that would bring to power a revolutionary government. That argument may well have convinced inquilinos to join the rebellion. Given the last three years of coups and the short-lived Socialist Republic as well as the Sindicato Agrícola Lonquimay's evident political weight and successful collective organizing to colonize Ránquil, the rebellion's leaders' claims that they were part of a revolutionary change in government would not have seemed far-fetched and would have reinforced their assumption of authority.

The group led by Simón Sagredo returned to Nitrito, bringing with them Víctor Vergara, Zapata and one of his sons, and one Peña and his two sons who lived in Nitrito. They bound Vergara and Zapata and had them watched by sentinels armed with sticks. They asked Sánchez Salazar, whom they had earlier taken prisoner, if he was willing to join their ranks and then freed him along with Peña when the two pledged their loyalty to the movement. Sánchez Salazar claimed that in Nitrito Simón Sagredo began to berate Víctor Vergara: "Do you know me now or not? Shameless swine [*sinverguenza cochino*]. Do you remember that it was because of you that I was bound and beaten with sticks? What would you say if I left you hanging right here? . . . I could kill you, but I won't. I'll be considerate with you, bourgeois [*te tendré consideración, burgués*]."[54]

An element of personal animosity in Sagredo's attack on Vergara was obvious. Vergara had overseen campesinos' expulsion from Nitrito, and in Sagredo's eyes he and his brother had been arrested, hung by the wrists, and beaten by carabineros at Vergara's behest. Later, witnesses would declare that Sagredo ordered Vergara killed, but Sánchez Salazar's vivid account appears to undermine this claim, which would have conveniently placed responsibility for Vergara's disappearance and death on Sagredo's shoulders. The conflicting testimony does not illuminate Víctor Vergara's fate, but at some point he was killed. The rebels also apparently executed the carabinero San Martín Calderón and Teofilo Zapata, although their bodies were never found. Zapata, like Vergara, was an old enemy of the union; following the fall of the Ibáñez regime in 1931 he had denounced the union leaders to the labor authorities for continually harassing him and refusing to follow his orders.[55] Jorge Valderrama testified that he and Zapata had been taken prisoner by a group of "around sixty individuals armed with carbines, sticks, revolvers, and knives." The rebels bound them and took them to Llanquén. They told them that if they did not join the movement they would be killed. Apparently Valderrama agreed, but Zapata did not. In the morning he went to find Zapata, but he was gone. "I had no doubt," he testified, that "the seditionists had killed him and since that moment he has not been seen again."[56]

During the afternoon of 28 June news of the rebellion arrived in Lolco. Luciano Gainza, a brother of José and Martín Gainza who apparently worked for Juan Olhagaray as an administrator on the estate, encountered five armed individuals on the opposite bank of the Biobío River who told him "in a threatening tone": "Go get your people to defend yourself." Gainza communicated this to Olhagaray, who sent his wife to the house of the mayordomo of the neighboring Villucura fundo for safety. That night they waited for the assault to come but since nothing happened they went to bed, sending a message to Dolores Charó de Olhagaray that she could return. On her way back to Lolco from Villucura, however, Charó saw a group of "individuals on horseback and on foot." Moments later she heard shots and noticed a fire that she thought came from the estate's big house. She was then captured by one of the revoltosos, who, pistol in hand, told her that the revolution had broken out in the entire country, demanded that she declare herself to be on the side of the "rich or the poor," and took her prisoner.[57]

According to police reports and witness testimony, at eight in the morning of 29 June a group of fifty men, some on horseback, some on foot, had arrived at Lolco and surrounded the house. Gainza and Olhagaray, one armed with a revolver and the other with a Winchester carbine, exchanged gunshots with the band of rebels, who then proceeded to set fire to a shed near the house as a threat to force Gainza and Olhagaray to surrender. The rebels also began to knock down the locked doors of the house with hatchets. Gainza and Olhagaray attempted to flee the house through the kitchen and exchanged rounds with the rebels. Surrounded, Gainza shot himself in the head. Olhagaray tried to hide but was caught.[58]

When Dolores Charó returned to the estate as a prisoner she saw that her husband was under detention and Gainza was dead. She testified that "fifty individuals had made themselves owners of the house." In yet another example of the rebels' symbolic inversion of the established social hierarchy, they dressed themselves in Olhagaray's clothing "and gave orders as if they were lords and masters [amos y señores])," forcing Charó de Olhagaray and her husband to serve them for the five days they remained their prisoners. One of the leaders of the assault on Lolco, José Troncoso, donned Olhagaray's suit, as in other instances of looting, a symbolic claim to badges of social prestige and authority. During the assault, Charó narrated, Ignacio Maripi, "cacique of the Ralco reducción," gouged out an eye and broke the jaw of Gainza's cadaver with an iron spit. If true, these acts reveal the animosity toward the gringo patrones and the sense of vengeance that shaped the movement's violence.[59] Both Olhagarays would survive their captivity and emerge unscathed after the rebellion's defeat.

A number of Pehuenches, many of them members of the Ralco community, joined the assault on Lolco, whose inquilinos, like those on Contraco, came from nearby Pehuenche communities. Eventually, twelve, or around 20 percent, of the detainees in Temuco's jail belonged to Pehuenche communities.[60] The testimony of José de Cármen Vega Tapia, who had been an inquilino and ocupante on Guayalí, sheds some light on Pehuenches' role in the rebellion. Vega Tapia had been expelled to Llanquén but because of Llanquén's inhospitable conditions had planned to move on to the town of Santa Bárbara. Instead, however, he found lodging with the *professor de indios*, Luis Muñoz, in Ralco Lepoy. He testified that on 28 June "José Sagredo, Benigno Avello, Alfredo Salazar, and one Loncona, and another who I believe is called Sepúlveda" arrived in Ralco Lepoy. They sent Vega Tapia to find the wife of Ignacio Maripi and charged him with delivering a message to Maripi's son. According to Vega Tapia, José Sagredo and Benigno Avello spent the day recruiting people in Ralco. They ordered Vega Tapia to deliver letters to "indios in Quepuca and Maya [Malla]," nearby Pehuenche communities, and "to the house of one Levi, where they were celebrating a nguillatún," an indigenous religious ceremony. Vega testified that the letters contained instructions to members of the Malla and Quepuca communities to "take over the launch in Callaquén and prevent all transport on it."[61]

The group led by José Sagredo headed to the Lolco estate, which had a large labor force composed of Pehuenches, many of them from Ralco. Following the revolt, carabineros arrested a number of members of the Ralco community for their role in the assault on Lolco. The detainees testified that they had joined the movement only because they were threatened with death by José Troncoso, "one of the leaders of the revolt." Domingo Pellao Gallina and Remigio Mariguan, accused of being cabecillas of the movement, also rejected accusations that they had sent messages to members of the Ralco community who worked as inquilinos on Lolco to join the rebellion. Instead, they avowed, they had sent messages to community members who worked on the estate, informing them about the nguillatún.[62] It would be a remarkable coincidence if the very morning of the assaults on Lolco, Contraco, and Guayalí, which included members of the Ralco community and the community's lonko, Ralco also happened to be holding a nguillatún unrelated to the rebellion. In all likelihood the community held the nguillatún in order to discuss the revolutionary movement led, in part, by its lonko, who had worked with Juan Segundo Leiva Tapia and the Sindicato Agrícola Lonquimay since 1930. In the end, a number of Pehuenches from local communities appear to have joined the rebellion, including inquilinos on Contraco and Lolco. This is not surprising given the union's organization of councils on estates neighboring Pehuenche reducciones and Pehuenches' presence in the union and at the assembly at Quilleime.

Like most of the campesino rebels, members of Pehuenche communities were less driven by the Communist Party's formal ideological propositions—the program of building soviets of indios and an Araucanian Republic—than by the concrete goal of winning back land they perceived to have been illegally taken over by the Bunster and Puelma families' large estates. Given that many Pehuenches labored on these estates as inquilinos, there may have been a labor component to the tensions between the landowners and their workers as well. If so, this might, for example, explain Ignacio Maripi's apparent hatred of Gainza, who would have appeared to be not only a gringo usurper of indigenous land but a detested patrón as well. As in the case of non-Pehuenche campesinos, members of Pehuenche communities occupied shifting social, occupational, and legal identities. While non-Pehuenche campesinos moved easily between the positions of ocupante and inquilino, many Pehuenches occupied the dual position of belonging to indigenous communities and laboring as inquilinos or gañanes on neighboring estates. To Pehuenche and non-Pehuenche campesinos alike, first the union and its councils and then the armed insurrection were tools for acquiring and settling estate land.

The Counterinsurgency

Following the combat in Llanquén on 29 June the carabineros and rebels retreated, the former to Troyo to spend the night and the latter to Lolco, where the forces led by the Sagredos were concentrated. On 1 July the twenty-five reinforcements commanded by Captain Alfredo Monreal arrived in Troyo. The next day they made their way north to Llanquén. They forded the Llanquén River and continued on toward Nitrito, apparently in search of the Sagredo brothers. While Monreal continued north toward Guayalí, Sublieutenant Fernández Frías, who had remained in the Nitrito and Llanquén area, dispatched a patrol of five men to search the huts in the area and arrest rebels who had taken flight. In Nitrito, they reported, they saw an armed individual come out of a hut and begin shooting at them with his carbine. They fired back and, as in almost every armed encounter, suffered no casualties, while killing the rebel, whom they identified as "one of the bloodthirsty Sagredo brothers." Police later identified him as Juan Sagredo. After collecting the carbine and ammunition, the carabineros continued their work, leaving Sagredo's cadaver behind. When they returned later, they reported, the cadaver had disappeared, "certainly the work of the revoltosos who always tried to hide their losses to prevent demoralization among their ranks."[63] Once again, as in the case of Leiva Tapia, one of the rebellion's leaders had been killed and disappeared. And once again carabineros placed the responsibility for the disappearance on the campesinos' shoulders.

Forty-six troops led by Délano and fifty led by Monreal continued to advance north along both sides of the Biobío River with the goal of bottling up the rebels in Lolco. Other reinforcements also headed to Lolco: twenty carabineros dispatched from Boca Norte under the command of Lieutenants Larenas and Fernández, who traveled to Lolco and the Las Juntas placers as well as forty troops from Temuco and fifty more from Los Ángeles.[64] In addition, twenty-five carabineros led by Lieutenant Arriagada crossed the Pemehue cordillera and went to the Villucura estate, where there had been word of an assault and sacking. Captain Valenzuela, at the head of fifty men, traveled from Loncopangue to Guayalí to continue on to Lolco.[65] By 1 July the number of carabineros mobilized to stamp out the rebellion had reached well over two hundred.

As Monreal's and Délano's men moved northward on either side of the Biobío toward Lolco, they coordinated with carabineros advancing from the north between the Tres Pinos cordillera and the Villucura River from Collipulli, Santa Bárbara, Mulchén, and Los Ángeles. Délano reported that as they approached Lolco his troops had been attacked a number of times by groups of "guerillas" and that they had killed several rebels in shootouts and recuperated large quantities of arms and ammunition, surely an exaggeration given how few arms the rebels possessed.[66] On 3 July Délano reported that four hundred rebels in Lolco had been surrounded and had surrendered.[67] The national Santiago papers *La Nación* and *El Mercurio*, using police sources, reported even larger numbers of rebels detained in Lolco ranging from four to six hundred. As the historian Jaime Flores has noted, these inflated figures were probably employed as a means of exaggerating the military threat posed by the rebellion and carabineros' corresponding glory in its defeat.[68]

By 4 July carabineros under Délano's command, including Fernández and forty-four men, had also taken control of Contraco. They reported that the revoltosos had dispersed into the cordillera, leaving behind "abandoned houses, and in others only women and children." That same day Captain Monreal took possession of Guayalí.[69] The next day *El Diario*

Austral reported that three hundred carabineros had encircled the rebel bands. Perhaps as a sign of the rebellion's persistence as a scattered guerilla struggle in the mountains, General Arriagada, the director of carabineros, departed Santiago with fifty men to extinguish the last embers of the movement. Meanwhile, small groups of rebels fled north pursued by carabineros. According to police reports, about seventy rebels had refused to surrender and instead fled and fought small skirmishes with carabineros. A number were killed during this last phase of the rebellion, including, reportedly, "the communist agitator Alarcón, who had come from Lota."[70]

For his part, Juan Pablo Ortíz fled northward to Loncopangue. Some days before, José Sagredo had traveled there to organize campesinos in the region to join the movement. Adolfo Sánchez Salazar told police that during the days leading up to the rebellion Sagredo had been in Loncopangue collecting news about what was happening outside the region. He was in the company of "two communist delegates" who were on their way to Santa Bárbara.[71] Armed with a pistol, Ortíz went to the house of Francisco Carrasco León. He informed him that "a communist revolution had broken out" and that Carrasco should join the movement, which would "kill carabineros and numerous residents in the region." Ortíz also asked him to send a telegram to Temuco with the news that a communist revolution had begun in Lonquimay. Ortíz's testimony was that he had been given the telegram by José del Carmen Sagredo Pacheco. Another witness testified that Ortíz had orders to mobilize campesinos from Loncopangue to Mulchén. This testimony appears to confirm the efforts of the movement's leaders to initiate a broader regional uprising throughout the south as well as reports of their network of contacts in southern towns.[72]

On 6 July, ten days after the assembly in Quilleime, *El Diario Austral* reported that the rebellion had come to an end. Rebels taken prisoner in Lolco would be transported to Temuco and put at the disposition of Franklin Quezada Rogers, the appellate court judge assigned by the Supreme Court to investigate the rebellion and crimes that violated the Internal Security of the State Law.[73] Later the paper announced that the rebels were being brought to Curacautín and then to Victoria, where Quezada would "interrogate the hundreds of detained rebels brought by Prefecto Délano." The prefect had sent word that he had arrived in Boca Sur with a "long caravan of detainees."[74]

Over the next week, as the caravan of prisoners made its way on foot to Curacautín and then on to Temuco by train their reported numbers dwindled. When the caravan finally reached Temuco, it was composed of only 56 prisoners. By September the number of campesinos detained in Temuco reached 62.[75] The strongest evidence that carabineros engaged in atrocities against detainees lies in this simple discrepancy. Even if Délano exaggerated the numbers of the rebels detained in Lolco (his reports certainly suggest a strong dose of hyperbole), it is difficult not to arrive at the conclusion that there must have been at least 150–200 rebels taken prisoner. The numbers of men in the different parties, the number in attendance at the Quilleime assembly, and the numbers recruited during the course of the rebellion point to figures in this range.

Carabineros tried to explain what had occurred.[76] They described, for example, scattered bands of rebels fleeing into the cordillera and crossing the border into Argentina. Simón, Benito, and Emelina Sagredo, for example, hid in the mountains under bushes and bramble, survived for days by eating snow and toasted flour, and finally made their way across the cordillera to Argentina. They were accompanied by Margarita Ramírez's sons Francisco and Pablo Cisternas, one of whom later died from pulmonary illnesses contracted while hiding in the mountains.[77] A police report noted that a group of more than one hundred rebels had fled into the mountains and attempted to cross into Argentina. The report suggested that many may have died in the snow. This figure, like most of the carabineros' numbers, appears to be inflated, an increase by thirty, for example, from the figure of seventy rebels who escaped into the mountains given above. What is known is that some rebels may have died in the mountains, but at least sixteen made it to the town of Loncopué across the border in Argentina. They were detained and told the local police that they had fled the Chilean police "since they had participated in the unfortunate events in Lonquimay."[78]

Despite the Chilean government's efforts to have them extradited or at least moved close to the international border where they could be captured, the group of sixteen Chileans was freed and employed in public works projects in Neuquén. By October their number had increased to twenty-nine, including a number of men and women who had played leadership roles in the rebellion: Juan Domingo Lagos and Elías Lagos as well as the Sagredos.[79] Perhaps others were not so lucky and died trying to cross the cordillera, as police tallies suggested. But the small number of rebels accounted for in Argentina implies that flight across the border cannot explain the whereabouts of a substantial number of disappeared campesinos.

The other explanation given in carabineros' reports is that a number of prisoners fled, most by jumping into the Biobío River, and perished in the river's icy currents. This account was taken up by the press. On 9 July, for example, *El Mercurio* reported General Arriagada's claim that "many revoltosos had fled, throwing themselves into the river."[80] Others were allegedly shot while attempting to flee. In one case, on 4 July, while carabineros were escorting a number of prisoners across the Biobío River, "more or less halfway across Daniel Quilodrán Palavecinos threw himself into the water, and it was impossible to save him."[81] In another case, carabineros reported that the prisoners Luis Roa and Manuel Astroza had been brought as guides from Lonquimay, fled, and been fired upon. Wounded, they fell into the Biobío, "the current taking them off."[82]

Another police report narrated how, as carabineros were transporting a group of prisoners from Lolco to Contraco, they were attacked by a group of rebels. During the ensuing combat, the prisoners escaped, and carabineros, after ordering them to halt, fired on them "but could not determine if any of them were wounded." The prisoners, José Troncoso Baeza, Eufemio Darío Cabezas Lagos, Luis Sepúlveda Canales, José Sagredo Uribe, José Cabezas Jara, Ignacio Maripi, Francisco Liñai, Exequiel Beroiza Espinoza, Juan de Dios Lagos, Pedro Rodríguez, Alfonso Pitrai, and Manuel Piñaleao (note the four Pehuenche last names), threw themselves into the Biobío and apparently disappeared since police reports contained no further information.[83] In a similar case, carabineros recounted that while transferring a large group of prisoners from Lolco to Contraco on 8 July they were attacked by a *montonera* (band of guerillas) composed of fifty men. In the confusion of combat the detainees escaped and threw themselves into the river. As in the other cases, carabineros reported that "it is not known if they were able to escape from the water even though it is believed that because of the torrential speed of the current they have perished, dashed against the numerous rocks strewn throughout the river." Among this group were two cabecillas, Juan and Pablo Sagredo, who were wanted dead or alive by the authorities. The Sagredo brothers were allegedly the first detainees to throw themselves into the icy winter waters and disappear.[84]

These were the carabineros' accounts. The campesinos' testimony differed dramatically. Recalling the events in a 1972 interview, Clementina Sagredo, who was not part of the rebellion and who had been taken prisoner in her home in Nitrito, related that as carabineros marched the long caravan of detainees from Lolco to Curacautín, they took groups of prisoners away who never returned: "They took many away from the column of prisoners and left. They said goodbye to us with sad smiles. After an hour the pacos returned by themselves. After assassinating them in cold blood, they threw their bodies into the Bio-Bio."[85]

Oral histories collected by Jaime Flores in 1991 similarly describe groups of prisoners executed and thrown into the Biobío. The wife of the Villucura estate's administrator described carabineros' execution of a group of fifteen rebels in front of the estate's houses. "They made them face the Bío-Bío River, bound, and they shot them in the back. The river is deep there." Another of Flores's sources remembered that "in Troyo five people died, among them, the *veterano* Lagos and Nacho Lagos. At the intersection of the Lolco and Bío-Bío, they killed around twenty." Other sources simply described in general terms the barbarities committed by carabineros in Ralco, Lolco, and Troyo.[86]

These oral accounts from 1991 are surprisingly consistent with descriptions of atrocities given by Alto Bío Bío's campesinos in 1934. After the rebellion's repression the FOCH sent a commission to investigate reports of massacres and violence committed against detained campesinos and their families. The investigators interviewed prisoners in Temuco as well as the family members of those killed or detained during the rebellion and then issued a report, which was published in the Universidad de Chile law school student publication *Llamas*. The report served as the basis for a series of legal accusations against carabineros in Concepción's military court brought by the lawyer Gerardo Ortúzar Riesco, a Communist Party militant commissioned by the FOCH to defend rebels detained in Temuco.

The report declared, in a sentence that resonates powerfully today, that during the repression "the carabineros took away groups of people who disappeared."[87] In Contraco, for example, "they took away fourteen and only two returned, Benigno Avello and Pedro Alarcón." In Troyo "they took away five in the direction of the river, and they never returned. Among them were Anselmo Orrego, Ernesto Lagos, Juan Lagos, one Merigno, and others." At Herminio Campos's house "they took away Ramón Quilodrán and Emilio Valenzuela." In addition, "in front of many colonos they assassinated Silverio Ortíz, Manuel Muñoz, Erasmo Baeza, Jose Dionisio Reyes, Juan Sagredo, Atanasio Peña, Segundo Pacheco, Luis León, Gregorio Videla."[88]

The FOCH commission met with a group of thirty women in the house of Modesto Acuña in Llanquén. Acuña's wife told them that carabineros had taken away the women's husbands and shot them. The group also met with "the widow Lagos," who told them that carabineros had taken away her husband and Juan Segundo Leiva Tapia and executed them.[89] Perhaps most dramatically, the account detailed the death of Leiva Tapia and others taken prisoner at the Lagoses' house: carabineros took Cesáreo Orrego, Luis Lagos, José Riquelme, Daniel Moreno, Juan Segundo Leiva Tapia, and Juan Lagos "out to the plaza," where "they were beaten ferociously with the butts of carbines, beaten and whipped cruelly." The prisoners were then taken on foot and tied to horses during the night through the snow six leagues to Llanquén. Campesinos interviewed by the commission stated that "they were assassinated in Llanquén." Carabineros, the report alleged, tied Leiva Tapia's corpse to a tree "to be eaten by condors." The other cadavers were left on the banks of the Biobío River.[90]

The report underlined that carabineros had targeted all eight members of the Sagredo family, including children and elderly people, by throwing them into the river and shooting them "as if they were shooting floating shells."[91] There appears to be no question that carabineros were especially focused on detaining the Sagredos and Leiva Tapia, who they knew to be the leaders of the rebellion. However, some of the evidence undermines the FOCH commission's account. By late July, Benito, Simón, and Emelina Sagredo had all appeared in Argentina, while José, Adán, and Clementina Sagredo were arrested and detained in Temuco. Yet one witness supplied a detailed, convincing account of atrocities committed against members of the family whom carabineros found at home in Nitrito. In August 1934 José del Carmen Sandoval, who had been imprisoned for his role in the rebellion, told Franklin Quezada Rogers that he wanted to make a declaration about the "fate of some members of the Sagredo family following the events investigated by the Court."[92]

On 2 July, Sandoval testified, carabineros arrived with a list of names in Nitrito. They asked him and his brother Luis if they had been involved in the so-called massacres and told them to return to their *ranchos* when they responded in the negative. Before they headed to their huts, however, they witnessed carabineros taking Erasmo Baeza, Silverio Ortíz (the father of a detainee with the same name), one Reyes, son of Gregorio Reyes (also a detainee), and one Salvador down to the banks of the Biobío River. They heard shots but never learned what had happened to the prisoners. The next day, however, Sandoval and another prisoner, Teodoro Hermosilla, witnessed carabineros taking three female members of the Sagredo family, Hortensia Sagredo, Ester Sagredo, and an old woman of eighty years, the Sagredos' mother, down to the Biobío, where they struck them in the neck with the butts of their carbines and threw them into the river.

Hermosilla narrated that one of the Sagredos who was disabled (an older sister of Clementina and Emelina) had been left alone, presumably because her family members had been arrested or killed or had fled. She died of hunger, he said, because carabineros prohibited anyone from bringing her food. Her body remained in the Sagredos' hut in Nitrito, where it was partially consumed by dogs and pigs.[93] Clementina Sagredo was released soon after her detention when it became clear that she had been mistaken for her sister Emelina and had played no part in the rebellion. But by then, apparently, it was too late, and the Sagredos' disabled sister had died of hunger.[94] Emelina Sagredo's account of the violence visited on her family during the rebellion's repression bears out some of the accusations in the FOCH report.[95] She recalled that her nephew Juan Sagredo, who was sixteen, was killed by carabineros in front of his mother, grandmother, and the family's other children, not in the shootout described by carabineros above. Carabineros then threw his body into the Biobío.

Violent beatings and torture of prisoners were not uncommon. The FOCH summarized how Manuel Arraneda, Pedro Rivera, and Eduardo Donoso had been arrested and beaten in Curacautín by carabineros after the rebellion. In addition, a number of detainees described being tortured after they were taken prisoner. Onofre Ortíz recalled his detention in Troyo, where carabineros beat him with the butts of their carbines while he was tied to his brother Juan, Adán Sagredo, "and one Riquelme." He was then transferred with other prisoners to Lonquimay, where at night carabineros took him out of his cell, threw water on him, and beat him again.[96] José Adán Sagredo Pacheco, also detained in Troyo, related how he was tied up with the others and beaten by carabineros, who slapped him and hit him with the butts of their rifles in the chest and stomach. Before arriving in Troyo he had been detained in Llanquén, where carabineros bound his feet, threw him into the water, and beat him with the butts of their carbines.[97] Juan Bautista Valenzuela Sagredo was detained by carabineros more than a week after the rebellion had ended on 16 July. He was imprisoned in Contraco, where Lieutenant Robertson had established his headquarters. Valenzuela Sagredo testified that Robertson and four other carabineros took him to the banks of an estuary, stripped him, and submerged him five times in the icy waters while they kicked him and beat him with their rifles, "interrogating me about the things I had knowledge about." He told them "what I knew, but they kept asking me for more information."[98]

In response to prisoners' declarations detailing the abuses they had suffered following their detention, a military court initiated an investigation of "crimes said to have been committed by carabineros in the suffocation of the uprising in Lonquimay." On 8 September the military prosecutor ordered an investigation of the whereabouts of Marcos Hermosilla, Cesáreo Orrego, Anselmo Orrego, Silverio Ortíz, Manuel Muñoz, José Benicio Reyes, Erasmo Baeza, Atanasio Peña, Pedro Antonio Valenzuela, José Troncoso, Darío Cabezas, José Cabezas, José del Rosario Sagredo, Ramón Quilandrón, Emilio Valenzuela, Pedro Riquelme, and one Alarcón, subpoenaing their wives to provide information about where they might be found. That same day he ordered an investigation of the FOCH commission's allegations of a massacre of hundreds of members of the Ralco community.[99]

On 12 September Prefect Délano issued a detailed statement in which he refuted the FOCH lawyer's charges. He referred to the detention of José, Adán, and Clementina Sagredo as evidence that carabineros had not, in fact, killed the entire Sagredo family. He noted only that they had killed Juan Sagredo in a shootout in Nitrito on 4 July. He did not mention or refute the charge that carabineros had executed three female members of the family. A number of rebels, he declared, including Marcos Hermosilla, had been killed during the battle at Ránquil Bridge, but other than Hermosilla's, none of their bodies had been found since the rebels themselves had thrown the cadavers into the Biobío River in order to make them disappear and thus "prevent the demoralization of their people." In fact, as noted above, carabineros used this as an explanation for the disappeared bodies of dead rebels on a number of occasions, as in the case of the disappeared bodies of rebels killed in the battle at Llanquén. Délano suggested that some of the disappeared campesinos described in the FOCH's legal brief must have been among those who died in combat and whose bodies were thrown into the river by their comrades. He assured the court that they had not been executed by carabineros.[100]

Délano also marshalled the explanation described above in the case of the deaths of José Troncoso, Darío Cabezas, José Cabezas, José del R. Sagredo, "and eight other individuals." They had escaped while Fernández and his men were under fire, thrown themselves into the Biobío, and disappeared. It was possible, he conjectured, that they had joined other fugitives across the border in Argentina. In fact, that assertion became something of a refrain. The prefect denied the charge that carabineros had assassinated Ramón Quilandrón, Emilio Valenzuela, Pedro Riquelme, and Alarcón. They were presumed, he stated, to have taken refuge in Argentina. As for the accusation that there had been a mass killing of members of the Ralco community, he noted that a number of the community's members had been arrested and jailed. Others had fled following their detention and "thrown themselves into the river."

On 12 September Captain Monreal gave his own account to the military prosecutor of the presumed death of Alarcón, which had been reported in the press on 5 July. He described how carabineros had detained Alarcón, who under interrogation confessed that his name was Juan Segundo Araneda and that he was from Lota. As the patrol of carabineros that had captured Alarcón/Araneda climbed a narrow path, they were attacked by a group of revoltosos and the prisoner escaped, "throwing himself into the river." They shot at him, but, as in the case of other escaped prisoners, his body was never found.[101] Both Monreal's and Délano's statements were accompanied by declarations from carabineros in charge of prisoners, all of whom denied that they had beaten detainees and confirmed the story of Alarcón's escape and plunge into the Biobío.[102]

On 13 September 1934, the day after Délano's statement explaining the deaths and disappearances of the fifteen men and one week after the military prosecutor began his investigation, congress passed Law No. 5,483, a general amnesty for political crimes committed since 1931 that included in its second article amnesty "for carabineros processed or condemned for crimes committed during acts of service." Délano immediately petitioned the military prosecutor to end the investigation.[103] On 25 September the military court brought the inquiry to a close, citing the amnesty law, "which totally extinguished carabineros' criminal responsibility."[104] None of the men whom campesinos had described to the FOCH commissioners as having been executed by carabineros were ever located. They number among Chile's earliest *detenidos-desaparecidos*.[105]

In the end, how many died? The rebels led by the Sagredos killed the three carabineros stationed on Guayalí as well as Guayalí's administrator Víctor Vergara and foreman Teófilo Zapata. They also killed José and Martín Gainza in Lolco and Luciano Gainza and Herminio Campos in Contraco. The groups led by Leiva Tapia targeted pulperías and their owners and employees. They killed Pedro Acuña, Juan Zolezzi, and Alfonso Zañartu. They also killed the mayordomo Manuel Salas on El Rahue. There were also credible accusations by witnesses that they had killed two campesinos who refused to join the rebellion: Heriberto Alegría and Segundo Hermosilla.[106] It is an irony that because the Puelmas and Bunsters did not reside on their estates only the immigrant Gainzas, who had rented Contraco and worked with Juan Olhagaray on Lolco, were killed by rebels. Not one landowner was killed. It was, instead, landowners' renters, administrators, and foremen, the immediate faces of their authority, who fell victim to the violence. Perhaps as a reflection of how badly armed the rebels were, no carabineros were killed during guerilla attacks, skirmishes (including the reported ambushes by groups of guerillas), or full-out battles.

As for how many campesinos died, because there was no judicial investigation any figure is only a rough estimate. Even establishing the number of campesinos involved in the rebellion is difficult. Police and press accounts ranged from 400 to 600. The director of the carabineros, General Arriagada, even floated numbers like 1,200 and 1,600, certainly gross exaggerations designed to exalt the carabineros' accomplishment in executing a successful counterinsurgency. A member of the FOCH commission, Cleofe Arriagada of the Federación de Maestros, arrived more realistically at 300 campesinos.[107] Adding the numbers in each of the parties that assaulted estates and pulperías, themselves rough figures drawn from witnesses' testimony, one arrives at a somewhat smaller number of 250–300. Flores's estimate of 300–350 may be valid as well, especially if the Pehuenche laborers recruited on the Contraco, Guayalí, and Lolco estates are included.

As for casualties, carabineros' reports of four hundred detained prisoners in Lolco were surely an exaggeration. Considering the number of rebels who fled and deserted over the course of the combat with carabineros and the number who were killed following battles in Llanquén and Ránquil, a number closer to two hundred may be more accurate. Carabineros' reports of escaped prisoners who threw themselves into the Biobío River account for roughly twenty-five men. Another twenty-nine were documented to have made it to Argentina. Eight were reported by carabineros to have died during the battle at the Ránquil Bridge and an unknown, but probably similar, number during the battle at the Llanquén River. Others may have died trying to cross the cordillera or in the scattered guerilla altercations described in carabineros' reports. Sixty-two were eventually jailed. This leaves a figure of around one hundred disappeared prisoners, probably more if one includes those who were alleged to have perished in the Biobío.[108]

CHAPTER TEN

History, Memory, and the Question of Campesino Insurgency

THE HEADLINES IN CHILE's leading newspapers during early July 1934 were shocking. *Zig-Zag* led the sensationalist reporting on the rebellion with a full-page spread featuring photos of a number of detained rebels with captions describing the outrages they were alleged to have committed. Clementina Sagredo's photo was accompanied by a caption that read "Clementina Sagredo, twenty-nine years old, called the *descuartizadora* [the one who quarters bodies]." Sofía Cisternas "sang and danced while her compañeros fought." Her mother, Margarita Ramírez, "passed the hours away singing and playing guitar" during the rebellion. Even though few women were directly involved in the movement, three of *Zig-Zag*'s six photos of rebels featured detained female campesinas.[1] Concepción's *El Sur* described how Clementina Sagredo "mutilated Corporal Bascuñán" and Margarita Ramírez "sang and played guitar while they quartered Bascuñán."[2] And Temuco's *El Diario Austral* reported that Clementina Sagredo had danced and played guitar while Juan Zolezzi was tortured to death. After she was released from prison and found to have played no part in the rebellion, the paper noted that "the bloodthirsty dancer was not Clementina Sagredo, but her sister Emelina." Emelina Sagredo, the paper reported, had "danced and sang" while Zolezzi was tortured.[3]

Neither the national nor the regional press reported on the harsh measures employed by carabineros to suppress the rebellion, including torture, mass executions of prisoners, and forced disappearance. Rather, newspapers published hyperbolic and often entirely apocryphal accounts of the violent depredations committed by the revolutionary movement. Like carabineros' exaggerations of the size of the revolutionary bands, these stories served to both eclipse and justify the brutal counterinsurgency in Alto Bío Bío. None of the accounts of the movement's alleged atrocities, including rape and mutilation, were even considered by Franklin Quezada Rogers, the appellate court judge charged with investigating crimes committed during the rebellion. Neither the judicial findings nor witness testimony put forth any evidence to support the accounts of rebel campesinos' atrocities published in the press. In fact, both the crimes Quezada Rogers established and the charges he brought were limited, and the handful of rebels charged and convicted were eventually freed under the September 1934 amnesty law.

Narratives of women's violence in the press served as a way to represent the campesino rebels as barbaric, their violation of gendered norms representative of the movement's broader assault on the social order. Like *Zig-Zag*, *El Diario Austral* published a number of fictional accounts of women's role in mutilating prisoners taken captive by the revolutionary movement. The paper drew on almost certainly fabricated stories of how the rebels "had a special place to kill as many patrones as fell into their hands, which they called "*el matadero* [slaughterhouse]."[4] Juan Olhagaray told the paper that "the executioners were Aníbal Sepúlveda and three women who afterward quartered the cadavers." Olhagaray claimed that "a woman was in charge of this [the execution of Víctor Vergara]. Vergara was tied to a tree, and then it was that woman, that true human hyena, who began to butcher him with a knife, member by member . . . until he succumbed."[5] Yet the Olhagarays were kept captive in Lolco and were never in *el matadero* in Llanquén, where Vergara had been detained and executed. Nor were Lolco's owners harmed during their days of captivity, despite the claim that the rebels' plan was to execute patrones.

Campesinos' reported rapes of female servants and the wives of estate and pulpería owners similarly served to accentuate their criminal depravity. Carabineros' official publication gave an account of the rebellion that celebrated police actions as necessary "to suffocate" campesinos' acts of banditry: "In the desolate region of Lonquimay, order was upended, private property sacked, citizens assassinated, women violated, and, as if this were not enough, cadavers were mutilated."⁶ Yet a number of men and women who did not belong to the rebel movement, including servants and the wives of pulpería and estate owners, testified as witnesses during the judicial investigation, and in no instance did they mention rape, though they provided evidence for charges of homicide and robbery with violence.⁷ In certain cases noted above, it is clear that Juan Segundo Leiva Tapia and Margarita Ramírez took measures to protect women from assault. Rape was not included among the crimes investigated by Franklin Quezada Rogers.

Numerous accounts in the press of how rebels mutilated the bodies of their victims also pointed to campesinos' barbarism. *El Diario Austral* reported that during the assault on the carabinero Bascuñán rebels stabbed and then bound him "even while he was still in agony, and they opened him up like a piece of beef, tying him to two pieces of wood, naked, and sliced him open, and threw him into the river."⁸ No part of this supposed execution came to the fore in the multiple accounts of Buscañán's death given to the court by imprisoned campesinos. Narratives of campesinos' depraved violence made it to the floor of congress, where the Liberal Party deputy Edmundo Fuenzalida cited *El Diario Austral*'s version that during the assault on his pulpería Juan Zolezzi "died, stabbed repeatedly. When he still wasn't dead, he was hung from a stick and his victimizers tortured him, treated him cruelly. And then his body was thrown into the Ránquil River."⁹ The Democratic Party deputy Anibal Gutiérrez read a letter from a number of Lonquimay's leading citizens, including José Frau, that described how, after Zolezzi and Zañartu were stabbed, each supposedly two hundred times, "they were thrown into the Bio Bio River, with guitar playing and singing and dancing." Guayalí's carabineros, they added, had been quartered, and the mob had "opened their chests as if they were killing pigs."¹⁰ Claims that Zolezzi was stabbed repeatedly were eventually contradicted by his death certificate, which described the cause of death as "a number of blows to the head."¹¹

These apocryphal descriptions of campesinos' violation of their victims' bodies signified, like the cruelty of the "female hyena," the violation of the social body, while implicitly justifying carabineros' repression of the rebellion. They also represented campesinos as irrational and prepolitical and their movement as criminal barbarity. As *El Diario Austral* editorialized, "The movement in Lonquimay displays only the characteristics of banditry. It is impossible to believe that these individuals have been fighting for ideals." Rather than participating in a collective political movement with a revolutionary program, the campesinos were "guided solely by their desire to pillage and massacre."[12]

The Chilean state initially worked to vacate the Ránquil rebellion's legitimacy as a revolutionary movement. It did so by building a narrative of the rebellion that made it less an organized insurgency with political goals than an unplanned outpouring of senseless violence that belonged in the realm of the premodern.[13] Both the government and the press sought to minimize the political content of the rebellion and to deny its organized, collective character by reducing it to individual acts of violent criminality. The interior minister and Radical Luis Salas Romo portrayed the rebellion not as an insurgency but as "a matter of banditry [*salteo*], an armed assault." As in any criminal case, he contended, the government was obligated "to make these delinquents submit."[14] Los Ángeles's Radical Party assembly echoed the interior minister's characterization of the rebels as common criminals when it declared that "Alto Bío Bío's campesinos have committed numerous common crimes, such as robberies, murders, and rapes; ... campesinos have acted with the cruelty of professional criminals."[15] Carabineros had acted not to repress an insurgency but to punish the crimes of a mob.

While sympathetic to the rebel campesinos, leftist parties and publications purged the rebellion of its insurgent politics either by stressing that the innocent, simple campesinos had been manipulated and duped by outside communist agitators or by defining the rebellion as a spontaneous response to immediate deprivation triggered by the April eviction from Nitrito. Democratic Party congressmen advocated on behalf of Alto Bío Bío's campesinos, petitioning the government to avoid a bloodbath in repressing the movement. They downplayed the rebellion's political content by emphasizing that the campesinos were honorable colonos, in the words of the deputy Arturo Huenchullán, who had been led astray by communist agitators: "People foreign to the colonos came through Curacautín, took advantage of the colonos. ... [T]here were two or three Communists ... who were the cabecillas. It was they who incited the colonos to kill. ... And that is the only explanation ... for why those colonos would have risen up with arms against sr. Zolessi and the owners of the fundos and the eleven citizens who have suffered cruel death."[16]

The Socialist Party deputy Carlos Alberto Martínez recited a detailed history of the rebellion's causes, accentuating campesinos' eviction from Nitrito and the abject conditions they suffered in Llanquén: "Last summer they proceeded to expel the ocupantes already settled by the

Ministry of Southern Property from agricultural land that can be worked during the entire year to move them to ravines in the cordillera where during winter months there are more than two meters of snow and where it is materially impossible to subsist. This is the reason all of that happened. Hunger and need have impelled those unhappy ocupantes to commit these outrages [*desmanes*]."[17] Like others, Martínez reduced the rebellion to criminal acts of violence, outrages, or excesses, even while underlining that the uprising had been sparked by campesinos' violent expulsion from the Nitrito Valley and subsequent starvation in Llanquén.

To members of the Communist Party, who defended both the campesinos and the act of rebellion itself, the movement was less an insurgency than a legitimate response to deprivation. Campesinos had acted in response to immediate conditions in an outpouring of outrage, not out of a developed political consciousness. Thus even while affirming that the party had circulated the manifestos urging campesinos and indígenas to organize self-defense committees and soviets throughout southern Chile, the Communist Party deputy Andrés Escobar contended that "the manifesto is the work of my party that calls on the residents of the city and the countryside not to let themselves die of hunger."[18] Escobar downplayed the insurgent character of the movement in Ránquil and the role of communist militants in leading it, while calling the rebellion a legitimate response to the abject conditions of starvation in the southern countryside. While the Communist Party deputy affirmed the movement's character as a rebellion, he minimized its revolutionary goals, although unlike his Radical, Democratic, and Socialist party colleagues he did not represent the rebellion as merely criminal outrages.

Franklin Quezada Rogers's judicial inquiry into the Ránquil rebellion confronted head-on the question of whether the rebellion constituted a revolutionary insurrection or simply an aggregation of criminal acts. However, a full-blown inquiry into campesinos' ideology was foreclosed by the September 1934 amnesty since the judge was precluded from investigating political crimes. The amnesty effectively shut down any attempt to wrestle with the question of campesinos' political consciousness and the rebellion's revolutionary dynamics. Quezada Rogers's investigation produced a narrative of the rebellion as an assortment of individual common crimes. Campesinos speak in the judicial record through their testimony under questioning. Because Quezada Rogers posed only questions and investigated charges related to common crimes, however, the testimony of both detained campesinos and nonparticipant witnesses described the revolutionary movement's violence as criminal and remained silent on campesinos' understanding of the insurrection's revolutionary politics. The September 1934 amnesty both made it impossible for the judicial inquiry to pursue the question of the rebellion's insurrectionary character and, paradoxically, reinforced the tendency to represent the rebellion's violence as the criminal acts of a mob even as the application of the amnesty presupposed that the movement had a political character.

Quezada Rogers's interrogations of prisoners rendered a rough outline, fragmentary and incomplete to be sure, of the campesino rebels' actions and intentions, even a sense of their political understanding of their collective movement. But the judge was resolutely uninterested in delving into the world of the rebels' political consciousness. He appeared to presume that most rebels, save for a handful of cabecillas, lacked political reason and that their actions constituted individual common crimes. Quezada Rogers's investigation of a list of ordinary crimes and efforts to locate those crimes' authors reflected the government's initial interest in stripping the rebellion of its political content and reducing the campesinos to the status of either common criminals or passive participants with little understanding of the nature of the movement they had joined. There may have been a legal strategy here as well. Were Quezada Rogers to interpret campesinos' violence as acts of political insurrection, their crimes would fall under the September amnesty law. In order for the judge to mete out punishment for the imprisoned rebels' crimes, they would have to be defined as nonpolitical.

On 22 July 1934 Quezada Rogers charged forty-seven adult prisoners and seven minors with the following crimes:

a. Armed uprising in the commune of Lonquimay, in the department of Victoria, with the goal of promoting a civil war and provoking a violent change in government.
b. Robbery with homicide against Juan Zolezzi and Alfonso Zañartu in Troyo, zone of Ránquil, commune of Lonquimay.
c. Robbery with violence against persons in the fundo Contraco, in which José and Martín Gainza were taken prisoner.
d. Robbery in the pulpería Frau with homicide of Pedro Acuña.
e. Robbery and violence against persons and setting fire to a shed filled with straw on the Lolco estate.
f. Violence and mistreatment of Corporal of Carabineros Rafael Bascuñán and soldier Fidel Montoya, while both were per-

forming acts of duty, resulting in their deaths in Nitrito in the zone of Lonquimay.
g. Opposition to the actions of Carabineros when these, in exercising their duties, arrived at the Ránquil bridge, resulting in a serious injury to Corporal José Reyes Lira and a light injury to carabinero Luis Maldonado.
h. Robbery with violence against persons in the houses of the Guayalí estate and the Carabineros barracks located in the same place (Los Guindos).
i. Robbery with violence against persons in the pulpería belonging to Bruno Ackermann.
j. Possession and distribution of subversive manifestos.

As the investigation proceeded over the subsequent months, Quezada ordered the arrest of an additional thirteen campesinos who had been identified as actors in the rebellion. He then elaborated a series of criminal charges but threw out charges against prisoners accused of violating the internal state security law. The amnesty law, he stated, "grants general amnesty to all authors, accomplices, and those who cover up crimes against the internal security of the state."[19] Thus all charges for crime "a" were dismissed, and Quezada did not include in his investigation the crime of "possession and distribution of subversive manifestos," for which the Communist Party leader Higinio Godoy had been arrested.[20] In September five prisoners who had not been charged with common crimes were released from prison under the amnesty law. Most prisoners, however, were charged with crimes that, according to Quezada Rogers, did not fall under the amnesty and remained in prison in Temuco.[21]

On 11 December 1934 Quezada Rogers declared his investigation complete. In most cases, he found that prisoners' part in crimes committed during the rebellion was either coerced or simply "passive." He accepted campesinos' testimony that they had acted under threat of violence from the movement's leaders.[22] The judge argued that "the prisoners ... maintain that they were forced to join the subversive movement in Lonquimay, participating in crimes because the cabecillas took control of the situation in Quilleime and threatened them with death." He noted that the fact that most had been armed only with sticks and that, according to witnesses, two campesinos, Heriberto Alegría and Segundo Hermosilla, had been killed for refusing to join the movement served as evidence confirming detained rebels' claim that they had been coerced to join the rebellion. "[Because] they did not play a central role in the events" and "since their participation was not voluntary," Quezada Rogers wrote, "the Tribunal believes they are not guilty of the crimes for which they are charged." On 12 December a large group of detained rebels were freed from prison.[23] In this case they were released not because of the amnesty law but because Quezada Rogers found that they had no legal responsibility with regard to their role in common crimes committed during the rebellion.

These imprisoned campesinos had also been amnestied for the initial charge of having a role in an armed uprising to provoke a violent change in government. However, following Quezada Rogers's legal logic, the amnesty was unnecessary since most of the campesinos' participation in the rebellion was coerced or passive. The judge adopted the prisoners' testimony that their actions had been involuntary as well as their determination to assign blame to a handful of cabecillas. Neither the detained campesinos nor the judge had any interest in exploring the rebellion's revolutionary politics. To some degree their reticence was consistent with the narrative articulated most forcefully by Democratic Party politicians that campesinos had joined the uprising because they had been duped or manipulated by outside communist agitators. Rather than sharing the collective movement's goals, campesinos had been led astray by a handful of communist cabecillas. To the Right, this reflected campesinos' barbarity and propensity to criminal violence; to Democrats and Socialists on the Left, their innocence and simplicity as well as the suffering that had made them vulnerable to the inducements of communist agitators.

After freeing the majority of imprisoned campesinos in December, Quezada Rogers charged a number of alleged cabecillas who, he argued, held criminal responsibility for the actions of the rebellious campesinos. Paradoxically, he chose to charge those campesinos who acted as cabecillas guided by their commitment to the revolutionary goals enunciated by Leiva Tapia, the Sagredos, and Alarcón, those men and women who probably had the clearest understanding of the rebellion's revolutionary purposes and strategy, with ordinary rather than political crimes. These included Onofre Ortíz, Juan Segundo Ortíz, Juan Bautista Valenzuela Sagredo, Margarita Ramírez, her son, Pablo Cisternas Ramírez, José Emiliano Balboa Benítez, Ismael Cartes, Federico Astroza, Modesto Acuña Sandoval, José Nieves Alegría Espinoza, Florentino Pino Valdebenito, Teodoro Hermosilla, Silverio Segundo Ortíz, and Eulojio Mardones Naverrete. All denied playing a leadership role in the rebellion. A number recanted their earlier confessions, drawing on the fact that witnesses had retracted their testimony that they had been leaders. In addition, they argued that they had only followed orders from the Sagredos or Juan Segundo Leiva Tapia and had been mere passive participants. Finally, a few admitted to occupying leadership positions in the Sindicato Agrícola Lonquimay but denied having been elected to the "revolutionary directorate" in the Quilleime assembly or having led any of the revolutionary bands in the assaults on pulperías and estates.[24]

The alleged cabecillas found unlikely support in the Temuco appellate court's public prosecutor, or *fiscal*. The prosecutor argued that all the crimes committed during the rebellion fell under the umbrella of the amnesty law. He contended that "the accumulated evidence demonstrates that, while a large number of the accused did not have a complete understanding of the goals [of the insurrection] and others acted because they were compelled by [the threat of] violence, the sucesos in Alto Bío-Bío were produced with the primary purpose of toppling the government and installing in its place a communist regime." He adduced as evidence the Communist Party's manifestos that had been distributed widely, "inciting obreros, campesinos, and *soldados* to revolt and strike." These same revolutionary goals, he pointed out, had been espoused by the Sagredos and Leiva Tapia during the assembly in Quilleime at which they announced the plan "to attack the pulperías and the big houses on the fundos" and "made it known that the revolution had broken out throughout the country."[25]

According to the fiscal, all the crimes committed in the rebellion, including homicides, arson, and violent assaults against people and property, constituted methods "employed by the subversives . . . to achieve the purpose of procuring a change of government." As in any revolution, "especially those of a communistic character," these crimes "were directed at instilling terror and producing the annihilation of the antagonists." The robberies, rather than looting or simple theft, "were directed at procuring the provisioning of the improvised troops." "In the acts of depredation and violence against persons and property," the fiscal continued, "none have been discovered in the investigation in which the actor acted on their own and in the interest of personal profit and outside of a revolutionary goal." The fiscal concluded that the September 1934 amnesty had to apply to every detained rebel. All the crimes perpetrated during the rebellion, he reasoned, were "crimes against the internal security of the state." To the fiscal, at least, it was clear that the sucesos in Alto Bío Bío constituted an organized insurrection rather than an unplanned outburst of mob violence.[26] The individual common crimes outlined by Quezada belonged to a collective revolutionary movement and were thus covered by the amnesty law.

Nonetheless, Quezada Rogers's view of the Ránquil rebellion as a criminal matter initially prevailed. On 21 January 1935 the fiscal elaborated a list of charges against a number of alleged cabecillas, following the judge's instructions. In the crime of "violence against the carabineros Bascuñán and Montoya," he noted that because Montoya's body had never been found, the court could prove the crime of homicide only in the case of Bascuñán. This case stands out because of all the crimes established by Quezada Rogers it most clearly fits the legal definition of a political crime that might have fallen under the amnesty law. That Quezada Rogers reduced the attacks on carabineros to homicide and assault reflects his determination to make the rebellion a criminal matter and to punish those found legally responsible. Despite a number of prisoners' confessions that they had engaged in the beating of the carabineros with sticks, the fiscal recommended charges against only one of the accused, Juan Bautista Valenzuela Sagredo, who had confessed that "he had been the first to stab one of the carabineros in the face."[27] He ignored Valenzuela's later recantation and statement that he had confessed while under torture.

In terms of the homicides of Alfonso Zañartu and Juan Zolezzi, disappeared cadavers posed a problem. Although witnesses had testified that they had seen the murders, the bodies had never been found, and there was, therefore, insufficient evidence to prove that homicides had been committed. But there was plenty of evidence of armed robbery and assault. The fiscal proposed charging only two of the prisoners: Onofre Ortíz Salgado and Juan Orellana Barrera. Ortíz had confessed to being a cabecilla of "the subversive movement" and the assault on the pulpería. He had also confessed that he had given Zolezzi the coup de grace with a knife (as noted above, Zolezzi was, in fact, killed not by a stab wound but by blows, perhaps evidence that Ortíz's confession was coerced under torture). The fiscal found that there was enough evidence to charge Ortíz with armed robbery or "robbery with violence against persons" for his role as a leader in the assault. The fiscal concluded that he had encouraged his men to commit "outrages" which, following Quezada's legal logic, "were not indispensable to obtain the goals of the subversives."[28] As in Ortíz's case, Juan Orellana Barrera's confession was a primary piece of evidence against him. According to Orellana Barrera, he was in the group that assaulted the Zolezzi pulpería, and he detained Zañartu, "handing him over to his compañeros who killed him" while also stabbing him himself.[29]

In the case of the assault on the Frau pulpería and the death of Pedro Acuña, homicide once again could not be proven since Acuña's body had never been found. However, there was enough evidence to prove theft "against objects or people." Despite Florentino Pino Valdebenito's confession that he had ordered Acuña's death, he was charged only with robbery. All the other detained men who had assaulted the pulpería and joined in the killing of Acuña had charges against them dropped for lack of evidence or because the judge found that they had acted under threat.[30] In the case of the assault on the Ackermann pulpería, almost all prisoners had, similarly, already had charges against them dropped because Quezada Rogers had agreed with their defense that they had acted under threat. Only Ismael Cartes remained in detention, accused of being the cabecilla of the group that looted the pulpería. Despite the fact that he had admitted to his role at the head of the group that assaulted the Ackermanns' pulpería, the fiscal found that there was only sufficient evidence to charge Cartes with being an accomplice to robbery. Charges against Cartes for leading rebels during the battle with carabineros at the Ránquil bridge had already been dropped because of the amnesty law.[31]

In terms of the assaults on Contraco, Guayalí, and Lolco, a similar pattern prevailed. Homicide was difficult to prove because rebel bands had thrown the bodies of their victims into the Biobío River, so the fiscal focused on charges of robbery with violence against persons and property. In the case of Contraco, a large group was detained and faced charges, but most had charges against them dismissed because Quezada Rogers found their actions in the assault to have been either coerced or passive. No charges for the deaths of the Gainzas could be brought because their bodies had not been found. Many detainees took part in the attack armed with sticks or knives but had not stolen anything and thus could not be charged with robbery. Only Juan Pablo Ortíz faced charges for the assault on Contraco. A number of witnesses testified that Ortíz had led the assault with Benito Sagredo. Because of the amnesty law, the fiscal made no mention of testimony from prisoners who told Quezada that Ortíz had been elected to the "revolutionary directorate" in the Quilleime assembly. Ortíz's role as a revolutionary leader might have underlined that his criminal responsibility fell under the amnesty law.[32]

Shockingly, the fiscal recommended bringing no charges for crimes committed during the assaults on Lolco and Guayalí, including the killing of the carabinero Bernardo San Martín Calderón. His death, like those of the Gainzas, Víctor Vergara, and others, could not be established as his body had not been located. The only crimes that could be proven and that did not fall under the amnesty law were robbery with violence against people and property. But the fiscal proposed no charges since the identity of those who had committed theft could not be established. Even in cases where the author of a robbery could be identified, the fiscal found that robbery was covered by the amnesty law since it served the purpose of the rebellion's revolutionary strategy. José Adán Sagredo Pacheco, for example, was accused by witnesses of transmitting orders from Benito Sagredo and acting as a cabecilla during the assault on Guayalí. He confessed to stealing "don Víctor Vergara's horse and spurs." However, the fiscal found that "the goods the prisoner took were destined to serve by their nature the revolutionary purposes he pursued." In the end, the fiscal recommended bringing charges against only six men: Juan Bautista Valenzuela Sagredo, Onofre Ortíz Salgado, Juan Orellana Barrera, Juan Pablo Ortíz, Florentino Pino Valdebenito, and Ismael Cartes.[33]

The judicial investigation did cover a number of homicides, but in most cases, because no bodies had been found or no authors of the alleged crimes identified, no charges could be brought. The disappearance of the bodies of both the victims and the rebels made it difficult to establish that crimes had been committed and to identify the crimes' perpetrators. As late as early January 1935 the corpses of José Gainza Irigoyen, Martín Gainza Irigoyen, Luciano Gainza Irigoyen, Manuel Salas, Bernardo San Martín Calderón, Fidel Montoya Villagrán, and Alfonso Zañartu had not been found. The corpses of Víctor Vergara, Teófilo Zapata González, and Herminio Campos Pedrazo had been found, but there was no witness testimony or evidence to determine who had killed them. The judge had also initiated an investigation into the deaths of two campesino rebels, Juan Segundo Leiva Tapia and Nolasco Sandoval, a campesino who had settled in Ránquil as an aspiring colono, but their corpses had also never been found. No investigation of the killing of detained prisoners other than in these two cases took place.

The Civil Registry in Lonquimay eventually issued death certificates for a number of people killed in the rebellion. However, these included only individuals believed to have been killed by the rebel bands: Rafael Bascuñán, Herminino Campos, Luciano Gainza, José Gainza, Manuel

Salas, and Juan Zolezzi.[34] Could it be that no corpses of campesino rebels were ever found? And if they were found, why were no death certificates issued and why were their deaths not recorded by Lonquimay's Civil Registry? If even Juan Zolezzi's body had been found and a death certificate issued in April 1935 is it possible that not one campesino rebel's body had been found and identified? It seems likely that the absence in the registry of deaths of any of the well more than one hundred campesinos killed by carabineros is owing to the state's effort to erase any traces of the mass executions of prisoners. That endeavor began with the September amnesty and the preemptive end to the Concepción military court's investigations, continued throughout Quezada Rogers's judicial investigation, and then was implemented at the local level by the Registro Civil.

The prisoners' lawyers responded to the formal legal accusations with a number of arguments. They repeated almost verbatim the fiscal's line of reasoning that none of the crimes were ordinary crimes since they all occurred as part of the "revolutionary political movement" and should thus be included under the broader legal umbrella of "crimes against internal state security and subversion of public order." The robberies and acts of violence were of a "collective nature," committed in a "collective effort to establish a new political, social, economic order" based on "common property." The rebellion's "communist goals" were demonstrated by the subversive manifestos and the speeches made by the Sagredos and Leiva Tapia at the Quilleime assembly. As further evidence of the revolutionary character of the rebellion, the defense cited the rebels' organization of a "tribunal to punish those who opposed the new [revolutionary] order and deserters."[35] Finally, the defense argued, there was ample evidence that Leiva Tapia, the Sagredo brothers, and a number of their followers threatened the accused: "Those who resisted or who were suspected by the leaders were detained, mistreated, and many disappeared." This strengthened the case that the six men had not acted voluntarily but were actually victims themselves who had acted under threat, compelled by an "unstoppable force or compelled by an insurmountable fear."[36]

On 5 March 1935 Quezada Rogers issued sentences for the accused men. He rejected the defense's arguments and imposed sentences ranging from three to ten years in prison. Quezada Rogers doubtless intended to make an example of the handful of men who had been identified as the rebellion's cabecillas. In doing so, he allowed more than fifty detained rebels to go free and, by reducing their acts to the level of ordinary crimes, minimized the political threat the movement they led posed to the status quo.³⁷ Stiff sentences would satisfy a public opinion incited by inflammatory articles in the press and the outrage of politicians across the political spectrum, especially the Conservatives, Liberals, and Radicals in government, while serving as a stern warning to any future "delinquents" and "communist agitators" who attempted to upend the social order.

Amnesty, *Olvido*, and Chilean Democracy

The defendants appealed to Temuco's appellate court, and this time they were successful. The panel of three justices fully endorsed the fiscal's original legal reasoning and rejected Quezada Rogers's efforts to define the campesinos' actions as ordinary crimes. On 23 March 1935 the court ordered all of the accused men to be freed under the 13 September 1934 amnesty law.³⁸ Like the fiscal, the court found that every crime committed during the rebellion was part of the broader collective movement to bring down the government and replace it with a "communistic" regime. None of the accused men had committed crimes motivated by "hatred, rancor, vengeance, profit, greed or simple self-gain [*egoismo*]." The court reviewed the long history of "crimes against the internal security of the State" in the criminal code, which stretched back to the Penal Code of 1874. It noted that while this legal concept had originally been elaborated to refer to political rebellions directed at changing the "Constitution of the State or its form of government or preventing the President or Congress or the Superior Courts from exercising their functions," it had evolved to include "economic-social movements that threaten the social order," as in the case of strikes and land invasions.

During his final days in power Ibáñez had imposed an expansion of state security laws (Decree-Law No. 143, 5 May 1931), which gave the government the right to sanction activities to protect the common good. The definition of such activities was sweeping. It included "the propagation of tendentious or false news or information designed to produce lack of confidence or disturbances in the country's order, peace, or security, in the monetary regime, or in the stability of the value of public commercial instruments." A second, more infamous internal state security decree-law imposed on 21 June 1932 (Decree-Law No. 50) during the Dávila regime employed both far more specific and broader restrictions. The law stated that anyone who propagated doctrines, either verbally or in writing, that advocated "the destruction through violence of the social order or the political organization of the State" would be considered an "enemy of the Republic." Among the "enemies of the Republic," the law included those who "incite the subversion of public order or revolt or uprising against the Government." The law's language was broad enough to criminalize strikes, land occupations, public protests, and even the act of distributing "subversive manifestos."

The justices pointed out that every act committed during the rebellion in Alto Bío Bío constituted a crime against the internal security of the state according to the definitions laid out in Decree-Law No. 50, including crimes against property rights and homicides that were committed "within the objectives propagated by the leaders of the insurrection." Homicides and robberies were not simple crimes but "acts of terrorism aimed at the destruction or disturbance of the social order" and thus constituted "crimes against the internal security of the State contemplated in the Decree Law [No. 50]." The crimes of the six accused cabecillas, no matter how "abominable and execrable," were committed as part of the "communist uprising in Alto Bío Bío" and hence fell under the amnesty law.

The appeals court underlined the role of amnesty laws in Chilean history. It noted that amnesty meant "the suppression of memory or *olvido* [oblivion]" and that amnesty laws for political crimes were essential to state and society given that "they provide good government and promote the general interest of society . . ., its harmony, peace, and the settling of spirits, that are obtained and conserved through olvido of the past." For amnesties to serve the purpose of reconsolidating the state and reunifying society no exceptions could be made for particular criminal actors or crimes, even in the case of the atrocities committed during the Ránquil rebellion. The olvido necessary to reuniting Chilean society so that the nation could move forward required amnesty laws that were imposed impartially and applied to all sides of political conflicts. The court ordered immediate freedom for the six convicted cabecillas.

Unlike Chile's most famous amnesty law, the 1978 law decreed by the Pinochet dictatorship, which became known as a self- or auto-amnesty and covered the regime's horrific and internationally condemned violations of human rights, the September 1934 law was approved in congress with the support of parties across the political spectrum. These included the parties in government, the Liberal, Conservative, and Radical parties, as well as representatives from the two Democratic parties (the party had split between left and right factions), the Communist Party, and the Trotskyist Communist Left. Though a number of dissenters, mostly from the Liberal, Conservative, and Socialist parties, voted against the law, the vote for amnesty and olvido was overwhelming. The only party to vote in a block against the amnesty was the Socialist Party.

When President Arturo Alessandri delivered the amnesty law to congress in September 1934 he requested an urgent vote.[39] The law's goal was to pardon all those who had been party to the 4 June 1932 military coup that brought Marmaduke Grove and the Socialist Republic to power. As Brian Loveman and Elizabeth Lira note, an ongoing judicial investigation into Alessandri's role in the 1932 overthrow of the Montero government may have precipitated the amnesty. The interior minister included in the law an amendment that gave amnesty to carabineros who had committed crimes while in service. This article was incorporated expressly into the amnesty law to cover the counterinsurgency in Alto Bío Bío.[40] The amnesty law arrived in congress just as Concepción's military court began its inquiry into atrocities committed by carabineros in the repression of the Ránquil rebellion and put a quick end to the investigation. Although it remained unstated, this may explain Alessandri's urgency in pushing the amnesty law through congress.

The sucesos in Ránquil and the prisoners in Temuco were mentioned only once and in passing during debate in the house. Deputies like the Radical Juan Antonio Ríos saw the sucesos of 4 June 1932 as "the principal cause for the legislation of this amnesty." While he condemned the coup, Ríos argued that the amnesty would bring about reconciliation and "noble olvido of the past" so that "the Chilean family can be one without rancor." The Conservative deputy Ricardo Boizard similarly endorsed the law because "the country needs to get back to work and be compensated for all the damage done by the moral and political perversion brought by dictatorships. It needs this process to come to an end once and for all. It needs peace to begin again." Boizard repudiated the crimes committed by the "dictatorships" of the previous years, as well as "enemies of order." But he contended that the criminal courts were not the place to resolve ideological conflicts and that the amnesty would constitute the foundation of the social and political order required for the country to move forward.[41]

To members of congress on the Left who supported the law, its benefit lay in granting liberty to the thousands of political prisoners jailed for violating Decree-Law No. 50. Deputies from the Socialist and Communist parties made ardent appeals for the derogation of the law, which had been used as a weapon to jail leftists who printed and distributed proclamas subversivas or who had simply engaged in labor or leftist activism. The Communist Party's Andrés Escobar voiced his support for the amnesty law because it would, he said, bring immediate freedom to political prisoners jailed for exercising what should have been their constitutional right to political speech. He told congress that the Communist Party would support the amnesty because it would free "two thousand political and social prisoners across the country, the majority of whom are workers jailed for insulting the president, for distributing manifestos considered subversive, and for other crimes against Decree-Law No. 50 that to the working class are not crimes." Escobar, like other deputies on the Left, called for the immediate repeal of the Internal Security of the State Law. Emilio Zapata of the Trotskyist Communist Left voiced his support for the amnesty because it would free "the prisoners condemned for crimes sanctioned by the legislation dictated by Dávila against the working class ... because it covers all the workers accused of violating the Internal Security of the State [Law], including the victims of the bloody sucesos in Ránquil."[42]

Unlike their fellow leftists, Socialists opposed the amnesty for two reasons. First, they rejected the characterization of their assumption of power in a military coup on 4 June 1932 as a crime in need of pardon. Rather, they reaffirmed the revolutionary and democratic goals of the Socialist Republic and claimed the regime enjoyed widespread popular support. As the deputy Alberto Merino put it, "We have never believed we have committed a crime in bringing down an oligarchic government and giving the government to the workers. ... [W]e never believed we were committing a crime when we aspired to bring justice to the persecuted." "We contend," he declared further, "that there was no crime and thus we reject the pardon." Second, Socialists argued that as long as Decree-Law No. 50 remained on the books, the amnesty was nothing but a farce. Once emptied, Chile's prisons would be filled again with political prisoners since the Alessandri regime had made enthusiastic use of the law as an instrument for crushing political dissent. Carlos Alberto Martínez argued that "if the amnesty law were sincere and honest it would have been paired with a declaration that the decree-law [No. 50] has no legal standing." Instead, he observed, the government had made widespread use of "this infamous Decree-Law No. 50 to keep itself in power."[43]

In the end, the legislature did Alessandri's bidding. It voted against any repeal of Decree-Law No. 50 while voting with an appreciable majority in favor of the amnesty law. The Radical Party deputy Arturo Olavarría, a political ally of Alessandri, cast a typical vote in defense of both the amnesty law and Decree-Law No. 50. He summed up, with a dose of cynicism, the structure of Chilean politics: "This happens with all amnesties and pardons. The laws that sanction the pardoned crimes remain in force." As the Radical Party deputy well understood, the two laws represented the twin pillars of Chilean democracy. The Internal Security of the State Law handed governments the legal tool they needed to employ widespread repressive measures, including sending political opponents into internal and external exile, cracking down on peaceful protests, restricting the distribution of dissident political publications, significantly curtailing free speech, and imposing limits on the activities of labor organizations. Frequent amnesty laws were a safety valve, resolving temporarily political conflicts, insurrections, and periods of social upheaval and state repression while emptying the prisons of those charged under draconian security measures.[44]

Revolution and Memories of Ránquil

The Chilean Communist Party's positions during this period reflected the broader politics of the times. On the one hand, the party threw in its lot with popular struggles in Chile's mines, cities, and countryside, hoping to organize revolutionary strikes and land invasions that would bring about a government of soviets in line with the Comintern's insurrectionary strategy of anti-imperialist agrarian revolution in Latin America. On the other, it followed a parliamentary strategy of participating in local and national elections. Even during the Comintern's "third period" of promoting an insurrectionary road to revolution, party candidates ran and were at times elected to congressional office in line with what was called the Recabarrenist tendency in the party founded by the typographer Luis Emilio Recabarren. In 1921 Recabarren himself had been elected deputy for the Socialist Workers Party (POS), which was affiliated with the communist international and became the Communist Party the following year.

The tension between insurrectionary popular revolution from below and an electoral path to social reform from above would shape the politics of the Chilean Left for the remainder of the twentieth century.[45] Only one year after the Ránquil rebellion, the Communist Party made a definitive choice to pursue the path of electoral politics and alliances with bourgeois parties, following the Comintern's antifascist Popular Front strategy. As Olga Ulianova argues, the party's efforts to build political alliances and work through the electoral system, which bore fruit in the 1938 election of Radical Party president Pedro Aguirre Cerda at the head of a Popular Front coalition that included both the Socialist and Communist parties, shaped historical narratives that deemphasized the party's role in organizing the Ránquil rebellion.[46] In addition, these narratives downplayed the rebellion's insurrectionary character, underlining instead the campesinos' spontaneous uprising against deprivation and the bloody repression they suffered. The olvido produced by the amnesty law applied not only to the massacres committed by carabineros but also to campesinos' own violence. As the Left became increasingly committed to an electoral path to socialism, the memory of Ránquil as a revolutionary movement was replaced by histories that emphasized the unplanned nature of the uprising and the atrocities committed by carabineros. Ránquil became an emblem for the Chilean Left, but not of its revolutionary roots in popular armed struggle. Instead, Ránquil entered historical memory as one of many violent massacres that had quelled popular movements throughout Chilean history.[47]

Nonetheless, the revolutionary character of the Ránquil rebellion remained a persistent, if muted, current in cultural memory, at odds with a more general tendency to isolate the campesino movement from politics and ideology. As early as 1941 Carlos Contreras Labarca's secretary Reinaldo Lomboy published a novel describing the rebellion and its origins: *Ránquil*.[48] Despite Contreras Labarca's report to the Comintern ascribing leadership of the insurrection to the Communist Party and FOCH, the novel mentioned neither the party and labor federation nor even Juan Segundo Leiva Tapia and the Sindicato Agrícola Lonquimay. Instead, Lomboy painted a richly textured portrait of the language, lifeways, and hardships of the southern cordillera's campesinos. The novel portrayed the violent abuse meted out by carabineros in their pursuit of campesinos who engaged in livestock contraband. It depicted vividly how carabineros had expelled campesinos from their land and burned their huts at the behest of landowners. Rather than a planned movement, Lomboy represented the rebellion as it would be remembered later by figures like the party and FOCH leader Elías Laferrte, as "a spontaneous rebellion, unplanned, an explosion of campesinos' rage" provoked by the appropriation of their "impoverished and scarce land" and punished by carabineros with brutal repression.[49]

Yet while Lomboy's campesinos were free of ties to the Left and the labor movement, they did express an embryonic revolutionary understanding of their movement. As the novel concluded, "The campesinos have known to die in order to indicate the path along which man will travel to find his dignity."[50] Even as the politics of the Popular Front era made it impossible for Lomboy to describe the rebellion as an insurrection led by the Communist Party, to the author and to the Chilean Left generally Ránquil signified both the potential of a grassroots revolution in the countryside and the violence of the state, which, as in the northern nitrate mines, employed massacre to repress popular mobilizations.

After Lomboy's novel was published, the massacre of campesinos in Alto Bío Bío acquired an iconic place in the historical memory of the Chilean Communist Party. In 1948 Pablo Neruda included the massacre in Ránquil in his poem "Los Muertos de la Plaza" (The Dead in the Square), which commemorated the 1946 gunning down of peaceful labor union protesters in Santiago and identified the deaths with infamous massacres in Chile's northern nitrate fields and ports. To Neruda, as to Lafertte and many others on the Left, Ránquil's meaning lay in campesinos' deaths at the hands of carabineros rather than their act of insurrection.[51]

For two decades Lomboy's hope that Alto Bío Bío's campesinado would show the road to revolution to the rest of the country remained unrealized. In politics, the Popular Front agreement that excluded rural workers from being covered by the 1931 labor laws and limited social reform to the urban sector shaped the politics of the Left.[52] During these decades an enduring silence surrounded the events in Ránquil. However, the 1967 agrarian reform and campesino unionization laws passed during the Christian Democratic government of Eduardo Frei Montalva launched a resurgence of rural protest and labor organizing in Chile. In this context Ránquil reemerged as a potent symbol of campesinos' revolutionary potential. In 1967 the rural labor federation led by the Communist Party, the Federación Nacional Campesina e Indígena, renamed itself the Confederación Nacional Campesina e Indígena Ránquil to honor the campesino victims of the 1934 massacre and to celebrate the earlier alliance of indigenous and nonindigenous campesinos in Alto Bío Bío.[53]

Two years later the writer Isidora Aguirre staged her play *Los que van quedando en el camino,* a phrase taken from a speech by Che Guevara—the title was translated into English as *Those Left by the Wayside.* The drama depicted in vivid detail the events of the Ránquil rebellion.[54] To do research for the work Aguirre interviewed some of the surviving leaders of the rebellion, including Benito and Emelina Sagredo, who now lived in Santiago. She located the Sagredos at the party-led construction workers' union hall and a local Communist Party office in Santiago. Aguirre's play marked a shift in Ránquil's place in the memory of Chile's Left. As she noted, the play's purpose was to reclaim the revolutionary role played by campesinos in Chilean history. To Aguirre, Ránquil signified more than massacre. She saw the rebellion as a revolutionary agrarian movement spearheaded by politically conscious campesinos who had exhausted all legal methods of struggle and taken up arms. Indeed, Aguirre intended the play to identify Ránquil with campesino movements sweeping Latin America since the Cuban Revolution and as a critique of both the moderate Christian Democratic agrarian reform and the legalist reformism of the Communist Party. At the end of the play, campesinos engage in a protest carrying a placard stating, "Legality is of no use to the poor campesino!"[55]

Aguirre was joined by the writer and musician Patricio Manns, who, during the years of Salvador Allende's democratically elected socialist Popular Unity (Unidad Popular, or UP) government, identified with the Movement of the Revolutionary Left (Movimiento de Izquierda Revolucionaria, or MIR) and its embrace of a Cuban path to revolution. In a short book on "major massacres" (*Las grandes masacres*) in Chilean history published in 1972 Manns included a brief chapter on Ránquil. He highlighted his view that the rebellion's protagonists were campesinos who organized the first guerilla movement in Latin America ("when Che Guevara was only seven") and had served as a precursor to the Cuban Revolution. To Manns, as to Aguirre, Ránquil's importance lay not only in the state violence employed to crush the rebellion but also in the "awakening of the campesinado and its true incorporation into active struggle."[56] Like Aguirre, Manns ignored the role of the rural labor movement and Communist Party in the rebellion, identifying it instead with armed revolutionary movements throughout Latin America inspired by the Cuban Revolution.

Also in 1972 the Communist Party magazine *Ramona* published an article commemorating the massacre of campesinos in Ránquil that included interviews with Emelina and Clementina Sagredo and Ismael Cartes. The article noted that *Los que van quedando en el camino* was playing at the Universidad de Chile theater and, in a stunning historical irony, starred the actress Carmen Bunster, a granddaughter of the Sagredos' old enemy Gonzalo Bunster, as the character identified with Emelina Sagredo. Much like *Los que van quedando en el camino*, the article depicted the rebellion as a grassroots insurgency that had emerged from the campesinos themselves and accentuated the campesinos' violent expulsion from their land in Nitrito and loss of harvests, the onerous conditions they confronted in Llanquén, and the bloody massacre that brought their movement to an end. To *Ramona* as to Aguirre, the campesino movement in Alto Bío Bío prefigured the agrarian reform underway in the countryside. But the article muted any mention of the party's role in organizing the rebellion.[57]

Consistent with the Communist Party's support of Allende's *vía chilena al socialismo*, a revolution made through coalition and at the ballot box, *Ramona* ignored the waves of land invasions in southern Chile that had radicalized the agrarian reform since 1971 and produced a revolution in the countryside. Its article on Ránquil underlined only that the state agrarian reform agency had expropriated some of the fundos (primarily Guayalí) claimed by campesinos in 1934. To the Communist Party publication, a campesino-led insurgency fit uneasily with its support for Allende's approach to building socialism within the legal framework of Chilean democracy. During the years of the Popular Unity government, the party was a resolute opponent of those on the Left, especially within Allende's own Socialist Party and the MIR, who, inspired by the 1959 Cuban revolution, promoted an insurrectionary approach to revolutionary change. In this sense, the divergent narratives of the Ránquil rebellion during the late 1960s and early 1970s reflected the division within the Chilean Left between those who, like Aguirre and Manns, identified with the Cuban Revolution and those who supported Allende's program of an incremental and democratic path to socialism. Campesinos' embrace of armed insurrection in 1934 occupied an uneasy position in the Chilean Left's historical memory marked by persistent olvido.

In August 1973, a month before the coup that would inaugurate seventeen years of military dictatorship in Chile, a pseudonymous author named Ránquil published a short, popular, revisionist history of Chile titled *Capítulos de la historia de Chile* (*Chapters in Chile's History*). That the author adopted Ránquil as a pseudonym spoke to the enduring momentousness of the rebellion and massacre in the memory of the Left.[58] *Capítulos de la historia de Chile* precipitated an avalanche of vitriolic criticism in the press and congress for its critical representation of two key moments in Chilean history: the war for independence and its leader, Bernardo O'Higgins, and the War of the Pacific with Bolivia and Peru, in which Chile appropriated the nitrate-rich provinces of Antofagasta and Tarapacá. In congress the president of the Bernardo O'Higgins Institute,

Senator Humberto Aguirre Doolan (a nephew of the Radical Party and Popular Front president Pedro Aguirre Cerda) denounced the brief book as a "serious distortion" and "falsification" of Chilean history written by Marxist enemies of the patria who should be prosecuted for violating the Internal Security of the State Law.[59] A group of retired military officers also chimed in, penning a letter in which they attacked Ránquil's book, which, they claimed, "vilified with extraordinary distortions the truth of the events that gave liberty to Chile." They demanded that Ránquil be sanctioned by both civilian and military courts.[60]

Deputies and senators from the opposition to the Popular Unity government sought to have a congressional commission investigate Ránquil's identity and sanction whoever it was for violating the Internal Security of the State Law. Their campaign was realized in part when the intellectual property office of the Dirección de Bibliotecas, Archivos y Museos revealed that the author was the artist Lucy Lortsch Revett.[61] Lortsch was not a historian but an accomplished painter and engraver whose sympathies lay on the Left and who had worked in organizing campesino unions during the 1960s. In adopting Ránquil as a pseudonym, Lortsch likely embraced the symbolism of armed peasant insurrection, igniting in part the outrage of the political opposition to Allende's socialist government as well as hostility from some sectors of Allende's coalition government.

The Chilean Communist Party distanced itself from the author Ránquil. The party declared that she was not a member of the party and that the party had had nothing to do with the publication of *Capítulos*. The book itself was not Marxist in methodology and suffered from serious "distortions" and "gaps." The party's newspaper, *El Siglo*, editorialized that Ránquil's focus on "a few figures from the history of Chile demonstrates a passionate bias that is inconsistent with a scientific study of the epoch." The party also characterized as anticommunist Ránquil's brief critique of the Popular Front government, which operated, she contended, as a means for the dominant classes to further their interests by taking advantage of working-class votes channeled through the Communist and Socialist parties. This contention was especially problematic because the Popular Front, in which Salvador Allende had served as Minister of Health, served as a template for the Popular Unity coalition and the Communist Party's support for a socialist revolution made within the context of Chile's democratic institutions.[62]

The import of both the Ránquil rebellion and Ránquil's short revisionist history as cultural and political flashpoints during the turbulent years of Allende's Popular Unity government was made clear following the 11 September 1973 military coup. The military collected copies of the book from libraries, bookstores, and kiosks and destroyed as many as it could find. Lortsch was detained in Chile's Estadio Nacional and then in the Buen Pastor women's prison in Santiago, not for any political activism but for her identity as Ránquil. She was tried by a military court for violating a 1958 iteration of the Internal Security of the State Law (Ley No. 12927, 6 August 1958), in her case the law's first article, which covered "those who gravely offend patriotic feeling." Lortsch suffered horrific torture by her interrogators while being held incommunicado for over a year. International pressure may have saved her life. Because of her prominence as an artist and writer, the Organization of American States and Amnesty International placed Lucy Lortsch's case in their reports on human rights violations under the Pinochet dictatorship and made regular inquiries about her whereabouts and legal status. She was eventually expelled from the country and went into exile in France. Like the bodies of massacred campesinos that disappeared in 1934 into the Biobío's icy waters, the records of the judicial investigation that vanished onto the dusty shelves of Temuco's Conservador de Bienes Raíces, relegated to oblivion by the 1934 amnesty law, and copies of Ránquil's *Capítulos* that were incinerated on bonfires set by Chile's new military rulers in 1973, Lucy Lortsch herself disappeared from the historical record, first into the Pinochet dictatorship's prisons and then into exile.[63]

In 1985, after more than a decade of dictatorship, Patricio Manns revisited the Ránquil rebellion in a novel titled *Actas del Alto Bío-Bío*.[64] Manns presents *Actas del Alto Bío-Bío* as an interview between the author and a Pehuenche lonko named Angol Mamalcucheo, who is probably based on the historical figure of Ralco's Ignacio Maripi. *Las grandes masacres* and the literary treatment that had gone before, especially works by Reinaldo Lomboy and Isidora Aguirre, largely ignored the presence of Pehuenche communities in the rebellion. But *Actas del Alto Bío Bío* described the Ránquil rebellion's protagonists as indigenous Pehuenches and relegated the nonindigenous "*criollo*" campesinos to the margins of the narrative.[65] The novel underlined as well the role of Juan Segundo Leiva Tapia—who is described as a Communist Party militant named José Leiva Tapia—in organizing Pehuenche communities, assisting them to rise from their historic slumber, and leading them in armed revolution. It is no coincidence that Manns wrote the novel at the moment the Communist Party had taken up the strategy of armed resistance to the Pinochet dictatorship and organized a military arm, the Frente Patriótico Manuel Rodríguez (FPMR), and Mapuche communities had inaugurated a new grassroots movement to regain land usurped by large estates. In fact, Manns wrote the FPMR's "anthem," *Himno FPMR*.[66]

Manns's novel was the first cultural representation of Ránquil on the Left that described Juan Segundo Leiva Tapia as a member of the Communist Party and ascribed the rebellion to his work as a militant organizing among Pehuenche communities in Alto Bío Bío. In conjunction with the party's embrace of armed struggle against the dictatorship, this novelistic treatment constituted memory work designed to recuperate the party's leadership role in a campesino insurrection for the contemporary historical moment and to identify the insurrection in Alto Bío Bío with revolutionary peasant movements in Cuba and Central America.

Ironically, *Actas del Alto Bío-Bío*'s depiction of a Mapuche rebellion led and organized by a nonindigenous Communist Party militant overlooked the historical dynamics of the movement for indigenous rights that had emerged in Chile during the late 1970s and 1980s. This movement began with the formation of Mapuche Centros Culturales in Temuco in response to a 1979 decree-law (Decree-Law No. 2658) dictated by the Pinochet dictatorship to subdivide into privately held parcels land belonging to indigenous communities. The Centros Culturales organized Ad Mapu, the first Mapuche organization to oppose the Pinochet dictatorship's scheme for breaking up Mapuche communities and putting their land on the market. While some of Ad Mapu's leaders had ties to political parties, including the Communist Party, by 1991, as Chile entered its transition to democracy, a number of Mapuche activists split from Ad Mapu to organize the All Lands Council (Consejo de Todas las Tierras, or Aukiñ Wallmapu Ngulam). The council promoted peaceful invasions to recuperate land usurped from communities over the years as well as a broader struggle for recognition of Mapuche linguistic, cultural, and political autonomy and territorial sovereignty.[67] At the same time, during the 1990s a number of communities embroiled in bitter conflicts with logging companies organized the Coordinadora de Comunidades en Conflicto Arauko y Malleko, which also shaped its militant demands for land in terms of Mapuches' rights to sovereignty over territory in southern Chile.[68]

One of the key moments in the emergence of the militant Mapuche movement of the 1990s and 2000s involved the Ralco community, which had been divided into two communities, Ralco-Lepoy and Ralco-Quepuca, in 1954. Ralco made national headlines, as it had in the twenties and thirties, when some of its members opposed plans by the transnational energy company ENDESA to build two dams on the Biobío River. The dams threatened to flood land belonging to the two Ralco communities and cause serious ecological disruptions that would undermine their subsistence base. To build the dams, ENDESA and the Chilean government would have to move the two communities off their land. The dams required the approval of both the indigenous affairs agency, the Corporacíon Nacional de Desarrollo Indígena (CONADI), and the government agency in charge of environmental regulation, the Comisión Nacional del Medio Ambiente (CONAMA), both of which initially issued reports unfavorable to the hydroelectric projects. Yet under pressure from the center-left coalition government of Eduardo Frei Ruiz-Tagle (1994–2000), the son of Eduardo Frei Montalva—which fired two Mapuche directors of CONADI who refused to give the indigenous affairs agency's approval to the dam projects—CONADI and CONAMA eventually issued reports favorable to the projects. The Pangue and Ralco dams displaced a large number of Ralco households, which were resettled further up the Biobío River.[69]

Ralco's conflict with ENDESA posed one of the first and most important challenges to the neoliberal economic policies and limited democratic arrangements handed down by the Pinochet dictatorship during Chile's transition to democracy. The community's efforts to defend its land from the ENDESA dam projects signaled the emergence of both indigenous and environmental rights as two poles of popular opposition to the policies of privatization and market-driven development that had made Chile a model throughout the Americas. During the debates, studies, and protests generated by the controversial dam megaprojects, however, Ralco's long history of political mobilization, including the part played by Ignacio Maripi and other community members in the Ránquil rebellion, went unspoken. Even the most outstanding anthropological study of Alto Bío Bío's Pehuenche communities, published at the time of Ralco's confrontation with ENDESA in 1997, made no mention of the 1934 rebellion.[70]

Just ten years after Manns's *Actas del Alto Bío Bío* consecrated Ralco and its lonko as precursors to a revolution in the countryside, the community's involvement in Chile's most important campesino rebellion appeared to have been relegated to oblivion once again. The narrative of a small indigenous community struggling to retain rights to ancestral land and standing up to a goliath of a transnational power company could not accommodate the history of Ralco's alliance with the Sindicato Agrícola Lonquimay and its embrace of armed insurrection. In addition, Ralco's ties to the union and non-Mapuche campesinos in the 1930s fit uncomfortably within the ideological framework of a Mapuche indigenous rights movement dedicated to the pursuit of ethnic political and territorial sovereignty.

During the transition to democracy after 1990, Chile reckoned with the horrific state terrorism unleashed by the Pinochet dictatorship through, first, a truth and reconciliation commission, then a national commission on torture, and, finally, numerous trials of military officers implicated in human rights abuses. For a Left committed to a stable transition to democratic rule, there was little room for nurturing historical memory of a moment when members of the Communist Party and Chilean and Pehuenche campesinos took up arms together to spark a national revolution. Throughout the 1990s and 2000s it was easier to commemorate Ránquil as another chapter in the state's violent repression of popular movements than to resurrect in historical memory a moment when sectors of the Left opted for armed revolution and Alto Bío Bío's campesinos organized a collective movement to bring down the oligarchic order in the countryside by force.[71] Olvido remained at the foundation of Chile's struggle to build a more democratic state and society.

Notes

Introduction

1. Reinaldo Lomboy, *Ránquil: novela de la tierra* (Santiago: Editorial Orbe, 1942); Isidora Aguirre, *Los que van quedando en el camino* (Santiago: Imprenta Mueller, 1970); and Patricio Manns, *Actas del Alto Bío-Bío* (Madrid: Ediciones Michay, 1985). Two memoirs narrate the history of the rebellion: Arturo Huenchullán, *Los sucesos de Alto Bio-Bio y el diputado Huenchullán* (Santiago: Imprenta Selecta, 1934), and Harry Fahrenkrog Reinhold, *La verdad sobre la revuelta de Ránquil* (Santiago: Editorial Universitaria, 1985). The most thorough historical work on the rebellion to date is Jaime Flores Chávez, "Un Episodio en la Historia Social de Chile: 1934, Ránquil. Una Revuelta Campesina" (MA thesis, Universidad de Santiago de Chile, 1993).
2. In his landmark study of Chile's agrarian history, *Chilean Rural Society from the Spanish Conquest to 1930* (Cambridge: Cambridge University Press, 1975), Arnold Bauer argues that Chile's hacienda system remained unchallenged by campesino labor organizing or revolts until the agrarian reform of the 1960s. According to Bauer, Ránquil was the only example of a campesino uprising in twentieth-century Chile.
3. This book builds on early work I published on the Ránquil rebellion in *La Frontera: Forests and Ecological Conflicts on Chile's Southern Frontier* (Durham: Duke University Press, 2014) and "Ránquil: Violence and Peasant Politics on Chile's Southern Frontier," in Gilbert M. Joseph and Greg Grandin, eds., *A Century of Revolution: Insurgent and Counterinsurgent Violence during Latin America's Long Cold War* (Durham: Duke University Press, 2010).
4. For critical analyses of Chile's transition to democracy, see Peter Winn, ed., *Victims of the Chilean Miracle: Workers in the Pinochet Era, 1973–2002* (Durham: Duke University Press, 2004); Paul Drake and Ivan Jaksic, eds., *El modelo chileno: democracia y desarrollo en los noventa* (Santiago: LOM Ediciones, 1999).

5. For a recent analysis of political violence in Chilean history see, among other works, Elizabeth Lira and Brian Loveman, "La Violencia Política en Chile: Contextos y Prácticas desde 1810," in Iván Jaksic and Juan Luis Ossa, eds. *Historia política de Chile, 1810–2010*, vol. 1: *Prácticas Políticas* (Santiago: Fondo de Cultura Económica, Chile, 2017); Lessie Jo Frazier, *Salt in the Sand: Memory, Violence, and the Nation-State in Chile, 1890 to the Present* (Durham: Duke University Press, 2007).
6. Catherine LeGrand, *Frontier Expansion and Peasant Protest in Colombia, 1850–1936* (Albuquerque: University of New Mexico Press, 1986); Michael Jiménez, "The Limits of Export Capitalism: Economic Structure, Class, and Politics in a Colombian Coffee Municipality, 1900–1930" (PhD diss., Harvard University, 1985); Aldo A. Lauria-Santiago and Jeffrey Gould, *To Rise in Darkness: Revolution, Repression, and Memory in El Salvador, 1920–1932* (Durham: Duke University Press, 2008); Barry Carr, "Mill Occupations and Soviets: The Mobilisation of Sugar Workers in Cuba 1917–1933," *Journal of Latin American Studies* 28, no. 1 (February 1996); Gillian McGillivray, *Burning Cane: Sugar Communities, Class, and State Formation in Cuba, 1868–1959* (Durham: Duke University Press, 2009).
7. For histories of anarchism in Chile, see Sergio Grez, *Los anarquistas y el movimiento obrero: la alborada de "la Idea" en Chile, 1893–1915* (Santiago: Lom Ediciones, 2007); *De la "regeneración del pueblo" a la huelga general: génesis y evolución histórica del movimiento popular en Chile (1810–1910)* (Santiago: DIBAM, Centro de Investigaciones Diego Barros Arana, 1998) and *La "cuestión social" en Chile: ideas y debates precursores (1804–1902)* (Santiago, DIBAM: Centro de Investigaciones Diego Barros Arana, 1995); Raymond Craib, *The Cry of the Renegade: Politics and Poetry in Interwar Chile* (Oxford: Oxford University Press, 2016). The anarchist-led workers' movement that most closely resembled the Ránquil rebellion was the regional rebellion on enormous sheep ranches in Patagonia, which included Chilean migrant workers from Chiloé. See Osvaldo Bayer's famous account of this rebellion in *La Patagonia rebelde* (Mexico, DF: Editorial Nueva Imágen, 1980). For a history of Chilean Communist Party organizing in the countryside after 1935, see Nicolás Acevedo Arriaza, *Un fantasma recorre el campo: Comunismo y politización campesina en Chile (1935–1948)* (Santiago: Editorial América en Movimiento, 2017).
8. Brian Loveman, *Struggle in the Countryside: Politics and Rural Labor in Chile, 1919–1973* (Bloomington: Indiana University Press, 1976) and *Chile: The Legacy of Hispanic Capitalism* (Oxford: Oxford University Press, 2001).
9. For works that refer to the campesino rebels exclusively as colono smallholders rather than inquilinos or obreros agrícolas, see Flores, "Un Episodio," 61–62; Loveman, *Struggle in the Countryside*, 144; Bauer, *Chilean Rural Society*, 222; Olga Ulianova, "Levantamiento Campesino de Lonquimay y la Internacional Comunista," *Estudios Públicos*, no. 89 (Summer 2003); and Sebastián Leiva, "El Partido Comunista de Chile y Levantamiento de Ránquil: ¿Plani-

ficación, Dirección, Apoyo?," *Cyber Humanitas*, no. 28 (Spring 2003) https://web.uchile.cl/vignette/cyberhumanitatis/CDA/texto_simple2/0,1255, SCID%253D6781%2526ISID%253D374,00.html, accessed 12 November 2018. This view of the social origins of the rebellion is reproduced most recently in Florencia E. Mallon, "Victims into Emblems: Images of the Ránquil Massacre in Chilean National Narratives, 1934–2004," *Labor: Studies in Working-Class History of the Americas*, 8, no. 1 (2011), and José Bengoa, *Historia rural de Chile central*, vol. 2, *Crisis y ruptura del poder hacendal* (Santiago: LOM Ediciones, 2016).

10. Loveman, *Struggle in the Countryside*, 145–51.
11. Claudio Robles-Ortíz, "Agrarian Capitalism and Rural Labour: The Hacienda System in Central Chile, 1870–1920," *Journal of Latin American Studies* 41, no. 3 (August 2009). An earlier work that emphasizes agrarian commercial expansion and the semi-proletarianization of the rural labor force is Gabriel Salazar, *Labradores, peones, y proletarios: formación y crisis de la sociedad popular chilena del siglo XIX* (Santiago: SUR, 1985).
12. William Roseberry, "Images of the Peasant in the Consciousness of the Venezuelan Proletariat," in *Anthropologies and Histories: Essays in Culture, History, and Political Economy* (New Brunswick: Routledge, 1989). See also Jeffrey Gould, *To Lead as Equals: Rural Protest and Political Consciousness in Chinandega, Nicaragua, 1912–1979* (Chapel Hill: University of North Carolina Press, 1990), 134–35.
13. See Roseberry, "Images of the Peasant," 55–59, for a critical discussion of the moral economy literature.
14. E. P. Thompson, "The Moral Economy of the English Crowd in the Eighteenth Century," *Past & Present* no. 50 (February 1971); James C. Scott, *The Moral Economy of the Peasant: Rebellion and Subsistence in Southeast Asia* (Princeton: Princeton University Press, 1976).
15. Germán Palacios Ríos, *Ránquil: la violencia en la expansión de la propiedad agraria* (Santiago: Ediciones ICAL, 1992).
16. Ulianova, "Levantamiento Campesino de Lonquimay y la Internacional Comunista"; Leiva, "El Partido Comunista de Chile y Levantamiento de Ránquil."
17. In Chile there are three types of laws implemented by decree: *decreto con fuerza de ley; decreto ley;* and *decreto* (or *decreto supremo*): *decretos con fuerza de ley* are promulgated under the authority delegated by congress to the president in which congress delegates to the president *facultades extraordinarias* (extraordinary powers); a *decreto ley* is implemented by an unelected de facto government, often one that has assumed power in a military intervention or coup; a *decreto* or *decreto supremo* is an administrative action taken by a ministry, under the president's constitutional authority. I thank Brian Loveman for raising this point and explaining these definitions, which he expands on with Elizabeth Lira in *Poder judicial y conflictos políticos: Chile, 1925–1958* (Santiago: LOM Ediciones, 2014).

18. This view of the authoritarian practices and policies sustained during the second Alessandri government differs from the conventional historical narrative, which sees the economic crisis produced by the Great Depression as leading to the fall of the authoritarian Ibáñez regime and the restoration of a multiparty democracy with Alessandri's election in 1932. See, for example, Alan Knight, "The Great Depression in Latin America: An Overview," in Paulo Drinot and Alan Knight, eds., *The Great Depression in Latin America* (Durham: Duke University Press, 2014).
19. Heidi Tinsman, *Partners in Conflict: The Politics of Gender, Sexuality, and Labor in the Chilean Agrarian Reform, 1950–1973* (Durham: Duke University Press, 2002), 33.
20. For a pathbreaking history of one Mapuche community's struggle for land, see Florencia E. Mallon, *Courage Tastes of Blood: The Mapuche Community of Nicolás Ailío and the Chilean State, 1906–2001* (Durham: Duke University Press, 2005).
21. The role of Pehuenche communities in the rebellion is discussed in Eduardo Téllez Lúgaro, Cristian Arancibia, Larisa De Ruit, Rodrigo Quinteros, and Yuri Quintupirray, "El Levantamiento del Alto Biobío y el Soviet y República Araucana de 1934," *Anales de la Universidad de Chile*, sixth series, no. 13 (August 2001), and Mallon, "Victims into Emblems."
22. Huenchullán, *Los sucesos de Alto Bio-Bio y el diputado Huenchullán;* Flores Chávez, "Un Episodio en la Historia Social de Chile: 1934"; Ulianova, "Levantamiento Campesino de Lonquimay y la Internacional Comunista"; Leiva, "El Partido Comunista de Chile y Levantamiento de Ránquil"; Téllez Lúgaro, Arancibia, De Ruit, Quinteros, Quintupirray, "El Levantamiento del Alto Biobío y el Soviet y República Araucana de 1934."
23. William Taylor, *Drinking, Homicide, and Rebellion in Colonial Mexican Villages* (Stanford: Stanford University Press, 1979), 114. In *Elementary Aspects of Peasant Insurgency in Colonial India* (Durham: Duke University Press, 1999), Ranajit Guha employs the term "insurrection" rather than "uprising" or "rebellion" to underline the organized and political character of peasants' violent collective actions in British colonial India.
24. Julio Pinto Vallejos, *Trabajos y rebeldías en la pampa salitrera: el ciclo del salitre y la reconfiguración de las identidades populares (1850–1900)* (Santiago: Universidad de Santiago, 1998) and *Desgarros y utopías en la pampa salitrera: la consolidación de la identidad obrera en tiempos de la cuestión social (1890–1923)* (Santiago: LOM Ediciones, 2007); Sergio González Miranda, *Hombres y mujeres de la pampa: Tarapacá en el ciclo de la expansión salitrera* (Santiago: LOM Ediciones, 2002); Eduardo Devés, *Los que van a morir te saludan: historia de una masacre, Escuela Santa María* (Santiago: LOM Ediciones, 1997); Frazier, *Salt in the Sand: Memory, Violence, and the Nation-State in Chile, 1890 to the Present.*
25. This is the argument of Bauer in *Chilean Rural Society*. See Robles, "Agrarian Capitalism" for a discussion of this point.

26. Lira and Loveman discuss the amnesty and judicial investigation into the Ránquil rebellion in *Poder judicial y conflictos políticos (Chile: 1925–1958)*.
27. Guha, *Elementary Aspects of Peasant Insurgency in Colonial India*, 8–13, and Ranajit Guha, "The Prose of Counter-Insurgency," in Ranajit Guha and Gayatri Chakravorty Spivak, *Selected Subaltern Studies* (Oxford: Oxford University Press, 1988). See also the discussion of Guha's seminal work in Gilbert Joseph, "On the Trail of Latin American Bandits: A Reexamination of Peasant Resistance," *Latin American Research Review* 25, no. 3 (1990).
28. Elizabeth Lira and Brian Loveman, *Las suaves cenizas del olvido: vía chilena de reconciliación política, 1814–1932* (Santiago: LOM Ediciones, 1999) and *Las ardientes cenizas del olvido: vía chilena de reconciliación política, 1932–1994* (Santiago: LOM Ediciones, 2000).

Chapter 1. San Ignacio de Pemehue

1. Francisco Puelma Tupper, *Esposición ante el H. Senado de los títulos de Francisco Puelma Castillo al fundo San Ignacio i algunas consideraciones jenerales* (Santiago: Editorial Universitaria, 1919), 10; Ministerio de la Propiedad Austral, Mensura de Tierras, "Informe de la Comisión Nominada por Decreto No. 265, de 27 de Marzo Último sobre el Problema del Alto Bío-Bío," Ministerio de Bienes Nacionales, Providencias 1930, vol. 107, Archivo Nacional de la Administración, Santiago (hereafter ARNAD).
2. Loveman and Lira, *Poder judicial y conflictos políticos*.
3. José Bengoa, *Historia del pueblo mapuche: Siglo XIX y XX* (Santiago: LOM Ediciones, 2000), 94–95. See also Raúl Molina and Martín Correa, *Territorio y comunidades pehuenches del Alto Bio Bío* (Santiago: CONADI, 1996), 11–14.
4. Sergio Villalobos, *Los pehuenches en la vida fronteriza* (Santiago: Ediciones Universidad Católica de Chile, 1989), 197.
5. Ibid., 73–74. See also Jorge Pinto Rodríguez, "Integración y desintegración de un espacio fronterizo," in Jorge Pinto Rodríguez, ed., *Araucanía: mundo fronterizo en América del Sur* (Temuco: Ediciones Universidad de la Frontera), 22–24.
6. Jorge Pinto Rodríguez, *La formación del Estado y la nación, y el pueblo mapuche: de la inclusión a la exclusión* (Santiago: DIBAM, 2003), 80–86.
7. Eduarda Poepping, *Un testigo de la alborada de Chile (1826–1829)*, 386, cited in Pinto Rodríguez, *La formación del Estado y la nación, y el pueblo mapuche*, 86. See also Bengoa, *Historia del pueblo mapuche*, 95–96.
8. Villalobos, *Los pehuenches*, 17.
9. Ibid., 20.
10. Carmen Norambuena and Guillermo Bravo, "Política y Legislación Inmigratoria en Chile, 1830–1930," *Revista de Historia de América*, no. 109 (January-June, 1990): 88–90.
11. Pinto Rodríguez, *La formación del Estado y la nación, y el pueblo mapuche*, 124–25, 185–86.

12. Raúl Molina and Martín Correa argue that the requirement that the governor or intendant approve land sales was ignored in all the land sales in Alto Bío Bío during the early 1880s in *Territorio y comunidades pehuenches del Alto Bío Bío*, 26.
13. Puelma Tupper, *Esposición ante el H. senado*, 10.
14. Ibid., 10–11.
15. Pinto Rodríguez, *La formación del Estado y la nación, y el pueblo mapuche*, 132–44.
16. Ibid., 138–39; Bengoa, *Historia del pueblo mapuche*, 180–83.
17. Pinto Rodríguez, *La formación del Estado y la nación, y el pueblo mapuche*, 145. See also Bengoa, *Historia del pueblo mapuche*, 167–72; Tomás Guevara, *Historia de la civilización de Araucanía* (Santiago: Imprenta Barcelona, 1902), 3:291.
18. Guevara, *Historia de la civilización de Araucanía*, 3:293.
19. *El Mercurio de Valparaíso*, 24 May 1859, and *El Ferrocarril*, no. 1054, May 1959, cited in Rodrigo Andreucci Aguilera, "La Incorporación de las Tierras de Arauco al Estado de Chile y la Posición Iusnaturalista de la Revista Católica," *Revista de Estudios Histórico-Jurídicos* 20 (1998): 48–49.
20. Cornelio Saavedra al Ministro de Estado en el Departamento de la Guerra, Valparaíso, 11 October 1861, in Cornelio Saavedra, *Documentos relativos a la ocupación de Arauco* (Santiago: Imprenta de La Libertad, 1870), 14.
21. Cornelio Saavedra, "Memoria de 1868, Establecimiento de la Línea de Malleco," Santiago, 8 May 1868, in ibid., 77–78.
22. Cornelio Saavedra al Ministro de Estado en el Departamento de la Guerra, Valparaíso, 11 October 1861, in ibid., 16.
23. Molina and Correa, *Territorio y comunidades pehuenches del Alto Bío Bío*, 27.
24. "Otorgamiento de Escrituras," Santiago, 16 October 1863, and "Otorgamiento de Escrituras," Santiago, 9 March 1873, in Julio Zenteno Barros, *Recopilación de leyes y decretos supremos sobre colonización* (Santiago: Imprenta Nacional, 1892), 144, 147–48.
25. Cornelio Saavedra, "Resumen y Apreciación Jeneral de los Datos e Ideas que Arrojan los Documentos Aquí Recopilados," in Saavedra, *Documentos relativos a la ocupación de Arauco*, 252.
26. Guevara, *Historia de la civilización de Araucanía*, 3:353.
27. Ibid., 3:373, 424.
28. Pinto Rodríguez, *La formación del Estado y la nación, y el pueblo mapuche*, 145.
29. Ibid., 241–43; Guevara, *Historia de la civilización de Araucanía*, 3:424–25.
30. Puelma Tupper, *Esposición ante el H. Senado*, 11–12.
31. Ibid., 12.
32. Ibid., 13.
33. Ibid., 12–14.
34. R. Fabián Berrios B., *Desde Caldera hasta Tacna: Testimonios de Rafael Segundo Torreblanca* (Santiago, 2012), 83.
35. Francisco Puelma Castillo, "Reseña Biográfica Parlamentaria," Biblioteca del Congreso Nacional, http://historiapolitica.bcn.cl/resenas_parlamentarias/

wiki/Francisco_Segundo_Puelma_Castillo (26 May 2017, 9:38AM); Gabriel Salazar Vergara and Carlos Altamirano Orrego, *Conversaciones con Carlos Altamirano: Memorias Críticas* (Santiago: Editorial Chile, 2011); Guevara, *Historia de la civilización de Araucanía*, 3:292.

36. Pedro Pablo Figueroa, *Diccionario biográfico de Chile* (Santiago: Imprenta Barcelona, 1897), 2:513–14.
37. Molina and Correa, *Territorio y comunidades pehuenches del Alto Bío Bío*, 20–21.
38. Ibid., 23–25; Guevara, *Historia de la civilización de Araucanía*, 3:476.
39. Guevara, *Historia de la civilización de Araucanía*, 3:469–70.
40. Hernán Ramírez Necoachea, *Obras escogidas* (Santiago: LOM Ediciones, 2007), 1:151; Oficina de Tierras y Colonización, Se Dicta su Reglamento, 28 December 1889, in Zenteno Barros, *Recopilación de leyes y decretos sobre colonización*, 25–26.
41. Puelma Tupper, *Esposición ante el H. Senado*, 14, 29; "Arrendamiento de Talajes en Alto Bío-Bío," 28 September 1887, and "Arrendamiento de Talajes en Alto Bío-Bío," 10 September 1889, in Zenteno Barros, *Recopilación de leyes y decretos sobre colonización*, 187–89.
42. Consejo de Defensa Fiscal, Informe No. 609 in Puelma Tupper, *Esposición ante el H. Senado*, 28–30.
43. Puelma Tupper, *Esposición ante el H. Senado*, 25.
44. Ibid., 30–31.
45. Ibid., 33.
46. For an interesting description of this oligarchy with an emphasis on the Orrego, Altamirano, and Puelma families, see Salazar Vergara and Altamirano Orrego, *Conversaciones con Carlos Altamirano*.
47. "Reclamación No. 57, Jorge Federico Bussey," in *Reclamaciones presentadas al tribunal anglo-chileno (1894–1896)* (Santiago: Imprenta y Librería Ercilla, 1896), 2:715–25.
48. Puelma Tupper, *Esposición ante el H. Senado*, 16.
49. Julio Zenteno Barros, *Recopilación de leyes y decretos supremos sobre colonización, Tercera Parte*, 2nd ed. (Santiago: Imprenta Nacional, 1896), 1325.
50. Consejo de Defensa Fiscal, Informe No. 609, in Puelma Tupper, *Esposición ante el H. Senado*, 25.
51. Puelma Tupper, *Esposición ante el H. Senado*, 12.
52. Ibid., 16–18.

Chapter 2. Campesinos, *Indígenas*, and Early Challenges to the Hacienda

1. For a description of the 1896 and 1898 laws as well as later colonization laws, including Decree No. 1,239, 15 October 1902, and Decree No. 9,622, 12 October 1908, which applied regulations for colonos who acquired land under the 1896 and 1898 laws, and Ley de Ocupantes Nacionales, Ley no. 2,087, 15 February 1908, see Congreso Nacional, Chile, *Comisión*

parlamentaria de colonización: informe, proyectos de ley, actas de sesiones i otros antecedentes (Santiago: Sociedad "Impr. y Litografía Universo," 1912), 223–29.
2. Ibid., 243.
3. Ministerio de Relaciones Exteriores, Santiago, 24 January 1907, and Santiago, 8 April 1907, in Ministerio de Relaciones Exteriores (hereafter MRREE), vol. 1343, ARNAD.
4. Oficio de ese Departamento (Inspección Jeneral de Tierras y Colonización), no. 179, 8 April 1907, a Intendencia de Cautín Oficio; Oficio No. 653, 7 May 1909; Oficio No. 1,036, 22 June 1909, and Decreto no. 560, 24 June 1909 in Ministerio de Tierras y Colonización (hereafter MTC), Oficio No. 73, 16 November 1918, Inspección Jeneral de Colonización, T. Urrutia, al Ministro de Colonización. Santiago, 20 November 1918 (Oficio No. 1,931) in Puelma Tupper, *Esposición ante el H. Senado*, 37–40.
5. Oficio No. 1,036, 22 June 1909, and Decreto no. 560, 24 June 1909, cited in MTC, Oficio No. 73, 16 November 1918. Inspección Jeneral de Colonización, T. Urrutia, al Ministro de Colonización. Santiago, 20 November 1918. (Oficio No.1,931) in Puelma Tupper, *Esposición ante el H. Senado*, 38–39.
6. Consejo de Defensa Fiscal, Informe No. 609, in Puelma Tupper, *Esposición ante el H. Senado*, 34; Jaime Flores Chávez, "La Construcción del Espacio: Una Mirada Histórica al Territorio Cordillerano de la Araucanía," in Andrés Núñez, Rafael Sánchez, Federico Arenas, eds., *Fronteras en movimiento e imaginarios geográficos: La cordillera de los Andes como espacialidad sociocultural* (Santiago: Instituto de geografía-RIL Editores, 2013), 433.
7. Consejo de Defensa Fiscal, Informe No. 609, in Puelma Tupper, *Esposición ante el H. Senado*, 34.
8. Ibid., 19–20.
9. Ibid., 34.
10. Ibid., 35.
11. MTC, Oficio No. 73, 16 November 1918, Inspección Jeneral de Colonización, T. Urrutia, al Ministro de Colonización. Santiago, 20 November 1918. (Oficio No. 1,931) in Puelma Tupper, *Esposición ante el H. Senado*, 37.
12. Oficio No. 1,036, 22 June 1909, and Decreto No. 560, 24 June 1909, cited in MTC, Oficio No. 73, 16 November 1918; Inspección Jeneral de Colonización, T. Urrutia, al Ministro de Colonización. Santiago, 20 November 1918. (Oficio No. 1,931) in Puelma Tupper, *Esposición ante el H. Senado*, 38–39.
13. Puelma Tupper, *Esposición ante el H. Senado*, 41.
14. *El Siglo de Los Ángeles*, 28 January 1926, 6.
15. Susana Bandieri, "Areas Andinas y Relaciones Fronterizas: Un Ajuste de Periodización," in Jorge Pinto Rodríguez, ed., *Araucanía y pampas: un mundo fronterizo en América del Sur* (Temuco: Ediciones Universidad de la Frontera, 1996), 195.
16. Carmen Norambuena Carrasco, "La chileanización de Neuquén," in ibid., 215.
17. Puelma Tupper, *Esposición ante el H. Senado*, 8.

18. Cámara de Senadores, *Boletín de Sesiones*, Sesión Ordinaria, 15 July 1919, Biblioteca del Congreso Nacional, Santiago (hereafter BCN).
19. Cámara de Senadores, *Boletín de Sesiones*, Sesión Estraordinaria, 23 January 1919, BCN.
20. Puelma Tupper, *Esposición ante el H. Senado*, 4.
21. Cámara de Diputados, *Boletín de Sesiones*, Sesión Ordinaria, 28 August 1905, BCN.
22. Puelma Tupper, *Esposición ante el H. senado*, 4–6.
23. Ibid., 6.
24. I narrate this history in more detail in *La Frontera*.
25. Puelma Tupper, *Esposición ante el H. senado*, 6.
26. Klubock, *La Frontera*, 46–52.
27. Puelma Tupper, *Esposición ante el H. senado*, 7.
28. Cámara de Diputados, *Boletín de Sesiones*, Sesión Ordinaria, 28 August 1905, BCN.
29. Congreso Nacional, Chile, *Comisión parlamentaria de colonización*, 257.
30. Cámara de Diputados, *Boletín de Sesiones*, Sesión Extraordinaria, 10 January 1910, BCN.
31. Ibid.
32. Puelma Tupper, *Esposición ante el H. Senado*, 8–9.
33. Sentencia, Juez Titular de Indios de Victoria, don Gustavo Bisquertt Susarte, November 1942, CONADI Archive, Archivo Regional de la Araucanía, Temuco (hereafter ARA).
34. The 1866 law on indigenous settlement employed colonial language to mandate the settlement of indigenous Mapuche in small communities, or reducciones. Títulos de Merced (land grant titles) were granted to communities organized around kinship groups headed by caciques or lonkos, which could demonstrate uninterrupted possession of their land. The process of settling Mapuches in reducciones began only in 1884 with the establishment of the Settlement Commission (Comisión Radicadora). The law radically reduced Mapuches' access to land and natural resources, while determining that members of small reducciones would hold land communally and that reducción land would be inalienable. In addition, the law created the position of Protector de Indígenas to represent indigenous reducciones' legal interests. The law and indigenous settlement are discussed in a number of works, including Fabián Almonacid, "El Problema de la Propiedad de Tierra en el Sur de Chile (1850–1930), *Historia* 42, no. 1 (June 2009).
35. Sentencia, Juez Titular de Indios de Victoria, don Gustavo Bisquertt Susarte.
36. For an account of this history, see also Molina and Correa, *Territorio y comunidades pehuenches del Alto Bío Bío*, 75–80.
37. Ministerio de Tierras y Colonización, 1930, vol. 64, Decreto 2243, cited in Mallon, "Victims into Emblems," 34.

38. Klubock, *La Frontera*, 34. This incident is documented in "Memoria de los trabajos llevados a cabo por el injeniero de la Comisión Radicadora de Indígenas que suscribe durante el año 1901," *Memoria de la Inspección Jeneral de Tierras i Colonización* (Santiago, 1905), 229–30.
39. Sentencia, Juez Titular de Indios de Victoria, don Gustavo Bisquertt Susarte.
40. Ministerio de Relaciones Exteriores, Culto i Colonización, Sección: Colonización; Solicitante Ignacio Maripí y otros; Materia: Piden que se les radique; Iniciada: 1912 in MRREE, vol. 1699, Sección Colonización, Solicitudes Particulares, 1912. Letras A a Ll, ARNAD; Klubock, *La Frontera*, 34.
41. Intendencia de Bio-Bio, Los Ángeles, 6 December 1919, vol. 1478, in Fernando Riquelme Barrera, "Adaptaciones y acomodos en los primeros años de las comunidades pewenche del Alto Bío Bío (1900–1930)," *Cuadernos de Historia* (Santiago), online version, December 2014, 10.
42. José Manuel Zavala Cepeda, "Documentos y Testimonios: El Pleito de Ralco en 1919," *CUHSO: Cultura, Hombre, Sociedad* (Universidad Católica de Temuco), 26, no. 2 (December 2016), 216–17. This document contains a letter from the Franciscan missionary Angel Saavedra to the Franciscan publication *El Misionero Franciscano* and a copy of a legal appeal to the Concepción appeals court by the Ralco community's lawyer, Domingo Ocampo, as well as a brief historical introduction by José Manuel Zavala Cepeda.
43. Ibid.
44. Ibid., 214–17.
45. Article from *Las Últimas Noticias*, republished in *El Siglo de Los Ángeles*, 2 December 1922, 4.
46. Ibid., 26 December 1922, 1.
47. *El Siglo de Los Ángeles*, 29 November 1924, 6, quoted in Riquelme Barrera, "Adaptaciones y acomodos," 9.
48. Ibid., 9.

Chapter 3. The *Inquilinos* Organize

1. *El Comercio*, 21 April 1929, 1 September 1929.
2. Sergio Grez Toso, "El Escarpado Camino Hacia la Legislación Social: Debates, Contradicciones y Encrucijadas en el Movimiento Obrero y Popular (Chile: 1901–1924)," Universidad de Chile, *Cyber Humanitatis*, no. 41 (Summer 2007): 2–5.
3. Sergio Grez Toso, *De la "regeneración del pueblo" a la huelga general: génesis y evolución histórica del movimiento popular en Chile (1810–1890)* (Santiago: DIBAM, 1998), 703–4.
4. Quoted in Nicolás Palacios, *La raza chilena* (Valparaíso: Imprenta y Litografía Alemana, 1904), 687–89.
5. *El Comercio*, 21 April 1929.

6. Information and documents about Juan Segundo Leiva Tapia and his family were provided to *El Diario Austral* by the notary Maximiliano González and the Conservador de Bienes Raíces in the city of Victoria and published after the rebellion in *El Diario Austral*, 4 July 1934, 5.
7. Fahrenkrog Reinhold, *La verdad sobre la revuelta de Ránquil*, *El Sur*, 22 July 1934.
8. Fahrenkrog Reinhold, *La verdad sobre la revuelta de Ránquil*, x.
9. Sindicato Agrícola Lonquimay al Intendente Cautín, 11 October 1929, Intendencia de Cautín (hereafter IC), vol. 324, Archivo Nacional, Santiago (hereafter AN).
10. Ibid.
11. For details on the estates' status, see Ministerio de la Propiedad Austral, Mensura de Tierras, "Informe de la Comisión Nominada por Decreto No. 265, de 27 de Marzo Último."
12. This process was remarkably similar in Colombia's coffee frontier region during the late 1920s and 1930s, where campesinos organized *ligas agrarias* (agrarian leagues) and unions, some affiliated with the Communist Party of Colombia and others with the populist Jorge Eliécer Gaitán's Unión Nacional Izquierdista Revolucionaria (UNIR). The leagues organized self-defense groups to combat evictions, invaded estates, and engaged in a wave of strikes. In addition, as in Chile, ocupantes petitioned the government for titles to public land they claimed had been usurped from the state by large estates. Arrendatorios on large estates similarly declared that they were colonos and that the land was public, not private, property. See LeGrand, *Frontier Expansion*, chapter 6.
13. For a description of *inquilinaje* during the 1920s and 1930s, see Loveman, *Struggle in the Countryside*, 29–34.
14. See *El Comercio*, 11 May 1930, for a description of payments to inquilinos. Loveman, *Struggle in the Countryside*, 49, also notes that in some regions by 1930 inquilinos had begun to earn wages as well as in kind payments, although this was not the norm nationally.
15. Fahrenkrog Reinhold, *La verdad sobre la revuelta de Ránquil*.
16. The gendered organization of production and reproduction within campesino households in Alto Bío Bío during this period resembles the case of the Aconcagua Valley in central Chile during the 1950s and 1960s, studied by Tinsman in *Partners in Conflict*.
17. For a study of how official documents in Chile elided women's labor, see Elizabeth Quay Hutchison, *Labors Appropriate to Their Sex: Gender, Labor, and Politics in Urban Chile, 1900–1930* (Durham: Duke University Press, 2001).
18. Notes from Isidora Aguirre interview with Emelina Sagredo, 1965, Apuntes de Investigación, Isidora Aguirre, Archivo Digital, http://isidoraaguirre.usach.cl/texto/ia-026-007-016/, 9 October 2019.
19. Fahrenkrog Reinhold, *La verdad sobre la revuelta de Ránquil*, x.

20. *El Comercio*, 10 June 1928, in Flores, "Un Episodio en la Historia Social de Chile," 81–82.
21. For the cases cited in this paragraph, see also Klubock, "Ránquil," 130.
22. *El Diario Austral*, 26 May 1934.
23. See, for example, Juzgado Militar de Concepción (hereafter JMC), Causa 187-34, Evasión de Detenidos; Causa 189-34, Desaparecimiento de Juan Jara; Causa 252-34, Flagelaciones a Alfonso Wenceslao—jornalero, ARNAD.
24. JMC, Causa 189-34, ARNAD.
25. Comunicación del Intendente al Prefecto de Carabineros, 9 December 1932, IC, vol. 387, AN.
26. George McCutchen McBride, *Chile: Land and Society* (New York: American Geographical Society, 1936), 294. Quoted also in Klubock, *La Frontera*, 93–94.
27. Mark Jefferson, *Recent Colonization in Chile* (New York: Oxford University Press, 1921), 5. Quoted also in Klubock, *La Frontera*, 94.
28. *El Siglo de Los Ángeles*, 14 July 1924, 5.
29. Quoted in Loveman, *Struggle in the Countryside*, 38.
30. *El Comercio*, 12 February 1928, in Flores, "Un Episodio en la Historia Social de Chile," 81.
31. Census of Guayalí ocupantes in Corte de Apelaciones de Temuco, Sucesos de Lonquimay, Antecedentes remetidos por el Ministerio de Tierras y Colonización, 3 September 1934, Conservador de Bienes Raíces, Temuco (hereafter CBBRR-T).
32. Notes from Isidora Aguirre interview with Emelina Sagredo.
33. Klubock, *La Frontera*, 94–95.
34. Cámara de Diputados, *Boletín de Sesiones*, Sesión Extraordinaria, 29 December 1931, BCN.
35. Ibid., 28 January 1936, BCN.
36. Dirección General de Tierras y Colonización al MTC, "Ley Sobre la Constitución de la Propiedad Austral: Anomalías y Omisiones en los Expedientes que Se Tramitan," November 1939, MTC, Providencias, 1939, vol. 1814. ARNAD. I discuss this in Klubock, *La Frontera*, 96.
37. Klubock, *La Frontera*, 96.
38. Loveman, *Struggle in the Countryside*, 41–43. See Jorge Rojas Flores, *La dictadura de Ibáñez y los sindicatos, 1927–1931* (Santiago: DIBAM, 1993), 61–64.
39. Fabián Almonacid, "El Problema de la Propiedad de la Tierra en el Sur de Chile (1850–1930)."
40. Quoted in M. C. Mirow, "Origins of the Social Function of Property in Chile," *Fordham Law Review* 80, no. 3 (December 2011): 1183.
41. *El Diario Austral*, 21 March 1926, 5.
42. Ministerio de Agricultura, Industria, Colonización, Informe del Abogado Consultar and Oficio al Ministerio del Interior, 5 February 1925, MTC, Oficios, 1–341, 1925, ARNAD.

43. Ministro de Tierras y Colonización al Ministerio del Interior, 22 May 1925 and 25 November; Ministro de Agricultura, Industria, Colonización al Ministro del Interior, 21 July 1925; Ministro de Tierras al Ministro de Justicia, 16 December 1925; Ministro de Tierras al Ministro del Interior, 30 December 1925, in Ministerio de Agricultura, MTC, Oficios, 1–341, 1925, and Ministerio de Tierras y Colonización reports on Nueva Italia, 30 April and 24 July 1925, in Ministerio de Agricultura, MTC, Sección Colonización, Decretos, 199–300, May-June 1925, ARNAD.
44. Cámara de Diputados, *Boletín de Sesiones*, Sesión Extraordinaria, 7 December 1926, BCN.
45. Loveman, *Struggle in the Countryside*, 63, 73–75. For a detailed study of both Ibáñez's repressive techniques and corporatist labor reforms, see Rojas, *La dictadura de Ibáñez*.
46. Ministerio de Fomento, *Memoria de Fomento, 1927* (Santiago, 1927), 11–13; Klubock, *La Frontera*, 97.
47. Ministerio de Fomento, *Memoria de Fomento, 1928*, (Santiago, 1928), 94; Klubock, *La Frontera*, 97–98.
48. Ministerio de Fomento, *Memoria de Fomento, 1928*; Klubock, *La Frontera*, 97–98.
49. Oficio del Intendente al Ministro de Fomento, 16 January 1928, IC, vol. 264, AN.
50. Oficio al Ministro de Fomento, 21 March 1928, IC, vol. 264, 1928, AN.
51. Víctor García Garcena, "El Problema de la Colonización: Estudio Sobre la Ley 5,604," Thesis, Facultad de Leyes, Universidad de Chile, 1936, 43. For the full text of the law establishing the Caja, see Ministerio de Fomento, Ley No. 4,496, 15 December 1928, BCN.
52. *El Comercio*, 16 December 1928. For the text of the law, see Ministerio del Fomento, Ley No. 4,531, 14 January 1929, BCN.
53. Ministerio del Interior, Decreto Supremo No. 2826, 30 April 1927, IC, vol. 269, AN.
54. Telegrama del Ministerio del Interior al Intendente, 3 Octubre 1929, IC, vol. 280, 1929, AN.
55. Letter to Señor Ministro del Interior, don Carlos Ibáñez del Campo, 9 April 1927, in Ministerio de Agricultura, Industria, y Colonización, Sección Colonización, Providencias, July-September, 1927, ARNAD. For this paragraph, see Klubock, *La Frontera*, 99.
56. Gobernación de Villarrica, Pitrufquén, Gobernador-Villarrica al Intendente de Cautín, 6 November 1929, IC, vol. 399, AN.
57. Comunicación del Gobernador de Villarrica al Intendente, 6 November 1929, and Comunicación del Gobernador de Villarrica al Intendente, 7 November 1929, IC, vol. 279, AN.
58. Circular del Ministerio de Fomento al Intendente, 29 April 1929, IC, vol. 281, 1929, AN. Also in Klubock, *La Frontera*, 100.

59. Comunicación del Intendente al Prefecto de Carabineros, 26 August 1933, IC, vol. 414, 1933, AN. Also in Klubock, *La Frontera*, 100.
60. Letter from Abelino Grandón. 15 August 1929; Surveyor's report to Agrimensor Regional, Angol, 8 December 1929, in MTC, Providencias, vol. 165, ARNAD.
61. Carlos Valenzuela Huerta, Intendente al Ministerio de Tierras y Colonización, MTC, Providencias, 1930, vol. 165, ARNAD.
62. *El Llanquihue*, January, 1929, in MTC, Providencias, 1930, vol. 167, ARNAD.
63. Ministerio de Propiedad Austral, Oficina de Osorno, 15 March 1930, MTC, Providencias, vol. 167, 1930, ARNAD. See also Klubock, *La Frontera*, 98.
64. Solicitud al Intendente de Pedro Ugalde Barrios, agricultor, 13 October 1928. IC, vol. 261, 1928, AN. See also Klubock, *La Frontera*, 100.
65. Solicitud al Intendente de Eduardo Slano Illanes y Santiago Viñuela, agricultores, 13 October 1928, IC, vol. 261, 1928, AN. Also in Klubock, *La Frontera*, 100.
66. Comunicación del Intendente Suplente al Prefecto de Carabineros, 10 April 1931, IC, vol. 376, AN.
67. Comunicación del Secretario de Bienestar a la Intendencia, 7 April 1930; Informe de Carabineros a la Prefectura de Cautín, 20 April 1930, IC, vol. 305, 1930, AN. Also in Klubock, *La Frontera*, 100.
68. Telegrama de Pedro Soto B. al Intendente, 27 December 1929. IC, vol. 298, AN.
69. Telegrama de Alfredo Lacourt al Intendente, 29 July 1929. IC, vol. 278, 1929, AN.
70. *El Siglo de Los Ángeles*, 7 February 1929, 4.
71. *Sindicatos blancos* had been organized since 1923 in a national federation of Catholic unions identified with the church's social teachings and, by 1927, the corporatist social policy of the Ibáñez regime. See Rojas Flores, *La dictadura de Ibáñez y los sindicatos*, 140–42.
72. Cámara de Diputados, *Boletín de Sesiones*, Sesión Ordinaria, 16 August 1926, BCN.
73. Oficio al Ministro de Fomento, 10 September 1928, IC, vol. 268, AN.
74. Telegrams from Carlos Ibáñez del Campo, Ministerio del Interior, to Gobernador de Traiguén, 11, 14, 15, 16 February 1927, in Cámara de Diputados, *Boletín de Sesiones*, Sesión Ordinaria, 15 January 1929, BCN.
75. Sumario mandado a instruir por la gobernación departamental por providencia No. 459 para establecer la efectividad de las actividades de agitadores del fundo Pellahuén. Fiscal: Capitán de Carabineros, D. Humberto Fuenzalida Espinoza, 16–26 October 1928, Ministerio del Interior (hereafter MI), ARNAD.
76. *Sesta Memoria del director de la Oficina de la Mensura de Tierras*, 148–49; Argentina, Ministerio de Relaciones Exteriores, Informes Consulares, 1905, *Boletín*, vols. 7–8, 11; Cámara de Diputados, *Diario de Sesiones*, Sesión Extraordinaria, 16 January 1914, BCN; Sindicato Pellahuén, "Demanda Sobre Posesión de este Fundo" (Santiago: Imprenta el Colono, 1906); Tomás

Ramírez, *Pellahuén: sus títulos y sus derechos, discursos pronunciados por el diputado Santiago don Tomás Ramírez Frías* (Santiago: Imprenta Universo, 1922). I summarize some of this history in Klubock, *La Frontera*, 44–45.
77. Comunicación del Ministerio del Interior al Intendente, 23 July 1930, IC, vol.306, 1930, AN.
78. Telegrama Carlos Ibáñez a Intendente, 5 May 1930, IC, vol.306, 1930, AN.

Chapter 4. Populism in the Countryside

1. See the full text of the interview between Ibáñez and Leiva Tapia in *El Comercio*, 9 December 1928.
2. *El Comercio*, 9 December 1928.
3. *El Comercio*, 31 March 1929.
4. *El Comercio* 12 May 1929.
5. *El Comercio*, 11 January 1931.
6. *El Comercio*, 26 April 1931.
7. *El Comercio*, 7 April 1929.
8. *El Comercio*, 28 April 1929.
9. Comunicación del Sindicato Agrícola de Lonquimay al Intendente, 29 September 1929, IC, vol. 278, AN.
10. Comunicación del Sindicato Agrícola de Lonquimay al Intendente, 29 September 1929, and Telegrama a Ibáñez del Campo, 27 September 1929, IC, vol. 279, AN.
11. Telegrama del subdelegado suplente Moraga al gobernador de Victoria, 6 October 1929; Comunicación del Gobernador de Victoria, 14 October 1929, IC, vol. 279, AN.
12. *El Comercio*, 20 October 1929.
13. *El Comercio*, 29 September 1929.
14. *El Diario Austral*, 9 December 1927, 7.
15. *El Diario Austral*, 20 April 1930, 14.
16. Informe a la Prefectura de Carabineros de Cautín, 17 January 1930, IC, vol. 298, AN.
17. *El Siglo de Los Ángeles*, 6 December 1928, 2; 11 December 1928, 2.
18. *El Siglo de Los Ángeles*, 30 April 1931, 3.
19. *El Siglo de Los Ángeles*, 19 March 1931, 3; 27 April 1931, 1.
20. Telegrama a Carlos Ibáñez del Campo, 20 September 1929, IC, vol. 399, AN.
21. "Telegrama Circular de S.E. el Presidente de la República" in *El Comercio*, 1 September 1929.
22. Comunicación de Gobernación de Victoria a la Intendencia, 12 November 1929, IC, vol. 279, AN; Telegrama de Carlos Ibáñez del Campo, 11 November 1929, IC, vol. 279, AN.
23. Comunicación del Prefecto de Carabineros al Intendente, 16 November 1929, Comunicación del Intendente al Prefecto de Carabineros, 14 October

1929, Comunicación de Prefecto de Carabineros a Intendente, 15 November 1929, IC, vol. 279, AN.
24. Comunicación de Gobernación de Victoria a la Intendencia, 12 November 1929; Telegrama de Carlos Ibáñez del Campo, 11 November 1929, IC, vol. 279, AN.
25. Telegrama de Carlos Ibáñez al Intendente, 23 January 1930, IC, vol. 298, AN.
26. Comunicación del Ministerio de Fomento al Intendente, 28 September 1929; Telegrama, Ministerio de Fomento a Intendente, 9 July 1929, IC, vol. 281, 1929, AN.
27. Telegrama subsecretario de Interior a Intendente, 15 October 1929, IC, vol. 283, 1929, AN.
28. Petition from directorate of the Sindicato Agrícola Lonquimay to President Carlos Ibáñez, nd, in IC, vol. 279, AN. The union leadership denounced "abuses by landowners" and "violent expulsions" in a letter to Cautín's intendant dated 10 October 1929, IC, vol. 324, AN.
29. Comunicación del Gobernador de Victoria Salomón Ascui G. al Intendente, 14 October 1929. IC, vol. 279, AN.
30. Telegrama de Gobernador de Lautaro Guillermo Carmona a Intendente, 10 July 1929, IC, vol. 299, AN. The case in Lautaro's court was no. 1522 against Benjamín Cáceres and others (1928).
31. Telegrama gobernador de Victoria a Intendencia, 14 February 1930, IC, vol. 297, AN.
32. Telegrama del Ministerio del Interior al Intendente, 24 December 1929, IC, vol. 280, AN.
33. Telegrama del Ministerio del Interior al Intendente, 24 December 1929.
34. Telegrama gobernador de Victoria a Intendencia, 14 February 1930, IC, vol. 297, AN.
35. Carabineros de Chile, Prefectura de Cautín no. 12, "Sub-Teniente Osterstein Axt, Comandante de la Tenencia de Curacautín a Prefectura de Carabineros 'Cautín,'" 24 April and 28 May 1929 IC, vol. 287, AN.
36. Telegrama de Gobernador Benavente (Mulchén) a Intendencia, 16 January 1930, IC, vol. 298, AN.
37. Telegrama Carlos Ibáñez a Intendente, 5 May 1930, IC, vol. 306, AN.
38. *El Comercio*, 17 November 1929; Cámara de Diputados, *Boletín de Sesiones*, Sesión Extraordinaria, 30 October 1929, BCN.
39. Cámara de Diputados, *Boletín de Sesiones*, Sesión Extraordinaria, 30 October 1929.
40. Gould describes a similar process in the politics of Nicaraguan campesinos in *To Lead as Equals*.
41. The language is that of the deputy Carlos Alberto Martínez in Cámara de Diputados, *Boletín de Sesiones*, Sesión Ordinaria, 9 July 1934, BCN.
42. The decree can be found in *Boletín de Tierras y Colonización*, no. 2, 1930, 27 March 1930, 42 and in IC, vol. 334, AN.

43. Cámara de Diputados, *Boletín de Sesiones*, Sesión Ordinaria, 9 July 1934, BCN.
44. *El Comercio*, 9 March 1930.
45. Intendente de Cautín al Ministerio del Interior, Propone vocales obreros para integrar Juntas Vecinos Provincia Cautín, Temuco, 28 July 1930, IC, vol. 309, AN.
46. *La Nación*, 18 January 1930, cited in Andrew Barnard, *El Partido Comunista de Chile, 1922–1947* (Santiago: Ariadne Ediciones, 2017), chap. 3, n. 267.
47. Rojas Flores, *La dictadura de Ibáñez y los sindicatos (1927–1931)*, 58.
48. Intendencia de Bío Bío, Los Angeles, 8 April 1930, Transcribe telegrama Sub-Secretario Interior, sobre un denuncio Sucesión Bunster, Intendencia de Bío-Bío (hereafter IBB), vol. 76, AN.
49. *El Siglo de Los Ángeles*, 8 April 1930, 3.
50. Memoria Anual de la Secretaría de Bienestar Social de la Provincia de Cautín, 1929, 2 January 1930, IC, vol. 299, AN.
51. Carabineros de Chile, Prefectura Bío Bío, Segunda Comisaría, no. 355, Informa sobre un denuncio de la Sucesión Luis Martín Bunster en contra del Sindicato Agrícola Lonquimay, 15 April 1930, IBB, vol. 76, AN.
52. Comunicación de Prefectura de Carabineros al Intendente, 22 April 1930, and Comunicación de la Subdelegación de Lonquimay a la Intendencia, 21 April 1930 in IC, vol. 305, AN.
53. Carabineros de Chile, Prefectura Bío Bío, Segunda Comisaría, no. 355, Informa sobre un denuncio de la Sucesión Luis Martín Bunster en contra del Sindicato Agrícola Lonquimay, 15 April 1930, IBB, vol. 76, AN.

Chapter 5. Agrarian Reform Arrives in Alto Bío Bío

1. *El Comercio*, 27 April 1930.
2. *El Comercio*, 11 May 1930.
3. Ibid.
4. Ibid.
5. Ibid.
6. Ibid.
7. *El Comercio*, 20 May 1930.
8. *El Comercio*, 1 June 1930.
9. Ministerio de Fomento, Decreto Número 1,730, 31 July 1930. This decree was published in its entirety in Cámara de Diputados, *Boletín de Sesiones*, Sesión Ordinaria, 9 July 1934, BCN.
10. Ministerio de la Propiedad Austral, Mensura de Tierras, "Informe de la Comisión Nominada por Decreto No. 265, de 27 de Marzo Último sobre el Problema del Alto Bío-Bío."
11. Ministerio de Fomento, Decreto Número 1,730, 31 July 1930.
12. Cámara de Diputados, *Boletín de Sesiones*, Sesión Ordinaria, 9 July 1934, BCN.

13. Ibid.
14. Decree, 2243, 26 August 1930, in Corte de Apelaciones de Temuco, Sucesos de Lonquimay, Antecedentes remitidos por el Ministerio de Tierras y Colonización, 3 September 1934, CBBRR-T.
15. Decree No. 2243, 26 August 1930.
16. Ministerio de Propiedad Austral, Decree No. 1,707 in Cámara de Diputados, *Boletín de Sesiones*, Sesión Extraordinaria, 1 December 1943, BCN.
17. *El Comercio*, 9 November 1930.
18. Ibid.
19. *El Comercio*, 24 December 1930.
20. Ibid.
21. *El Diario Austral*, 1 November 1930, 7.
22. Juzgado de Indios de Victoria, Radicación, no. 2099, 19 January 1939, CONADI Archive, ARA.
23. Juzgado de Indios de Victoria, Radicación, no. 2099, 19 January 1939.
24. Notes from Isidora Aguirre interview with Emelina Sagredo.
25. Florencia Mallon makes this argument in *Courage Tastes of Blood*.
26. *El Comercio*, 18 and 28 January 1931.
27. *El Comercio*, 1 February 1931.
28. Letter from Francisco Vial Freire por Sucesión Luis Martín Bunster to President, Cámara de Diputados, 17 February 1932, in Cámara de Diputados, *Boletín de Sesiones*, Sesión Extraordinaria, 17 February 1932, BCN.
29. Report of Intendente del Bío Bío L. E. Julio, to Ministro del Interior, 1 June 1931, in Cámara de Diputados, *Boletín de Sesiones*, Sesión Extraordinaria, 17 February 1932, BCN.
30. The police reports are included with the other documentation cited above in Cámara de Diputados, *Boletín de Sesiones*, Sesión Extraordinaria, 17 February 1932, BCN.
31. *El Comercio*, 30 August 1931 in Flores, "Un Episodio en la Historia Social de Chile," 75–76.
32. *El Comercio*, 14 June 1931.

Chapter 6. The Fall of Ibáñez and Political Radicalization in Southern Chile

1. *El Siglo de Los Ángeles*, 16 April 1931, 1.
2. Loveman, *Chile*, 185–87. For the social impact of the Great Depression in Chile, see Ángela Vergara, "Chilean Workers and the Great Depression, 1930–1938," in Drinot and Knight, eds., *The Great Depression in Latin America*.
3. Loveman, *Chile*, 187; Michael Monteón, *Chile and the Great Depression: The Politics of Underdevelopment, 1927–1948* (Tempe, AZ: Center for Latin American Studies Press, Arizona State University, 1998), 42–47.

4. William F. Sater, "The Abortive Krontadt: The Chilean Naval Mutiny of 1931," *Hispanic American Historical Review* 60, no. 2 (1980); Paul W. Drake, *Socialism and Populism in Chile, 1932–1952* (Urbana: University of Illinois Press, 1978), 64–65; Carlos Alfaro Hidalgo, "La Sublevación de la Armada de Chile de 1931: ¿Revindicaciones Laborales o Infiltración Comunista?," *Cooperativa de Estudios Históricos y Ciencias Sociales, Revista Norte Histórico*, no. 1 (2014); Olga Ulianova and Alfredo Riquelme Segovia, *Chile en los archivos soviéticos, 1922–1991* (Santiago: DIBAM-LOM Ediciones, 2009), 2:34–42.
5. Drake, *Socialism and Populism in Chile*, 64–65; Monteón, *Chile during the Great Depression*, 73.
6. Ulianova and Riquelme Segovia, *Chile en los archivos soviéticos, 1922–1991*, 2:41–43.
7. *El Diario Austral*, 4 October 1931, cited in Bengoa, *Historia rural de chile*, vol. 2, chap. 6, n. 10.
8. *El Mercurio*, 4 October 1931, in Palacios Ríos, *Ránquil*, 62.
9. Monteón, *Chile and the Great Depression*, 75–81.
10. Informe sobre Colonización en Alto Bío-Bío. Del gobernador de Victoria al Ministro de Tierras y Colonización, 5 January 1932, IC, vol. 378, AN.
11. Informe sobre Colonización en Alto Bío-Bío.
12. Ibid.
13. Monteón, *Chile and the Great Depression*, 81–83.
14. Drake, *Socialism and Populism in Chile*, 82.
15. Elizabeth Lira and Brian Loveman, *Arquitectura política y seguridad interior del estado 1811–1999* (Santiago: DIBAM/Centro de Investigaciones Diego Barros Arana, 2002), 97–100.
16. Monteón, *Chile and the Great Depression*, 83–84.
17. Quoted in Felipe Portales, *Los mitos de la democracia chilena* (Santiago: Editorial Catalonia, 2010), 204.
18. Ibid., 205.
19. Manuel Concha Pedregal, Director General de Carabineros al Ministerio del Interior, 23 March 1932, MI, vol. 8146, ARNAD.
20. *El Diario Austral*, 29 September 1932, 7.
21. *El Diario Austral*, 7 September 1932, 7, and 29 October 1932, 9.
22. Comunicación de la Dirección de Distrito de Pucón al Intendente, 8 August 1932, IC, vol. 421, AN.
23. Carabineros de Chile, Prefectura de Cautín, no. 12, Copias de telegramas recibidos de Pucón, 27 August 1932; Telegrama del Gobernador Carlos Bravo a la Intendencia, 24 August 1932; Telegrama al Ministerio de Tierras y Colonización de Carlos Holzapfeld, Federico Kaun (for Percy Compton), Alberto Ansorena, Roberto Geis, Arnaldo Sindia-Como, Luis Gomez, Emilio Meldher, Pedro Ansorena, 20 August 1932; Telegrama de Percy Compton al Intendente de Temuco, 18 August 1932, in IC, vol. 382, AN. Telegrama del Gobernador Carlos F. Bravo, Pucón, al Intendente, 22 August 1932, IC, vol. 387, AN.

24. *El Diario Austral*, 29 September 1932, 7.
25. *El Diario Austral*, 15 January 1933, 7.
26. Comunicación del Gobernador de Villarrica al Ministerio del Interior, 10 November 1932, IC, vol. 403, AN.
27. Ministerio de Tierras y Colonización, "Ocupación indebida de terrenos en Pucón," 16 December 1932 and "Da cuenta de los hechos ocurridos durante la mensura de los terrenos de Palguin," November 1932; Comunicación de la Dirección General de Tierras y Colonización al Ministro del Interior, recibida en Temuco 21 December 1932, IC, vol. 404, AN.
28. "Informa Reclamación de don Gonzalo Bunster Gómez contra Sindicato Agrícola Lonquimay," 5 January 1933, IC, vol. 400, AN. See also the account of this incident in *El Diario Austral*, 20 December 1932.
29. Telegrama del Intendente de Bío Bío al Intendente de Cautín, 19 December 1932, IC, vol. 400, AN.
30. "Informa Reclamación de don Gonzalo Bunster Gómez contra Sindicato Agrícola Lonquimay."
31. "Documentos referidos a la denuncia del Sindicato Agrícola Lonquimay contra Gonzalo Bunster G."; "Damos cuenta al señor Subdelegado de que somos víctimas de atropellos y amenazas de parte del señor Gonzalo Bunster Gómez," 16 December 1932; "Informa Reclamación de don Gonzalo Bunster contra Sindicato Agrícola Lonquimay," IC, vol. 400, AN.
32. "Documentos referidos a la denuncia del Sindicato Agrícola Lonquimay contra Gonzalo Bunster G."; *El Comercio*, 8 January 1933.
33. *Justicia*, 10 February 1933.
34. *El Diario Austral*, 19 August 1931, 8.
35. Drake, *Socialism and Populism in Chile*, 70; Elías Lafertte, *Vida de un comunista* (Santiago: np, 1961), 245.
36. *El Sur*, 22 and 27 January 1933.
37. *El Diario Austral*, 30 January 1933, 1–2.
38. Telegrama a Intendencia, 27 October 1932. IC, vol. 383, 1932, AN.
39. *El Diario Austral*, 27 January 1933, 7.
40. Ibid. Comunicación de la Compañía Agrícola y Ganadera de Toltén, 9 November 1932. IC, vol. 403, AN.
41. Comunicación de la Compañía Agrícola y Ganadera de Toltén al Gobernador del Departamento de Villarrica, 9 November 1932, IC, vol. 403, AN.
42. See, for example, Telegrama Ministro de Tierras a Intendente, 18 November 1932, IC, vol. 384, AN.
43. Comunicación de la Comisaría de Pitrufquén a la Prefectura de Carabineros de Cautín, 15 January 1933, IC, vol. 403, AN.
44. *El Diario Austral*, 31 March 1933, 4.
45. *El Sur*, 10 March 1933.
46. Intendencia de Bío-Bío al Ministro del Interior, "Sobre aplicación Circular ocupación violenta de terrenos de terceros," 5 May 1933, MI, vol. 8676, ARNAD.

47. Comunicación del Ministerio del Interior al Intendente, 6 April 1933, IC, vol. 342, AN.
48. Dirección de Investigaciones al Ministerio del Interior, "Actividades comunistas," 8 April 1933, MI, vol. 8375, ARNAD.
49. Ministerio de Relaciones Exteriores, Confidencial No. 21, 26 May 1933, and Confidencial No. 13, 29 April 1933, in MI, vol. 8375, ARNAD.
50. *El Comercio*, 5 November 1933. See also Lafertte, *Vida de un comunista*.
51. Lafertte, *Vida de un comunista*, 255–63, 274; Ulianova and Riquelme Segovia, *Chile en los archivos soviéticos*, 2:418.
52. Ulianova and Riquelme Segovia, *Chile en los archivos soviéticos*, 2:418–22. Ulianova provides one of the most complete analyses of the Communist Party's role in the Sindicato Agrícola Lonquimay and the 1934 rebellion. It is based on her research in Comintern archives, in this book, and in her article "Levantamiento Campesino de Lonquimay."
53. Ulianova and Riquelme Segovia, *Chile en los archivos soviéticos*, 2:427.
54. Lira and Loveman, *Arquitectura política y seguridad interior del estado 1811–1999*, 23, cited in Portales, *Los mitos de la democracia chilena*, 206.
55. Verónica Valdivia Ortíz de Zárate, *La Milicia Republicana: los civiles in armas, 1932–1936* (Santiago: DIBAM, 1992), 14.
56. Ibid., 15.
57. Ibid., 17–18.
58. Monteón, *Chile during the Great Depression*, 184–86. See also Luis Corvalán Márquez, "Orígenes, Trayectoria e Identidades Ideológicas de la Milicia Republicana, 1932–1936," *Izquierdas*, September 2016.
59. Monteón, *Chile during the Great Depression*, 185.
60. *El Sur*, 22 July 1934.
61. A copy of the Consejo's memorandum to the Ministerio de Tierras y Colonización was printed in *El Diario Austral*, 22 July 1934, 1.
62. *El Sur*, 22 July 1934.
63. Copy of decree in Corte de Apelaciones de Temuco, Sucesos de Lonquimay, Antecedentes remetidos por el Ministerio de Tierras y Colonización, 3 September 1934, CBBRR-T.
64. Telegrama del Subsecretario de Tierras a Intendente, 27 March 1933; Telegrama a Intendencia, 27 March 1933; Comunicación de la Intendencia al Ministerio del Interior, 29 March 1933; Comunicación del Intendente al Prefecto de Carabineros, 31 March 1933; Comunicación de la Prefectura de Carabineros al Intendente, 11 April 1933, IC, vol. 404, AN.
65. Comunicación del Intendente al Prefecto de Carabineros, 26 August 1933, IC, vol. 414, AN.
66. *El Diario Austral*, 6 and 8 May 1933, 1.
67. Ibid.
68. *El Diario Austral*, 4 February 1934, 7.
69. Comunicación entre Intendencia y Ministerio del Interior, 12 January 1933, IC, vol. 413, AN.

70. *La Opinión,* 12 April 1934.
71. *La Opinión,* 19 May 1934.
72. *La Opinión,* 26 March 1934.
73. Ibid. I also narrate these events in *La Frontera.*
74. *El Diario Austral,* 21 April 1934, 5.
75. *El Diario Austral,* 23 April 1934, 3.
76. *El Diario Austral,* 6 May 1934, 7.
77. *El Diario Austral,* 12 May 1934, 1.
78. *El Diario Austral,* 6 November 1933, 6.
79. Ibid.
80. *El Diario Austral,* 8 November 1933, 1.
81. Bengoa, *Historia del pueblo mapuche,* 391–98. See also José Bengoa, *Historia de un conflicto: el estado y los mapuches en el siglo XX* (Santiago: Planeta, 1999), and Mallon, "From Victims to Emblems."
82. "Sesión Inaugural de la Segunda Convención Nacional de la Central Socialista de Colonización," 5 November 1933 in MI, vol. 8099, ARNAD; *El Diario Austral,* 6 November 1933, 6.
83. *El Diario Austral,* 6 November 1933, 6.
84. Carabineros de Chile, Dirección General, al Ministro del Interior, "Sobre contestación dada por el Partido Comunista al Manifiesto de S.E. el Presidente de la República," 27 January 1933 in MI, vol. 8375, ARNAD.
85. Ibid.
86. Comité Regional del Partido Comunista, Concepción, "Ante el Segundo Aniversario de la Insurrección de los Marineros, Obreros, Empleados, Campesinos, Profesores," 1 September 1933, MI, vol. 8373, ARNAD.
87. Ibid.
88. Ibid.
89. Julio Pinto Vallejos and Verónica Valdivia Ortíz de Zárate, *Revolución proletaria o querida chusma: socialismo y Alessandrismo en la pugna por la politización pampina (1911–1932)* (Santiago: LOM Ediciones, 2001).

Chapter 7. Expulsion from the Nitrito Valley

1. Dirección General de Tierras y Colonización, Comisión Guayalí da cuenta de su cumplimiento, Santiago, June 1934, in Corte de Apelaciones de Temuco, Sucesos de Lonquimay, Antecedentes remetidos por el Ministerio de Tierras y Colonización.
2. Comunicación del Ministerio de Tierras y Colonización al Intendente, 29 January 1934, IC, vol. 418, AN.
3. Orden de Citación, 17 January 1934, Campamento Guayalí; Ordén de Citación, 27 January 1934, Campamento Guayalí; Notificación, Campamento de Guayalí, 1 February 1934; Notificación, Guayalí, 6 February 1934; Notificación, Campamento Guayalí, 15 February 1934; Notificación, Campamento Guayalí, 16 February 1934, all in Corte de Apelaciones de Temuco,

Sucesos de Lonquimay, Antecedentes remetidos por el Ministerio de Tierras y Colonización.
4. "Solicitud" in Corte de Apelaciones de Temuco, Sucesos de Lonquimay, Antecedentes remetidos por el Ministerio de Tierras y Colonización.
5. Dirección General de Tierras y Colonización, Comisión Guayalí da cuenta de su cumplimiento.
6. Census taken by government surveyor in Corte de Apelaciones de Temuco, Sucesos de Lonquimay, Antecedentes remetidos por el Ministerio de Tierras y Colonización.
7. Solicita se notifique personas que indica el decreto 4834 del Ministerio de Tierras, Campamento de Guayalí, 29 January 1934, in Corte de Apelaciones de Temuco, Sucesos de Lonquimay, Antecedentes remetidos por el Ministerio de Tierras y Colonización.
8. "Actas de Declaración," 18, 21, and 22 January 1934, in Corte de Apelaciones de Temuco, Sucesos de Lonquimay, Antecedentes remetidos por el Ministerio de Tierras y Colonización.
9. Dirección General de Tierras y Colonización, Comisión Guayalí da cuenta de su cumplimiento.
10. Tinsman, *Partners in Conflict*. My analysis here is influenced by Tinsman's study of the subordination of female campesinas' labor to both male inquilinos and patrones in the Aconcagua Valley.
11. Dirección General de Tierras y Colonización, Comisión Guayalí da cuenta de su cumplimiento.
12. *El Diario Austral*, 31 January 1934, 4.
13. *El Diario Austral*, 4 February 1934, 7; 8 February 1934, 2.
14. *El Diario Austral*, 22 July 1934, 1.
15. Intendencia de Cautín a Carabineros de Chile, Regimiento "Cautín," 13 February 1934, in file of uncatalogued documents of the Intendencia de Cautín related to the Sucesos de Lonquimay, ARA.
16. Dirección General de Tierras y Colonización, Comisión Guayalí da cuenta de su cumplimiento.
17. Telegrama, Arturo Fernández Correa, 18 February 1934, in Corte de Apelaciones de Temuco, Sucesos de Lonquimay, Antecedentes remetidos por el Ministerio de Tierras y Colonización.
18. Dirección General de Tierras y Colonización, Comisión Guayalí da cuenta de su cumplimiento.
19. Ibid.
20. Telegrama del Director de Tierras al Intendente, 13 March 1934, IC, vol. 419, AN.
21. Telegrama, Intendencia de Cautín, 13 March 1934, in file of uncatalogued documents of the Intendencia de Cautín related to the Sucesos de Lonquimay.
22. A. Aguilera, Surveyor to Sr. Jefe de La Comisión del Ministerio de Tierras y Colonización en Guayalí, March 15, 1934, in Corte de Apelaciones de Temuco, Sucesos de Lonquimay, Antecedentes remetidos por el Ministerio de Tierras y Colonización.

23. Ministerio del Interior, Intendencias y Gobernaciones, Intendencia de Cautín, Sobre Lanzamiento Fundo Guayalí, Temuco, 26 March 1934, IC, vol. 419, AN.
24. Telegrama, 21 March 1934, IC, vol. 419, AN.
25. Arturo Huenchullán in Cámara de Diputados, *Boletín de Sesiones*, 3 July 1934, in Huenchullán, *Los sucesos del Alto Bío-Bío y el diputado Huenchullán*, 23–24.
26. Dirección General de Tierras y Colonización, Comisión Guayalí da cuenta de su cumplimiento.
27. Ibid.
28. Huenchullán, *Los sucesos del Alto Bío-Bío y el diputado Huenchullán*, 26–27.
29. Carabineros de Chile, Prefectura Cautín, no. 16, "Da cuenta de su regreso de Lonquimay, después de haber dado cumplimiento al lanzamiento de los ocupantes de fundo Huayalí," 7 April 1934, IC, vol. 419, AN.
30. Juzgado de Victoria, Causa Criminal No. 5021, 6 April 1934, "Subvertir el Orden Público," Conservador de Bienes Raíces, Victoria (CBBRR-V).
31. Comunicación de Carabineros, 7 April 1934, IC, vol. 419, AN.
32. Juzgado de Victoria, Causa Criminal No. 5021, 6 April 1934, "Subvertir el Orden Público."
33. Ibid.
34. Ibid.
35. See Tinsman's analysis of gender and patriarchy during the 1966–73 agrarian reform in *Partners in Conflict*.
36. Notes from Isidora Aguirre interview with Emelina Sagredo.
37. Intendente de Bío Bío al Ministro del Interior, Los Ángeles, 7 July 1934, Sobre detención del profesor primario de Ralco, MI, vol. 8676, ARNAD.
38. "Manifiesto de los Colonos de Nitrito a los Campesinos, Obreros e Indígenas de la Región," MI, vol. 8676, ARNAD.
39. "En Defensa de los Colonos del Alto Bío Bío," MI, vol. 8676, ARNAD.
40. The election results were reported in *El Mercurio*, 14 May 1934, 3.
41. *Ramona*, 4 April 1972.
42. Ibid.
43. Comunicación del Sindicato Agrícola de Lonquimay al Intendente, 29 September 1929, IC, vol. 278, AN.
44. A number of these cases can be found in the Juzgado Laboral de Los Ángeles, 1928–33, ARNAD.
45. For a discussion of labor courts, see Diego Ortúzar and Ángela Vergara, "Bringing Justice to the Workplace: Labor Courts and Labor Laws in Chile, 1930s–1980s," in Leon Fink and Juan Manuel Palacio, eds., *Labor Justice across the Americas* (Urbana: University of Illinois Press, 2017).
46. Ministerio del Bienestar Social, Inspección General del Trabajo, Tribunal del Trabajo, No. 756, José Contreras, demandante, Gustavo Neuman, demandado, 11 January 1932, in Juzgado del Trabajo, Los Ángeles, Caja, 14 April 1930–3 February 1932, ARNAD.

47. Ministerio del Bienestar Social, Inspección General del Trabajo, Tribunal del Trabajo, No. 757, Pedro María Arévalo, demandante, Maces Medis, demandado, 11 January 1932, in Juzgado del Trabajo, Los Ángeles, Caja, 14 April 1930–3 February 1932, ARNAD.
48. Ministerio del Bienestar Social, Inspección General del Trabajo, Tribunal del Trabajo, No. 1054, Baldomero Jara Jara, demandante, Benjamín Carrasco, demandado, 21 November 1932, in Juzgado del Trabajo, Los Ángeles, Caja, 14 April 1930–3 February 1932. Other similar cases involving inquilinos or inquilinos–medieros suing their patrones for restitution for crops they had planted and for harvests they had lost following their dismissals in the same caja include Tribunal del Trabajo, No. 1060, Celedino Escobar, demandante, Luis Cornejo, demandado, 24 November 1932; Tribunal del Trabajo, No. 1073, Angel Aguilera, demandante, Demetrio Rebolledo, 5 December 1932, ARNAD.
49. Cámara de Diputados, *Diario de Sesiones*, Sesión Extraordinaria, 13 February 1934, BCN.

Chapter 8. "All You See Is Yours"

1. "True account of the events that occurred in Lonquimay before and during the criminal movement of the seditious of Ránquil etc.," in Cámara de Senadores, *Boletín de Sesiones*, 30 July 1934, BCN; Subdelegado de Lonquimay Schweitzer a Señor Juez de Crimen Victoria, Lonquimay, 8 July 1934, in file of uncatalogued documents of the Intendencia de Cautín related to the Sucesos de Lonquimay.
2. Subdelegado de Lonquimay Schweitzer a Señor Juez de Crimen Victoria.
3. "True account of the events that occurred in Lonquimay."
4. The telegram was signed by subdelegate Augusto Schweitzer, communal treasurer Rigoberto Jara, head of customs Roberto Pezoa, municipal secretary Custodio Tapia, postal director Raúl Moreno, municipal inspector Jorge España, inspector of the gold placer mines (*lavaderos*) Humberto Carrasco, Father Jesualdo, and the merchants Luis Moraga, César Chávez, Pablo Siade, José Frau, Miguel Rodríguez, Abraham Rodríguez, Marcos López, Carlos Labayru, Francisco Rojas, Nicolás Siade, Alejandro Sorensense, among many others. Cámara de Senadores, *Boletín de Sesiones*, 30 July 1934, BCN.
5. Ángela Vergara, " 'Busquemos Oro': Trabajo, Lavaderos de Oro y Ayuda Fiscal durante Tiempos de Crisis, Chile, 1930–1936," *Revista Tiempo Histórico*, Year 6, no. 11 (July-December 2015), 75–76.
6. Ibid., 83–84.
7. Ibid., 84.
8. Monteón, *Chile and the Great Depression*, 179.
9. *El Comercio*, 27 August 1933 and 22 January 1934, in Flores, "Un Episodio en la Historia Social de Chile," 84–85.

10. Servicio de Investigaciones, Sub Comisaría de Bío Bío, Los Ángeles, Collipulli, 7 July 1934, "Da cuenta hechos de Lonquimay con detenido," MI, vol. 8676, ARNAD.
11. *El Diario* Austral, 3 July 1934, 3.
12. *Justicia*, 10 November 1933, 2.
13. MI, vol. 8720, ARNAD and *El Comercio*, 29 April 1934, in Flores, "Un Episodio en la Historia Social de Chile," 85.
14. *El Diario Austral*, 30 June 1934, 5.
15. Carabineros de Chile, Prefectura Cautín No. 16, Parte No. 1490, 15 July 1934, in Intendencia, in file of uncatalogued documents of the Intendencia de Cautín related to the Sucesos de Lonquimay and also in MI, vol. 8676, ARNAD.
16. Cámara de Senadores, *Boletín de Sesiones*, 30 July 1934, BCN.
17. *El Diario Austral*, 29 June 1934, 1.
18. Report from Intendente de Cautin to Minister of Interior, Los Ángeles, 6 July 1934, in Cámara de Senadores, *Boletín de Sesiones*, Sesión Ordinaria, 16 July 1934, BCN.
19. Carabineros de Chile, Prefectura Cautín No. 16, Parte No. 1490, 15 July 1934.
20. *El Diario Austral*, 11 July 1934, 5.
21. *El Diario Ilustrado*, 12 July 1934, reprinted in *Gaceta de los Carabineros de Chile*, 26 July 1934, 28.
22. Carabineros de Chile, Prefectura Bío Bío, Primera Comisaría, Detenido por cómplice de sedicioso y por la responsabilidad que pueda afectarle en el Alto Bío-Bío," 10 July 1934, MI, vol. 8676, ARNAD.
23. Godoy's name, given as Reginio Godoy, and basic biographical information are included in a list of fifty-six detainees following the revolt in Carabineros de Chile, Prefectura Cautín No. 16, Parte No. 1490, Temuco, 15 July 1934.
24. *El Diario Austral*, 18 July 1934, 8.
25. The manifestos and case against Godoy are contained in "Contra Remigio Godoy Ortega por Circulación de Impresos Subversivos," Corte de Apelaciones, Temuco, CBBRR-T and referred to in Sentencia no. 104 Contra Onofre Ortíz y Otros, Sucesos de Lonquimay, Temuco, 5 March 1935, and Segunda Instancia, 23 March 1935, Archivo de la Corte de Apelaciones, Temuco (ACA-T).
26. Ulianova and Riquelme Segovia, *Chile en los archivos soviéticos*, 2:441.
27. Ministerio del Interior, Intendencias y Gobernaciones, Gobernación de Mulchén, "Denuncio de Constancio Cortés F.," MI, vol. 8676, ARNAD.
28. *El Diario Austral*, 5 July 1934, 5.
29. Ministerio del Interior, Intendencias y Gobernaciones, Gobernación de Mulchén, "Denuncio de Constancio Cortés F."
30. Carabineros de Chile, Prefectura de Cautín No. 16, "Detenido por complicidad en la subversión del Alto de Bío-Bío," 21 September 1934, in Corte de Apelaciones de Temuco, Sucesos de Lonquimay, Contra Onofre Ortíz Salgado y Otros, 21 September 1934, CBBRR-T.

31. Corte de Apelaciones de Temuco, Sucesos de Lonquimay, Segundo Cuaderno Principal, Contra Onofre Ortíz Salgado y Otros, 21 September 1934, CBBRR-T.
32. Carabineros de Chile, Prefectura de Bío-Bío, No. 10. a Intendencia de la Provincia, Los Ángeles, 7 July 1934, MI, vol. 8676, ARNAD.
33. Servicio de Investigaciones, Sub Comisaría de Bío Bío, Los Ángeles, Parte No. 951, 6 July 1934, "Amplia parte sobre detenidos sublevación revoltosos Lonquimay," MI, vol. 8676, ARNAD.
34. Servicio de Investigaciones al Segundo Juzgado de Crimen, Parte No. 559, Remite detenidos por transgresión al Decreto Ley No. 50, Valdivia, 9 July 1934, MI, ARNAD, vol. 8676.
35. Copy of Report from the Concepción Regional Committee of the Communist Party found on detained Communist in Corral, 9 July 1934, MI, vol. 8676, ARNAD.
36. *El Diario Austral*, 9 July 1934, 1.
37. Servicio de Investigaciones, Memorandum, "Sociedades," No. 181, 30 June 1934, MI, vol. 8679, ARNAD.
38. Ibid.
39. "Transcripción de Reunión del Secretariado Latinoamericano Realizada en Moscú (fragmentos de estenograma), 25 March 1935, included as appendix in Ulianova, "Levantamiento Campesino de Lonquimay," 218.
40. Carta del Emisario de KOMINTERN, "Horacio," al Lender-Secretario Latinoamericano en Moscú, 1 January 1935, in Ulianova and Riquelme Segovia, *Chile en los archivos soviéticos*, 2:455–56.
41. Ibid.
42. Transcripción de Reunión del Secretariado Latinoamericano Realizada en Moscú (fragmentos de estenograma).
43. *Bandera Roja*, Year 10, no. 14, 28 July 1934.
44. Eduardo Téllez Lúgaro et al., "El Levantamiento del Alto Bío Bío y el Soviet y la República Araucana de 1934."
45. Testimony of Juan Orellana Barrera in Sentencia no. 104 Contra Onofre Ortíz y Otros, Sucesos de Lonquimay, Temuco, 5 March 1935.
46. Corte de Apelaciones de Temuco, Delito Contra la Seguridad Interior del Estado, Sublevación Lonquimay, Asalto a la Pulpería Frau (Acuña), 18 July 1934, CBBRR-T; Testimony of Florentino Pino Valdebenito in Sentencia no. 104 Contra Onofre Ortíz y Otros, Sucesos de Lonquimay, Temuco, 5 March 1935.
47. Carabineros de Chile, Prefectura de Cautín, No. 16, Detenido por haber tenido participación en los sucesos de Ránquil, Parte No. 6 in Corte de Apelaciones de Temuco, Sucesos de Lonquimay, Segundo Cuaderno Principal, Contra Onofre Ortíz Salgado y Otros, 21 September 1934.
48. Corte de Apelaciones de Temuco, Delito Contra la Seguridad Interior del Estado, Sublevación Lonquimay, Asalto a la Pulpería Frau (Acuña), 18 July 1934. See also testimony of Juan Bautista Valenzuela Sagredo, Onofre Ortíz,

and Juan Orellana Barrera in Sentencia no. 104 Contra Onofre Ortíz y Otros, Sucesos de Lonquimay, Temuco, 5 March 1935.
49. Testimony of Juan Bautista Valenzuela Sagredo in Sentencia no. 104 Contra Onofre Ortíz y Otros, Sucesos de Lonquimay, Temuco, 5 March 1935.
50. Servicio de Investigaciones, Sub Comisaría de Bío Bío, Los Ángeles, Collipulli, 7 July 1934, "Da cuenta hechos de Lonquimay con detenido."
51. Carabineros de Chile, Prefectura Bío Bío, Primera Comisaría, Detenido por cómplice de sedicioso y por la responsabilidad que pueda afectarle en el Alto Bío-Bío," 10 July 1934.
52. Testimony of Florentino Pino Valdebenito in Corte de Apelaciones de Temuco, Delito Contra la Seguridad Interior del Estado, Sublevación Lonquimay, Asalto a la Pulpería Frau (Acuña), 18 July 1934.
53. Testimony of Manuel Astroza Dávila in Corte de Apelaciones de Temuco, Delito Contra la Seguridad Interior del Estado, Sublevación Lonquimay, Asalto a la Pulpería Frau (Acuña), 18 July 1934.
54. Testimony of Onofre Ortíz Salgado in Sentencia no. 104 Contra Onofre Ortíz y Otros, Sucesos de Lonquimay, Temuco, 5 March 1935.
55. Testimony of José Nieves Alegría Espinoza in Corte de Apelaciones de Temuco, Delito Contra la Seguridad Interior del Estado, Sublevación Lonquimay, Asalto a la Pulpería Frau (Acuña), 18 July 1934.
56. Carabineros de Chile, Prefectura de Cautín, No. 16, Detenido por haber tenido participación en los sucesos de Ránquil, Parte No. 6, Corte de Apelaciones in Corte de Apelaciones de Temuco, Sucesos de Lonquimay, Segundo Cuaderno Principal, Contra Onofre Ortíz Salgado y Otros, 21 September 1934.
57. *El Comercio*, 5 November 1933; Ulianova and Riquelme Segovia, *Chile en los archivos soviéticos*, 2:428–29.

Chapter 9. Rebellion and Repression

1. In this chapter I rely chiefly on accounts in police reports located in the archives of the interior ministry and the testimony provided by detained campesinos during the judicial inquiry located in the Conservador de Bienes Raíces, Temuco, as well as the judicial sentence issued by Temuco's Corte de Apelaciones and reports in Temuco's *El Diario Austral*.
2. Guha, *Elementary Aspects of Peasant Insurgency in Colonial India*, 107–8; Joseph, "On the Trail of Latin American Bandits," 21. For "reading against the grain," see Guha, "The Prose of Counter-Insurgency." For the need to interpret subaltern subjects' actions in the absence of documentary sources like letters and diaries, see Dipesh Chakrabarty, "Conditions for Knowledge of Working-Class Conditions," in Guha and Spivak, *Selected Subaltern Studies*.
3. Notes from Isidora Aguirre interview with Emelina Sagredo.
4. Testimony of Delia Rosa Ortega Espinosa and Florentino Pino Valdebenito in Corte de Apelaciones de Temuco, Delito Contra la Seguridad Interior del

Estado, Sublevación Lonquimay, Asalto a la Pulpería Frau (Acuña), 18 July 1934. See also the account of the assault in Sentencia no. 104 Contra Onofre Ortíz y Otros, Sucesos de Lonquimay, Temuco, 5 March 1935.
5. Report of the FOCH and the Socorro Rojo Internacional in Cámara de Diputados, *Boletín de Sesiones*, 26 June 1935, BCN.
6. Notes from Isidora Aguirre interview with Emelina Sagredo.
7. The phrase is originally from Christopher Hill's study of radical movements in seventeenth-century England, *The World Turned Upside Down: Radical Ideas During the English Revolution* (New York: Penguin Books, 1991).
8. Testimony of Delia Rosa Ortega Espinosa in Corte de Apelaciones de Temuco, Delito Contra la Seguridad Interior del Estado, Sublevación Lonquimay, Asalto a la Pulpería Frau (Acuña), 18 July 1934.
9. Testimony of Florentino Pino Valdebenito and José Nieves Alegría Espinoza in ibid.
10. Testimony of Delia Rosa Ortega Espinosa in Corte de Apelaciones de Temuco Sucesos de Lonquimay, Segundo Cuaderno Principal, Contra Onofre Ortíz Salgado y Otros, 21 September 1934.
11. For a discussion of looting during peasant insurrections, see Guha, *Elementary Aspects of Peasant Insurgency in Colonial India*.
12. This witness testimony was not borne out by Zolezzi's death certificate, which described his death as due to blows to the head. Certificado de Defunción, Juan Zolezzi, Registro Civil, Lonquimay.
13. Carabineros de Chile, Prefectura Cautín No. 16, Parte No. 1490, 15 July 1934.
14. Carabineros de Chile, Prefectura Cautín No. 16, Parte No. 1490, 15 July 1934.
15. "Regularización del procedimiento, subsidiariamente, acusa, i pide sobreseimientos," in Corte de Apelaciones de Temuco, Sucesos de Lonquimay, Segundo Cuaderno Principal, Contra Onofre Ortíz y Otros, 21 September 1934.
16. Carabineros de Chile, Prefectura Cautín No. 16, Parte No. 1490, 15 July 1934.
17. "Regularización del procedimiento, subsidiariamente, acusa, i pide sobreseimientos."
18. See testimony of witnesses in ibid. and in Corte de Apelaciones de Temuco, Delito Contra la Seguridad Interior del Estado, Sublevación Lonquimay, Asalto a la Pulpería Frau (Acuña), 18 July 1934.
19. Corte de Apelaciones de Temuco, Delito Contra la Seguridad Interior del Estado, Sublevación Lonquimay, Asalto a la Pulpería Frau (Acuña), 18 July 1934.
20. Sentencia no. 104 Contra Onofre Ortíz y Otros, Sucesos de Lonquimay, Segunda Instancia, Temuco, 23 March 1935.
21. Testimony of Víctor Reyes Burgos and Ismael Cartes in Corte de Apelaciones de Temuco, Sucesos de Lonquimay, Segundo Cuaderno Principal, Contra

Onofre Ortíz y Otros, 21 September 1934; Carabineros de Chile, Prefectura Cautín No. 16, Parte No. 1490, 15 July 1934.
22. Testimony of Víctor Reyes Burgos in Corte de Apelaciones de Temuco, Sucesos de Lonquimay, Contra Onofre Ortíz Salgado y Otros, 21 September 1934; Carabineros de Chile, Comisaría Victoria, Comisaría Lonquimay, Parte 2, detenido en cumplimiento a orden competente in Corte de Apelaciones de Temuco, Delito Contra la Seguridad Interior del Estado, Sublevación Lonquimay, Asalto a la Pulpería Frau (Acuña), 18 July 1934.
23. Testimony of Ismael Cartes in Corte de Apelaciones de Temuco, Sucesos de Lonquimay, Segundo Cuaderno Principal, Contra Onofre Ortíz y Otros, 21 September 1934.
24. *Ramona*, 4 April 1972.
25. *El Diario Austral*, 10 July 1934, 1; Testimony of Antonio Ortíz Palma in Servicio de Investigaciones, Sub Comisaría de Bío Bío, Los Ángeles, Collipulli, 7 July 1934, "Da cuenta hechos de Lonquimay con detenido," MI, vol. 8676, ARNAD.
26. Carabineros de Chile, Prefectura Cautín No. 16, Parte No. 1490, 15 July 1934.
27. Salas's death is referred to in a letter from Lonquimay's leading residents to congress and published in Cámara de Senadores, *Boletín de Sesiones*, 30 July 1934. His death was also referred to in the Fiscal's findings in "Regularización del procedimiento, subsidiariamente, acusa, i pide sobreseimientos." Salas's body was not registered by the Registro Civil in Lonquimay until January 1935, which meant that, as with others, his disappeared corpse had not been found until months after the rebellion, and his death remained outside of the judicial investigation. According to his grandson, Francisco Salas, he had worked as a mayordomo on both Ránquil and Rahue (interview with author in December 2019, Ránquil).
28. *El Diario Austral*, 10 July 1934, 1.
29. Carabineros de Chile, Prefectura Cautín No. 16, Parte No. 1490, 15 July 1934; *El Diario Austral*, 11 July 1934, 5. *El Diario Austral* reported on 10 July 1934 that Leiva Tapia had been killed in a shootout when carabineros attempted to detain him at the Lagoses' house. This account is contradicted by the paper's later reporting and by subsequent police reports that described his capture and death during the "combat at Llanquén" as well as accounts by campesinos who describe how Leiva Tapia and others were simply executed by carabineros. These conflicting accounts are described below.
30. *El Diario Austral*, 29 June 1934, 1.
31. *El Diario Austral*, 30 June 1934, 5.
32. Telegrama de Délano, Prefecto, Temuco, 29 June 1934, in file of uncatalogued documents of the Intendencia de Cautín related to the Sucesos de Lonquimay.
33. Carabineros de Chile, Prefectura Cautín No. 16, Parte No. 1490, 15 July 1934; *El Diario Austral*, 10 July 1934, 1.

34. *El Diario Austral*, 11 July 1934, 1.
35. *El Diario Austral*, 12 July 1934, 1.
36. Carabineros de Chile, Prefectura Cautín No. 16, Parte No. 1490, 15 July 1934.
37. Ibid. See also testimony of Juan Bautista Sagredo Valenzuela and José Carlos Riquelme Zurita in "Regularización del procedimiento, subsidiariamente, acusa, i pide sobreseimientos" and account in Sentencia no. 104 Contra Onofre Ortíz y Otros, Sucesos de Lonquimay, Temuco, 5 March 1935.
38. Servicio de Investigaciones, Sub Comisaría de Bío Bío, Los Ángeles, Parte No. 951, 6 July 1934, "Amplia parte sobre detenidos sublevación revoltosos Lonquimay."
39. Carabineros de Chile, Prefectura Cautín No. 16, Parte No. 1490, 15 July 1934.
40. Testimony in "Regularización del procedimiento, subsidiariamente, acusa, i pide sobreseimientos."
41. Testimony of Adolfo Sánchez Salazar in Servicio de Investigaciones, Sub Comisaría de Bío Bío, Los Ángeles, Parte No. 951, 6 July 1934.
42. Testimony in "Regularización del procedimiento, subsidiariamente, acusa, i pide sobreseimientos"; Testimony of Wenceslao Millar Yáñez in Sentencia no. 104 Contra Onofre Ortíz y Otros, Sucesos de Lonquimay, Segunda Instancia, Temuco, 23 March 1935.
43. Testimony of Adolfo Sánchez Salazar in Servicio de Investigaciones, Sub Comisaría de Bío Bío, Los Ángeles, Parte No. 951, 6 July 1934; Testimony of Wenceslao Millar Yáñez in Sentencia no. 104 Contra Onofre Ortíz y Otros, Sucesos de Lonquimay, Segunda Instancia, Temuco, 23 March 1935.
44. Corte de Apelaciones de Temuco, Sucesos de Lonquimay, Segundo Cuaderno Principal, Contra Onofre Ortíz Salgado y Otros, 21 September 1934.
45. Testimony of Adolfo Sánchez Salazar in Servicio de Investigaciones, Sub Comisaría de Bío Bío, Los Ángeles, Parte No. 951, 6 July 1934.
46. Carabineros de Chile, Prefectura Cautín No. 16, Parte No. 1490, 15 July 1934.
47. See report of Fiscal in "Regularización del procedimiento, subsidiariamente, acusa, i pide sobreseimientos."
48. Testimony of Adolfo Sánchez Salazar in Servicio de Investigaciones, Sub Comisaría de Bío Bío, Los Ángeles, Parte No. 951, 6 July 1934.
49. Carabineros de Chile, Prefectura Cautín No. 16, Parte No. 1490, Temuco, 15 July 1934. While Martín Gainza's body was not found, his brother José's body was recovered, and a death certificate was issued by Lonquimay's Registro Civil on 9 January 1935. The cause of death was attributed not to gunshots but to "two blows with sticks to his brain."
50. Campos's death from "blows to the head" in Contraco on 1 July 1934 is recorded in his Certificado de Defunción, Registro Civil, Lonquimay in Sucesos de Lonquimay and referred to by the public prosecutor in "Regularización del procedimiento, subsidiariamente, acusa, i pide sobreseimientos."

51. Carabineros de Chile, Prefectura Cautín No. 16, Parte No. 1490, 15 July 1934.
52. Ibid.
53. Guha, *Elementary Aspects of Peasant Insurgency*, 195–97. Guha quotes Hobsbawm and Rudé from Eric Hobsbawm and Georges Rudé, *Captain Swing* (London: Phoenix Press, 1969), 212.
54. Servicio de Investigaciones, Sub Comisaría de Bío Bío, Los Ángeles, Parte No. 951, 6 July 1934.
55. See labor inspector's 1931 report attached to Informe sobre Colonización en Alto Bío-Bío. Del gobernador de Victoria al Ministro de Tierras y Colonización, 5 January 1932. IC, vol. 378, 1932, AN.
56. Corte de Apelaciones de Temuco, Sucesos de Lonquimay, Segundo Cuaderno Principal, Contra Onofre Ortíz y Otros, 21 September 1934.
57. Carabineros de Chile, Prefectura Cautín No. 16, Parte No. 1490, 15 July 1934.
58. Ibid. See also witness testimony in "Regularización del procedimiento, subsidiariamente, acusa, i pide sobreseimientos."
59. Carabineros de Chile, Prefectura Cautín No. 16, Parte No. 1490, 15 July 1934. Gainza's death certificate in the Registro Civil in Lonquimay (January 1935) only ascribes his death to a bullet wound in the head. It does not mention violence allegedly done to his face.
60. This figure is based on Aburto Panguilef's petition for freedom for prisoners in which he refers to the twelve indígenas and sixty prisoners overall as well as an analysis of prisoners' last names. Transcripción acuerdos oficiales del 14. Congreso Araucano de Plom-Maquehue, 25 December–1 January 1935, IC, vol. 430, 1935.
61. Corte de Apelaciones de Temuco, Sucesos de Lonquimay, Segundo Cuaderno Principal, Contra Onofre Ortíz Salgado y Otros, 21 September 1934.
62. Ibid.
63. Carabineros de Chile, Prefectura Cautín No. 16, Parte No. 1490, 15 July 1934.
64. Telegram, Intendente of Cautín to Ministerio del Interior, nd, in file of uncatalogued documents of the Intendencia de Cautín related to the Sucesos de Lonquimay.
65. Información del Intendente Bío Bío al Ministro del Interior in file of uncatalogued documents of the Intendencia de Cautín related to the Sucesos de Lonquimay.
66. *El Diario Austral*, 6 July 1934, 5.
67. *El Diario Austral*, 7 July 1934, 1.
68. *La Nación*, 7 and 9 July 1934, and *El Mercurio*, 7 July 1934, in Felipe Portales, "Primeros Detenidos Desaparecidos en Chile: la Masacre de Ránquil," *Punto Final*, 12 December 2014.
69. Telegram Intendente Cautín to Ministro del Interior, 4 July 1934, in file of uncatalogued documents of la Intendencia de Cautín related to the Sucesos de Lonquimay.

70. *El Diario Austral*, 5 July 1934, 1, 5. Later it would emerge that Alarcón had been detained, interrogated, and then killed while allegedly attempting to escape carabineros.
71. Servicio de Investigaciones, Sub Comisaría de Bío Bío, Los Ángeles, Parte No. 951, 6 July 1934.
72. Sentencia no. 104 Contra Onofre Ortíz y Otros, Sucesos de Lonquimay, Temuco, 5 March 1935.
73. *El Diario Austral*, 6 July 1934, 5; Comunicación de la Corte de Apelaciones de Temuco a la Intendencia, 3 July 1934, IC, vol. 420, AN.
74. *El Diario Austral*, 9 July 1934, 1.
75. A list of fifty-six prisoners can be found in Carabineros de Chile, Prefectura Cautín No. 16, Parte No. 1490, 15 July 1934. In addition, a 21 September 1934 list of sixty-two prisoners detained for their participation in the rebellion can be found in Corte de Apelaciones de Temuco, Sucesos de Lonquimay, Contra Onofre Ortíz Salgado y Otros, 21 September 1934.
76. In their chapter on the Ránquil rebellion, Brian Loveman and Elizabeth Lira use some of the same police reports and cases in Concepción's military court that I employ here to describe the rebellion and its repression as well as the judicial investigation by Franklin Quezada Rogers, the appellate court justice assigned to the case. See Loveman and Lira, *Poder judicial y conflictos políticos*.
77. *Ramona*, 4 April 1972.
78. Consulado de la República de Chile, Neuquén, Argentina, Da cuenta de los chilenos que se internaron en Argentina y tomaron parte en los sucesos de Lonquimay, Neuquén, 18 July 1934, MI, vol. 8678, ARNAD.
79. Carabineros de Chile, Dirección General, al Ministro del Interior, comunica resultado comisión para ir a buscar fugitivos a la Argentina, Santiago, 29 October 1934, MI, vol. 8678, ARNAD.
80. *El Mercurio*, 10 July 1934, in Portales, "Primeros Detenidos Desaparecidos en Chile."
81. Carabineros de Chile, Prefectura Cautín No. 16, Parte No. 1490, 15 July 1934.
82. Telegrama Intendente Cautín al Ministro del Interior, nd, in file of uncatalogued documents of the Intendencia de Cautín related to the Sucesos de Lonquimay.
83. Fiscalía de Carabineros, JMC, Causa 187-34, "Por Evasión de Detenidos," contra Teniente de Carabineros René Sepúlveda Fernández, 18 July 1934, ARNAD. Also in MI, vol. 176-356, cited in Flores, "Un Episodio en la Historia Social de Chile," 114.
84. *El Diario Austral*, 9 July 1934, 1.
85. *Ramona*, 4 April 1972.
86. Flores, "Un Episodio en la Historia Social de Chile," 143-44.
87. Report of the FOCH and the Socorro Rojo Internacional. See also a summary of the FOCH commission investigation and legal accusations against

carabineros by Gerardo Ortúzar Riesco in Fiscalía de Carabineros, JMC, Causa 195-34, "Por Diferentes Delitos contra Carabineros de Cautín," 18 July 1934, ARNAD. Carabineros made an official response denying the FOCH accusations in Carabineros de Chile, Prefectura de Cautín No. 16, "Contesta Oficio No. 350 sobre delitos imputados a Carabineros," 12 September 1934 in JMC, Causa 195-34, ARNAD.
88. Report of the FOCH and the Socorro Rojo Internacional.
89. Carabineros de Chile, Dirección General al Ministro del Interior, transcribe oficio de la prefectura de Cautín," Santiago, 13 December 1934, MI, vol. 8678, ARNAD.
90. Report of the FOCH and the Socorro Rojo Internacional.
91. Ibid.
92. JMC, Causa 195-34, Contra Carabineros, "Por Diferentes Delitos," 18 July 1934, Statement of José del Cármen Sandoval, 7 August 1934, ARNAD.
93. JMC, Causa 195-34, Contra Carabineros, "Por Diferentes Delitos," 18 July 1934, Statements of José del Cármen Sandoval and Teodoro Hermosilla, 7 August 1934, ARNAD.
94. *El Diario Austral*, 20 July 1934, 1.
95. Notes from Isidora Aguirre interview with Emelina Sagredo.
96. JMC, Causa 195-34, "Por Diferentes Delitos," Declaración de Onofre Ortíz Salgado, 8 September 1934, ARNAD.
97. JMC, Causa 195-34, "Por Diferentes Delitos," Declaración de José Adán Sagredo Pacheco, 8 September 1934, ARNAD.
98. JMC, Causa 195-34, "Por Diferentes Delitos," Declaración de Juan Bautista Valenzuela Sagredo, 8 September 1934, ARNAD.
99. JMC, Fiscalía de Carabineros de Cautín a la Subcomisaría de Carabineros de Lonquimay, No. 353, 8 September 1934, ARNAD.
100. JMC, Causa 195-34, Carabineros de Chile, Prefectura de Cautín No. 16 a la Fiscalía de Carabineros de Cautín, 12 September 1934, "Contesta oficio No. 350 sobre delitos imputados a Carabineros," ARNAD.
101. JMC, Causa 195-34, "Por Diferentes Delitos," Declaración de Alfredo Monreal Cabello, 12 September 1934, ARNAD.
102. JMC, Causa 195-34, "Por Diferentes Delitos," Declaraciones de Agapito Figueroa Figuera, Juan Celis Ravanal, Arturo Rivera Canto, and Juan Leal Salazar, 15-24 September 1934, ARNAD.
103. JMC, Causa 195-34, Fernando Délano Soruco, "Amnestía," ARNAD.
104. JMC, Causa 195-34, Lucio Para P., Auditor de Ejército, and Humberto Gordon B., Coronel y Juez Militar, 25 September 1934, ARNAD.
105. Portales makes this point in "Primeros Detenidos Desaparecidos en Chile."
106. In the case of Alegría and Hermosilla, see testimony of Mateo Alegría, who saw Alegría's cadaver, and of Francisco Vial in 11 December 1934 decision of Franklin Quezada Rogers, Corte de Apelaciones de Temuco, Sucesos de Lonquimay, Segundo Cuaderno Principal, Contra Onofre Ortíz Salgado y Otros, 21 September 1934.

107. Servicio de Investigaciones, Memorándum, Federación de Maestros, Santiago, 14 December 1934, MI, vol. 8678, ARNAD.
108. In congress, Arturo Huenchullán stated that he had been told by people in Lonquimay that more than sixty campesinos and miners had been killed (Cámara de Diputados, *Boletín de Sesiones*, Sesión Ordinaria, 13 July 1934). In her 1971 interview in *Ramona*, 4 April 1972, Emelina Sagredo speaks of more than one hundred campesinos killed. As for historians, Jaime Flores estimates at least one hundred killed in "Un Episodio."

Chapter 10. History, Memory, and the Question of Campesino Insurgency

1. Jaime Martínez Williams, ed., *Así lo Vió Zig-Zag* (Santiago: Empresa Editora Zigzag, nd), 86.
2. *El Sur*, 14 July 1934.
3. *El Diario Austral*, 24 July 1934, 1.
4. In fact, "el matadero," or slaughterhouse, was the name given to Llanquén by the campesinos evicted from Nitrito.
5. *El Diario Austral*, 11 July 1934, 5.
6. *Gaceta de los Carabineros*, no. 38 (26 July 1934).
7. In *To Rise in Darkness*, 190–91, Lauria-Santiago and Gould similarly note in the case of the 1931–32 campesino revolution in El Salvador that baseless rumors and news stories about rapes committed by hordes of Indians circulated widely. They note that there was no evidence to confirm these accounts.
8. *El Diario Austral*, 12 July 1934, 1.
9. Cámara de Diputados, *Boletín de Sesiones*, 13 July 1934, BCN.
10. Cámara de Senadores, *Boletín de Sesiones*, 30 July 1934, BCN.
11. Registro Civil, Lonquimay, Certificado de Defunción, Juan Zolezzi, 25 April 1935. Flores Chávez also notes the discrepancy between the press coverage and the information in Zolezzi's Certificado de Defunción in "Un Episodio en la Historia Social de Chile: 1934." Other deaths recorded by the Lonquimay Registro Civil in 1934 and 1935 include Herminino Campos (24 August 1934), Luciano Gainza (7 January 1935), bullet wound to right side of brain, José Gainza (9 January 1935), two wounds to the brain caused by sticks, Manuel Salas, blow with a machete to the face (17 January 1935).
12. *El Diario Austral*, 2 July 1934, 1.
13. In *Elementary Aspects of Peasant Insurgency in Colonial India*, Guha demonstrates how the British colonial state in India similarly consigned peasant insurgencies to prepolitical and premodern forms of criminal behavior and to the realm of uprisings and *jaqueries*.
14. Cámara de Senadores, *Boletín de Sesiones*, 2 July 1934, BCN.
15. Cámara de Diputados, *Boletín de Sesiones*, 13 July 1934, BCN.
16. Cámara de Diputados, *Boletín de Sesiones*, 13 July 1934, BCN.

17. Cámara de Diputados, *Boletín de Sesiones*, 18 July 1934, BCN.
18. Ibid.
19. Corte de Apelaciones de Temuco, Sucesos de Lonquimay, Contra Onofre Ortíz Salgado y Otros, 21 September 1934.
20. Corte de Apelaciones de Temuco, Sucesos de Lonquimay, Segundo Cuaderno Principal, Contra Onofre Ortíz Salgado y Otros, 21 September 1934; *El Diario Austral*, 18 July 1934, 8.
21. Corte de Apelaciones de Temuco, Sucesos de Lonquimay, Segundo Cuaderno Principal, Contra Onofre Ortíz Salgado y Otros, 21 September 1934.
22. Ibid.
23. Ibid.
24. Ibid.
25. Fiscal, Corte de Apelaciones, Temuco, 14 December 1934, in ibid.
26. Ibid.
27. "Regularización del procedimiento, subsidiariamente, acusa, i pide sobreseimientos."
28. Ibid.
29. Ibid.
30. Ibid.
31. Ibid.
32. Ibid.
33. Ibid.
34. All death certificates except for Bascuñán's are located in Lonquimay's Registro Civil in the volumes for 1934 and 1935. That of Bascuñán is located in Corte de Apelaciones de Temuco, Sucesos de Lonquimay Segundo Cuaderno Principal, Contra Onofre Ortíz Salgado y Otros, 21 September 1934.
35. The quote is from Sentencia no. 104 Contra Onofre Ortíz y Otros, Sucesos de Lonquimay, Temuco, 5 March 1934. This is the only mention of the "revolutionary tribunals" in the judicial inquiry. Indeed, none of the witness testimony that I have been able to review mentions revolutionary tribunals. However, in his report to the Comintern, Carlos Contreras Labarca described how the movement had organized "a revolutionary tribunal to carry out immediate class justice." Cited in Ulianova, "Levantamiento Campesino de Lonquimay," 198. Given that the defendants' lawyer was a Communist Party militant it may be that the aspirational notion that the campesinos had organized a revolutionary tribunal circulated not among the detained campesinos, who were not party militants, but via Contreras Labarca through the party leadership.
36. "Contesta la acusación, deduce tachas, presenta lista de testigos y minuta puntos de prueba, e impugnan una tasación" in Corte de Apelaciones de Temuco, Sucesos de Lonquimay Segundo Cuaderno Principal, Contra Onofre Ortíz y Otros, 21 September 1934.
37. Sentencia no. 104, Contra Onofre Ortíz y Otros, Sucesos de Lonquimay, Temuco, 5 March 1934.

38. Sentencia no. 104, Contra Onofre Ortíz y Otros, Sucesos de Lonquimay, Segunda Instancia, Temuco, 23 March 1935.
39. See the discussion of the law in Cámara de Diputados, *Boletín de Sesiones*, 10 and 11 September 1934, BCN.
40. See the discussion of the amnesty law and debate in congress in Loveman and Lira, *Las ardientes cenizas del olvido*, 33–41.
41. Cámara de Diputados, *Boletín de Sesiones*, 12 September 1934, BCN.
42. Ibid.
43. Cámara de Diputados, *Boletín de Sesiones*, 11 September 1934, BCN.
44. On the role of amnesties in Chilean history, see Loveman and Lira, *Las suaves cenizas del olvido* and *Las ardientes cenizas del olvido*.
45. See Peter Winn's foundational analysis of the "revolution from below" and "revolution from above" during the government of Salvador Allende in *Weavers of Revolution: The Yarur Workers and the Chilean Road to Socialism* (Oxford: Oxford University Press, 1988).
46. Ulianova, "Levantamiento Campesino de Lonquimay."
47. On Ránquil as an emblem, see Mallon, "Victims into Emblems." Mallon also discusses historical memories of the Ránquil rebellion in many of the texts discussed below.
48. Lomboy, *Ránquil*. Ulianova also discusses Lomboy's novel and many of the texts discussed below in "Levantamiento Campesino de Lonquimay."
49. Lafertte, *Vida de un comunista*, 274.
50. Lomboy, *Ránquil*.
51. Pablo Neruda, "The Dead in the Square," translated by Robert Brittain in *Let the Rail Splitter Awake and Other Poems* (New York: Masses & Mainstream, 1950), 41.
52. This is the pioneering argument of Loveman in *Struggle in the Countryside*.
53. Almino Affonso, *Trayectoria del movimiento campesino chileno* (Santiago: ICIRA, 1972), 18.
54. Aguirre, *Los que van quedando en el camino*. A copy of the 1988 English translation of the play by Frances Horning Barraclough can be found at the digital Isabel Aguirre archive: http://isidoraaguirre.usach.cl/texto/ia-004-009-001 /3 February 2020.
55. Aguirre describes the political messages of the play in notes she wrote down during the late 1960s in "Notas sobre compromiso político obra Lonquimay (Los que van quedando)," Isidora Aguirre, Archivo Digital, http://isidora aguirre.usach.cl/texto/ia-026-007-014/3 February 2020. The quote is from Aguirre, *Los que van quedando en el camino*, 69.
56. Patricio Manns, *Las grandes masacres* (Santiago: Editora Nacional Quimantú, 1972), 58.
57. *Ramona*, 4 April 1972.
58. Ránquil, *Capítulos de la historia de Chile* (Santiago: Editora Nacional Quimantú, 1973).
59. *La Tercera de la Hora*, 19 July 1973, 12.

60. *Las Últimas Noticias*, 16 July 1973, 31.
61. *El Mercurio*, 25 August 1973, 26; Chile, Senado, *Diario de Sesiones*, 19 August 1973, BCN.
62. *El Siglo*, 23 August 1973, 7.
63. Amnesty International, "For the Record, Amnesty Report: Writers and Journalists in Prison" (1974); Naciones Unidas, Consejo Económico y Social, Comisión de Derechos Humanos, "Estudio de los Informes de Violaciones de los Derechos Humanos en Chile, con Particular Referencia a la Tortura y Otros Tratos o Castigos Crueles, Inhumanos o Degradantes," Información Presentada por la Federación Democrática Internacional de Mujeres, 11 February 1974; Organization of American States, Inter-American Commission on Human Rights, "Report on the Status of Human Rights in Chile, 25 October 1974" and "Annual Report, 1975." The full text of the 1958 law is available on the website of the Biblioteca del Congreso Nacional: https://www.leychile.cl/Navegar?idNorma=27292 (19 January 2020). I am grateful to the historian Manuel Fernández-Cunque who provided some of the information on the publication of *Capítulos* and Lucy Lortsch's detention and torture in a personal communication.
64. Manns, *Actas del Alto Bío-Bío*.
65. As the historian Florencia Mallon notes in "Victims into Emblems," none of the fictional narratives of the Ránquil rebellion took up the role of Pehuenche communities in the movement. This reflected a subordination of indigenous communities' movements to recuperate land usurped by large estates to a broader campesino movement for agrarian reform and the unionization of rural labor.
66. See Mallon, "Victims into Emblems" for an illuminating discussion of Manns's book.
67. This brief summary is based on Diane Haughney, *Neoliberal Economics, Democratic Transition, and Mapuche Demands for Rights in Chile* (Gainesville: University Press of Florida, 2006), 59–75.
68. Ibid., 167. I discuss Mapuche conflicts with forestry companies in depth in *La Frontera*.
69. For discussions of Ralco and the hydroelectric projects, see Domingo Namuncura, *Ralco: ¿represa or pobreza?* (Santiago: LOM Ediciones, 1999); Haughney, *Neoliberal Economics*; Barbara Johnston and Terrence Turner, "The Pehuenche, the World Bank Group, and ENDESA S.A.: Report of the Committee for Human Rights," American Anthropological Association, March 1998; Jorge Moraga R., *Aguas turbias: la central Ralco en el Alto Bío Bío* (Santiago: Observatorio Latinoamericano de Conflictos Ambientales, 2001).
70. Correa and Molina, *Territorio y comunidades pehuenches del Alto Bío Bío*.
71. The most recent example of this is Portales's "Primeros Detenidos Desaparecidos en Chile."

Index

Aburto, Luis, 220
Ackermann, Bruno, 72; involvement in Sindicato Agrícola Lonquimay, 71, 103, 110–11, 112, 168; pulpería of, 72, 192, 197, 221–22, 249
Ackermann, Jorge, 72; involvement in Sindicato Agrícola Lonquimay, 71, 117, 120, 168; pulpería of, 72, 197, 221–22
Acuña, Albino, 139, 151, 152–53
Acuña Lobos, Pedro, 192, 217, 218, 219, 241, 248, 253
Acuña Sandoval, Modesto, 151, 169, 172–73, 237–38, 250
Adrian, Vicente, 48, 49
Agrarian Cooperatives and Colonies Law, 100
Agricultural Cooperatives Law (1929). *See* Law No. 4531
Agua de los Padres estuary, 26, 122
Aguirre, Isidora, 262; *Los que van quedando en el camino*, 2, 262–63
Aguirre Cerda, Pedro, 261
Aguirre Doolan, Humberto, 265
Alarcón, 215; actions during rebellion, 214; death of, 234, 240, 241, 303 n.70; organizing activities by, 193, 194, 199, 206, 208–9

Alarcón, Jervasio, 96
Alarcón, Pedro, 237
Alegría, Daniel, 115
Alegría, Heriberto, 242, 249
Alegría, Juan Pablo, 50
Alegría Espinoza, José Nieves, 211, 250
Alessandri, Arturo, 5, 13–14, 21, 67, 87, 154–55, 188, 258; 1920 election, 84; 1931 election, 144–45; 1932 election, 21, 148–49, 158–59; Liberal Alliance, 84; Nitrito Valley evictions, actions regarding, 172, 173, 176; relationship with Sindicato Agrícola Lonquimay, 160–61
Allende, Salvador, 3, 24
Almonacid, Fabián, 85
Alto Bío Bío, 1, 28, 45, 123, 210
Altos de Cule, 35
Álvarez, Héctor, 95
amnesty, 19, 20–21, 241, 247, 249, 251, 256–60
Ampuero, Juan de Dios, 186
Andes cordillera, 26, 28, 35, 39, 41, 122, 124
Anguita, Héctor, 63
Anguita, Octavio, 62, 63
Anguita, Rafael, 60, 62
Araucanía, 3, 6, 27, 34
Arévalo, Pedro María, 185

309

Argentina: border with Chile, 124; migration to and from Chile, 27–28, 51–52, 81
Arraneda, Manuel, 239
Arriagada, Cleofe, 242
Arriagada, General, 234, 242
Arriagada, Lieutenant, 233
Astroza, Federico, 250
Astroza Dávila, Manuel, 130, 134, 140, 146, 168, 210, 236
Astudillo, 195–96, 199, 200–201
Avello, Benigno, 231, 237

Baeza, Agustín, 42, 50, 96, 111, 113
Baeza, Erasmo, 139, 224, 237, 238, 240
Baeza, Lisandro, 115
Balboa Benítez, José Emiliano, 193–94, 208, 250
Balmaceda, José Manuel, 37, 38
Bandieri, Susana, 51
Barros Arana, Diego, 40, 124
Barros Borgoño, Manuel, 40
Bascuñán Rodríguez, Rafael, 224, 243, 245, 248, 252, 254
beets, sugar, 54–56
Belmar, Arturo, 95
Beroiza Espinoza, Exequiel, 236
Biobío River, 39, 41, 268
Bisquertt Susarte, Gustavo, 60–61
Blanche, General Bartolomé, 148
Boizard, Ricardo, 258
Briones, Colonel Ramón, 223
Budi, El, 149–50, 156
Bulnes Pinto, Manuel, 33–34, 49, 110, 113, 122
Bulnes Prieto, Manuel, 29, 33, 34
Bunster, Carmen, 263
Bunster, Gonzalo, 115, 118–19, 151, 152–53, 175, 182–83, 263
Bunster, José, 31, 64
Bunster, Luis Martín, 48–49, 60, 62, 63–64, 65, 66, 67, 133
Bunster, Mario, 175
Bunster, Martín Bryan, 62, 64
Bunster family, 60–68, 114–15, 139, 160, 173, 174–75
Bussey, Jorge Federico, 40, 41

Cabezas Jara, José, 236, 240
Cabezas Lagos, Eufemio Darío, 236, 240
Cabrera Urrutia, Lieutenant Luis, 188–89, 192, 222–23
Cáceres, Benjamín, 107, 109–10, 117
Caja de Colonización Agrícola, 89–90, 99, 136, 161–62, 172, 173
Campaign for Gold, 189
campesino, 6
Campos Pedrazo, Herminio, 227, 241, 254, 301 n.50
Canio, Antonio, 64
carabineros, 99, 222; abuses by, 20, 79, 178, 235, 236–40; attacks on, 215, 224–25, 227; justifications offered by, 235–36; reports of, 215; repression by, 86, 87, 90, 95, 173, 176–78; suppression of rebellion by, 188, 222–24, 232–42
Cárdenas, Antonio, 115
Carrasco, Benjamín, 185
Carrasco, Domingo, 115
Carrasco, Humberto, 189
Carrasco, Marcos, 164
Carrasco León, Francisco, 234
Cartes, Ismael, 131, 183, 221, 222, 250, 253, 254, 263
Casanova, Oscar, 82–83
Central Socialista de Colonización, 162, 164–65
Chanks Camus, Oscar, 185–86
Charó, Juan Bautista, 73, 119
Charó de Olhagaray, Dolores, 229–30
Chau-Chau estate, 92

Chilpaco estate, 40, 73, 121, 131, 136; improvements on, 131; union activities on, 126
Cid, Baldovino, 221
Cisternas, Sofía, 76, 216, 243
Cisternas Ramírez, Francisco, 235
Cisternas Ramírez, Pablo, 206–7, 235, 250
Claro, Emilio, 96, 97
class, 111–12, 219
colonization of southern Chile, 9–10, 15, 41–42; heads of households, 45; 1845 law, 28, 45; 1896 law, 44; 1898 law, 44; 1908 law, 44; 1925 law, 85–86; national colonization, 44, 70; of Nitrito Valley, 117, 131–32, 134–35, 145; of Ránquil, 134–35, 145, 160, 163, 173
colonos, 6, 44–45, 46, 74, 82
Comisión Nacional del Medio Ambiente (CONAMA), 268
Comité Social Obrero de Curacautín, 140
Communist Party, 4–5, 16, 143–44, 148, 166–67, 247, 260, 262, 265; *Bandera Roja*, 203–4; international conference (1933), 157–58; manifestos, 176–77, 180; *Ramona*, 182–83, 263, 264; repression of, 88; role in insurrection, 12, 192–205, 216
Compañia de Salitre y Ferrocarril, 35–36
Compton, Percy, 150, 161
Concha, Malaquías, 70
Confederación Nacional Campesina e Indígena Ránquil, 2, 262
Confederación Republicana de Acción Cívica (CRAC), 114
Constitution (1925), 85
contraband. *See* smuggling
Contraco estate, 225–27, 233, 237, 253

Contreras, José, 184–85
Contreras Labarca, Carlos, 200, 201, 202–3, 213
cooperativism, 101
Corporacíon Nacional de Desarrollo Indígena (CONADI), 268
Correa, Martín, 32
Cortés, Constancio, 196
counterinsurgency, 232–42

Dávila, Carlos, 147–48, 154, 177
Decree-Law No. 2658 (1979), 267
Decree No. 3,871 (14 August 1929), 102, 160
Decree No. 265 (27 March 1930), 112–13, 160
Decree No. 1730 (31 July 1930), 132, 134, 160
Decree No. 1693 (13 March 1931), 160
Decree No. 2243 (2 August 1930), 160, 170
Decree No. 143 (5 May 1931), 256
Decree No. 258 (20 May 1931), 139, 160
Decree No. 50 (21 June 1932), 148, 177, 194, 256–57, 258–60
Decree No. 4834 (24 November 1933), 160
Délano, Fernando, 223, 233, 240, 241
Democratic Party, 3, 69, 70, 88
Deramond, Carlos, 220
Díaz Norambuena, Domingo, 174
Donoso, Eduardo, 239
Drake, Paul, 148
Drouilly, Martín, 37, 132

education, public, 101–2
Edwards Ossandón, Agustín, 35
El Rahue estate, 40, 46–47, 73, 121, 130–31, 136; evictions on, 47, 102–3; improvements on, 130–31; union activities on, 126, 138

ENDESA, 268
Errázuriz Echauren, Federico, 42
Escobar, Andrés, 247, 259
Espinosa Orrego, Francisco, 109
Evans, Enrique, 63
evictions, 56–57, 58; from El Rahue, 47, 102–3; Ibáñez promise to not support, 99–100, 102, 106; from Nitrito Valley, 168–87, 198, 213; from Ralco, 64; from Ránquil, 102–3; timing of, 182–86

Fahrenkrog Reinhold, Harry, 72, 75, 78, 221
Federación Obrera de Chile (FOCH), 143, 157; 1934 Congress, 200–201; insurgency fomentation by, 192, 195, 202–3; relationship with Sindicato Agrícola Lonquimay, 12, 71, 153–54, 168, 204; report on Ránquil rebellion, 237–38, 239; unionization efforts
Fernández, Roque, 48, 49, 50, 110
Fernández Correa, Arturo, 168–69, 169, 170, 171, 172–73, 174, 175, 182
Fernández Frías, Sublieutenant, 232, 233
Fierro, Captain, 179, 180
Flores, Jaime, 15, 18, 48, 233, 237, 305 n.108
FOCH. *See* Federación Obrera de Chile (FOCH)
fraud: against inquilinaje, 82–83; land, 29, 31–33, 41, 48, 60–61, 66, 82–84, 96, 111
Frau Pujol, José, 190, 192, 217
Frei Montalva, Eduardo, 24, 262
Freire, Esteban, 96
Frei Ruiz-Tagle, Eduardo, 268
Friere, Vial, 169
Fuentealba, Joaquín, 30
Fuenzalida, Edmundo, 245

Gainza Irigoyen, José, 220, 225, 226–27, 241, 248, 254, 301 n.49
Gainza Irigoyen, Luciano, 229–30, 241, 254
Gainza Irigoyen, Martín, 220, 225, 226–27, 241, 248, 254, 301 n.49
Galindo Quilodrán, José, 134
gañanes, 7
gender: employment, gendered, 75–78, 125, 171; participation in rebellion, 216–17; property rights, 45, 170–71. *See also* men; women
Gerlach, Mario, 120
Gibbs, William, 35
Godoy, Higinio, 194, 195, 204, 249
gold, payment for, 217–18
gold placers, 189–91; concessions, 11, 189–90; unionization of, 190
Gómez Bunster, Celmira, 133
Grandón, Abelino, 92
Great Depression, 142, 143
Grove, Marmaduke, 84, 147–48, 258
Guayalí estate, 36, 60, 62, 67, 132–33, 136, 139–40, 145, 233; carabineros on, 115, 215, 227; evictions from, 128, 168–79, 214; union activities on, 133, 136, 138; unrest on (1932), 151–53; workers on, census of, 81
Guha, Ranajit, 215, 228
Guiñez, Nemesio, 93–94
Gutiérrez, Anibal, 245
Gutiérrez, Artemio, 174–75, 188
Gutiérrez, José Miguel, 73, 131

Henríquez Argomedo, Carlos, 155–56
Hermosilla, Manuel Antonio, 50
Hermosilla, Marcos, 225, 240
Hermosilla, Segundo, 242, 249
Hermosilla, Teodoro, 238–39, 250
Hernández, Manuel, 193
Herrera, Amelia, 91
Horacio, 201–2

Huenchullán, Arturo, 164, 165, 174, 176, 188, 246, 305 n.108

Ibáñez del Campo, Carlos, 14, 84, 87–88; commission (1930), 112, 113, 117–32; communication with Leiva Tapia (September 1929), 103; meeting with Leiva Tapia (December 1928), 98–100; repression by, 142; resignation of, 143; support of campesinos, 3, 14, 90, 95, 97, 105–6, 110, 112, 139; tour of Bío-Bío, 104
Ibáñez del Campo, Javier, 88
inquilinaje, 7, 74–84
inquilinos, 6–7, 74, 82, 118, 124–25, 281 n.14
Internal Security of the State Law. *See* Decree No. 50 (21 June 1932)
Irarrázaval Zañartu, Alfredo, 57–58
Izquierda Comunista, 144

Jara, Cipriano, 131
Jara Jara, Baldomero, 185
Jefferson, Mark, 80
Joseph, Gilbert, 216

Labor Code (1931), 15
laboring conditions, 79–80
labor relations, 46–47
Labrín Díaz, Froilán, 146, 169, 227
Lacourt, Alfredo, 93–94
Lafertte, Elías, 145, 148, 154, 157, 158, 200, 209
Lagos, Elías, 220, 235
Lagos, Ernesto, 237
Lagos, Juan de Dios, 236, 237, 238
Lagos, Juan Domingo, 217, 220, 235
Lagos, Luis, 238
La Laja, 60, 61
land: dispossession of indigenous people from, 29, 31–33, 83, 137–38, 150, 156, 165; frontier, 6, 9; speculation in, 30, 34. *See also* fraud; public land
Lara, Juan Sebastián, 206
Larenas, Alberto, 39–40, 41, 96, 111, 123
Larenas, Lieutenant, 233
Las Ñiochas estate, 93
Las Raíces tunnel, 191, 192, 195, 204
Law No. 4054, 105
Law No. 4531, 72, 89–90
Law No. 4301 (February 1928), 14, 88–89, 90, 102, 106, 162, 172
Law No. 3420 (19 February 1934), 172
Law No. 5,483 (13 September 1934), 241, 257–58. *See also* amnesty
Law No. 12927 (6 August 1958), 266
Leiva, Sebastián, 12
Leiva Ramos, Juan Segundo, 71
Leiva Tapia, Juan Segundo, 71–72, 117, 120, 134, 140; actions during rebellion, 214, 215, 220, 221, 245; appointment to CRAC, 114; arrest of, 157–58; capture of, 223; communication with Ibáñez (September 1929), 103; death of, 224, 238, 254, 300 n.29; education, report about, 101–2; insurrection planning by, 194, 196, 199, 208, 211–13, 215; literature, disseminating, 108–9; meeting with Ibáñez (December 1928), 98–100; political affiliations, 112, 144–45, 157–58, 164–65, 181; subdelegate appointment, 106
León, Carmen, 225
León, Luis, 237
Lepeman, Manuel, 67
Liñai, Francisco, 236
Lira, Elizabeth, 21, 258
livestock, 47, 74–75
Llafenco hacienda, 150–51
Llaima colonization concession, 91, 149
Llanquén, 134, 161, 168, 169, 174

Llanquén River, 224
Lolco estate, 40, 73, 117, 119, 121, 128–29; assault on, 229–31, 233; improvements on, 127, 128–29; massacre on (1882), 36–37; union activities on, 126, 136, 138
Lomboy, Reinaldo, 261; *Ránquil*, 2, 261–63
Long-Long estate, 93
Lonquimay, 28, 36, 45, 46, 57, 123, 189
looting, 219, 220, 221, 222, 225, 226, 230
Lortsch Revett, Lucy, 265, 266; *Capítulos de la historia de Chile*, 264, 265, 266
Loveman, Brian, 5, 8, 21, 85, 258

Maldonado, Ernesto, 112, 113, 118, 119, 134, 135
Maldonado, Luis, 249
manifestos, 176–77, 179–80, 188, 193, 194, 195, 203, 216
Manns, Patricio, 263; *Actas del Alto Bío Bío*, 2, 266–67
Mapuche, 6, 27, 137–38, 163, 267–68; combat against, 33, 36; dispossession of, 29, 83, 137–38, 150, 156, 165
Mardones Naverrete, Eulojio, 250
Mariguan, Remigio, 231
Marihuan, Antonio, 64
Maripi, Benicio, 64
Maripi, Ignacio, 15, 16, 60, 64, 65–66, 67, 68, 138, 236, 268; actions during rebellion, 230; alliance with Sindicato Agrícola Lonquimay, 136, 205, 231
Martínez, Carlos Alberto, 246–47, 259
Matte, Eugenio, 147
McBride, George, 80
media. *See* press
mediería, 7
Medis, Meces, 185

men: employment of, 76; heads of families, 14–15, 45, 75–76, 125, 170–71, 178
Mendes, Luis, 196
Merillán, José, 218
Merino, Alberto, 259
migration. *See* mobility of labor
mobility of labor, 10; to and from Argentina, 27–28, 51–52, 81; south to north, 80, 81
Molina, Raúl, 32
Molina Villar, Juan Evangelista, 114
Monreal, Captain Alfredo, 223, 232, 233, 241
Montero, Juan Esteban, 143, 144, 145, 147
Montoya Villagrán, Fidel, 248, 252, 254
Montoya Villagrán, Raúl, 224–25
Montt, Manuel, 27, 28, 31
Moraga, Juan de Dios, 162
Morales, Julio, 120
Moreno, Daniel, 238
Moreno, Francisco, 124
Mulchén River, 26, 35, 39, 41, 122
Muñízaga, Francisco, 42, 46
Muñoz, Delicia, 170–71
Muñoz, Luis, 179, 180, 195, 196–97, 199, 231
Muñoz, Manuel, 237, 240

Nahuel, 26, 29, 49, 113, 122
Nahuelcheo, Eloi, 115
naval mutiny, 143
Navarrete, Manuel, 110
Navarro Puelma, Sara, 40, 73, 131, 132
Neruda, Pablo, 262
Neuman, Gustavo, 184–85
nitrate mines, 11, 35–36, 142–43; repression at, 17–18, 167
Nitrito, 37, 232
Nitrito Colonos Defense Committee, 171, 178, 179, 203, 216; manifestos, 179–80, 203, 216

Nitrito Valley, 49, 81, 152; colonization of, 117, 131–32, 134–35, 145; expulsion from, 168–87, 213
Nueva Italia, 86–87, 156, 163

ocupantes, 6, 74, 82, 118
Olavarría, Arturo, 259–60
Olhagaray, Juan Bautista, 73, 230, 244
Olhagaray, Juan Cadet, 73
Orellana Barrera, Juan, 206, 221, 252–53, 254
Orrego, Anselmo, 237, 240
Orrego, Cesáreo, 220, 238, 240
Orrego, Juan Antonio, 40, 73, 132
Orrego, Blanca Aurora, 220, 221
Ortega Espinosa, Delia Rosa, 217, 218–19, 221
Ortíz, Juan Pablo, 115, 151, 169, 172–73, 174, 239, 253, 254; actions during rebellion, 224, 225, 234; insurrection planning by, 199, 206
Ortíz, Juan Segundo, 250
Ortíz, Silverio, 237, 238, 240
Ortíz, Silverio Segundo, 250
Ortíz Palma, Antonio, 190, 197, 208
Ortíz Salgado, Onofre, 211, 220, 226, 239, 250, 252–53, 254
Ortúzar Riesco, Gerardo, 237
Ossa Lynch, Eugenio, 107
Ovalle, Manuel, 130–31

Pacheco, Segundo, 237
Pacheco Sepúlveda, Manuel Segundo, 115
Paillaleo, José, 218
Paiñaleo, José, 222
Palacios, Germán, 12
Panguilef, Manuel Aburto, 165
Parra, Paulo, 50
Parra, Ramón, 131
Partido Obrero Socialista (POS), 70. *See also* Communist Party

Patriotic Leagues, 159
Pavian, Manuel, 64
Paz, José, 73, 102, 129, 131, 175
Pehuenche, 7, 27–28, 60, 63–68, 77; campaign of the desert, 36; combat against, 34; involvement in rebellion, 15–16, 205, 226, 230–32, 236, 268; involvement in the rebellion, 308 n.65; labor organizing of, 136–37; massacre of (1882), 36–37; property rights, understanding of, 29. *See also* Mapuche
Pellahuén estate, 94–95, 96, 133–34
Pellao Gallina, Domingo, 231
Pemehue cordillera, 39, 122, 124
Peña, Atanasio, 151, 237, 240
Peña Campos, Abraham, 151, 225
Pérez, José Joaquín, 31
Pérez, Otilia, 50
Piñaleo, Isidoro, 226
Piñaleo, Manuel, 236
Piñaleo, Segundo, 66
Pino, Juan, 115
Pino Alegría, Arturo, 207
Pino Valdebenito, Florentino, 206, 217, 218, 250, 253, 254
Pinto, Jorge, 31
Pinto, Julio, 167
Pitrai, Alfonso, 236
pobladores, 71
Popular Front, 5, 261, 262, 265
press, 215, 236, 243–45
property rights, 3, 118
public land, 6, 9, 13, 46, 74, 82, 95, 113, 118, 123, 125; auctions of, 37–38, 44; restoration of, 88
Puelma Castillo, Francisco, 34, 35–36, 40–41, 49, 110–11, 113, 122; challenges to property rights of, 13, 38–39; death of, 40
Puelma Tupper, Adelaida, 40, 41
Puelma Tupper, Alfredo, 40
Puelma Tupper, Elisa, 40, 41, 111

Puelma Tupper, Francisco, 35, 39, 40, 73, 107, 130, 132; challenges to property rights of, 13, 42–43, 46–59
Puelma Tupper, Guillermo, 40, 54
Puelma Tupper, Manuel, 40, 73
Puelma Tupper, Rosa, 40, 73, 129–30, 132, 145, 160, 173, 175
Puelma Tupper, Teresa, 40, 73
Puelma Tupper and Company, 40, 41
Puga, General Arturo, 147
pulperías, 78, 190, 191; Ackermann, 72, 192, 221–22; attacks on, 1, 192, 215, 217–24; Frau, 190, 192, 217–20; inflated prices at, 75, 217–18; looting at, 219, 220, 221, 222, 225, 226; Rubilar, 225–26; Zolezzi, 190, 192, 219, 220–21

Queco estate, 36; union activities on, 136, 138
Quellillanca, General, 67
Quevedo, Abraham, 82
Quezada Rogers, Franklin, 19, 219, 234, 238, 244, 247–50, 255
Quilleime assembly, 206–13, 214, 216
Quilodrán, Galindo, 131
Quilodrán, Ramón, 237, 240, 241
Quilodrán Palavecinos, Daniel, 236
Quilodrán San Martín, Fermín, 222
Quilondrán, Cesáreo, 218
Quilondrán, José, 109
Quiroga, Bernardo, 48, 49

Rahue River, 39, 41, 215
Raiman, Mainuquilias, 67
Ralco, 15, 60–68, 138, 267–68; evictions from, 64; union activities in, 136–37, 138
Rambeaux, Gaston, 73, 129, 175
Ramírez, Margarita, 76, 206, 243; actions during rebellion, 216, 220, 221, 245, 250; property rights of, 171
Ramos, Segundo, 169
Ránquil bridge, 215, 221–23, 224
Ránquil estate, 40, 49, 73, 105, 121, 129–30, 132; colonization of, 134–35, 145, 160, 163, 173; evictions on, 102–3; improvements on, 129–30; union activities on, 126, 138, 192
Ránquil-Rahue Cooperative, 103, 107
Ránquil rebellion, 1–3; bridges, guarding, 215, 221; carabineros, attacks on, 215, 224–25, 227; causes of, 11–13, 214, 215–16; commencement of, 192, 206–13, 215–16; Communist Party involvement in, 195–205, 216; Lolco estate, attack on, 229–31; media reports of, 215, 236, 243–45; memories of, 2, 260–69; plan of attack, 215; pulperías, attacks on, 192, 215, 217–24, 225–27; as uprising, 17; women's participation in, 216, 243, 244. *See also* looting
Recabarren, Luis Emilio, 69–70, 260
reducciones, 6, 65–66
reform, land, 84–97, 119, 121–41
Renaico River, 26, 35, 122, 123
Republican Militias, 159, 167, 177, 192
Reyes, José Benicio, 240
Reyes, José Miguel, 150
Reyes Burgos, Víctor, 222
Reyes Lira, Corporal José, 249
Reyes, José Dionisio, 237
Rieloff Vargas, Carlos Humberto, 198
Ríos, Juan Antonio, 258
Riquelme, José, 238
Riquelme, Pedro, 240, 241
Risopatrón, Luis, 65
Rivera, Froilán, 72, 101, 110, 114, 145
Rivera, Pedro, 145, 239
Rivera Muñoz, Pedro, 172
Roa, Luis, 236

robbery. *See* looting
Robertson, Lieutenant, 223, 239
Robles, Claudio, 8
Rodríguez, José María, 26, 29, 30, 33, 49, 110, 113, 122
Rodríguez, Pedro, 236
Rodríguez Cerda, Enrique, 40
Rodríguez Viscarra, Alberto, 198
Rojas, Victor, 140
Rosa Cofré, Juan, 140
Rubilar, Adolfo, 225
Rudé, Georges, 228
rural labor movement, 5–10

Saavedra, Ángel, 66
Saavedra, José, 73
Saaverda, Cornelio, 30, 31–32, 33, 34–35, 49, 110, 113, 122–23
Saez, Eujenio, 50
Sagredo, Adán, 238, 239, 240
Sagredo, Benito, 81, 170, 262; actions after rebellion, 235, 238; actions during rebellion, 214, 215, 224, 225, 226, 253; arrest and torture of, 176–78, 224; insurrection planning by, 199, 215
Sagredo, Clementina, 76, 236–37, 239, 243, 263; detention of, 216, 238, 240
Sagredo, Emelina, 243; actions after rebellion, 235, 238; actions during rebellion, 216–17, 224, 225; carabinero attack on, 178–79; remembrances by, 77–78, 81, 137, 182–83, 216–17, 218, 239, 262, 263, 305 n.108
Sagredo, Ester, 238–39
Sagredo, Hortensia, 238–39
Sagredo, José, 236, 238, 240
Sagredo, José del Rosario, 240
Sagredo, Juan, 232, 236, 237, 239, 240
Sagredo, Lindor, 169
Sagredo, Pablo, 236
Sagredo, Rosendo, 226

Sagredo, Simón, 81–82, 107, 115, 119, 139–40, 146, 151, 170, 182; actions after rebellion, 235, 238; actions during rebellion, 214, 215, 224, 226, 227, 229; arrest and torture of, 176–78, 224; insurrection planning by, 172–73, 194, 196, 199, 206, 207, 208, 211, 215
Sagredo Pacheco, José Adán, 239, 254
Sagredo Pacheco, José del Carmen, 231, 234
Sagredo Valenzuela, Juan Bautista, 224
Salas, Manuel, 223, 241, 254, 300 n.27
Salas Romo, Luis, 246
Salazar, Alfredo, 231
Salazar, Prudencio, 115
Sánchez, Carlos, 140
Sánchez, Darío, 56
Sánchez Salazar, Adolfo, 197, 204, 225–26, 229, 234
Sandoval, José del Carmen, 238
Sandoval, Manuel, 139
Sandoval, Nolasco, 254
Sandoval Maldonado, Lorenza Elena, 227
San Ignacio de Pemehue estate, 26–43, 49, 73, 110; borders of, 26, 34–35, 39–40, 41, 42, 49, 50, 113, 122–25; founding of, 30; Lot A, 38, 39, 42; Lot B, 38; Lot C, 38; Lot D, 38, 39, 42, 49, 60; Lot E, 38, 42; Lot F, 38; Lot G, 38, 39, 42; massacre of Pemehue on, 36–37; as public land, 46, 123; surveys of, 123
San Juan de Trovolhue estate, 93
San Martín Calderón, Bernardo, 227, 229, 254
Santa Elena estate, 34
Santa Graciela, 117–18, 141, 161
Santiago Smith, Felipe, 92, 161
Santos Ossa, José, 35
schists, 57, 58
Schmidt, Roberto, 54

Schmidt colonization concession, 53, 54–55, 56
Schweitzer, Augusto, 120, 188, 189
Scott, James, 11
Seguel de Zolezzi, Carmen Luisa, 220, 221
Sepúlveda, Anibal, 244
Sepúlveda Canales, Luis, 236
Sepúlveda Leal, Ramón, 87
shale, 57, 58
Siade, Nicolás, 197
Siade, Pedro, 197
Silva Ricci, Luis, 149–50
Sindicato Agrícola Lonquimay, 7, 8, 86, 101, 107, 126, 140; assembly (January 1931), 138; assembly (June 1934), 206–13; gendered labor in, 171; insurrection planning by, 1, 194, 196, 199, 208, 211–13, 215; legal status, 72–73; meetings with Maldonado (1930), 134–36; meeting with commission (1930), 117–20; organization of, 69–73; political alliances, 3, 12, 69–70, 71, 144, 153–54, 181, 204; power of, 113–14, 209; Quilleime assembly, 206–13; radicalization of, 168; registration of, 72, 103, 105; relationship with Alessandri, 160–61; relationship with Ibáñez, 3, 14, 98–101, 114, 139; report (1929), 72; report (1931), 146–47; size of, 145–46
Sindicato Blanco de Obreros, 94–95
Sindicato Pellahuén, 95–96
smuggling, 47–48, 51–53, 58–59
social security registration, 104–5
Sociedad Agrícola Pellahuén, 96
Sociedad Olhagaray y Charó, 73, 109, 121, 128, 132
Soto, Pedro, 93
Southern Property Law. *See* Law No. 4301 (February 1928)
Staeding, Juan, 57

Staeding colonization concession, 46, 52, 53, 54, 57–59
surveys, 41, 42, 123

Taylor, William, 17
Thompson, E. P., 11
timbering, 55
Tinsman, Heidi, 15
Títulos de Merced, 63, 68, 137, 138
Toltén, 97, 151, 156, 162, 163
Torrealba, Zenón, 52–53, 59, 110
Torres, Pascual, 115
Torres de Schweitzer, Ema, 120
transhumance, 27, 29, 52
Trapa Trapa, 36
Troncoso Baeza, José, 230, 231, 236, 240
Troyo, 135, 217, 223, 232, 237
Trucco, Manuel, 143
23 de Enero, 141

Ulianova, Olga, 12, 158, 194, 195, 260

Valderrama, Jorge, 227, 229
Valdivia, Verónica, 167
Valenzuela, Captain, 233
Valenzuela, Emilio, 237, 240, 241
Valenzuela, Pedro Antonio, 240
Valenzuela Sagredo, Juan Bautista, 239–40, 250, 252, 254
Vega Díaz, José, 149
Vega Tapia, José del Cármen, 115, 196–97, 231
Vergara, Edmundo, 91
Vergara, Víctor, 146–47, 152, 169, 175, 198; capture and death of, 227, 229, 241, 254
Vial, Francisco, 115
Vicuña Mackenna, Benjamín, 31
Vidal Muñoz, Gregorio, 174
Videla, Gregorio, 237
Villucura estate, 40, 73, 121, 126–28; improvements on, 127; union activities on, 126, 127
violence, 16–25, 79

women: employment of, 76–78, 171; participation in rebellion, 15, 216–17, 243; property rights, 15, 170–71; violence by, 243–44; violence to, 78, 244–45
Wood, Santiago, 87

Yáñez, Eliodoro, 41, 42, 50, 111, 113, 123

Zañartu Rodríguez, Alfonso, 192, 220, 241, 245, 248, 252, 254
Zapata, Emilio, 259
Zapata González, Teófilo, 227, 229, 241, 254
Zolezzi, Juan: death of, 192, 220, 241, 243, 245, 248, 252, 255; pulpería, 190, 192, 197, 219, 220–21
Zurita, José Ignacio, 50